STRESS AND ANXIETY

Volume 9

Series Editors

Charles D. Spielberger

University of South Florida

and

Irwin G. Sarason

University of Washington

Guest Editor of This Volume

Peter B. Defares

University of Wageningen, The Netherlands

 HEMISPHERE PUBLISHING CORPORATION

Washington   New York   London

DISTRIBUTION OUTSIDE THE UNITED STATES
McGRAW–HILL INTERNATIONAL BOOK COMPANY

Auckland   Bogotá   Guatemala   Hamburg   Johannesburg
Lisbon   London   Madrid   Mexico   Montreal
New Delhi   Panama   Paris   San Juan   São Paulo
Singapore   Sydney   Tokyo   Toronto

This volume contains papers from two conferences on Stress and Anxiety convened in 1980 at the Netherlands Institute for Advanced Study in the Humanities and Social Sciences, Wassenaar, The Netherlands.

STRESS AND ANXIETY: Volume 9

1 2 3 4 5 6 7 8 9 0   E B E B   8 9 8 7 6 5 4

Library of Congress Cataloging in Publication Data

Advanced Study Institute on Stress and Anxiety in Modern Life, Murnau, Ger., 1973.

Stress and anxiety: [proceedings] /edited by Charles D. Spielberger, Irwin G. Sarason. Washington: Hemisphere Pub. Corp.
    v.   : ill.: 24cm. (v. 1–2: The Series in clinical psychology
    v. 3–5: The Series in clinical and community psychology)

"Sponsored by the Scientific Affairs Division of the North Atlantic Treaty Organization."
    Includes bibliographies and indexes.
    1. Stress (Psychology)—Congresses. 2. Anxiety—Congresses.
I. Sarason, Irwin G., ed. II. Spielberger, Charles Donald, date, ed.
III. North Atlantic Treaty Organization. Division of Scientific Affairs.
IV. Title. [DNLM: 1. Anxiety. 2. Stress, Psychological. WM 172 S755a]

BF575.S75A38 1973 616.8'522 74-28292
                                    MARC
ISBN 0-89116-310-7
ISSN 0146-0846
ISSN 0364-1112

This volume is dedicated to the memory of Dr. Roger C. Smith, a pioneering researcher on stress and performance in air traffic control specialists. Dr. Smith was Chief of the Clinical Psychology Research Unit, Aviation Psychology Laboratory, Federal Aviation Administration Center, Oklahoma City. After presenting an outstanding paper at the Conference on Stress and Anxiety in The Netherlands in June 1980, Roger died in a tragic automobile accident while returning home. His distinguished contributions to stress research are greatly valued by his colleagues; his future contributions will be sorely missed.

Contents

II
ENVIRONMENTAL STRESS AND ANXIETY

V
STRESS AND HEART DISEASE

Contributors

VERNON L. ALLEN, University of Wisconsin, Madison, Wisconsin, USA

LAURIE ANDERSON, Boston University School of Medicine, Boston, Massachusetts, USA

A. APPELS, Rijksuniversiteit Limburg, Maastricht, Holland

F. C. BAKKER, Vrije Universiteit, Amsterdam, The Netherlands

J. BASTIAANS, University of Leyden, Leyden, The Netherlands

JAMES C. BUELL, University of Nebraska Medical Center, Omaha, Nebraska, USA

M. A. CHESNEY, Stanford Research Institute, Menlo Park, California, USA

ROSARIO S. CRANE, University of South Florida, Tampa, Florida, USA

P. B. DEFARES, University of Wageningen, Wageningen, The Netherlands

THEODORE M. DEMBROSKI, Eckerd College Stress and Cardiovascular Research Center, St. Petersburg, Florida, USA

ANN L. DENSON, The Pennsylvania State University College of Medicine, Hershey, Pennsylvania, USA

ROBERT S. ELIOT, University of Nebraska Medical Center, Omaha, Nebraska, USA

HANS J. EYSENCK, University of London, London, England

NICO H. FRIJDA, University of Amsterdam, Amsterdam, The Netherlands

PETER GLANZMANN, Johannes Gutenberg University, Mainz, West Germany

A. GOSTAUTAS, Kaunas Medical Institute, Kaunas, Lithuania SSR

P. GROSSMAN, Institute for Stress Research, Wageningen, The Netherlands

VERNON HAMILTON, Reading University, Reading, England

RUGH HENDERSON, The Pennsylvania State University College of Medicine, Hershey, Pennsylvania, USA

MICHAEL W. HURST, Boston University School of Medicine, Boston, Massachusetts, USA

IRVING L. JANIS, Yale University, New Haven, Connecticut, USA

C. DAVID JENKINS, University of Texas Medical Branch, Galveston, Texas, USA

BERNARD E. KREGER, Boston University School of Medicine, Boston, Massachusetts, USA

LOTHAR LAUX, University of Bamberg, Bamberg, West Germany

JANET LEWIS, The Pennsylvania State University College of Medicine, Hershey, Pennsylvania, USA

JAMES M. MACDOUGALL, Eckerd College Stress and Cardiovascular Research Center, St. Petersburg, Florida, USA

DAVID MAGNUSSON, University of Stockholm, Stockholm, Sweden

F. NIJHUIS, Rijksuniversiteit Limburg, Maastricht, Holland

J. F. ORLEBEKE, Vrije Universiteit, Amsterdam, The Netherlands

ROBERT M. ROSE, University of Texas Medical Branch, Galveston, Texas, USA

R. H. ROSENMAN, Stanford Research Institute, Menlo Park, California, USA

DAISY SCHALLING, Karolinska Institute, and University of Stockholm, Stockholm, Sweden

PAUL SCHAFFNER, Johannes Gutenberg University, Mainz, West Germany

JIM L. SHIELDS, National Institutes of Health, NHLBI, Bethesda, Maryland, USA

ROGER C. SMITH (deceased), formerly FAA Civil Aeromedical Institute, Oklahoma City, Oklahoma, USA

R. J. M. SOMSEN, Vrije Universiteit, Amsterdam, The Netherlands

CHARLES D. SPIELBERGER, University of South Florida, Tampa, Florida, USA

SIEGFRIED STREUFERT, The Pennsylvania State University College of Medicine, Hershey, Pennsylvania, USA

SUSAN C. STREUFERT, The Pennsylvania State University College of Medicine, Hershey, Pennsylvania, USA

M. W. VAN DER MOLEN, Vrije Universiteit, Amsterdam, The Netherlands

HENK M. VAN DER PLOEG, University of Leyden, Leyden, The Netherlands

L. J. P. VAN DOORNEN, Vrije Universiteit, Amsterdam, The Netherlands

P. C. W. VAN WIERINGEN, Vrije Universiteit, Amsterdam, The Netherlands

Preface

Almost a decade has passed since the publication in 1975 of the first volume in the *Stress and Anxiety* series. During this time, stress research has continued to proliferate, and demands for practical solutions for stress-related problems have accelerated at an even faster pace. While much has been learned about the nature of stress and its impact on behavior, dedicated multidisciplinary efforts by social, behavioral, and medical scientists will be required to make further progress in this highly complex field.

Growing evidence of the effects of stress on such medical disorders as coronary heart disease has stimulated demands for stress reduction and stress management programs. There remains, however, a tremendous gap between the wide variety of programs designed to ameliorate the effects of stress and the knowledge base on which such programs must depend. In the United States, stress has become a major growth industry, and there is an urgent need for stress modification efforts to be firmly based on a solid foundation of empirical research.

The *Stress and Anxiety* series was originally created to disseminate research findings based on papers presented at international scientific conferences and advanced study institutes organized by the editors and sponsored by the Scientific Affairs Division of the North Atlantic Treaty Organization. Volume 8, which marked an important departure from the past, was based on two international conferences held in Israel on Psychological Stress and Adjustment in Time of War and Peace. The organizer of these conferences, Professor Norman A. Milgram, served as Guest Editor for that volume.

The present volume is based on papers presented at two international conferences on Stress and Anxiety convened in 1980 at The Netherlands Institute for Advanced Study in the Humanities and Social Sciences (NIAS), Wassenaar, The Netherlands. These conferences were organized and coordinated by Peter B. Defares and Charles D. Spielberger, and supported in part by grants from the Dutch Ministry of Education, The Netherlands Heart Foundation, and The Netherlands Institute for Stress Research. Professor Defares has served as Guest Editor for this volume, which is based primarily on papers initially presented at the NIAS conferences.

The editors of this continuing series would like to express our deep appreciation to Professor Defares for his many contributions to the NIAS Stress and Anxiety conferences, and his effective work in reviewing and co-editing the manuscripts for this volume. We would also like to extend our thanks to Professor H. A. J. F.

Misset, Director of NIAS, and his staff for placing the resources of the Institute at our disposal in planning and carrying out the conferences, and for serving as such gracious hosts. Special thanks are due to Katherine Murphy and Diane L. Gregg for their dedicated efforts in coordinating the administrative arrangements for the conferences, and for their expert technical and clerical assistance in processing and preparing the manuscripts for publication.

Charles D. Spielberger
Irwin G. Sarason

I

STRESS, COGNITION, AND PERSONALITY

1

Toward a Model of Emotion

Nico H. Frijda
University of Amsterdam

INTRODUCTION

This paper presents the outline for a model of emotion. "Model" is meant here as a collection of procedures and of information which would generate the phenomena concerned—emotions in this case—if the model were operational. The present effort follows the philosophy of computer modelling.

The purpose of constructing a model of emotion is to attempt to order the available insights concerning emotions into a coherent whole. More precisely, it should aid in investigating whether such ordering is feasible, what gaps are encountered when doing so, what assumptions have to be made, and what empirical questions appear to have as yet produced insufficient answers. The construction of a model is primarily a heuristic endeavor with, of course, the additional thrill of trying to compete with Nature.

The present paper described a model of human emotion, rather than the empirical evidence which might indicate its adequacy as a model. It adopts, mostly, the artificial intelligence viewpoint: what a system should look like that meaningfully manifests emotion. In order to take this point of view, it is necessary to give emotion a functional interpretation. "Emotion" is here considered as a subsystem signalling the world's state with respect to the satisfaction of the system's driving forces, and indicating what, if anything, should be done about possible discrepancies between states desired and states obtained.

The emotion-system has, as its input, a stream of events. It is secondary to the functioning and purpose of the system whether these events be external, or internal like thoughts or memories; it is also secondary whether the input consists of true events, or of stationary situations to which the system, for some reason, pays attention. As its output the system has either no emotion ("nothing"), or an emotional response consisting of behavior, physiological response, and experiential reaction.

OUTLINE OF THE EMOTION PROCESS

The process of emotional reaction embodied in the model may be briefly described as follows:

1. Events are encountered, perceived, and interpreted: Event Coding.
2. Interpreted events are evaluated in terms of their relevance for the system's concerns: its interests, values and sensitivities. This relevance can be positive, when

the event signals some fulfillment or promise thereof; it can be negative when it involves some harm, frustration, or dissatisfaction, or threat thereof; or it can be neutral or undetermined, but just "of interest" to the concern. We call this "Relevance Evaluation."

3. If the event indeed has some relevance, and when this relevance exceeds some threshold, the process continues; otherwise, nothing happens, the system awaits further events, and "Emotion" remains silent or continues its current operation.

4. An evaluation is performed of the context of the relevant event. By "context of the event" is here meant the nature of the total situation, beyond the event as such and its relevance, and including the spatial and temporal setting and also including the subject himself and his properties, as appreciated by himself. If relevance evaluation determines whether there is to be an emotion, "Context Evaluation" determines which emotion it is to be.

5. There is an evaluation of the seriousness of the threat, hurt, dissatisfaction or fulfillment, and of the risks of doing something about it. The result of this "Seriousness Evaluation" determines both the strength of the impulse as motivated by Relevance Evaluation and shaped by Context Evaluation, and a possible dampening of this impulse. If relevance evaluation determines the fact of an emotion, and context evaluation the nature of the emotion, seriousness evaluation determines the *intensity* of the emotion.

6. The evaluations are shaped into an emotional impulse on the basis of correspondence between such impulses and the evaluations: Action Tendency Generation.

7. The impulse is translated into overt expression: autonomic arousal or dearousal; motor expression; plans for purposive action. That is: from the repertories of arousal and behavior possibilities, those actions are selected which are appropriate to both the action tendency and the specific situation. We call this the Behavior Generation process. During, or previous to, execution of these expressions, this execution is regulated according to the effects obtained or anticipated.

The output of each phase—in particular the cognitive ones—is fed back to the event coding phase, and may influence subsequent cycles of the process. The emotion process is diagrammed in Fig. 1.

COMPONENTS OF THE SYSTEM

In order for a system to be capable of executing the process just sketched, it needs a number of components—information structures, if you wish—indicated alongside the flow diagram.

Cognitive Dispositions

These enable the system to understand an external event, or form the materials out of which a thought or a memory is constructed. The general nature of these dipositions is not specific for emotions, and is known from recent work on text understanding, in particular from the work of Schank and Abelson (1977). "Understanding" an event involves categorizing the entiries participating in the event in terms of known concepts, and categorizing their relationships and the transformations they undergo or effect in terms of the components of event schemata or of "scripts." Also, it involves constructing a causal network within and around the

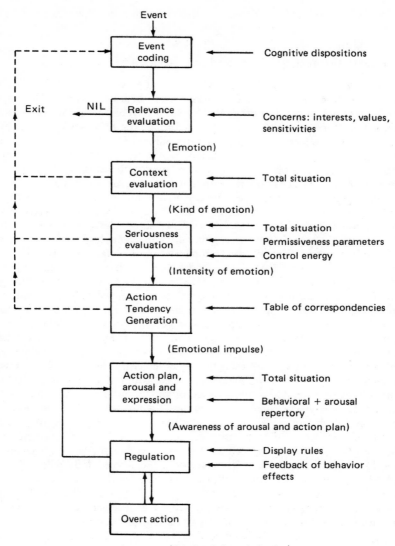

Figure 1 The process of emotion.

event, in terms of available scripts or of plan and goal schemata. In addition to interpretation, these cognitive dispositions enable the system to make predictions or entertain expectations, such as those of forthcoming physical harm when a tree is seen falling or of one's own abandonment when a dear person is perceived departing.

Event coding is based not solely upon the event plus existing cognitive dispositions. It is also based upon willingness to utilize this or that disposition, and the selectivity and bias this implies. Such willingness may be considered as determined primarily by the system's concerns and the emotional implications of the event. Hence the feedback loops, indicated by dashed lines in the flow diagram.

Concerns, Interests, Values, and Sensitivities

The assumption of the model is, obviously, that emotions emerge because some concern is touched upon: it is hurt or threatened to be hurt by the event, it appears unsatisfied because an event (a thought, an association) brings up the representation of an unsatisfactory state of affairs, or it is fulfilled, or promises to do so, by the event. The term "concern" is borrowed from Klinger (1975). It is used to denote those dispositions which, when mobilized, urge the system to act or react and which control its attention. The notion corresponds functionally to that of "response tendencies" in behavioristic formulations (e.g., Brown & Farber, 1951) or to that of "plans" or "structures" in cognitive ones (e.g., Mandler, 1975), and their "being touched" with "interference" and "interruption," respectively.

The overtones in the term "concern," with its subspecies—"interests," "values," and "sensitivities"—appear to be more generally applicable, however. "Sensitivities" is included because of the emotional implications of certain sensory events, such as physical pain or disgusting tastes or odors, and of the aftereffects of previous experiences, particularly disagreeable ones. For the purposes of understanding or modelling emotion it is not necessary to develop an extensive theory of motivation, in which basic motives are distinguished or the genesis and derivations of motives and values are represented. Functionally important, in view of the process of emotion, is only the fact that given concerns exist at a given time, such that an event may appear as discordant or concordant with what the system values: states like safety, absence of pain, self-esteem, cognitive clarity, being liked, possessions, the ownership of a given boat, honor, etc. The assumption is that emotions are evoked by basic or general, pervading concerns and by quite specific ones.

Clearly, then, a system which is to manifest the process of emotion should contain a "store" of interests, values, and sensitivities. The properties of "interests" which are relevant here—relevant, that is, for the detection of discordant or concordant events—are reasonably well understood through the work of Schank and Abelson (1977), and in particular its extension in a dissertation by Wilensky (1978) and its application to emotion by Wegman (1979). In those studies "goals" and "themes" correspond to what here is referred to as interests. "Themes" are information structures specifying attitudes, or sets of attitudes (such as "liking someone"), with goals associated to them. "Goals" are information structures specifying some desired end-state. Associated with these desired end-states are "plans"— possible ways to achieve the goal ("desiring information" is a goal, "asking" a plan), subgoals which may be instrumental in achieving the goal, and themes or more basic goals from which intermediate goals may spring. Themes, goals, and plans can be (and are, in the work referred to) represented in such a way that specific actions, plans or goals can be recognized as instances of the more general ones.

Concerns are assumed to vary in strength and it may be necessary to let them do so in several ways, by means of several different parameters. A "centrality-parameter" determines the intensity of reactions upon its frustration; the parameter represents the number and importance of implications of the concern, such as the number of behaviors which depend upon it. A "sensitivity parameter" determines the range of events which may touch the interest; it represents, let us say, the leniency of the decision rule which defines event relevance. A "priority-parameter" determines control of the action system, or relative readiness to assume such control—a process which lies outside the processes involved in the present model but to which we will briefly come back at the end of this paper. Whether the supposed parameters are meaningful in view of the empirical facts of emotion, whether they are independent, how they relate to their antecedent or constituent conditions, are open questions. There is at present hardly any information on which to base answers to these questions.

Concerns, in the context of the model, are assumed to lie dormant, except for one or a few which control the action system at a given moment. The dormant concerns, though, are awakened by events relevant to them, in a manner familiar from so-called pandemonium models (cf. Lindsay & Norman, 1977).

It is fairly clear how events may awaken concerns, and, at the same time, how the direction of relevance may be evaluated. Event-types refer to their possible consequent states (a threat to possible harm, for instance), and to plans from which constituent actions may derive. Also, the compatibility between states and goal end-states can be recognized: the incompatibility between goals, between states and goals, or between states and plans can be represented in the form of "rules," or may be inferred on the basis of such rules. Scolding implies rejection, and rejection is opposed to being liked; both Wilensky (1978) and Wegman (1979) give examples of such inference processes. Obviously, knowledge representation and inference processes must be very extensive and complex for adequate and naturalistic relevance evaluation, but the principles are shown working in the studies discussed.

The notion of emotion as arising from relevance of events for concerns, of course, is closely akin to the theories of emotion as the consequence of frustration (Brown & Farber, 1951), of phase-sequence disruption (Hebb, 1949), of plan interruption (Mandler, 1975), and of goal blocking (Wegman, 1979).

Context Evaluation

Essential for the emergence of a specific emotion, it is assumed, is evaluation of context. The system, therefore, must have at its disposition a set of *evaluation categories* in terms of which the total emotional situation is analyzed. The assumption here is that a given emotion is shaped by the pattern of situational aspects. "Emotion being shaped" means two things. First, the emotional experience (of "anger," "sorrow," etc.) is determined partly by the situation as the subject perceives it; such perception is a constituent of emotional experience, jealousy, for instance, being pain felt due to someone else's envied pleasure. Second: given the conditions for an emotion, as a result of relevance evaluation, the pattern of situational aspects determines the tendencies for action; and both emotional experience and the classification of emotional response are largely defined by these tendencies for action (cf. Arnold, 1960). Situational pattern and action tendency fit together, as cause and consequence.

Of course, what is involved here is the "cognitive process" of which much is made in present-day theorizing on emotion (e.g., Schachter, 1964; Mandler, 1975). The present effort to model emotion intends to specify these cognitive processes, as well as to indicate their place and mode of operation in the evolvement of the emotional experience and emotional response. It is hypothesized that a given emotional experience is characterized by a specific profile of cognitive features, which profile is determined by situational aspects—the latter being a product of what the situation in fact offers, what the subject is predisposed to see there, and what he adds by way of association, etc.

A satisfactory system of evaluation categories—satisfactory in enabling the distinctions between emotions which experience or behavior distinguishes—is something to be developed, and to be tested against the distinctions mentioned. So far, only a tentative listing of what appear to be some of the major variables can be presented; the listing has no pretense of completeness or of mutual independence of its entries.

(*a*) Constraints of action versus freedom for action. The event is seen as blocking or restricting a person's actions. Or, alternatively, the event allows a person freedom of action, is open to his approach, or permits access to desired situations. Constraints dominate, it seems, in situations leading to anger ("frustration," as usually conceived, is exactly this), to feelings of oppression, disappointment, loneliness. The subject feels that he is running up against a wall, that other people are unattainable, or not yielding. Freedom of action dominates in many positive emotions such as elation, personal warmth and safety, and sense of liberty, power, and ability.

(*b*) Responsibility, or psychological mutability of the event's agent: a truly attributional attribute. Anger, it seems, requires an animate, responsible agent, or at least the event's cause should temporarily be seen as responsible: damning fate presupposes that fate hears what you shout at it. In the positive emotions it plays an equivalent role—turning joy into love or gratitude, for instance. Love, says Spinoza, is pleasure, accompanied by the idea of an external cause. A specific variant of this aspect is involved when the agent is the subject himself, which is a necessary component of emotions such as feeling of guilt, remorse, or pride.

(*c*) Controllability or uncontrollability of the situation. Feelings of power, safety, familiarity, competence, contain this aspect as one of their components, with their opposites of helplessness, uncertainty, strangeness, incompetence, and disorientation. Following recent research findings and opinions, this aspect appears as an important condition for anxiety and many fears, for insecurity and possibly for depression.

(*d*) Openness or closedness of the situation. Situations may differ in the degree to which they present actual or potential ways of escape. Escape routes may exist, or they may be absent but desired, both in space and in time, as perspectives on ultimate changes in the situation, or they may consist in the possibility of outside help. The degree of actual or potential openness of the situation may decide whether the emotion turns into fear rather than anxiety or despair, or whether it turns into fear rather than anger (the cornered animal which switches into attack). Appreciation of the closedness of a situation may be the essential element for the reaction upon personal loss becoming grief, rather than protest or whatever other element of mourning, since grief involves acceptance of the finality of the loss. Angry protest remains as long as there is hope, or else it serves to ward off the sense of finality.

(*e*) Time perspective. Closedness of the situation is, in part, a function of time perspective: the expected duration, or repetitiveness of the event. In addition, expected duration, or duration or frequency of similar events so far, by itself influences the weight of the situation, and are constitutive of such emotions as hope and despair, trust and distrust, feelings of confidence or discouragement in the face of stress.

(*f*) Objectivity. By "objectivity" I mean the attribution to the emotional object of inherent properties, and, in particular, such properties as are relevant to values. Indignation, admiration, and moral disgust—all three are emotions with such an "objective" reference. Being moved, feelings of tenderness, and, quite generally, the aesthetic emotions seem to belong to the same class, or at least to be closely related.

(*g*) Degree of reality. An event may or may not be taken seriously. It may be considered a threat or a game or a formal, ceremonial, activity; it may, consequently, be the cause of fear, or of amusement, or of respectful neutrality. Decisive are the cues to reality (cf. the notion of keying in Goffman, 1974), as well as the mastery of the subject over the event (cf. Sroufe & Waters, 1976). The importance of this aspect shows in the drastically different emotions caused by events when merely imagined and when they really happen, as, for instance, described by Proust.

In order for context evaluation to be properly performed, the system should have at its disposition mechanisms for analyzing the emotional situation in terms of variables like the above. In addition, it should be in possession of a correlation table, relating evaluation profiles to emotions in an unambiguous and complete manner.

Obviously, formalizing the process of context evaluation will be difficult, since the cues for the attributions are unclear and, no doubt, subtle. In addition, it depends upon subject variables whether one aspect or the other is emphasized. Such variables may be conceptualized as idiosyncratic preference parameters (for some subjects, every misfortune is blamed upon someone else, and for others everything stems from immovable fate), or as parameters having been influenced by previous experience. It is also open to the subject to emphasize now one aspect of the situation and then another, on the basis of sequential scanning or tendencies for cognitive change. The result is emotional vacillation—the shifting of emotions aroused by one and the same event. A personal loss leads to disbelief, to protest, to despair, to depression, and finally to grief, by a mere change in focus on attributes as mentioned.

In the processes described thus far, emotion results from the interaction of event information with internal dispositions—concerns on the one hand, context evaluation dispositions on the other. The current pattern of attributes is registered in terms of these dispositions and determines the subsequent phases of the process. This does not imply awareness, by the system, of the concerns involved, nor of the prevailing context attributes, nor even of the attributes determining relevance evaluation. Most of the context attributes are "background variables," in the sense that the attentional focus is usually directed at the central event processed in the relevance evaluation phase. When getting angry one does not necessarily realize the antagonist's attributed responsibility, even though this responsibility attribution is a determining condition for the anger that is experienced. The present model is made to fit conceptions of the emotion process such as brought forward by Nisbett and Wilson (1977) and Zajonc (1980), rather than those by Schachter (1964) or Mandler (1975). The cognitive processes under discussion need not be conscious. In fact, the processes of taking cognizance and its efforts are, so far, not represented in the model.

Seriousness Evaluation

Intensity of emotion, it is assumed, is determined by two variables: an estimate of the intrinsic seriousness of the event, and the momentary amount of internal control. Both have, of course, to be based upon relevant information, which therefore has to be available to the system. It should be available in the form of *combination rules* and *permissiveness categories*. In addition, one needs a *control energy store*.

Various variables should go into the estimate of intrinsic seriousness. One of the major variables is an estimate of the extent of the event's consequences: the amount of injury involved, the duration and severity of the deprivation, the value of the person or property lost. The second, equally vital, variable is the importance of the concern or concerns involved, at that particular moment. "Importance" is some function of the three strength parameters mentioned earlier. In addition, it is likely, and meaningful, that blocking the action currently executed is worse, other things being equal, than threatening dormant concerns. Other contributing variables may be the expected time perspective, the amount of recent event change (contrast effects), and, particularly, the subject's estimate of his resources to cope with the event or to endure it—Lazarus' (1966) concept of primary coping.

How these various contributing factors combine can at present only be a matter of mere speculation, but it certainly is a subject for empirical investigation. There may be evidence in the literature concerning arousal as a function of both degree of food deprivation and suddenness or duration of subsequent food withdrawal, or concerning the relation between fear, shock intensity, and expected or previous duration of shocking, etc.

The nature of the second variable determining intensity—amount of internal control—is less evident. It is assumed that, apart from the intrinsic seriousness of the event, emotional intensity depends upon the degree to which the system prevents itself from being carried away. There is a functional aspect to such control, since the emotional activity may desequilibrate the system, cause carelessness, and interfere with other activities. Broadly speaking, amount of internal control is assumed to be a function both of the permissiveness of the situation and of the available control energy. "Permissiveness" in its turn is thought to depend upon the presence or absence of other urgent business, at that moment; upon the permissiveness of the social situation; upon the physical and social risks of losing self-control (say, the presence of either a 'Loving Understanding Person' or of a 'Critical Pestering Person'); and upon the possible advantages of being subject to an emotion (say, because of the presence of 'Manipulatable Persons'). Here, too, information upon which scaling rules can be based is lacking, or at least unknown to the present author.

One may wonder why evaluation of seriousness and of relevance are so clearly separated, and why control is introduced at such a relatively early stage of the process, before overt emotional response is under construction. The answer is both functional and psychological. As for the first: it appears advantageous to have a rapidly working evaluation system—rapidly working in the sense of having to bother with only a few informational attributes and capable of skipping the complex Seriousness Evaluation. The system may thus operate on the principle of "shoot first, ask questions later." As for the second: there is evidence suggesting the relative independence of emotion and emotional reality testing, or appropriate control. Pathology (neuropathology mostly) suggests that control can be weakened or lost (Mark & Ervin, 1970). At the same time, this control appears to operate upon emotion proper, and not only upon its overt expression. The implication, of course, of the way such control is modelled here, is that loss of control is not specific to a given drive or emotion such as anger. Whether this holds in view of the evidence remains to be investigated.

The present model of emotion, thus, is one in which the system is first set for maximal response, this setting being dampened on second consideration. The dampening is, among other things, dependent upon the available control energy. The notion of "control energy" is related to Kahneman's (1973) capacity for effort, and is introduced for somewhat extraneous reasons. Psychologically, it would seem that effort is required to partially or wholly discount the urgent requests of emotional evaluations, to postpone responding until the other evaluations are made, and to persist with coping. So far the model does not render this assumption necessary; but evidence concerning the effects of exhaustion upon coping and emotional control makes it empirically plausible.

Action Tendency Generation

Once the kind and degree of emotion are computed, the results of this computation have to be translated into a response. Emotional responses manifest a certain flexibility, an adaptivity to situational constraints and opportunities. In anger one may hit or kick or shout or shoot, according to the circumstances. In fright one may flee or freeze, or hide under cover when such is available. Thus, one should assume the "purpose" of such actions to exist separately from the different response modes. In other words: the emotional event shapes an action tendency, as the basis for selection from the response repertory.

There is another reason to interpose a level of action tendencies between event evaluation and response. Some emotions are characterized not so much by an overt response as by an absence of response due to lack of incentive (as in depression) or lack of opportunity for effective action (as often in anxiety or, in quite different fashion, in sheer excitement). Put differently: the system may on occasion be robbed of any reason for action or the event may render any action useless or impossible. The resulting action tendencies are null-states; the corresponding behavior does not consist of true responses, but is nothing more than the manifestation of absence of the impulse or the absence of impulse direction.

In order to produce an action tendency (in a somewhat broad sense of that term, including Null-States), the system has to possess a *repertory of action tendencies* to choose from, and a means to correlate the action tendencies with the current emotional state as embodied in evaluation profile and seriousness estimate. A set of action tendencies, or rather action tendency components, is suggested by the work of Davitz (1969). In his study, a cluster analysis was performed on the frequencies with which descriptive statements concerning emotions were applied together when subjects had to define given emotions by means of these statements. The resulting clusters qualify as action tendency components. They are labelled by Davitz as: activation, hypo-activation, hyperactivation, moving toward, moving away, moving against; comfort; discomfort; tension; enhancement; incompetence-dissatisfaction; and inadequacy. One may also need to add attention as a relatively nonspecific component.

The action tendencies are to be linked to the current emotional state (that is, to evaluation profile and seriousness estimate) by means of a table of correspondencies. Such a table might have, as one entry, the emotions, and, as another entry, the action tendency components. Davitz' analysis has produced exactly such a table, in which each emotion is represented by a profile of action tendency component scores. "Admiration," for instance, corresponds with scores on Activation, Moving Toward and Comfort. ("Comfort" I interpret here as the tendency to remain in the given situation); "Boredom" corresponds with Moving Away and a very high score on Hypo-activation; and "Contempt" is represented by Hyperactivation, Moving Against, and Tension.

In fact, a table like this might be superfluous. The correlation between evaluation profiles and action tendencies might be produced directly, by means of a single table having the context evaluation categories and action tendency components as its entries, rather than being produced indirectly by two tables, each with emotion labels as one of their entries. The choice between the two representations is not entirely arbitrary. Funnelling both categories agrees with conceptions concerning "discrete emotions" (Izard, 1977), but would seem to impose rigidities or restrictions upon the possible links between situational antecedents and response consequents.

The correspondence between evaluation profiles and action tendencies, as would be embodied in the suggested table, is not an arbitrary, purely empirical one. The action tendencies are such as to overcome the discrepancy (or sustain the correspondence) between actual state and the desired state, given the relevant concern, as signalled by Relevance Evaluation, and to do this in a fashion indicated by Context Evaluation. Physical threat conflicts with need for pain avoidance, and, in fear, gives rise to an aim to prevent the threat to materialize. Moving away is one way of doing this.

Theoretically, the underlying assumption for the present process is that emotions, as distinguished by verbal labels, can be characterized by their evaluation profiles and by their action tendencies. Some labels are more strictly defined by the first, and cover widely different action tendencies ("fright" always involves some threat, but may refer to flight, or to protection, or to impotent rigidity); others point more to the latter ("rage" implies Moving Against, whatever the eliciting situation). There is, it is supposed, a strict one-to-one correspondence between context evaluation profiles and action tendencies, since the latter should be the "answers" to the requests presented by the first. This supposition clearly has yet to prove itself.

Arousal and Expression

Emotional response consists of two components: overt behavior, in particular expressive behavior, and physiological response. The system should possess a *repertory of behaviors*, and the necessary information to find the behaviors appropriate to fulfill the action tendencies. The behavior repertory consists of the expressive behaviors as described in the literature (e.g., Ekman & Friesen, 1975), as well as to a large collection of learned expressive and instrumental behaviors.

Expressive behavior may be regarded as intrinsically and systematically related to the action tendency components (Frijda, 1969). Each expressive pattern can be characterized by its values on a set of dimensions such as Pleasantness–Unpleasantness, Activation–Passivity, Interest–Disinterest. A mapping can be made which links these values to the action tendencies and the seriousness estimate. Such a mapping should offer little difficulty, since the dimensions based upon Davitz' analysis of descriptive statements and those based upon Frijda's analysis of expression ratings are rather similar. Alternatively, scoring of expressive features such as eye closure, frowning, smiling and the like could be directly projected upon the action tendencies, considering the correlations between those expressive features and the values on the dimensions of expressive meaning (Frijda, 1969). It should, in fact, be possible not only to select from among available expressions, but to construct expressions from the relevant feature dimensions. The sequence from event to expression can then be produced rather smoothly. Blocking of strong interests of a competent subject by a responsible agent in a permissive setting should lead to strong Moving Against, and hence to intent looking, bracing oneself, clenched fists and clenched teeth.

In addition to these expressions, there will be many which can be connected to the action tendencies in only *ad hoc* fashion; pouting and biting one's lip may be examples. As for instrumental behaviors in emotion—escaping, insulting, seducing the antagonist's wife—they are clearly related to the aims with which the action tendencies are linked. Apart from these behaviors as such, or their plans, information should be available to the system concerning the goals served by these behaviors, or their consequences which might fit these goals. Moving Against aims at Unpleasantness for the Antagonist; unpleasantness is achieved by Disagreeable Behaviors; seducing the antagonist's wife clearly is such behavior. All this information, again, is of the same sort as that involved in story understanding, and of the same sort as is needed for decoding events and assessing their relevance.

Emergence of physiological response may follow a course similar to expression, although the evidence concerning the determinants of autonomic reactions is confusing. One may, as is implied by most of the emotion literature, locate "autonomic arousal" differently from where it had been placed in the present model; one may tie it directly to the relevance estimation or to the seriousness estimate. Here, however, physiological response is considered tied to the motor demands of the action tendency, hence its place at this point. "Autonomic arousal" (meaning predominantly sympathetic response) is to be linked to "active" action tendencies, such as Activation, Hyperactivation, Moving Against and the like. Heart rate deceleration may be linked to Attention. Autonomic deactivation or para-sympathetic dominance may be tied to Hypoactivation, or whatever "action tendency" may turn out to adequately represent such reactions as giving up, helplessness, or as passive receptivity in happiness or meditation.

Regulation of Overt Action

Behavior planned is not necessarily executed, or not necessarily executed as planned. In addition to the control which operates upon the emotional impulse, there is a regulation that operates upon behavior, and possibly (for some Yogis) upon physiological response. There are two different reasons for submitting emotional behavior to further control. One is the issue of situational appropriateness of overt responding, which can be formulated in terms of *display rules* (Ekman & Friesen, 1969b). The other concerns the anticipated or perceived effects of expressive behavior upon other people (Frijda, 1982). Others may dislike it or take advantage of it; or they may be impressed by it, becoming intimidated by fits of anger, mellowed by tears or solicitous by manifest sorrow or helplessness. There are, then, reasons and occasions for both suppression and enhancement of overt response; they are founded in actual or anticipated feedback from one's own responding.

Control of execution may have still other reasons, and go further than just suppression or enhancement. There is also feedback from the behavior as experience—actual or anticipated—upon the subject himself. He may want to deny his helplessness, or he may dislike being carried away. The control—Lazarus' secondary coping—may be conscious and operating upon the response, as well as more automatic and operating on the impulse. Under such conditions emotional behavior, as dictated by the action tendency, may be transformed into, or replaced by, different behavior. A laughing fit takes the place of weeping, or arrogance that of dependent yielding. Clearly, then, in order to implement such regulation, behavior execution should be monitored by assessment of its effects, and be evaluated in terms of goals and interests different from those which led to the behavior in the first place.

EMOTIONAL EXPERIENCE AND SEQUENCING

One may wonder where in the model emotional experience does emerge since no output is provided for it. The answer is that it emerges nearly everywhere; it springs from nearly every operation in the process. The bracketed labels alongside the diagram indicate the contributions made by each of them. These labels should not be understood to mean that, at a particular point, the particular component of the experience is felt subjectively. They are meant to indicate what component is contributed by what operation. The corresponding experience *might* arise if the process were to be interrupted, or would end, at that point, or when the other phases would be skipped. Relevance evaluation without context evaluation, and consequently without the generation of a directed action tendency, would lead to mere "emotion"—the undifferentiated feeling of being emotionally aroused, etc.

Emotional experience in its full developed form is assumed to be composed of the person's appraisal of the event and of the total situation, to the extent that he is aware of them or makes assumptions and post-hoc attributions about them; further, of his awareness of his action tendencies, feedback from his overt behavior and autonomic arousal, or physiological response generally. Take away any of these, and the experience becomes indeterminate or vague or confused, or mere feeling, or cold.

Emotional experience, then, is the result of monitoring the entire process. It may be assumed that such monitoring should have a function, or at least an effect upon the process itself. The model does not include such function or effect since it is by no means clear what these might consist of. One may think of emotional experience as modifying or co-determining the action tendency and emotional behavior, in ways described by attribution theorists.

Implied in the preceding paragraph is the assumption that the emotion process is not necessarily run through in its entirety. If we assume that each operation takes time, distraction, or too brief a confrontation with the event may block the process after some of its steps, or at least after any of the first three. It seems plausible that from the fourth step, seriousness estimation, onward, the remainder runs on its own, without needing further external input. Obviously, regulation may block the two operations which surround it.

The first four steps would not seem to have to follow each other in the sequence indicated. They may run in parallel, with some sort of integration thereafter, or the order may be changed. One can perceive an event as potentially dangerous, or potentially accessible, without any of one's own concerns getting involved until later, or until the event becomes more imminent; there may be other possibilities as well.

CONCLUSION

Implementation of the present outline of a model of emotion depends in part upon information representation and information processing of quite complex kinds; these are not specific to the domain of emotion, however, and are familiar from work on story understanding. It does not seem, therefore, that the model will turn out inappropriate or inadequate for reasons pertaining to such matters.

The adequacy and feasibility of the model also depends upon the appropriateness of the various correspondence assumptions. It remains to be demonstrated that concern relevance, context evaluation and seriousness evaluation unambiguously determine action tendency (and that means, to some extent, the emotion label) and emotional behavior. Also, it remains to be demonstrated that context evaluation categories and seriousness combination rules can be unambiguously defined. As for the main points of the theory, such as the generality of the asserted dependence of emotion upon concerns (and of emotional intensity upon concern strength) and the determinants of physiological response, these raise both empirical and conceptual issues, such as the fruitfulness of assuming that interest, values or sensitivities are determinants of every emotion.

In one basic respect the model is distinctly inadequate. Emotion is depicted as an isolated process, serving only its own ends. Obviously it is not. The process of emotion, it may be said, serves the interests of concerns and action, and should be subsumed under those, rather than having "concerns" as one of its inputs. Put otherwise: "emotion" should be considered an auxiliary process in the superordinated process of concerns and of actions dictated by those concerns. The current goal, current action, and concerns motivating those should be considered the major sources of emotion, rather than "events" impinging upon an otherwise passive system. This implies, as hinted at before, that "current concern" probably has more weight than other concerns; and that "emotion" feeds back primarily to decisions concerning the continuation or interruption of current action, and to those concerning which concern is to be the current one. In that perspective, emotion turns out to be a monitor system (Pribram, 1970), and an interrupt system as outlined some time ago by Simon (1967). At the same time, emotion is clearly motivational, considering the action tendency. Expression and arousal are only some of the realizations of such tendency and the position of instrumental behavior such as fleeing, or constructing a shelter, or killing one's rival by poison, is not essentially different.

Another basic limitation of the model stems from the fact that it only models the emergence of "an emotion"—of a single emotional response. Events are stretched out over time, and so is emotional responding. Events are modified by the emotional reaction, both objectively and cognitively: helplessness occurs only after previous coping attempts have proved fruitless. Emotional reactions exert influence upon succeeding ones, if only by depleting the "energy store" and by strengthening secondary coping attempts.

REFERENCES

Arnold, M. B. *Emotion and Personality*, Vol. I. New York: Columbia University Press, 1960.

Brown, J. J. & Farber, I. Emotions conceptualized as intervening variables—with suggestions toward a theory of frustration. *Psychological Bulletin*, 1951, *48*, 503–507.

Davitz, J. R. *The Language of Emotion.* New York: Academic Press, 1969.

Ekman, P. & Friesen, W. V. The repertoire of nonverbal behavior: Categories, origins, usage, and coding. *Semiotica*, 1969, *1*, 49–98.

Ekman, P. & Friesen, W. V. *Unmasking the Face.* Englewood Cliffs: Prentice Hall, 1975.

Frijda, N. H. Recognition of emotion. In L. Berkowitz (ed.), *Advances: Experimental Social Psychology*, Vol. 4. New York: Academic Press, 1969, pp. 167–223.

Frijda, N. H. The meanings of emotional expression. In M. Ritchie Key (ed.), *Nonverbal Communication.* Berlin: Mouton, 1982, pp. 103–120.

Goffman, E. *Frame Analysis.* New York: Harper, 1974.

Hebb, D. O. *The Organization of Behavior.* New York: John Wiley, 1949.

Izard, C. E. *Human Emotions.* New York: Plenum Press, 1977.

Kahneman, D. *Attention and Effort.* Englewood Cliffs: Prentice Hall, 1973.

Klinger, E. Consequences of commitment to and disengagement from incentives. *Psychological Review*, 1975, *82*, 1–25.

Lazarus, R. S. *Psychological Stress and the Coping Process.* New York: McGraw-Hill, 1966.

Lindsay, P. H. & Norman, D. A. *Human Information Processing*, 2d ed. New York: Academic Press, 1977.

Mandler, G. *Mind and Emotion.* New York: Wiley, 1975.

Mark, V. & Ervin, F. *Violence and the Brain.* New York: Harper & Row, 1970.

Nisbett, R. E. & Wilson, T. D. Telling more than we can know. *Psychological Review*, 1977, *84*, 231–259.

Pribram, K. H. Feelings as monitors. In M. B. Arnold (ed.), *Feelings and Emotions: The Loyola Symposium.* New York: Academic Press, 1970, pp. 41–53.

Schachter, S. The interaction of cognitive and physiological determinants of emotional state. In L. Berkowitz (ed.), *Advances in Experimental Social Psychology*, Vol. 1. New York: Academic Press, 1964, pp. 41–53.

Schank, R. C. & Abelson, R. P. *Scripts, Plans, Goals, and Understanding.* Hillsdale, N.J.: Lawrence Erlbaum, 1977.

Simon, H. A. Motivational and emotional controls of cognition. *Psychological Review*, 1967, *74*, 29–39.

Sroufe, L. A. & Waters, E. The ontogenesis of smiling and laughter: A perspective on the organization of development in infancy. *Psychological Review*, 1976, *83*, 171–189.

Wegman, C. Psychoanalyse en cognitieve psychologie. Ph.D. thesis, University of Nijmegen, 1979.

Wilensky, R. Understanding goal-based stories. Research Report No. 140, Department of Computer Science, Yale University. Mimeo.

Zajonc, R. B. Feelings and thinking: Preferences need no inferences. *American Psychologist*, 1980, *35*, 151–175.

2

A Cognitive Model of Anxiety

Implications for Theories of Personality and Motivation

Vernon Hamilton
Reading University, England

ANXIETY AS COGNITIVELY CODED INFORMATION

An extensive literature is available which describes human anxiety and its development, and unanimously confirms the impairing role of high, and not necessarily pathological, anxiety in many types of performances. I have reviewed this material recently in some detail (Hamilton, 1976a, 1976b, 1979a, 1979b), as well as the apparent inadequacies of models to account for this interaction. There are two major shortcomings in past theorizing: (1) no one was willing to offer a new definition of anxiety consistent with developments in cognitive processing theory, thus avoiding the question of *"what"* anxiety is, and (2) no one offered an explanation of *"why"* and *"how"* the unfavorable interaction with performance could actually occur. First attempts at a cognitive/informational specification of anxiety (Hamilton, 1972, 1975), were readily accepted by Sarason (1975) in a general way without reference, however, to the necessary cognitive operations and processes required for a processing capacity explanation. To account for the impairing effect of high anxiety in terms of interference from preoccupations with "worries," negative self-evaluations of anticipated threats or dangers (e.g., Liebert & Morris, 1967; Wine, 1971; Sarason, 1975), does not fully conceptualize what it is that is measured by criterion questionnaires of anxiety, nor by what interacting processes interference with an externally presented task can occur. I have argued, therefore, that anxiety should be considered as a particular set or network of connotative data, which on the basis of past experience and autonomous elaboration of their cognitive structures provide a store of long-term memories. These are available for retrieval when stimulated, just like other long term memory data.

Plausibility for this interpretation may be gained from various sources. *Anticipation* of any form of danger, *expectancies* of threats, the *probability* that any one of a number of painful, unpleasant, or aversive outcomes may be contingent on, say, what a person does at any given moment, or on how well he thinks he is doing it, or on where he is journeying with what type of transport, all of these must depend on having available knowledge of potential outcomes. This, however, requires a store of information, reality-based or fantasied, by which to anticipate, expect, and calculate the probability of an event which will be aversive and threatening for the person. My emphasis at this point is not only on the organization or consistency of structures, but on the *amount* of aversive information, its general-ization to objects, events or persons which characterize the high anxious person, and on the method of encoding the information. This information is usually un-related to and irrelevant for the task which a person is asked to carry out, and which contains its own quantum of information processing demands. However, the greater the predisposition to generate ideas of aversive expectancies of be-havior outcomes, the greater the appropriate memory store, the lower the retrieval threshold for this type of information; and the greater the response bias toward a primary attentional process of identifying and avoiding real or potential aversive-ness. If this analysis is correct, then it follows that the high anxious person when performing any task, is, in fact, in a dual task situation, which requires multiple channels and parallel cognitive processes.

Only one additional factor is required to provide a parsimonious reason to explain why high anxiety impairs performance. This is to be found in the generally acceptable propositions of data and resources limitations in human information processing capacity (e.g., Broadbent, 1971; Kahneman, 1973; Norman & Bobrow, 1975). An early, neat illustration of this was provided by Conrad (1951) when investigating limitations of human vigilance. As with performance by high anxious subjects, there were two sources of information to be observed in this experiment: signal rate and number of dials. Predictably, the number of responses possible is a decreasing function of the total information processing load.

If for high anxious individuals anxiety is cognitive information with low retrieval thresholds and high priorities for directing attention to stimuli which have no specific relationship to the task, and if the processing resources of the person are limited at any given time, then two general predictions can be made. First, high anxious subjects should perform worse than low anxious subjects when a task becomes more difficult, that is, when there is a substantial increase in its informa-tion processing demands. (Worse here is defined by either increased slowness, *or* increased errors to avoid the awkward trade-off effect.) Second, these performance deficits should not covary necessarily with levels or changes in levels of peripheral arousal.

There appears to be now a growing conviction that the implications of recent work on the interaction between arousal and performance may have to be recon-sidered (e.g., Poulton, 1976, 1977). The absence of any precise distinction between arousal, emotionality, stress, and anxiety (see for instance Easterbrook, 1959; Broadbent, 1971) has always seemed to be a curious gap in theorizing, particularly in view of the non-specificity of the physiological defining criteria. In cognitive terms, physiological changes in heart rate, muscle tension, and skin conductance, including their analysis by superordinate identifying schemata, involve only small amounts of information, most of which appears to be gross and undifferentiated (Ursin, Baade, & Levine, 1978). Its role in performance decrements, therefore, must be small and no more than indirect in setting up positive feedback loops between disturbing, distracting or interrupting information retrieval, matching and inte-grating processes, and concomitant physiological reactivity. Furthermore, there is only a tenuous relationship, if any, between peripheral-autonomic and electro-cortical arousal, where it is the latter and not the former which is implicated in changes in selective attention and in short-term, working memory capacity (War-burton, 1979).

Four experiments have been carried out which appear to support a cognitive interpretation of anxiety and of a cognitive processing load explanation of "*why*" high anxiety impairs performance in cognitive tasks, which do not support an arousal explanation (Hamilton, 1976a; 1979a; 1979b; 1980). Two tasks included an experimental manipulation of anxiety and/or arousal. In all four studies anxiety was assessed by Test Anxiety questionnaires (Sarason, Davidson, Lighthall, Waite, & Ruebush, 1960; I. G. Sarason, 1972) depending on whether the subjects were clinically normal students or school children.

The results showed that high anxiety subjects were significantly slower on word recognition, dual-task RT's, and problem solving, particularly on the more difficult items of a mathematical substitution problem series with systematically increasing information content; and very short term memory capacity (using Sperling's method) was significantly lower. Performance differences did not covary with levels or changes in levels of heart rate or skin conductance, and anticipation of electric shock (never given), and self-esteem threatening verbal feedback on performance affected high anxious subjects more than low anxious subjects, although the groups were undifferentiated on the arousal measures. In fact, the attempt to induce raised arousal levels *improved* the performance of high anxious subjects compared with their performance under nonthreatening conditions. This paradoxical result requires explanation in terms other than changes in arousal.

Since the most pronounced differences between the experimental groups were defined by their responses to anxiety questionnaire items, the most plausible explanation of these and similar studies on the effects of anxiety need to be sought in those organized cognitive structures from which subjects deduced or induced their response to questionnaire items. In other words, the type and intensity of self-generated cognitive interference appears to be a function of the content and elaboration of long term memory schemata which encode the subjective experience, knowledge, anticipation, and response requirements of potential threats and dangers. Thus, the interaction of one particular personality and motivational system—anxiety—with external situations is governed by cognitive processes which integrate external-temporary, and internal-more durable goal-directed processes.

INFORMATION PROCESSING CAPACITY LIMITS AND TASK–IRRELEVANT MOTIVATION

Effect of Experimenter-pacing and Test Anxiety on Problem Solving

Paradoxical results require an explanation. High anxious subjects should not have performed better under stressed compared with nonstressed conditions. Since high anxious students are frequently also high on achievement motivation, i.e., motivated to avoid failure, two explanations which could also serve as predictions were offered:

(1) Exposing high anxious subjects to ego-stressors would generate energy reserves through failure-avoidance motivation to enable them to improve their performance even with difficult tasks. This should be possible only, however, for relatively short periods.

(2) If the time allowed for problem solving is reduced, however, which is really another type of stressor, this extra coping effort would be of little avail since in these conditions high anxious subjects would be deprived of adequate processing

time as well as processing space for short term memory and selective attention operations.

An experiment was designed, therefore, to test for the interaction between problem solving and anxiety in a mixed design to enable the effects of stressing and nonstressing instructions and experimenter pacing and nonpacing to be assessed in all possible combinations. Groups of high test anxious ($\bar{X}$ TAS Score = 23), and low test anxious ($\bar{X}$ TAS Score = 9) subjects, respectively, were first randomly assigned to each of the instructions conditions, and within each of these to an initial paced or nonpaced condition as shown in Table 1. Each subject was tested on two parallel versions of a symbolic problem solving test of systematically increasing order of difficulty. Within each cell of Table 1 half the number of subjects were given Test 1 first, while the other half commenced with Test 2. The problem solving tests consisted of mathematical-symbolic statements and series of re-expressions of the same statements followed by a question of the identity or non-identity of a final symbolic equation (see Hamilton & Moss, 1974; Hamilton, 1980). Each test consisted of four levels of difficulty which were defined by the minimum number of necessary symbolic substitutions or steps required to affirm or disconfirm the final equation. There were three problems at each difficulty level, and solution times as well as errors were the dependent variables.

In addition, heart beats per minute were systematically sampled in all experimental conditions and at all problem difficulty levels. The subjects were first year university students majoring in a number of subjects, including psychology. The time limitation and stressor conditions were embedded in the instructions to subjects. Self-esteem anxiety was stimulated in the instruction condition by creating dissonance between the self-evident difficulty of the problems and the statement that students find them easy. In the nonstressing instruction the difficulty of the task was emphasized as well as giving reassurance about insufficient solution time and the possibility of errors. The time limit in the paced method of problem administration was set at 70 percent of the mean time for problems at each level of difficulty obtained in pilot testing for subjects commencing with the paced condition, or 70 percent of subjects' own unpaced performance which preceded the paced condition.

A selection of the experimental results is shown in Figs. 1, 2, and 3.[*] Figure 1 illustrates the solution time variable for the unpaced condition which was employed in all previous studies. It could not be computed for the paced condition because the large number of errors by subjects gave too small a set of error free data. The most important result is the replication that high anxious subjects improve in performance with the kind of ego-stressor usually embedded in instructions

---

[*]This experiment was conducted by Reine LeGall.

Table 1 Experimental design

Order of first condition	High anxious		Low anxious	
	Paced (P)	Unpaced (U-P)	Paced (P)	Unpaced (U-P)
Nonstressing instructions (N-S)	4	4	4	4
Stressing instructions (S)	4	4	4	4

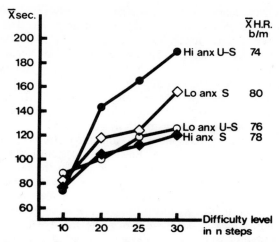

Figure 1 Unpaced solution times for blocks of three problems per difficulty level (U-S = Unstressed, S = Stressed Conditions) (N's = 8).

($F(1, 56) = 4.59$, $p < 0.05$). Furthermore, with nonstressing instructions high anxious subjects were considerably slower ($F(1, 56) = 5.43$, $p < 0.025$) than low anxious subjects. With stressing instructions, there was no significant main effect for anxiety. A special feature is the reversal of high and low anxious subjects' performance with stressing instructions, compared with previous findings. To judge by the large number of errors made by the low anxious when unstressed and their improvement when stressed, it was concluded that this group was relatively unmotivated when given nonstressing instructions. This interpretation is supported by the data in Fig. 3 and other evidence.

Figure 2 shows the effect of experimenter pacing on errors. The main effect of increased errors from pacing was highly significant ($F(1, 28) = 9.99$, $p < 0.01$),

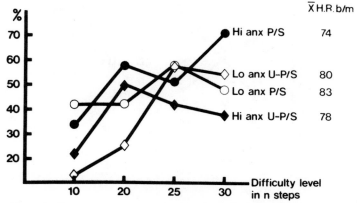

Figure 2 Errors and heart rates for Paced/Stressed (P/S) Conditions and Unpaced/Stressed (U-P/S) Conditions (N's = 8).

but without any significant interactions. The previously shown instruction effect clearly contributed to this by attenuating a general trend. The prediction was particularly directed at performance on the most difficult task (*n* steps = 30). Here a Mann-Whitney test shows significantly more errors for the high anxious ($U = 10.5$, $p < 0.014$), whereas the performance of the low anxious at this level of difficulty is (nonsignificantly) in the opposite direction.

Figure 3 summarizes the results across all levels of the difficulty factor (which in every analysis was the most significant main effect) in order to demonstrate the interaction between stressing by instruction and by pacing. The slopes of the graphs indicate that pacing had the most impairing effect on the high anxious group as predicted. Figure 3, as well as Figs. 1 and 2, additionally shows that the heart rate arousal measure played no systematic role in the results obtained. Furthermore, at difficulty level *n* steps = 30, slowness of processing was paired with lower error rates only for the low anxious group and for the high anxious only when nonpaced. From this the most plausible explanation needs to be in terms of time and space limitations in cognitive processing for the high anxious, who by prediction are also processing task-irrelevant aversive information. Evidence for this interpretation remains incomplete, however, until even more difficult tasks can be designed which produce an even higher load on short term working memory and selective attention, and until the effect of systematically increasing the *duration* of a test session at these higher levels of difficulty can be assessed. Moreover, evidence must be made available to show that all task-irrelevant motivational preoccupations deplete the data processing capacity of the cognitive system. One type of this evidence was aimed for in the study discussed next.

Effect of "Eroticism" on Problem Solving

It can be argued that if male subjects are invited by an attractive female experimenter to examine photographs of the "soft porn" variety, they are likely to

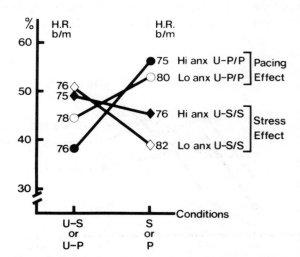

Figure 3 Grand mean percent errors for combined problem difficulty levels (*N*'s = 16 U-P/P; *N*'s = 8 U-S/S).

become sexually aroused in the physical as well as the cognitive sense. It can also be argued that the degree of arousal should be concomitant with scores on a questionnaire aimed to establish levels of sexual interest and activity. If instructions to experimental subjects require them to rehearse for subsequent recall the visually presented sexual material while at the same time they are engaged in a difficult problem solving task, we have a test situation which is probably analogous to placing high and low anxious subjects into an ego- or self-esteem threatening situation while engaged in a similarly demanding problem solving task. If, however, sexual preoccupation is not only less aversive but consists also of less finely differentiated and elaborated cognitive structures in long term memory than has been proposed for cognitive anxiety, then the interference or intrusion effect should be less marked than the interference from cognitive anxiety. Conversely, if what matters is a consistent and stubborn intrusion effect from a second task whose content occupies a high position in a hierarchy of characteristic goal-directed dispositions which has been deliberately stimulated, then the sensitization of "eroticism," as it is called here, should have a similar effect to that of ego-threat on anxiety.

Twenty-one male undergraduate students were given Sarason's Test Anxiety Scale and a questionnaire derived from items aimed at sexual interests previously published (Eysenck, 1976). High and low scoring subjects were assigned to four criterion groups each with $N = 7$. There was a small but quite insignificant positive correlation between these two measures. All subjects were given the two parallel tests described in the pacing study previously discussed in counter-balanced order. The instructions were relatively stressing in that they asked for great care, and fast and error-free performance. After completion of the first set of problems (pre-intrusion task) each subject was required to examine eight numbered photographs each depicting a man and a woman engaged in sexual play, and to place them in rank order of degree of sexual arousal. They were then asked to rehearse for subsequent correct recall the ranked number of the pictures with the advice that rehearsal of content would help them to do so. The second set of problems was then administered with the same instructions as before, and this was followed by the request to recall the numbers of the previously ranked sexual material.

Heart rate was monitored throughout. Exposure to the ranking task led to a significant rise in beats per minute ($p < 0.01$) but this increase was not maintained during the postintrusion task. The small *negative* correlation between "eroticism" score and heart rate during picture ranking was not significant, and it is possible that the low 'eroticism' scores may not be fully valid.*

A selection of the results is presented in Figs. 4, 5, and 6 for pre- and post-intrusion problem solution times and errors. Figure 4 shows once again the slowness of high anxiety subjects compared with a low anxiety group ($F(2, 72) = 3.13$, $p < 0.05$), but this time also the similarity to the low anxiety subjects, prior to sexual stimulation, of the 'eroticism' criterion groups. Furthermore, before exposure to sexually arousing material the high and low 'eroticism' groups perform virtually identically. Task difficulty is not a significant factor for these groups, though it is highly significant for the anxiety groups ($F(3, 72) = 8.77, p < 0.001$).

Figure 5 gives the solution times after the sexual material had been inspected and graded and while subjects attempted to remember the rank order of their

*This experiment was conducted by Linda Inglis.

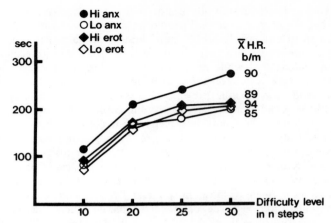

Figure 4 Mean preintrustion task solution times (blocks of 3 problems, N's = 7).

sorting exercise. The anxiety main effect is now no longer present, but a significant difficulty factor for the "eroticism" groups now appeared which was absent for the preintrusion task ($F(3, 72) = 12.26$, $p < 0.001$). In other words, after exposure to sexual material and with an ongoing rehearsal of that material, successive problems took progressively longer to solve. As a corollary it may be suggested that the absence of a significant main effect for anxiety was due to the motivational irrelevance of the sexual material for subjects differing in test anxiety rather than "eroticism."

Figure 6 shows the errors for the four criterion groups before and after exposure to the sorting and memory task. Apart from confirming again the special difficulty of high test anxious subjects with the most difficult tasks, the comparison of pre-

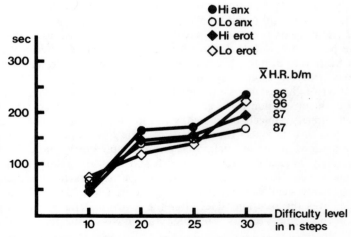

Figure 5 Mean postintrusion task solution times (blocks of 3 problems, N's = 7).

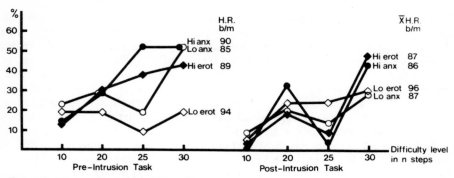

Figure 6 Mean percent errors (N's = 7).

with postintrusion performance shows an improvement for the high and low anxious, but a deterioration for the eroticism subgroups. Whereas the preintrusion error difference between the eroticism groups had been significant ($F(3, 72) = 4.25$, $p < 0.01$), this was no longer present in the postintrusion task. It suggests again that the low eroticism group was more susceptible to sexual arousal than reflected by their questionnaire answers. It is difficult to say that this is also reflected in their higher heart rates. No systematic peripheral arousal factor is present in Figs. 3, 4, and 5 relatable either to sexual arousal, or to problem solving capacity, or an interaction between these. If Lacey is correct (e.g. Lacey, 1967) then sexual arousal and heart rate deceleration during problem solving should work in opposite directions, and electrocortical, or tomographic measures (Lassen, Ingvar, & Skinhøy, 1978), may have to be employed in more definitive experiments.

The evidence from this experiment is not conclusive. The difference between high and low "eroticism" groups describes an only roughly similar pattern to that of high and low test anxious groups for solution times and errors in problem solving of systematically increasing difficulty. It seems plausible to conclude, however, that the presence of characteristic goal-directed dispositions, in which the connotative content of different cognitive structures defines the goals, acts as a source of interference and of processing capacity limitation, even if much of the content is mediated by visual or proprioceptive imagery. If this conclusion is correct then the nature of the interfering connotative data needs to be examined in order to find plausible mediators for the proposed interaction. Since it is no longer possible to cite arousal as the dominant explanatory variable, and since cognitive processing limitations have supplied a consistent fit for anxiety-related performance deficits, I want to cast a brief new look on what is actually implied by cognitive structures representing personality and motivation.

TOWARD A COGNITIVE–SEMANTIC MODEL

Two related conceptual steps seem to be required to generalize from the cognitive interpretation of anxiety and "eroticism": (i) to identify the *nature* of the cognitive data which is able to interact with the operations involved in problem solving, and (ii) to examine the possibility that all personality and motivational characteristics use cognitive data which are similar or identical to the data employed in problem solving. To this end I am putting forward a number of propositions which are derivable from the cognitive conception of human anxiety and stress (Hamilton & Warburton, 1979).

First, the signal or data language of the human responding and processing system must be a common language for interactions between cognitive problem solving operations and personality and motivation to occur. An integrated goal-directed response is not possible without it. Second, the unitary and coordinated nature of human behavior suggests that this language is the language of cognitive codes representing a large variety of stored information. Third, the cognitive codes and structures carrying this information and which also subserve personality and motivation, are represented by cognitive networks of functionally related experience, anticipated behavioral outcomes and by stimulus and goal attributes. Fourth, because the organization and interpretation of all nonreflexive adaptive behavior requires an analysis of stimulus meaning and of the implications of alternative responses, the networks of informational codes need to be *semantic networks.* Fifth, semantic networks serving personal goals and their precedence, constitute *semantic memories,* and have established functional and adaptive utility over a large range of response requirements. Sixth, the generalized utility of attributional semantic networks suggests that personality and motivational semantic memories are *organized in schemata.* Seventh, where individuals possess highly elaborated, characteristic goal-directed semantic schemata with *low retrieval thresholds,* internal, self-relevant cognitive activities will affect the objective utilization of external, objective stimuli, and personality-cognition interactions will occur which can be experimentally demonstrated.

A full discussion of these propositions required a monograph (Hamilton, 1983). and I will confine myself here to a relatively superficial exercise in pointing to theoretical analogues which appear to support my attempt to synthesize. The analogues I have chosen relate to existing notions of the cognitive-semantic organization of meaning and to elaborations of the concept of the schema. From these I will sketch by way of illustration a possible model of the cognitive-semantic structure of one aspect of social introversion.

Before I go on to this exercise, I would like to point to some important consequences of the cognitive interpretation of personality and motivation. If this has any validity at all, then one of the most widely used constructs in cognitive psychology is so misleading that it may actually be false. I am referring to Easterbrook's (1959) hypothesis that emotionality reduces the range of cue utilization. Another implication of the cognitive approach is the doubt which it throws on the ultimate utility of theories of personality-cognition interaction which have been derived from questionnaire criterion measures of personality or emotionality such as anxiety, neuroticism, repression-sensitization, internal-external control, introversion or extraversion. It is not only a question of the validity of regarding opposite ends of a factorial dimension as *opposite* traits, nor is it only the very limited identification of personality traits that can be achieved by the questionnaire technique. The real question seems to be whether trait-cognitive performance interactions have yielded a genotypical explanation, rather than evidence of covariation. This kind of evidence is important, of course, but it does not contribute to knowledge of the methods or nature of interaction. For this purpose, the concept of arousal has been proposed, and the various trait dimensions which I have cited have been considered as systematically related to it. Quite apart from my own data on the limited role of high arousal in cognitive performance deficits, we have here a logical problem. By definition, peripheral and electrocortical arousal processes are facilitators and carriers of information. Any information which they convey to an analyzing system is gross and nonspecific, even though the state of activation is intrusive. Thus, arousal is essentially without connotative content and thereby becomes a necessary but not sufficient process and explanatory concept in personality-cognition interaction.

Let us now remind ourselves of how the human cognitive processing system is currently conceived. Figure 7 is meant to summarize what are believed to be the major components of the information processing system for the acquisition of skills and capacities, and for the selection of stimulus-appropriate responses. It is a model of how information may be received, manipulated, coded and stored for subsequent use. It is the kind of system hypothetically required for the accumulation and elaboration of knowledge and memory of the objects and attributes of our *shared* environment.

One suggestion of how the organization of functionally related attributes may be cognitively coded was made nearly ten years ago. The hierarchical links of the semantic networks shown in Fig. 8 may be structurally incorrect, or the form of the functional organization across conceptual boundaries may be rather different (e.g. Rips, Shoben, & Smith, 1973). It provides one illustration, however, of the proposition that attributes which define objects or situations to which a response has to be made, and which have related definitions and *meaning* for the responder, are represented by semantic data networks in permanent memory.

Except when we are forced to use language precisely, we seem to be preoccupied with a wider range of meanings than concept definition. It seems plausible to

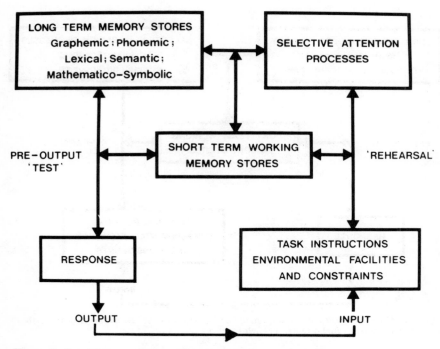

Figure 7 Cognitive processing components and operations for the acquisition and elaboration of information.

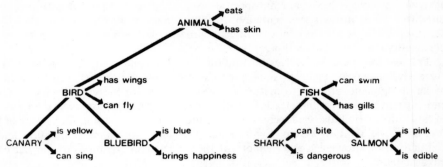

Figure 8 Hierarchical structure of portion of semantic memory. (After Collins and Quillian, 1969).

suggest, therefore, that the semantic memory store of characteristics, attributes, and strategies of definition, includes *higher order semantic codes of the nature of the responses* required from us, of expectancies of goal-directed alternative responses, and of the nature and attributes of the goals themselves. This suggestion is consistent, I believe, with Neisser's construct of the "executive" in perception (1976), and Erdelyi's (1974) suggestion that higher order selective attention operates in "perceptual defense." Figure 7 can be redrawn, therefore, as in Fig. 9, to show that permanent memory and selective attention, when not elicited in a

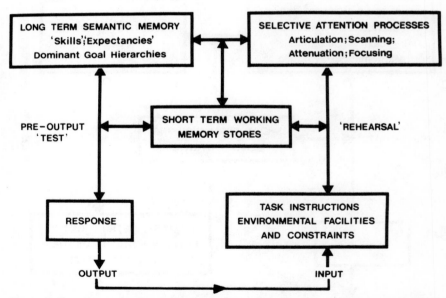

Figure 9 Cognitive processing components and operations for the acquisition and elaboration of characteristic goal-directed behavior.

narrow-focus laboratory setting, may need to go beyond the analysis and inter-pretation of sensory features. As an example let us take a person who is faced with a difficult interpersonal relationship problem, or one who is required to fulfil his usual occupational role following bereavement or after experiencing a serious blow to self-esteem. All these are stressors which make substantial demands on the differential allocation of attentional strategies and the retrieval and integration of a variety of response capabilities in order to achieve the most preferred adaptive state. To achieve the most preferred outcome external stimuli must have been completely analyzed and conceptualized in relation to dominant interpreting strategies. I would argue that these processes are not intrinsically different from those employed in other types of problem solving involving meanings of words or conceptual attributes, except that in the more complex examples, semantic net-works guide a *social* response.

Let me illustrate with an example from intelligence testing. Baddeley (1976) suggests that semantic memory may be the required cognitive process for solving the Picture Arrangement subtest of the Wechsler Intelligence Scale for Children, which has the solution code "FISHER". We may ask whether semantic data based on dictionary or lexical definition are the only semantic data needed. It can be argued that complex cognitive-semantic schemata are actually stimulated here if it is agreed that prior experience with, and interest in gardening and fishing facilitate performance on this task, and if a sense of humor helps, as in this example in which a man prefers fishing and dreaming by the river to the company of his nagging wife. All these ascribed characteristics and attributes figure directly or implicitly in personality trait or type theory, and, moreover, reflect differential motivational strength. The semantic basis is evident not only because the reasons for the arrange-ment of the pictures is *reportable*, but it so happens that this particular example actually has *two* fully correct normative solutions!

Let me now assume for the moment that there are no intrinsic objections to the proposition that cognitive codes, subserving meaning, have semantic content and representation. How then is this semantic information organized? I have already proposed that the concept of the schema supplies an appropriate organizing system. It remains to examine the utility of this concept more closely.

The role of schemata in perception and memory was first investigated syste-matically by Bartlett (1932). He proposed that remembering is influenced by a process of "effort after meaning" which is a reflection of individual strategies of simplifying, elaborating, focussing, naming and conventionalizing in encoding and retrieval operations. In *Cognition and Reality*, Neisser (1976) has further refined this complex and elusive construct by analogy with computer language format, with plans, patterns of and for action, frames of reference, and with geno-typical potentialities for development. Neisser's schema is an information pro-cessing and coding system with structural nervous system potentials which become manifest in anticipations, particularly, it may be added, in the presence of am-biguity and low informational redundancy.

We have at least two physiological construct theories which can conceivably supply a neurological basis for the concept of structural nervous system potential which is able to give rise to a hierarchically organized, subjective, and idiosyncratic memory system appropriate for the analysis of stimulus input. Hebb's (1949) construct of the cell assembly with its numerous links between cells in some form of hierarchical arrangement is a system by which individual differences in set and selective attention can trigger both different and similar identifiers depending on context. More recent and probably more sophisticated is Pribram's (1971) hologram model of neurological functioning. It retains Hebb's notion of patterns of cell activity, but introduces new concepts of the economy of information storage. The importance of the neurological constructs to date lies in their suggestions for the registration and coding of functionally related events by relevant cross-referenced classification or grouping, and hence for the organization of experience along subjectively coherent and even consistent lines. Since the presence and participation of schemata in perceptual and mnemonic activities are inferred from responses depending on the interpretation of meaning, it need not be implausible to suggest that holograms or cell assemblies in the final analysis can also encode semantic information.

One further step is required in this initial attempt to conceptualize personality and motivational attributes as cognitive-semantic data: to apply the notion of semantic networks or schemata to the concepts of traits and types. The evidence of a regularly performed skilled habit, such as lighting a pipe under many different conditions and in a variety of situations, is not only similar to Bartlett's famous example of the schematic characteristics of the tennis stroke, but to evidence that the meaning of situations, conditions, facilitations, and constraints have been correctly identified and integrated. At a higher conceptual level, we may say that, for example, the social introvert's identification of the to him aversive characteristics of a pre-Christmas party, *and* his rapid exit, similarly reflect the operation of the application of meaning, in this case, to the behavior of others in the context of self-image and interest schemata. I would argue that the concepts underlying person perception and self-images are not fundamentally different from other concepts, and that semantic networks schematically organized and structured represent them, just as other semantic networks contain the attributes of triangularity, of osmosis, or of ethnic prejudice. Figure 10 is a first approximation of the content and elaborations of the semantically coded schemata of a social introvert who on our most frequently used questionnaires, affirms that he likes being on his own. The "Interest Schemata" are, of course, very complex structures with many subsidiary specifiers, some of which may actually be shared by other people, including extraverts. The illustration also tries to show in a primitive way the overlap between attributes organized in different schemata. The more wholehearted the state of introversion, the greater the elaboration of appropriate schemata, the greater the amount of space, cell-assemblies or holograms they utilize in permanent memory, and the lower the retrieval thresholds of the consonant cognitive structures.

The proposition that personality and motivation can be fundamentally described by cognitive schemata, clearly has only superficial similarity to Kelly's (1955) personal constructs. The present analysis of personal goal-relevant memory content has greater affinity with the notion of conceptual belief systems (Harvey, Hunt, & Schroder, 1961). This is particularly so because Harvey's later studies (Harvey & Felknor, 1970) suggest sets of socialization and developmental antecedents which are similar to my own suggestions of the effects of suboptimal mothering on cognitive development (Hamilton, 1972, 1975).

There is considerable support now from animal learning (e.g. Estes, 1978), as well as from social learning theorists (e.g., Mischel, 1973; Cantor & Mischel, 1977; Bandura, 1977) that uncomplicated S-R models of behavior require cognitive

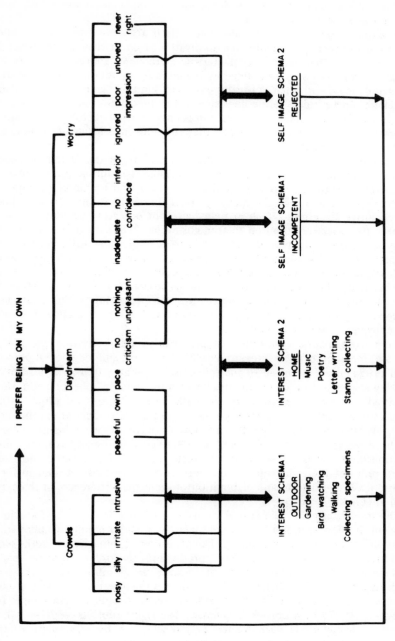

Figure 10 Interest and self-image schemata implied by a Social Introversion Questionnaire item.

mediating processes. The cognitive-semantic model of personality and motivation aimed at a more genotypic level of definition and explanation seems fully consistent with these conceptual developments.

The cognitive-semantic model also lends itself to a resolution of the uneasy relationship between personality and motivation. Here it may be proposed that the relationship is that between characteristic methods of approaching or avoiding goals, and hierarchies of goals defined by the intensity, duration, and intermittency of behavior they elicit. What is usually overt is a kind of "grammar" of organized goal-seeking whose rules define consistency and predictability. Consistency may well not be demonstrated, but then consistency is itself merely a reflection of superordinate coherence, and evidence that rule governed behavior includes rules of when and how to depart from them.

Operations on permanent memory schemata need be neither wholly dependent on external stimulation, nor need they be reportable. The autonomous processes in remembering illustrated by Bartlett and many others, and the developmental basis of adult semantic and pictorial memory, furthermore contribute to the idiosyncratic cognitive structures which at many levels of operation facilitate or impede fully objective selective attention to stimulus events. While the basic framework of the physical and social environment appears to be homogeneously and successfully transmitted to all physiologically intact people, we have enough evidence to maintain an important role for the unobservable operations which change veridicality into subjective coherence, or into incongruous anxieties. It seems, therefore, that there is as much justification for postulating self-protecting coding strategies of displacement, projection or reaction-formation, as for the development of a universal, convergent, and predictable lexicon.

A cognitive-semantic conception of personality and motivation provides the means and medium for their interactions with perceptual and judgmental processes. Erdelyi (1974) drew attention to the role of selective attention in an information processing sequence to account for the "perceptual defense" phenomenon. He left unspecified, however, the nature of the data, and the means by which data organized at one point in a sequence is able to integrate with data at another point. He also avoided the crucial question of how cognitive style or cognitive control could be displayed by a behavior system described traditionally as noncognitive. The proposition that this system must be seen as a cognitive-semantic information network removes these difficulties, and furthermore provides a paradigm for the acquisition, differentiation, and elaboration of individual differences in characteristic goal-directed behavior.

Is the model testable? The answer must be yes if one is searching for evidence of concept development and conceptual hierarchies, and a number of pilot studies are now in progress in this laboratory. Direct testing of semantic networks serving characteristic goal hierarchies by word production or word recognition reaction times may well be unprofitable, however, because various inhibitory processes may lead to unsystematic data. What may be required is the investigation of hemispheric differences during respectively verbal and nonverbal problem solving tasks (e.g., Underwood, 1977; Davidson & Erlichman, 1980) by subjects with known differences in characteristic goal-directed preferences, and by manipulating experimentally the strength of approach or avoidance preoccupations.

Though it may appear reactionary to suggest it, a projective approach to the semantic coding model for personality and motivational profiles may be of initial benefit. Some relevant earlier psychometric work, albeit for diagnostic purposes, was carried out with interesting results (e.g., Balken & Messerman, 1940; Zubin, Eron, & Schumer, 1965). The prediction would be that subjects' dominant characteristics as obtained from preliminary questionnaires and other self-assessment data, would be reflected in the degree of elaboration emerging in the verbal description of suitably labelled stimulus figures and in the goal-directed intentions which subjects ascribe to them. It would also have to be predicted that attributes and strategies generated by subjects in this situation, would be best remembered in suitable recognition experiments if they reflect previous evidence of their own dominant characteristics. It is even likely that dominant trait-relevant attributes will lead to a significant number of trait-relevant "false positives" in a recognition experiment.

One further prediction suggests itself at this early stage. If personality characteristics and their hierarchies of goals are correctly defined by conceptual, cognitive-semantic structures, then "problem solving" tests previously confined to affectively neutral knowledge, and conceptual operations involving it, should demonstrate the level of development of affectively important schemata. Test situations which specify the goal hierarchy of a test figure and his/her previously preferred methods of goal-achievement can be designed in which subjects are required to elaborate the different ways in which the test figure with characteristics "A to F," can achieve a particular goal "G," given environmental constraints and facilitations "H to Z." The semantic content of subjects' responses may then be taken as evidence of the elaboration of particular cognitive-semantic schemata.

Ultimately, behavioral science requires direct rather than inferred evidence for its theories. There are many reasons why developments in technological sophistication and biological theory will eventually produce the data necessary for that level of validation.

REFERENCES

Baddeley, A. D. *The psychology of memory*. New York: Harper & Row, 1976.

Balken, E. R. & Masserman, J. H. The language of phantasy: III the language of the phantasies of patients with conversion hysteria, anxiety state and obsessive-compulsive neurosis. *Journal of Psychology*, 1940, *10*, 75–86.

Bandura, A. *Social learning theory*. Englewood Cliffs, N.J.: Prentice-Hall, 1977.

Bartlett, F. C. *Remembering*. Cambridge: Cambridge University Press, 1932.

Broadbent, D. E. *Decision and stress*. London: Academic Press, 1971.

Cantor, N. & Mischel, W. Traits as prototypes: effects on recognition memory. *Journal of Personality and Social Psychology*, 1977, *35*, 38–48.

Conrad, R. Speed and load stress in sensorimotor skill. *British Journal of Industrial Medicine*, 1951, *8*, 1–7.

Davidson, R. J. & Erlichman, H. Lateralized cognitive processes and the electroencephalogram. *Science*, 1980, *207*, 1005–1006.

Easterbrook, J. A. The effect of emotion on cue-utilization and the organization of behavior. *Psychological Review*, 1959, *66*, 183–201.

Erdelyi, M. H. A new look at the New Look: Perceptual defense and vigilance. *Psychological Review*, 1974, *81*, 1–25.

Estes, W. K. On the organization and core concepts of learning theory and cognitive psychology. In W. K. Estes (ed.), *Handbook of learning and cognitive processes*. Hillsdale, N.J.: Lawrence Erlbaum, 1978.

Eysenck, H. J. *Sex and personality*. London: Open Books, 1976.

Hamilton, V. Maternal rejection and conservation: An analysis of suboptimal cognition. *Journal of Child Psychology and Psychiatry*, 1972, *13*, 147–166.

Hamilton, V. Socialization and information-processing: A capacity model of anxiety induced performance deficits. In I. G. Sarason & C. D. Spielberger (eds.), *Stress and anxiety*, Vol. 2. Washington, D.C.: Hemisphere, 1975.

Hamilton, V. Motivation and personality in cognitive development. In V. Hamilton & M. D. Vernon (eds.), *The development of cognitive processes*. London: Academic Press, 1976. (a)

Hamilton, V. Cognitive development in the neuroses and schizophrenias. In V. Hamilton & M. D. Vernon (eds.), *The development of cognitive processes*. London: Academic Press, 1976. (b)

Hamilton, V. Personality and stress. In V. Hamilton & D. M. Warburton (eds.), *Human stress and cognition: An information processing approach*. Chichester: Wiley, 1979. (a)

Hamilton, V. An information processing approach to neurotic anxiety and the schizophrenias. In V. Hamilton & D. M. Warburton (eds.), *Human stress and cognition: An information processing approach*. Chichester: Wiley, 1979. (b)

Hamilton, V. An information processing analysis of environmental stress and life crises. In I. G. Sarason & C. D. Spielberger (eds.), *Stress and anxiety*, vol. 7. Washington, D.C.: Hemisphere, 1980.

Hamilton, V. *The cognitive structure of human personality and motivation*. Chichester: Wiley, 1983.

Hamilton, V. & Moss, M. A method of scaling conservation of quantity problems by information content. *Child Development*, 1974, *45*, 737–745.

Hamilton, V. & Warburton, D. M. (eds.). *Human stress and cognition: An information processing approach*. Chichester: Wiley, 1979.

Harvey, O. J., Hunt, D. H., & Schroder, H. M. *Conceptual systems and personality organization*. New York: Wiley, 1961.

Harvey, O. J. & Felknor, C. Parent-child relations as an antecedent to conceptual functioning. In R. A. Hoppe, G. A. Milton, & E. C. Simmel (eds.), *Early experiences and the processes of socialization*. New York: Academic Press, 1970.

Hebb, D. O. *The organization of behavior*. New York: Wiley, 1949.

Kahneman, D. *Attention and effort*. Englewood Cliffs: Prentice-Hall, 1973.

Kelly, G. *The psychology of personal constructs*. New York: Basic Books, 1955.

Lacey, J. I. Somatic response patterning and stress: Some revisions of activation theory. In M. H. Appley & R. Trumbull (eds.), *Psychological stress*. New York: Appleton-Century-Crofts, 1967.

Lassen, N. A., Ingvar, D. H., & Skinhøy, E. Brain function and blood flow. *Scientific American*, 1978, *239*, 50–59.

Liebert, R. M. & Morris, L. W. Cognitive and emotional components of test anxiety: A distinction and some initial data. *Psychological Reports*, 1967, *20*, 975–978.

Mischel, W. Toward a cognitive social learning reconceptualization of personality. *Psychological Review*, 1973, *80*, 252–283.

Neisser, U. *Cognition and reality: Principles and implications of cognitive psychology*. San Francisco: Freeman, 1976.

Norman, D. A. & Bobrow, D. G. On data-limited and resource-limited processes. *Cognitive Psychology*, 1975, *1*, 44–64.

Poulton, E. C. Arousing environmental stresses can improve performance whatever people say. *Aviation, Space and Environmental Medicine*, 1976, *47*, 1193–1204.

Poulton, E. C. Continuous intense noise mask auditory feedback and inner speech. *Psychological Bulletin*, 1977, *84*, 977–1001.

Pribram, K. H. *Languages of the brain*. Englewood Cliffs, N.J.: Prentice Hall, 1971.

Rips, L. J., Shoben, E. J., & Smith, E. E. Semantic distance and the verification of semantic relations. *Journal of Verbal Learning and Verbal Behavior*, 1973, *12*, 1–20.

Sarason, I. G. Experimental approaches to test anxiety: Attention and the uses of information. In C. D. Spielberger (ed.), *Anxiety—Current trends in theory and research*. New York: Academic Press, 1972.

Sarason, I. G. Anxiety and self-preoccupation. In I. G. Sarason & C. D. Spielberger (eds.), *Stress and anxiety*, vol. 2. Washington, D.C.: Hemisphere, 1975.

Sarason, S. B., Davidson, K. S., Lighthall, F. F., Waite, R. R., & Ruebush, B. K. *Anxiety in elementary school children*. New York: Wiley, 1960.

Underwood, G. Attention, awareness and hemispheric differences in word recognition. *Neuropsychologia*, 1977, *15*, 61–67.

Ursin, H., Baade, E., & Lewis, S. (eds.). *Psychology of stress: A study of coping men.* New York: Academic Press, 1978.

Warburton, D. M. Physiological aspects of anxiety and schizophrenia. In V. Hamilton & D. M. Warburton (eds.), *Human stress and cognition: An information processing approach.* Chichester: Wiley, 1979.

Wine, J. Test anxiety and direction of attention. *Psychological Bulletin*, 1971, 76, 92–104.

Zubin, J., Eron, L. D., & Schumer, F. *An experimental approach to projective techniques.* New York: Wiley, 1965.

3

Stress, Personality, and Smoking Behavior

H. J. Eysenck
University of London

In this paper I hope to highlight certain difficulties and complexities which beset the general area of stress research. These difficulties are disregarded by many investigators, with the result that experiments are often uninterpretable and un-replicable, and that the general theory of stress reaction is in a very undeveloped state. Some of these difficulties can be illustrated by pointing to the linguistic perversion which makes us talk about "stress" when what we really mean is "strain." The failure to distinguish clearly between these two quite different concepts, a failure which is almost universal, is a survival of early behavioristic S-R theories, and antedates mediational hypotheses from Hull's original r_g-s_g notion to later and more sophisticated constructs, such as Osgood's (McGuigan, 1978). *Stress* is the stimulus, applied on the outside and directly observable; *strain* is the mediational concepts we use to direct attention to the internal and largely unobservable behavior of the organism. Whether *strain* is regarded as an intervening variable or a hypothetical construct is not important at the moment; my own preference would be for the former alternative.

Strain is a concept bound up with the evaluation of the stressful stimulus; identical stimuli may be evaluated as anxiety-provoking, neutral, or even pleasant by different persons. Thus, observation of the stimulus (stress) may tell us nothing about the subjective reaction of the person to whom the stimulus is applied; unless we can relate the stressful stimulus to personally experienced strain we have no right to talk about the stressful nature of the stimulus at all! Some stimuli of course are almost universally found to produce strain in most people (torture, starvation, asphyxiation), but psychologists are seldom concerned with stimuli of this kind. Certainly stimuli used in the laboratory are frequently considered as stressful by some people, not so by others; unless we have some way of looking at the strain produced by these stimuli we cannot generalize our conclusions in any way.

I have on previous occasions suggested that it may be useful in this connection to look at the concept of stress and strain as defined in Young's Modulus. Consider Hooke's law of elasticity: Stress = $k \times$ strain, where k is a constant (the modulus of elasticity) which depends upon the nature of the material and the type of stress used to produce the strain. This constant k, i.e., the ratio stress/strain, is called Young's Modulus, and is illustrated (with certain simplifications) in Fig. 1a. A and B are two metals differing in elasticity; they are stressed by increasing loads, and the elongation corresponding to each load plotted on the abscissa. It will be seen that identical loads θ give rise to quite divergence elongations, and Fig. 1b illustrates

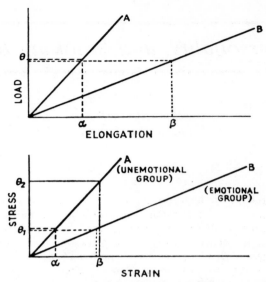

Figure 1 An analogy between Hooke's Law (top) and stress-strain effects in rats (bottom).

the similar analysis of rat behavior in an experimental situation productive of emotion. Again the stress (independent variable) is plotted on the ordinate, and the strain (dependent variable) on the abscissa; A and B represent unemotional and emotional strains of animals respectively. Identical stress θ_1 gives rise to quite different strains α and β. It would require stress θ_2 to make the strain in A animals equal to that produced by θ_1 in B animals.

Differences between θ_1 and θ_2 are the kinds of differences traditionally studied by experimental psychologists; differences between A and B are the kinds of differences traditionally studied by personality psychologists, believers in the importance of constitutional factors, and clinical psychologists. Physicists have never attempted to make a choice between these two sets of variables, or to study them in isolation; it seems equally futile for psychologists to do so. Provided the modulus employed is even moderately correct, and more than a mere analogy, the experimental possibilities suggested by this method of approach seem promising.

This way of looking at the problem suggests that we should try to measure strain in behaviorally meaningful terms, preferably by deductions from general theories, and to formulate laws relating the strain to the stress. It would seem to follow from our Fig. 1 that, to some extent, and under certain circumstances, stress and k are interchangeable. In the case of human beings and animals, of course, k corresponds to personality differences. These personality differences are as important in the study of stress reactions as is the modulus of elasticity in the case of Hooke's law; no meaningful and replicable relations can be postulated without keeping these sources of individual variation in mind.

An example may make clear what is intended here. Consider some early experiments carried out by Rosenbaum (1953, 1956). He used as his measure of strain the generalization of a voluntary response, the threat of shock (of varying intensity) as a stress, and measures of anxiety as task relevant indices of k (personality). He found that threat of a strong shock led to greater generalization of a voluntary response than did threat of a weak shock, and that the anxious subjects showed greater generalization to identical stimuli (i.e., threats of a given shock intensity) than did non-anxious subjects. In other words, Rosenbaum found that as far as strain is concerned we can trade personality (in this case trait anxiety) against stress (in this case, threat of shock of varying intensity). The crucial element in all this is the amount of strain, here conceptualized in terms of response generalization. In principle this approach should make it possible to devise algorithms in terms of which we could quantify strain and personality traits on a common metric. Other examples for this general proposition can be found in our own animals studies on emotionality (Savage & Eysenck, 1964).

It is important to consider another aspect of k which also has an analogue in human behavior. In the statement of Hooke's law, k depends upon the nature of the material (which we have equated with "personality" in human beings) *and the type of stress used to produce the strain.* This suggests that in psychology too different types of stress may produce quite different results, and as an example we may use the argument presented by Saltz (1970) who summarizes his review of the literature by saying that "persons who score as high anxious are those who show disruptive behavior under failure-induced stress, but not necessarily under pain-induced stress; persons who score as low anxious are those who show disruption under pain-induced stress, but not necessarily under failure" (p. 568). Saltz continues: "This position accounts for most of the conditioning and verbal learning data published to date" (p. 568).

Eysenck (1973b) has provided a review of the literature, with special reference to Spence's theory of anxiety as a drive; there seems to be no doubt that shock in particular produces effects which do not replicate those produced by other types of stress, suggesting the importance of this aspect of k in psychological research on stress. Most researchers, unfortunately, have taken it for granted that one type of stress is pretty well equivalent to another ("equipotentiality"). The lack of replicability of so much of the work done suggests that this may have been an overly simplistic view.

The first point on which I think it is essential to insist, therefore, is that *individual differences are all-important in the study of stress and strain.* Disregard of individual differences is of course characteristic of most approaches to the problem by experimental psychologists. This position in the field of negative reinforcement (stress) is mirrored in the field of positive reinforcement, where also we find very great individual differences, but little attempt to make any systematic study of these differences. Positive reinforcers cannot in the majority of cases be identified as applying uniformly to all subjects (leaving out certain obvious exceptions such as food in the case of hunger, water in the case of thirst, etc.). There is no common term to identify a concept parallel to "strain," but denoting pleasurable effects; perhaps the terms positive and negative hedonic tone may serve to identify the internal complement to external stimulation by positive reinforcers and by stressors. Behaviorists will of course reject purely subjective and introspective identification of positive and negative hedonic tone, but will prefer objective behavioral indices, such as adient and abient behavior.

One example of the importance of individual differences in defining reactions to identical stimuli is the relationship between level of stimulation (as objectively determined) and induced hedonic tone. The example chosen will also demonstrate at the same time another important source of difficulty in the general field of stress reactions which is unfortunately often disregarded, namely the general tendency of regressions in this connection to be nonlinear. Figure 2 (Eysenck, 1963) shows the curvilinear relationship between hedonic tone and level of stimulation, from low (sensory deprivation) to high (pain). It will be seen that excessively low or high levels of stimulation are characterized by negative hedonic tone (stressors), while intermediate levels of stimulation have positive hedonic tone (positive reinforcers). This relationship, however, must be looked at in terms of what Berlyne (1960, 1974) has called "arousal potential," here identified in terms of the level of intro-version or extraversion of the subject of the experiment. There is much evidence to support the hypothesis that introverts have a higher resting level of arousal than ambiverts, and ambiverts a higher level than extraverts. Thus the arousal potential of the introverts is higher than that of the extraverts, which displaces the optimum level of arousal of the introverts to the left in the diagram, and that of the extra-verts to the right. It will be seen that extraverts and introverts, therefore, differ very much in respect to the optimum level of stimulation (O.L.) that produces the highest level of positive hedonic tone.

Another consequence of the differences in arousal between extraverts and introverts is shown quite clearly by looking at points A and B on the abscissa. At these points, the hedonic tone of the average person is at the indifference level; stimulations of these particular intensities are characterized by neither a positive nor a negative hedonic tone. For introverts and extraverts, however, this is not so. At point A, the level of stimulation, interacting with the arousal level of the person has a negative hedonic tone for extraverts and a positive hedonic tone for intro-verts. At level B, the positions are reversed; here the relatively high level of stimu-lation produces a negative hedonic tone in introverts, a positive hedonic tone in extraverts. Clearly the "stressor" is identical in physical terms, but the strain, i.e., the negative hedonic tone experienced by extraverts, ambiverts, and introverts, is quite different, and would be predicted to result in quite different types of be-havior.

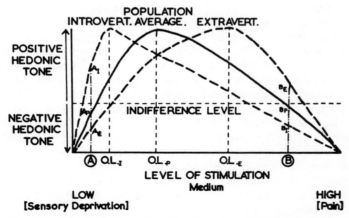

Figure 2   Relation between level of stimulation and hedonic tone for introverts, ambiverts, and extraverts.

The curvilinear regression between level of stimulation and hedonic tone shown in Fig. 2 is not the only curvilinear relationship which we find in this general area. The organism does not passively experience stimulation; it modulates incoming stimulation as already hypothesized by Pavlov in his "law of transmarginal inhibition." Pavlov used this concept (also sometimes called "protective inhibition" by him) to limit the "law of strength," which postulated that increasing strengths of the US would lead to increased strength of the CS. Discovering that there was an optimal level beyond which increasing the strength of the US led to a *decrement* in CS, he postulated that cortical neurones "protected" themselves against too strong stimulation by producing inhibition. While the pseudo-physiological explanation given by Pavlov is unacceptable, the phenomenon has been replicated too many times, in connection with too many different systems, to be in any real doubt. Examples are work on conditioning (Eysenck & Levey, 1972) who showed that with low intensities of US introverts conditions significantly better, whereas with strong US extraverts did; Shigehisa and Symons (1973), who looked at the influence of ambient sensory stimulation in one field on sensory thresholds in another; and the effect of different intensities of light on averaged evoked responses (Zuckerman et al., 1974).

This modulation of incoming sensory stimuli in terms of augmenting or reducing is thus a coping feature of the intact organism, and affects the strain properties of given stresses. There appears to be a relationship between cortical augmenting and extraversion, on the one hand, and cortical reducing and introversion on the other. Thus here again we see that there are complex interactions between stress, strain, and personality, linked together through a curvilinear relationship—a complex system which makes nonsense of any attempt to understand the facts in terms of a simple linear S-R model.

The modulation hypothesis links stimulation and cortical effects; it goes beyond the well-known Yerkes-Dodson Law and the equally well-known inverse-U relationship between stimulus and response. In the Zuckerman et al. experiment at least the "response" (the averaged evoked potential) is, as it were, a direct measure of cortical arousal, suggesting that the relationship is not necessarily between arousal (drive) and performance, as the inverse-U law would have it, but that modulation involves the cortical arousal level itself. It will be useful to bear this in mind in looking at another level of complication, namely, the interaction between stress, personality, and drugs known to affect the arousal level. The particular drug chosen to illustrate this is nicotine, administered through the smoking of a cigarette.

The problem which the experiment next to be recounted attempted to solve is a well-known one. Nicotine is a stimulant drug, yet many people smoke in order to calm their apprehensions and reduce their anxiety and their level of arousal. Yet others apparently smoke because they are bored, and wish to increase their level of arousal (Frith, 1971). Thus, tobacco apparently has two contradictory effects on the human organism; it may act to reduce one kind of strain (anxiety) by *reducing* anxiety levels, and to reduce another type of strain (boredom) by *increasing* arousal levels. Truly nicotine must be a wondrous drug to act in two opposite directions!

There are two possible ways to explain this dual and contradictory action. In an earlier paper I tried to explain it in terms of amount of nicotine ingested (Eysenck, 1973a). The hypothesis (for which there is a certain amount of evidence, both with animals and with humans) suggested that *small* amounts of nicotine increased arousal, whereas *larger* amounts of nicotine decreased arousal. Thus, the contradictory effects of nicotine could be explained in terms of the choice of cigarette (high versus low nicotine content) or the mode of smoking. While this explanation is still viable, it certainly is not capable of explaining all the known facts. In particular, it fails to take into account personality differences, which on the evidence so far submitted, should have a crucial influence on the effects of nicotine in delaying the strain produced by given stressors.

In order to take personality into account in connection with this general paradigm, I put forward the hypothesis shown in diagrammatic form in Fig. 3 (Eysenck & O'Connor, 1979; O'Connor, 1980). Using the contingent negative variation (CNV) on the EEG as a measure of arousal, the aim of the experiment was to contrast the reactions of extraverts and introverts to smoking a single cigarette, taking measures under sham smoking conditions (i.e., conditions where the subject manipulated the unlit cigarette as if he were smoking) and real smoking conditions, i.e., with the subject smoking one cigarette of known nicotine content, with puff frequency controlled and nicotine intake measured by analysing the stub of the cigarette at the end of the experiment.

The predictions made will be ovious from the diagram. Under sham smoking conditions, introverts are predicted to show a *higher arousal potential* than extraverts, as indexed by greater CNVs. Smoking a cigarette will push both extraverts and introverts along the curvilinear regression line, increasing the CNV for the extraverts, and decreasing it for the introverts. Positive results would tend to substantiate the hypothesis; negative results would be somewhat ambivalent, because one cigarette might not be sufficient to produce the predicted results.

At an early stage in the investigation of novel phenomena, there is little knowledge of the necessary parameter values in order to make a crucial experiment. O'Connor (1980) was fortunate, however, in hitting upon a degree of nicotine intake which was just right to demonstrate the predicted phenomenon. The actual experiment was carried out in a sound-proofed cubicle. S.L.E.9 mm silver/silver chlorided cup electrodes were attached to Cz and Fz (vertex and frontal) 10/20

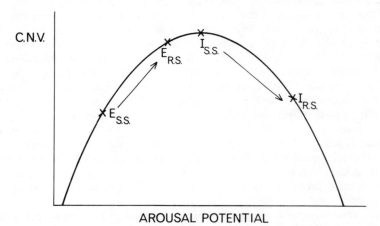

Figure 3 Diagrammatic representation of hypothesis linking arousal potential (extraversion vs. introversion), CNV measures of arousal, and sham smoking (SS) vs. real smoking (RS).

placement and connected with common reference to linked earlobe placements. An electrode on the nosebridge served as a ground. The EEG signals were fed through pre-amplifiers with time constants of 10 sec. and high frequency cut off 6 dB down at 30 Hz. Eye movements were measured ultrasonically by means of a Piezo electric transducer which converted the Doppler difference of reflected sound waves into a change of voltage level proportional to lateral excursion of the eyeball. Eye movements were calibrated during each session and any trial showing movement greater than 3° of visual angle was rejected from subsequent analysis.

Stimulus presentation was controlled by a Linc-8 computer which triggered relays via sense lines to the experimental room. The warning stimulus (S_1) was either a red or green light on for 100 msec. Lights were situated at eye level on a visual display panel mounted 4 ft in front of the subject. The response stimulus (S_2) was a continuous 600 Hz tone set comfortably loud at 40 dB above arbitrary zero and relayed binaurally through earphones. The tone was terminated by a motor response which consisted of pressing one of two push buttons, situated on the right and left arms of the subject's chair and pressed with right and left hands, respectively. The subject room was adjacent to the experimental recording room and was separated by a Venetian window, through which the subject could be observed. Communication was maintained via an intercom system. Time of day testing was standardized to 9.00 a.m.

The CNV was recorded both within conditions of simple RT and choice RT paradigm, and within each of these conditions under both a fixed constant foreperiod (FF) set at 1.25 sec., and a variable foreperiod (VF) in which a 1.25 or 4.0 sec. ISI was equally probable on any trial. The ISI length of 1.25 sec. was chosen as an anchor paradigm for replication of previous studies; the use of a 4.0 sec. ISI permitted the separation of early and late components of the CNV.

Each subject was tested under four conditions in both sham and real smoking condition sessions. Conditions were randomized across subjects according to an appropriate Latin square design. Puff frequency during the real smoking sessions was standardized over conditions and subjects; puff volume was measured by means of a Grass differential pressure transducer. The cigarettes smoked were standardized experimental cigarettes, and the butts were analyzed after the experiment to determine amount of nicotine absorbed.

Figure 4 shows the averaged CNVs for extraverts and introverts during the simple RT 1.25 sec. ISI paradigm, and Fig. 5 shows results for the 4.0 sec. ISI paradigm. It will be seen that the CNV peak latency occurs later for introverts under sham smoking, for extraverts under real smoking conditions. This is as predicted, because, as particularly apparent in Fig. 5, the strength of the CNV continues to *rise* for introverts after sham smoking, for extraverts after real smoking, but *declines* for introverts after real smoking, for extraverts after sham smoking. These relationships are shown particularly clearly in Fig. 6.

The experiment disclosed many other results which have been reported by O'Connor (1980) that tend to substantiate the hypothesis that introverts are in a higher state of arousal. Thus introverts' blink frequency was considerably higher than extraverts', and this has been suggested by Tecce et al. (1978) to be a good measure of arousal. Extraverts were found to have a larger puff volume than introverts; which may indicate the need for a steep rise up the arousal curve from an initially low level, while the introverts may have required less nicotine to push them over the top to transmarginal inhibition. In addition, there are significant differences

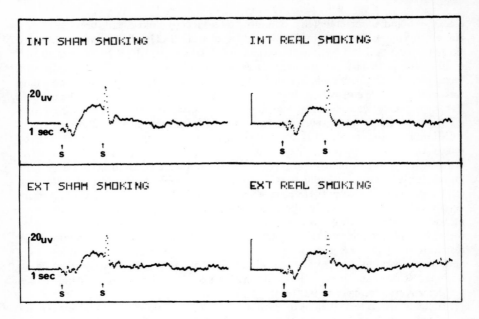

GROUP AVERAGE   1·25 sec I S I

Figure 4   Average CNVs for extraverts and introverts during simple RT 1.25 sec. ISI paradigm.

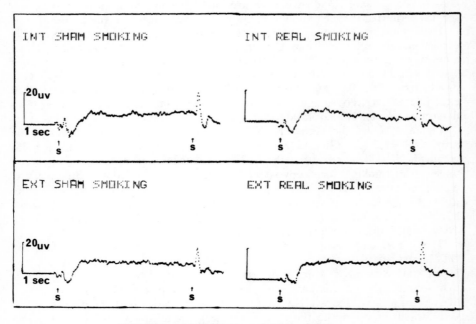

GROUP   AVERAGE   4·0 sec I S I

Figure 5   Average CNVs for extraverts and introverts during simple RT 4.0 sec. ISI paradigm.

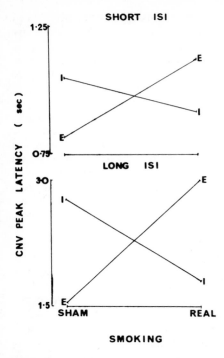

Figure 6 Crossover effects for extraverts and introverts on short and long ISI CNV experiments respectively. Peak latencies plotted on ordinates.

between introverts and extraverts in the development of the slow positive waves (SPW) occuring 200–400 msec. post S_1 and preceding the development of the slow negative wave (SNW) with which we have been concerned hiterto. Gaillard (1978) relates SPW magnitude to the input process by which stimulus information is integrated and evaluated, and Loveless (1980) suggests that it may indicate an effort to control irrelevant activity prior to deciding on an appropriate response, citing evidence that large positivities related to fast reaction. Introverts generally show a more cautious strategy in preparing for response, and the greater positivity of the introverts could suggest an initial emphasis on inhibiting rather than launching into activity.

This study is quoted here mainly in order to illustrate the crucial points in the theoretical analysis developed in the earlier parts of the chapter. It illustrates the importance of personality variables (in this case extraversion-introversion) in mediating stress and producing strain (in this case indexed by CNV arousal). Secondly, the experiment illustrates the need for accepting the reality of curvilinear regression in relation between stimulation and response, in this case between stress and strain. Simplistic questions like: "Does nicotine produce relaxation or arousal?" simply do not admit of an answer in that form; we can only answer such questions with respect to a particular personality type, under specified conditions, in which there is some control over nicotine intake. It is suggested that what is true of this particular example is true quite generally, and that the failure in this general field of study to develop acceptable and replicable general laws is due to neglect of this important point.

The difficulties in analyzing the relationship between stress, strain and behavior extend of course into the response field, where again an overly simplistic view has been taken of such response systems as "anxiety." Anxiety, as has often been pointed out, has three different measurable components, which do not by any means cohere together so closely as to enable us to adopt what has been called a "lump theory" of anxiety (Eysenck, 1975). When we look at these three components, which may be defined as physiological, behavioral, and introspective, we find that there is a considerable degree of desynchrony; in other words, anxiety elicited along one of these lines is not necessarily correlated with anxiety as manifested in behavior along the other two lines (Grey et al., 1979; Hodgson & Rachman, 1974; Rachman & Hodgson, 1974). The person may report anxiety, but show little or no physiological arousal or behavioral avoidance; he may show avoidance behavior without any physiological arousal or introspective reports of anxiety, and finally he may show physiological anxiety without any verbal or behavioral manifestations. This type of desynchrony is more apparent under relatively low emotional arousal, but of course that is precisely the condition which is usually encountered in the laboratory and in most life situations; really strong emotional arousal is relatively rare in civilized society.

It is possible, again, to seek for personality correlates of desynchrony; it seems likely that people whose scores on some physiological measures do not correlate with self-perception may be either "sensitizers" or "repressors," i.e., they may either exaggerate or deny the occurrence of autonomic reactions (Sackeim & Gur, 1978). There is some evidence that the discrepancy between self-reported and physiological measures is related to how people cope with stress. For example, Weinstein et al. (1968) found a significant relationship between measures of denial and physiological and self-reported discrepancies. Deniers reported less change in anxiety as a function of threat than was evident from their physiological reactions. Burish and Houston (1976) found that a high lie score on the MMPI predicted a disposition to employ defensive maneuvers against the threat of an electric shock. It was found that defensive strategies used by high lie scorers facilitated performance at the expense of increased physiological arousal. The authors concluded that "possibly the greater physiological arousal was due to the psychic cost of coping with stress."

Recently Weinberger et al. (1979) showed that self-perceptions are particularly inaccurate in people who score high on the Marlowe-Crowne Social Desirability Scale, which is essentially another form of the Lie Scale. For subjects showing low trait anxiety on the Taylor Manifest Anxiety Scale, they found that the Marlowe-Crowne scale predicted a repressive coping style which involved an avoidance of disturbing cognitions accompanied by a relatively high physiological arousal. This suggests that "repressors" tend to underestimate the physiological arousal which may have implications for psychosomatic research (Schwartz, 1977). When "repressors" were asked to describe their most important characteristics it appeared that they were preoccupied with rigorously controlling their emotions, clearly taking a rational and unemotional approach to life. Another group of subjects, called "sensitizers" had high trait anxiety and low defensiveness scores. "Sensitizers" tended to amplify their self-perceptions of anxiety. Both "repressors" and "sensitizers" coped ineffectively with stress as compared with truly low-anxious people. (See also Mandler et al., 1961, and Neilson et al., 1976.)

In a recent unpublished study by Gudjonsson, 36 male subjects were administered the Eysenck Personality Inventory and the Marlowe-Crowne Social Desirability Scale; they were also asked to rate their subjective feelings of disturbance during an emotionally arousing task, and their skin resistance was recorded. It was predicted that subjects whose self-reports showed more anxiety than their physiological reactions warranted (sensitizers) could be discriminated from those showing the opposite pattern (repressors) by having high N and low L scale scores. Repressors were expected to have high L scale scores and low N scores. Both predictions were verified at a reasonable level of statistical significance, and there was also a suggestion that "repressors" were more extraverted, "sensitizers" more introverted. It thus seems that personality is intimately connected with the occurrence of desynchronization, in a predictable manner. It would seem that in future work on stress and anxiety personality measures should be used in connection with the quantification of the response to stress also.

I would like now to make certain general suggestions for research planning which would seem to emerge from the considerations advanced above. In the first place, I think it is important to make the clearcut distinction between stress and strain advocated here, and always to provide for the measurement of strain in addition to recording the stimuli supposititiously producing stress. Strain, measured in this fashion, may be related to ultimate behavior in quite a different fashion to the observable relations between stress and behavior. Thus, in the O'Connor experiment described above, reaction time, as a response measure, covaried with strain rather than with stress.

Our second proposal is the very obvious one that no experimental studies in psychology should be done without the inclusion of provisions for the measurement of the major dimensions of personality, in particular extraversion-introversion and neuroticism (anxiety)-stability (Eysenck, 1980). Personality variables should not, of course, be included on a random basis, but a careful theoretical analysis of the whole experiment should precede their inclusion, and lead to specific and testable hypotheses regarding their interaction with the experimental variables.

The third consideration applies to the choice of parameter values, and the need for greater knowledge in respect to the kind of predictions that can be made on a quantitative basis. We may take it for granted that curvilinear relations are the rule rather than the exception in this field, but we have very little knowledge of the rules relating to the point at which optimal conditions occur, and the law of strength changes into the law of transmarginal inhibition. This should be an important area of research, but as far as I know very little has been done in this respect.

This failure to analyze the problem on a quantitative basis may be due in part to the fact that while many people have recognized the existence of the inverse-U relationship, there has not really been an adequate discussion of the many different *types* of inverse-U relationship which can be found in the literature. We have recognized several quite different ones in this chapter. First, we have the relationship between intensity of stimulation and hedonic tone. Second, we have the relationship between arousal (drive) and performance. Third, we have the relationship between arousal potential and arousal, as shown in Fig. 3. Next we have the relationship specified by Pavlov's law of strength and transmarginal inhibition, which do not seem to be identical with any of the others mentioned hitherto. This is an area where clarification is urgently needed, and prior to such clarification it will be difficult to carry out any reasonable quantification along experimental lines.

The importance of paying attention to parameter values and inverse-U relations is brought out very forcefully in Stelmack's (1980) survey of the "psychophysiology of extraversion and neuroticism." He finds, for instance, again and again, that conditions most conducive to discovering differences between extraverts and introverts are those which are described as "moderately arousing," the conclusion already anticipated by Gale (1973) in his survey of studies of extraversion and the EEG. It will be seen from Fig. 2 why, on theoretical grounds, this should be so; conditions of strong stimulation produce high arousal in all subjects, and would seem to eliminate differences between introverts and extraverts, even where they do not invert these through "transmarginal inhibition," while conditions of very low-intensity stimulation have strong negative hedonic tone for extraverts, but not for introverts, and thus produce arousal in the former which again can eliminate observable differences. It is unfortunate that much experimental work is still done in this field without regard to considerations of this kind.

Differences in stress-intensity are reasonably predictable on theoretical grounds, but other parameter values which appear to be important are less obvious to account for. Thus, Stelmack reports that the determination of differences between introverts and extraverts may be facilitated by employing low frequency auditory stimulation, and may be obliterated when high frequency auditory stimulation is employed. This agrees with the finding by Davis and Ferlin (1966) and Rothman (1970) that inter-individual variability of the AER is greater at low frequency than at high frequency, and this finding too is not easy to understand theoretically. These and many other parameter values have to be borne in mind in designing experiments in the attempt to link stress, anxiety, and personality.

Above all, what is needed is the development of theoretical concepts which will guide experimental investigations. One such theory was Spence's attempt to treat anxiety as a drive, and apply Hullian principles; this theory has been uniquely successful in many ways, although it has crucial weaknesses (Eysenck, 1973b). Recent years have seen no development in this field, but rather a shying away from the development of theories of this kind. Electicism and anti-theoretical pragmatism are not likely to solve the very real problems which arise in research on stress and anxiety. Only the development of better theories will succeed in doing this.

REFERENCES

Berlyne, D. E. *Conflict, Arousal and Curiosity.* New York: McGraw-Hill, 1960.

Berlyne, D. E. *Studies in the New Experimental Aesthetics.* London: Wiley, 1974.

Burish, T. G. & Hausham, B. K. Construct validity of the lie scale as a measure of depressiveness. *Journal of Clinical Psychology*, 1976, *32*, 310–314.

Davis, H. & Ferlin, S. Acoustic relations of the human vertex potential. *Journal of the Acoustical Society of America*, 1966, *39*, 109–116.

Eysenck, H. J. (ed.). *Experiments with Drugs.* London: Pergamon Press, 1963.

Eysenck, H. J. Personality and the maintenance of the smoking habit. In W. L. Dunn (ed.), *Smoking Behavior: Motives and Incentives.* Washington: Winston/Wiley, 1973a.

Eysenck, H. J. Personality, learning and "anxiety." In H. J. Eysenck (ed.), *Handbook of Abnormal Psychology.* London: Pitman Medical Press, 1973b.

Eysenck, H. J. The measurement of emotion: Psychological parameters and methods. In L. Levi (ed.), *Emotions: Their Parameters and Measurement*, pp. 429–467. New York: Raven Press, 1975.

Eysenck, H. J. (ed.). *A Model for Personality.* London: Springer, 1980.

Eysenck, H. J. & Levey, A. Conditioning, introversion-extraversion and the strength of the nervous sytem. In V. P. Nebylitsyn & J. A. Gray (eds.), *Biological Bases of Individual Behaviour.* New York: Academic Press, 1972.

Eysenck, H. J. & O'Connor, K. Smoking, arousal and personality. In A. Remond & C. Izard (eds.), *Electrophysiological Effects of Nicotine.* Amsterdam: Elsevier/North Holland, 1979.

Frith, C. Smoking behaviour and its relation to the smoker's immediate experience. *British Journal of Social and Clinical Psychology*, 1971, *10*, 73–78.

Gaillard, A. W. K. *Slow Potentials Preceding Tasks Performance.* Amsterdam: Akademische Press, B.V., 1978.

Gale, A. The psychophysiology of individual differences: Studies of extraversion and the EEG. In P. Kline (ed.), *New Approaches in Psychological Measurement.* New York: Wiley, 1973, 211–256.

Grey, S., Sartory, G., & Rachman, S. Synchronous and desynchronous thoughts during fear reduction. *Behaviour Research and Therapy*, 1979, *17*, 137–147.

Hodgson, R. & Rachman, S. Desynchrony in measures of fear. *Behaviour Research & Therapy*, 1974, *12*, 319–326.

Loveless, K. Event-related slow potentials of the brain on expressions of orienting function. In H. Kimmel et al. (eds.), *Orienting Reponse in Humans, 1980.* (In press)

McGuigan, F. J. *Cognitive Psychophysiology: Principles of Covert Behavior.* New Jersey: Prentice Hall, 1978.

Mandler, G. M., Mandler, J. M., Kreinen, I., & Sholiton, R. D. The response to threat: Relations among verbal and physiological indices. *Psychological Monographs*, 1961, *75*. Whole No. 513.

Neilson, T. C. & Petersen, K. E. Electrodermal correlates of extraversion trait anxiety and schizophrenism. *Scandinavian Journal of Psychology*, 1976, *17*, 73–80.

O'Connor, K. The contingent negative variation and individual differences in smoking behavior. *Personality and Individual Differences*, 1980, *1*, 57–72.

Rachman, S. & Hodgson, R. Synchrony and desynchrony in fear and avoidance. *Behaviour Research & Therapy*, 1974, *12*, 311–318.

Rosenbaum, R. Stimulus generalization as a function of level of experimentally induced anxiety. *Journal of Experimental Psychology*, 1953, *45*, 35–43.

Rosenbaum, R. Stimulus generalization as a function of clinical anxiety. *Journal of Abnormal & Social Psychology*, 1956, *53*, 281–285.

Rothman, H. H. Effects of high frequencies and intersubject variability in the auditory evoked cortical response. *Journal of the Acoustical Society of America*, 1970, *47*, 569–573.

Sackeim, H. A. & Gur, R. C. Self-deception, self-confrontation and consciousness. In G. E. Schartz & Shapiro (eds.), *Consciousness and Self-Regulation: Advances in Research and Theory*, vol. 2. New York: Plenum Press, 1978.

Saltz, E. Manifest anxiety: Have we misread the data? *Psychological Review*, 1970, *77*, 568–573.

Savage, R. D. & Eysenck, H. J. The definition and measurement of emotionality. In H. J. Eysenck (ed.), *Experiments in Motivation.* London: Pergamon Press, 1964.

Schwartz, G. E. Psychosomatic disorders and biofeedback: A psychobiological model of dysregulation. In J. D. Mazer & M. E. P. Seligman (eds.), *Psychopathology: Experimental Models.* San Francisco: Freeman Press, 1977.

Shigehisa, T. & Symons, J. R. Effect of intensity of visual stimulation on auditory sensitivity in relation to personality. *British Journal of Psychology*, 1973, *64*, 205–213.

Stelmack, R. M. The psychophysiology of extraversion and neuroticism. In H. J. Eysenck (ed.), *A Model for Personality.* London: Springer, 1980.

Tecce, J. J., Saviguano-Brown, J., & Cole, J. O. Drug effects on CNV and eyeblinks: The distraction-arousal hypothesis. In M. A. Lipton (ed.), *Psychopharmacology: A Generation of Progress.* New York: Raven Press, 1978.

Weinberger, D. A., Schwartz, G. E., & Davidson, R. J. Low-anxious, high-anxious and repressive coping styles: Psychometric patterns and behavioral and physiological responses to stress. *Journal of Abnormal Psychology*, 1979, *88*, 369–380.

Weinstein, J., Averill, J. R., Upton, E. M., & Lazarus, R. S. Defensive styles and discrepancy between self-report and physiological indices of stress. *Journal of Personality and Social Psychology*, 1968, *10*, 406–413.

Zuckerman, M., Murtaugh, T., & Siegel, J. Sensation seeking and cortical augmenting-reducing. *Psychophysiology*, 1974, *11*, 535–542.

4

Coping Patterns among Patients with Life-threatening Diseases

Irving L. Janis
Yale University

MALADAPTIVE RESPONSES

Prior psychological research on patients suffering acute coronary attacks or other life-threatening illnesses indicate that their behavior is frequently so maladaptive as to reduce their chances of survival (cf., Antonovsky & Hartman, 1974; Hackett & Cassem, 1969; Moss, Wynar, & Goldstein, 1969; Simon, Feinleib, & Thompson, 1972). For example, on the basis of their own observations and studies by other investigators, Hackett and Cassem (1975), describe a characteristic type of maladaptive behavior among patients with acute myocardial infarctions. While having a heart attack, the typical response is to attribute the symptoms to indigestion and to delay calling a physician for 4 or 5 hours, even though the chest pains are more intense and qualitatively different from whatever prior attacks of indigestion the person may have had. When the person thinks of the possibility that it might be a heart attack, he or she is likely to assume that "it couldn't happen to me."

The delay of treatment is not usually attributable to unavailability of medical aid or transportation delays; approximately 75% of the delay time elapses before the patient decides to call a physician. As Hackett and Cassem (1975) put it, "the decision making process gets jammed by the patient's inability to admit that he is mortally sick" (p. 27). In some cases, according to these investigators, the denial reaction is not confined merely to failure to call a doctor or to other such acts of omission. A sizeable number of patients take active steps to demonstrate to themselves that their acute chest pains could not be a heart attack. They run up stairs, do pushups, or deliberately engage in other vigorous actions that can augment heart damage.

A delay of several hours significantly increases a patient's chances of dying; over 60 percent of coronary deaths occur during the first hour following the onset of pain. Hackett and Cassem (1975) estimate that about half of these deaths can be prevented if the patients are treated promptly. If so, in the United States alone the psychological problem of delay results in over 300 avoidable deaths each day, since the rate of coronary deaths in this country is about 1,000 per day.

The delay phenomena have been found among patients in both sexes and in all

Preparation of this chapter was supported by Grant No. MH 32995-02 from the National Institute of Mental Health.

socioeconomic, age, and educational levels. Patients who have had a prior heart attack show just as much delay as those who have not (Hackett & Cassem, 1975).

Maladaptive delays have also been frequently observed among patients suffering from other life-threatening diseases, most notably those confronted with noticeable and persistent growths that are symptoms of cancer (e.g., Blackwell, 1963; Kasl & Cobb, 1966). One study found that over 30 percent of a sizeable sample of cancer patients postponed seeing a physician for three months or longer after the onset of symptoms that they knew were ominous danger signs (Goldsen, Gerhardt, & Handy, 1957). Ignorance does not seem to account for the majority of instances of procrastination because it has been found that patients who had decided to postpone having a medical examination were even more familiar with the danger signs of cancer than patients who had decided to seek medical aid promptly (Goldsen, Gerhardt, & Handy, 1957; Kutner, Makover, & Oppenheim, 1958).

Antonovsky and Hartman (1974) report an interaction effect between knowledge of disease and fear. People who know a great deal about the symptoms of cancer and who display a high level of fear tend to delay, whereas those who know just as much but display a low level of fear are less likely to delay. Their results, like those of other investigators, indicate that the problem of delay frequently, and perhaps for the vast majority, is not a matter of ignorance. If so, the problem cannot be solved for many patients simply by giving them more information about the symptoms that require prompt medical attention.

THE CONFLICT–THEORY MODEL

Studies of psychological stress evoked by external threats help to illuminate the determinants of maladaptive behavior displayed by seriously ill patients (see, for example, Horowitz, 1976; Janis & Mann, 1977; Sarason & Spielberger, 1975). From an analysis of the psychological stress literature bearing on how people respond to danger signs, such as acute pain and authoritative verbal warnings of the need for protective action to avert health hazards, Leon Mann and I have described five different patterns of coping with realistic threats (Janis & Mann, 1977). These coping patterns are shown in Fig. 1, which presents a summary of our conflict-theory model. The model specifies the psychological conditions for each of the five coping patterns, which were inferred from the research literature on stress and anxiety.

Unconflicted Inertia

Two of the coping patterns shown in Fig. 1 are directly relevant to the maladaptive delay phenomena just discussed. The first pattern, designated as *unconflicted inertia*, is largely ascribable to ignorance, which may be the reason for delay in a small minority of the cases. It consists of complascently ignoring the threat, continuing business-as-usual without taking any protective action in the face of realistic oncoming danger. This pattern is based on misjudgments about the risks from failing to take protective action. Such misjudgments arise when people receive insufficient or erroneous information about the probability that the threat will actually materialize or about the magnitude of the danger to be expected if it does materialize. When these misjudgments occur in medical patients, they can be

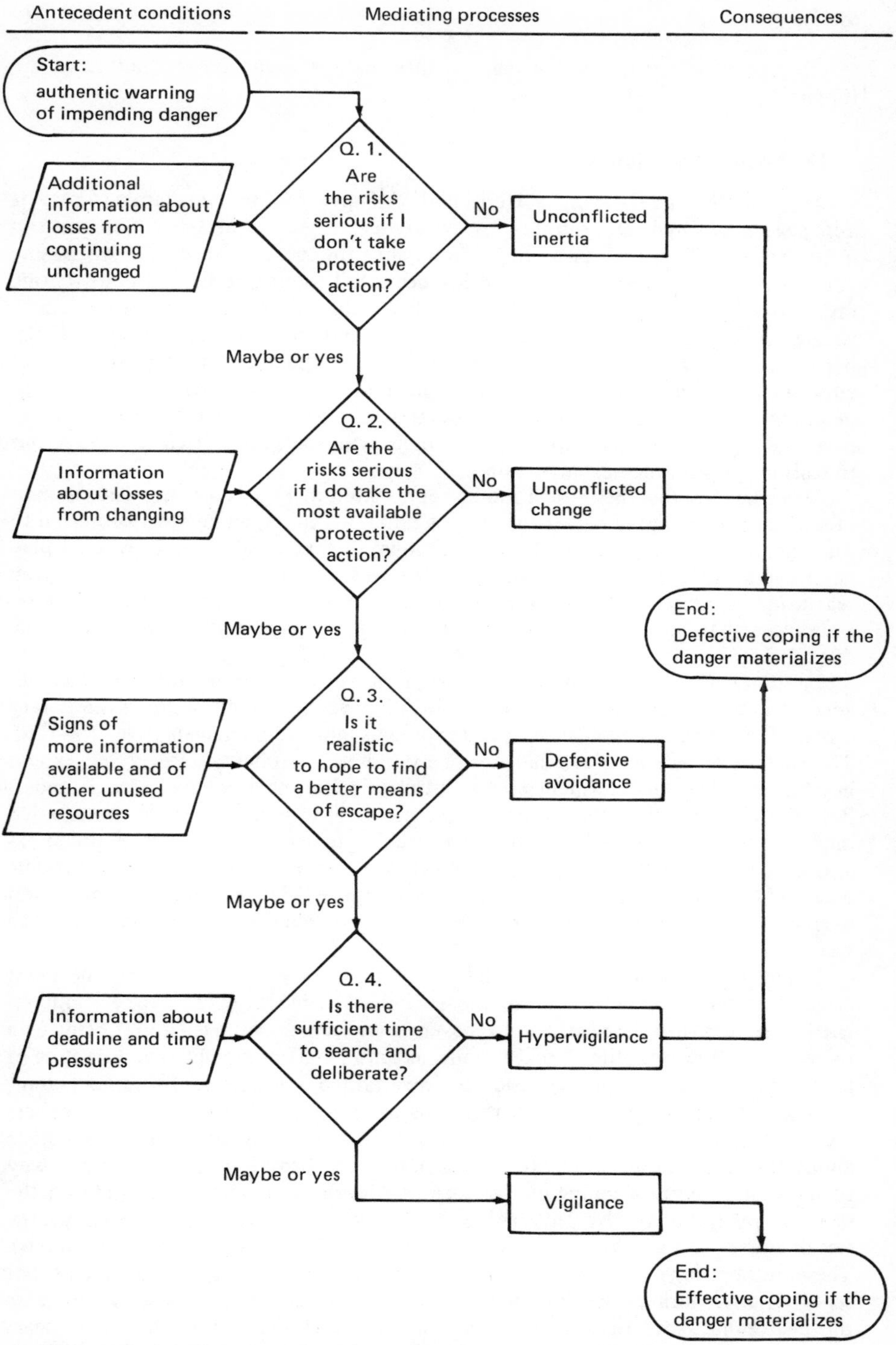

Figure 1 A conflict-theory model showing basic patterns of emergency decision making evoked by warnings of impending danger. (Based on Janis & Mann, 1977.)

readily corrected by impressive medical information about the real nature of the threat.

Defensive Avoidance

Another defective coping pattern that can give rise to maladaptive delay is *defensive avoidance*. It cannot be so easily corrected or prevented by realistic information. When this pattern is dominant, the person wards off distressing conflict by shifting responsibility for the decision to someone else, by constructing rationalizations to bolster the least objectionable alternative, or by procrastinating. In order to prevent the arousal of anxiety or other painful affects, the person displaying the defensive avoidance pattern is selectively inattentive to threat cues, including corrective communications that contain realistic warnings. This defective coping pattern probably characterizes a large percentage of those coronary and cancer patients who deny that their symptoms are sufficiently dangerous to warrant prompt medical attention.

According to the theoretical model represented in Fig. 1, a major determinant of this defective coping pattern is lack of hope of finding an adequate solution to the dilemma posed by the threat. It follows that medical patients who display defensive avoidance will be less likely to ignore realistic warnings if they are given reassuring information about the efficacy of available treatments and other reassurances that build up their hopes of finding a satisfactory way to resolve the dilemma.

Hamburg, Coelho, and Adams (1974) point out that although defensive avoidance sometimes has positive value for enabling people to surmount a temporary crisis, "the long-term avoidance of real problems tends to be maladaptive" (p. 426). The pattern of defensive avoidance is likely to have detrimental effects that extend beyond the delay of treatment at the outset of a life-threatening disease. It underlies failure to complete the course of treatments or to adhere to the recommended medical regimen after the patients have decided to seek medical aid. A prime example of the latter type of maladaptive behavior has been observed among patients diagnosed as suffering from coronary heart disease who continue to smoke and overeat, do not get sufficient exercise, or do not take essential medications (see Kasl, 1975; Stone, 1979).

It has been widely observed that many patients who have undergone heart attacks become depressed during the period of convalescence, worry about recurring attacks, lose hope of fully recovering and feel discouraged about being able to return to a normal life. Hackett and Cassem (1975) point out that this type of post-coronary depression can lead to unwarranted invalidism. To some extent, according to their account, such reactions are induced by physicians and others on the hospital staff who talk a great deal about all the restrictions but say little about the favorable prospects for recovering and returning to a fairly normal way of life. They quote a young convalescent cardiac patient who commented on the onerous restrictions: "No smokes, no booze, low salt, low fat, low energy, low sex or no sex—I feel like a cardiological capon!" (Hackett & Cassem, 1975, p. 36). These authors urge the hospital staff to counteract the depression and anxiety that so often arise during convalescence following a coronary attack by giving patients the heartening news that most people can work and lead normal lives after heart attacks. According to the Janis and Mann model, as represented in Fig. 1, such information should reduce the tendency to resort to defensive avoidance in response to the life-threatening illness by building up *hope* of arriving at a satisfactory outcome. By providing information about positive outcomes, the hospital staff can facilitate a vigilant coping pattern that may lead to effective action.

Several studies indicate that patients with coronary disease who develop a reactive depression are less likely to adhere to the recommended medical regimen necessary for rehabilitation than the equally ill patients who show less depression and less anxiety (Gentry, Foster, & Haney, 1972; Hackett, Cassem, & Wishnie, 1968; McGill, 1975). These findings are sometimes interpreted as suggesting that denial is beneficial, because the heart patients who seem to deny their illness do better than those who do not. But "denial" may be a misleading term for characterizing those patients who are not depressed, discouraged, or worried. The crucial factor may be that they feel *hopeful* about surmounting the threat to their health and display a vigilant pattern of coping; they decide to do whatever is necessary to recover. In contrast, those who remain hopeless may display a pattern of defensive avoidance by procrastinating and bolstering a do-nothing stance, or by pinning all their hopes on the physician's protective powers.

Unconflicted Change

A third coping pattern represented in Fig. 1 is *unconflicted change*, which occurs when the person is aware of the threat and wants to avoid anticipated losses by taking protective action but does not recognize that the new course of action could also result in potential losses. This pattern is maladaptive when it occurs in seriously ill patients who are uninformed about the usual suffering and deprivations to be expected from the course of medical treatments or surgery recommended by their physicians (see Janis, 1958). It is manifested when patients promptly agree to do whatever the physician says to do, with no signs of awareness of what they are letting themselves in for and with no manifestations of conflict.

When unconflicted acceptance of physicians' recommendations occurs in surgical patients, the main source of defective coping lies in the *lack of psychological preparation* for whatever distressing events take place in the operating room and during postoperative convalescence, which leads the patients to become angry and disillusioned with the hospital staff and to be uncooperative when routine postoperative treatments are administered (see Janis, 1958; Vernon & Bigelow, 1974). Numerous field experiments with patients in hospitals and clinics, reviewed by Janis and Rodin (1979), indicate that this defective coping pattern can be prevented to some extent by giving preparatory communications that convey a realistic picture of what is to be expected along with appropriate reassurances. Such communications apparently stimulate the patients to develop their own reassuring conceptions, which can provide "stress inoculation." They are then psychologically prepared to meet painful events and setbacks with "positive self-talk" that at least partially alleviates feelings of hopelessness and anxiety. This process, which is referred to as the "constructive work of worrying" (Janis, 1958), requires mental rehearsal of unpleasant events:

> *Before the operation, upon receiving preparatory information about what specifically is in store for them, these patients start to worry about the postoperative period and wonder how bad it is really going to be. As they mentally rehearse undergoing the*

predicted pains and deprivations, they are much less calm than those who are uninoculated. The inoculated patients work hard at regaining some degree of equanimity by developing reassuring conceptions of each of the different types of threat they are worried about (e.g., 'Most of the pains from the incision will last only a short time'; 'If any pains get to be unbearable I will be given a pain-killing drug'). Insofar as the patients have realistic information about the threat, the reassurances they develop continue to function effectively, without being undermined when the threat materializes. Consequently, throughout the convalescent period these patients are able to maintain a basically optimistic outlook about surviving each ordeal intact and can feel a sense of pride about being able to 'take it,' without ever becoming severely frightened, angry, or regretful about their decision. (Janis & Mann, 1977, p. 392).

Stress inoculation for surgery or other painful treatments is probably effective with initially uninformed patients who without it would unperturbedly agree to do whatever the physicians recommend. It may also be effective with many conflicted patients who bolster their decision to undergo surgery with rationalizations based on wishful thinking (e.g., "I won't feel a thing"), which is a form of defensive avoidance that may be frequent among hospitalized patients.

Some problems arise, of course, concerning the proper dosage of fear-arousing material in preparatory communications. The problem of working out appropriate dosages to avoid exceeding the optimal level of emotional arousal is discussed at length by Janis (1967, 1971) and McGuire (1969). Studies of reactions to warnings suggest that attempts at stress inoculation are effective only if they build up the patients' confidence that they can cope with the anticipated threats.

Hypervigilance

A fourth defective coping pattern represented in Fig. 1 is *hypervigilance*, which is dominant when a person is in a state of panic or near-panic. In such a state, the person becomes obsessed with thoughts about all the horrible things that may happen and engages in frantic search for a way out of the dilemma. The person may become overwhelmed by informational overload in an attempt to take account of the deluge of warnings, advice, and rumors to which he or she indiscriminately pays attention and takes seriously. When hypervigilance is the predominating coping pattern, the decision makers tend to over-react to bits of unreliable information about potential threats and to show extreme vacillation as first one course of action and then another seems most dangerous. In an excited state of hypervigilance, people are likely to commit themselves impulsively to a hastily contrived course of action without taking fully into account its undesirable consequences. Usually mental efficiency is temporarily impaired as a result of extremely high emotional arousal, which can result in perseveration, reduced memory span, and simplistic thinking.

Among the prime mediating conditions leading to hypervigilance, as shown in Fig. 1, are signs leading the person to anticipate having insufficient time to find an adequate means of escaping from rapidly oncoming danger at a time when all available courses of action appear to be extremely risky. Such conditions occur during large-scale fires, tornadoes, and other disasters when people face imminent entrapment, especially if they can see that escape routes are rapidly being closed off as the danger approaches.

Perceived entrapment in danger sometimes occurs in surgical wards and in intensive care units when a patient anticipates catastrophic loss or death at any moment. This results in extreme fright of panic proportions, and in maladaptive efforts to struggle against essential treatments (Hackett & Cassem, 1975; Janis, 1958). Such hypervigilant reactions may be mediated by overwhelming feelings of helplessness to avert catastrophe.

When people are required to make emergency decisions under conditions of danger, a number of environmental factors, in addition to those already discussed, increase the probability of hypervigilance. Among the other environmental conditions are restriction of activity, sensory deprivation (such as total darkness), and lack of contact with supportive persons. All of these conditions are likely to beset hospitalized patients, especially at night, unless the staff takes special steps to counteract them. Hypervigilance is sometimes seen among patients suffering from only minor discomforts during the prolonged recovery period from cardiac disease or other illnesses. Each individual episode of stress may be relatively mild, but as the stresses accumulate day after day without letup, the patient may become increasingly demoralized, feeling more and more hopeless as well as helpless, which gives rise to a mixture of depression with anxiety (see Janis, 1971). The patient undergoing a prolonged convalescence of unrelenting misery may show an alternation of defensive avoidance and hypervigilance—a pseudo-calm facade periodically puncutated by episodes of panic or near-panic when pains or threat cues are so salient that defensive efforts are ineffective.

Perhaps the most potent of all the antecedent conditions that make for hypervigilance consists of undergoing near-miss experiences, as when a disaster victim sustains some degree of serious injury but survives. After recovering from temporary emotional shock, survivors may remain jittery and hypervigilant for a long time, sometimes for months or years, constantly recalling how close they came to being permanently mutilated or killed (see Horowitz, 1976).

Similar, although less persistent, effects can occur as a result of witnessing another person being badly injured or dying in agony, especially if it is someone with whom it is easy to empathize or identify. Hackett and Cassem (1975) desscribe the profound emotional impact on patients in a coronary care unit when they see a fatal cardiac arrest in another patient. Although only a minority (about 20 percent) admit being frightened after witnessing such a distressing event, there are clear-cut indications of increases in behavioral symptoms of anxiety, in systolic blood pressure, in requests for tranquilizers, and in complaints about chest pains. At a time when such symptoms are evoked, one could expect to find that the hypervigilant pattern is predominant, with characteristic manifestations of indiscriminate responsiveness to information and rumors and with vacillation followed by impulsive choice when the patients are required to make important decisions about whether or not to accept a recommended treatment or surgery.

Undergoing cardiac arrest is undoubtedly one of the most extreme forms of near-miss experiences, far worse than merely seeing it happen to someone else. Every year, according to statistics cited by Hackett and Cassem (1975), there are hundreds of thousands of people who sustain a cardiac arrest and survive. In the mid and late 1960s the psychological aftermath of recovery from a cardiac arrest typically included key symptoms of traumatic neurosis, such as recurrent nightmares, jitteriness, and other anxiety symptoms (Druss & Kornfeld, 1967). When patients are in such a state, any recurrence of chest pains is likely to evoke paniclike reactions, with the extreme misjudgments and impulsive decision making that characterizes the hypervigilant pattern.

Nowadays anxiety symptoms and panic reactions rarely occur following cardiac arrests, probably because patients are routinely given reassuring explanations of what has happened to them (Dobson, Tattersfield, Adler, & McNicol, 1971; Hackett & Cassem, 1975). These reassurances may counteract the loss of self-confidence concerning personal invulnerability and the accompanying feelings of helplessness that appear to be the mediating attitude changes in cases of traumatic neurosis following actual victimization or near-miss experiences (see Janis, 1971).

Vigilance

In contrast to the four defective coping patterns just discussed, vigilance generally leads to effective problem-solving behavior that reduces or minimizes the threat. When this pattern is dominant, the decision maker searches painstakingly for relevant information, assimilates new information in an unbiased manner, and appraises alternatives carefully before making a choice. The main determinants of this adaptive pattern, as shown in Fig. 1, involve expectations concerning risks, hope, and the time available before being required to choose a course of protective action.

The behavioral consequences of vigilance as compared with the other four coping patterns are summarized in Tables 1 and 2. The column headings in the first table specify the major criteria that can be used to judge whether or not a person's decision is of high quality with regard to the problem-solving procedures that lead up to the act of commitment. These criteria were extracted from the extensive literature on effective decision making (see Janis and Mann, 1977, Chapters 1 and 2). The second table includes other behavioral consequences pertaining to overt manifestations of conflict and symptoms of stress.

The five patterns delineated in Fig. 1 and Tables 1 and 2 comprise the rudiments of a theoretical model of decisional conflict. A number of testable implications of the model have been investigated and at least partially confirmed—for example, hypotheses concerning the conditions that determine whether the decision-makers' information search will be cursory or thorough, whether their deliberations will be biased or unbiased, and whether adherence to their decisions will be short-lived or persistent. (Numerous relevant studies are reviewed in Janis & Mann, 1977, Chapters 4–12.)

On the basis of the conflict-theory model, a number of interventions have been developed that counselors can use to counteract the defective patterns of coping with the stresses of decisional conflict and to foster the vigilance pattern in their clients for the purpose of improving the quality of their decisions when they are about to make a vital choice concerning their health or other personal matters. Several controlled experiments have been carried out, which indicate that some of these interventions are sufficiently effective to warrant widespread clinical use. For example, Langer, Janis, and Wolfer (1975) developed an intervention procedure designed to boost decision-makers' hope of finding a satisfactory solution and, thereby, to establish one of the conditions for vigilance. They investigated the effectiveness of the procedure in a sample of hospital patients awaiting major surgical operations. In this setting, stress is very high and defensive avoidance rather than vigilance is often the dominant coping pattern. Patients were assigned on a random basis to experimental and control groups that were or were not given the coping device.

Table 1 Predecisional behavior characteristic of the five basic patterns of decision making (From Janis & Mann, 1977)

| Pattern of coping with challenge | Criteria for high-quality decision making | | | | | | | |
| | (1) Thorough canvassing of alternatives | (2) Thorough canvassing of objectives | (3) Careful evaluation of consequences | | (4) Thorough search for information | (5) Unbiased assimilation of new information | (6) Careful reevaluation of consequences | (7) Thorough planning for implementation and contingencies |
			a. of current policy	b. of alternative new policies				
Unconflicted adherence	−	−	−	−	−	+	−	−
Unconflicted change	−	−	+	−	−	+	−	−
Defensive avoidance	−	−	−	−	−	−	−	−
Hypervigilance	−	−	±	±	±	+	+	+
Vigilance	+	+	+	+	+	+	+	+

KEY: + = The decision maker meets the criterion to the best of his ability.

— = The decision maker fails to meet the criterion.

± = The decision maker's performance fluctuates, sometimes meeting the criterion to the best of his ability and sometimes not.

All evaluative terms such as thorough and unbiased are to be understood as intrapersonal comparative assessments, relative to the person's performances under the most favorable conditions that enable him to display his cognitive capabilities to the best of his ability.

Table 2 Manifestations of conflict and related symptoms of stress for each of the five basic patterns of decision making (From Janis & Mann, 1977)

Pattern of coping with challenge	Subjective beliefs (indicators of mediating psychological conditions specified in Fig. 1)	Level of stress	Degree of vacillation of preference for alternative courses of action
Unconflicted adherence	No serious risk from current course of action	Low: persistently calm	No vacillation
Unconflicted change	Serious risk from current course of action	Low: persistently calm	No vacillation
Defensive avoidance	Serious risk from current course of action Serious risk from new course of action No better solution can be found	Variable from low to high (predominantly pseudo-calm, with breakthrough of high emotional arousal when signs of threat become salient)	Little or no vacillation (except when signs of threat are salient)
Hypervigilance	Serious risk from current course of action Serious risk from new course of action A better solution might be found Insufficient time to search for and evaluate a better solution	High: persistently strong anxiety	Very high rate of vacillation, but occasionally practically none as a result of perseveration
Vigilance	Serious risk from current course of action Serious risk from new course of action A better solution might be found Sufficient time to search for and evaluate a better solution	Moderate variations within intermediate range, with level depending upon exposure to threat cues or reassuring communications	Moderate to high rate of vacillation (depending on content of new information)

The coping device, inserted in brief counseling sessions, involved encouraging an optimistic reappraisal of anxiety-provoking events to build up hope in the realistic possibility of dealing effectively with whatever setbacks or losses might be encountered. Each patient was given several examples of the positive or compensatory consequences of his or her decision to undergo surgery (e.g., improvement in health, extra care and attention in the hospital, temporary vacation from outside pressures). Then the patient was invited to think up additional examples that pertained to his or her individual case. Finally he or she was instructed to rehearse these compensatory consequences when feeling upset about the unpleasant aspects of the surgical experience. Patients were urged to be as realistic as possible about the compensatory features in order to emphasize that what was being recommended was not equivalent to trying to deceive oneself. The instructions were designed to promote warranted optimism and awareness of the anticipated gains that outweighed the losses to be expected from the chosen course of action.

The findings supported the prediction that cognitive reappraisal would reduce stress both before and after an operation. Patients treated with the coping device scored lower on nurses' blind ratings of preoperative stress and on unobtrusive postoperative measures of the number of times pain-relieving drugs and sedatives were requested and administered.

Evidence of the value of encouraging cognitive coping strategies also comes from a study by Kendall, Williams, Pechacek, Graham, Shisslak, and Herzoff (1977), which deals with patients who had agreed to undergo cardiac catheterization. This is a particularly stressful medical procedure that involves working a catheter into the heart by inserting it into a vein in the groin. One group of patients was given a stress inoculation procedure that focussed on the stresses to be expected and that encouraged them to develop their own cognitive coping strategies by suggesting various reassurances, modeling, and reinforcing whatever personal coping responses the patient mentioned. Two other equivalent groups of patients were given different preparatory treatments—an educational communication about the catheterization procedure and an attention placebo intervention. There was also a no-treatment control group. The patients given the stress inoculation procedure showed higher stress tolerance during the cardiac catheterization than those in the other three treatment groups, as assessed by self-ratings and ratings made by observers (physicians and medical technicians). Additional field experiments dealing with clinically relevant interventions that affect the patients' coping patterns are reviewed in Janis and Mann (1977, Chapters 13 and 14) and in Janis (1982).

PERSONALITY DETERMINANTS OF VIGILANCE*

According to the conflict-theory model, three conditions are essential for vigilant search and appraisal in response to a serious threat: (1) belief that there are serious risks for whichever alternative course of action is chosen; (2) belief that it is realistic to be optimistic or hopeful about finding a better alternative solution than the objectionable ones that are being contemplated; (3) belief that

*This section is based in part on my chapter entitled "Personality differences in responsiveness to counseling procedures" in I. Janis (ed.), *Counseling on personal decisions: Theory and research on short-term helping relationships.* New Haven, Conn.: Yale University Press, 1982.

there is adequate time in which to search and deliberate before a final decision is required. A person who is generally unresponsive to authentic information that promotes one or another of these beliefs would be expected to show a consistently defective coping pattern that generally would lead either to no change at all or to a poorly worked out decision without adequate contingency planning, which would soon be followed by reversal of the decision in response to acute postdecisional regret.

There are various bits and pieces of evidence from prior research on personality differences that appear to be in line with these assumptions. For example, a number of studies employing Byrne's (1964) repression-sensitization scale and Goldstein's (1959) closely related "coper versus avoider" test suggest that persons diagnosed as chronic repressors or avoiders tend to minimize, deny, or ignore any warning that presents disturbing information about impending threats. Such persons appear to be predisposed to display the characteristic features of defensive avoidance. Unlike those who are predisposed to be vigilant, they do not respond adaptively to pre- paratory information that provides realistic forecasts about stressful experiences to be expected along with reassurances and coping suggestions. Some relevant findings are to be found in the reports on two field experiments conducted on surgery wards by Andrew (1970) and DeLong (1971). In both studies, patients awaiting surgery were given Goldstein's test in order to assess their preferred mode of coping with stress and then were given preparatory information. The reactions of the following three groups were compared: (1) copers who tended to display vigilance or sensitizing defenses; (2) avoiders, who displayed avoidant or denial defenses; and (3) nonspecific defenders who showed no clear preference.

In Andrew's (1970) study, preparatory information, which described what the experience of the operation and the postoperative convalescence would be like, had an unfavorable effect on the rate of physical recovery of avoiders. But the information had a positive effect on nonspecific defenders. Copers recovered well irrespective of whether they were given the preoperative information. In DeLong's (1971) study, avoiders were found to have the poorest recovery regardless of whether they were given the preparatory information. Copers showed the greatest benefit from receiving the information.

Although not completely consistent with each other, the findings from the two studies appear to agree in indicating that persons who display defensive avoidance tendencies do not respond well to preoperative counseling that presents preparatory information. This conclusion seems to be in line with evidence on stress tolerance obtained in some (though not all) of the laboratory stress experiments in which differences between repressors (or avoiders) versus sensitizers have been studied. For example, Davidson and Bobey (1970) found that repressors showed a decrease in tolerance for experimentally-induced pain following an initial exposure to the painful stimulus whereas sensitizers showed a trend in the opposite direction. In a laboratory experiment by Olson and Zanna (1979), which required subjects to make a minor decision, repressors displayed selective exposure in the form of avoiding exposing themselves to dissonance-producing perceptions whereas sensi- tizers did not.

The findings from the various studies cited above are suggestive, but they bear only indirectly on the main implications of the conflict-theory analysis of coping patterns with respect to personality predispositions. The following propositions specify how, according to the theory, personality predispositions are expected to contribute to faulty decision making in response to challenging communications or events that call attention to serious risks from continuing defective courses of action or inaction:

1. If a person has a consistently high threshold for assimilating information about risks—such as lack of vivid imagery, which dampens the salience and emotional impact of the warnings—he or she will show: (a) unconflicted adherence to his or her current course of action in response to challenging events or communications that induce most other people to change their behavior; or (b) unconflicted change to a new course of action, without adequate preparation for avoiding acute post-decisional regret.

2. If a person has a consistently high threshold for assimilating information that for most people promotes optimism about finding an acceptable solution to the challenging event or communication—for example, because of pessimistic expectations resulting from a chronic mood of depressive self-disparagement—he or she will generally display a defensive avoidance pattern. This pattern can take the form of chronic procrastination, shifting responsibility to someone else, or bolstering the least objectionable alternative with rationalizations, all of which involve denying or minimizing the risks and interfere with developing plans that lead to stable changes in behavior.

3. If a person has a consistently high threshold for assimilating information that leads most people to expect to have sufficient time for search and appraisal before being required to make a choice among alternative courses of action—for example, because of a chronic sense of time urgency, as has been found among "Type A personalities" who are at high risk with regard to coronary heart disease (Glass, 1977)—hypervigilance will frequently be displayed in response to challenging events or communications. This pattern is characterized by emotional excitement, vacillation, and cognitive deficiencies, which lead to impulsive, ill-considered, and unstable decisions.

The examples of predispositional variables given in the above three propositions refer to personality traits that are so broad in scope that they would affect all types of decision, whether they involve health, career, marriage, social affiliations, or even policy making in an executive role. But most psychologists have learned to be skeptical about being able to make significant predictions on the basis of such broad predispositional attributes because so much prior research shows that personality traits, as measured by the most widely used tests and rating scales, do not show high consistency across different situations and do not account for very much of the variance in observable behavior change (see Mischel, 1968). Some more recent studies, however, indicate that general personality traits are not quite in such bad shape as they seemed in 1968 (see Epstein, 1977, 1980; Sechrest, 1976). In any case, the above three propositions do not necessarily need to be so imperialistic in scope; they can be reformulated in terms of predispositions that pertain to a more limited domain of decision making. The propositions could be confined, for example, to the home territory of just one type of decision, such as actions pertaining to health risks.

There is no reason, in my opinion, to be pessimistic about the prospects of finding consistent individual differences in the three thresholds specified in the above propositions. I expect that in some persons such thresholds may be consistently high and in others consistently low due to a variety of causes, including both persistent personality traits and social circumstances, such as continuous exposure to demoralizing or sensitizing events that could affect a person's responsiveness to information bearing on more than one type of decision.

Recent findings on level of self-esteem from field experiments that my colleagues and I have carried out in a weight-reduction clinic appear to be pertinent to the proposition concerning defensive avoidance. The results from two such studies indicate that the clients who benefit most from the type of short-term counseling provided in the dieting clinic are those who initially have a relatively low level of self-esteem, as manifested by their answers on a personality inventory dealing with feelings of personal inadequacy (Dowds, Janis, & Conolley, 1982; Conolley, Janis, & Dowds, 1982). These findings seem to be inconsistent with the second proposition, which carries the implication that overweight people who are lacking in self-esteem are likely to be lacking in hope about finding a satisfactory solution to their overeating problem, and therefore are unlikely to carry out successfully a decision to stay on a low-calorie diet. But among the overweight persons who come to our weight-reduction clinic, the majority who obtain low self-esteem scores may not be asserting a lack of confidence about succeeding on the diet, but, rather, expressing feelings of guilt or shame about their past failures to control overeating, which is a different component of low self-esteem.

In other studies, we have observed a minority of clients with a syndrome of pessimism combined with manifestations of defensive avoidance, which usually takes the form of procrastination or shifting responsibility to others. In some of these cases, pessimism about finding a successful solution to their overweight problem seems to be the result of a series of past failures at dieting, but in other cases the causes seem to be quite different. Whatever the causes, however, the relatively hopeless clients, those who express very low confidence about attaining their goal of bringing their weight down to a normal level and keeping it down, were found to be more likely to fail to adhere to the recommended diet than those who are more hopeful (Janis & Quinlan, 1982; Quinlan & Janis, 1982). This observed phenomenon might be explained by the second proposition, which is compatible with the recent reemphasis on self-efficacy as a key determinant of successful behavior change by Bandura (1977) and other behavior theorists.

In future research, investigations of individual differences in self-confidence and in feelings of hope could provide the type of data needed for more rigorous testing of the second proposition. By using appropriate questions in pretreatment interviews and questionnaires, it should be possible to determine whether such individual differences are related to manifestations of the defensive avoidance pattern and whether those manifestations, in turn, are predictive of failure to adhere to a counselor's recommendations.

Appropriate questions could also be devised in order to assess individual differences in the predispositional variables specified by the first and third propositions. Obviously, it is worthwhile to start off using pertinent measures that are already in the literature, such as the measures of time urgency developed by Glass (1977), which is suggested in the formulation of Proposition 3 on hypervigilance. If such measures fail to discriminate very well, the next step should be to develop new measures designed to tap more directly the predispositional factors specified in the three propositions. Insofar as the theory is correct, we can expect that some of those theoretically-based measures will prove to be more predictive of behavior change than the predispositional measures currently being used in research on counseling, psychotherapy, and attitude change.

REFERENCES

Andrew, J. M. Recovery from surgery, with and without preparatory instruction, for three coping styles. *Journal of Personality and Social Psychology*, 1970, *15*, 223–226.

Antonovsky, A. & Hartman, H. Delay in the detection of cancer: A review of the literature. *Health Education Monographs*, 1974, *2*(2), 98–125.

Bandura, A. Self-efficacy: Toward a unifying theory of behavioral change. *Psychological Review*, 1977, *84*, 191–215.

Blackwell, B. The literature of delay in seeking medical care for chronic illnesses. *Health Educ. Mono.* 1963, *16*, 3.

Byrne, D. Repression-sensitization as a dimension of personality. In B. A. Maher (ed.), *Progress in experimental personality research*, Vol. 1. New York: Academic Press, 1964.

Conolley, E., Janis, I. L., & Dowds, M. Effects of variations in the type of feedback given by the counselor. In I. L. Janis (ed.), *Counseling on personal decisions: Theory and research on short-term helping relationships*. New Haven, Conn.: Yale University Press, 1982.

Davidson, G. C. & Bobey, M. J. Repressor-sensitizer differences on repeated exposure to pain. *Perceptual and Motor Skills*, 1970, *31*, 711–714.

DeLong, D. R. Individual differences in patterns of anxiety arousal, stress-relevant information and recovery from surgery. Unpublished doctoral dissertation, University of California, Los Angeles, 1971.

Dobson, M., Tattersfield, A. E., Adler, M. W., & McNicol, M. W. Attitudes in long-term adjustment of patients surviving cardiac arrest. *British Medical Journal*, 1971, *3*, 207–212.

Dowds, M., Janis, I. L., & Conolley, E. Effects of acceptance by the counselor. In I. L. Janis (ed.), *Counseling on personal decisions: Theory and research on short-term helping relationships*. New Haven, Conn.: Yale University Press, 1982.

Druss, R. G. & Kornfeld, D. S. Survivors of cardiac arrest: Psychiatric study. *J.A.M.A.*, 1967, *201*, 291–296.

Epstein, S. Traits are alive and well. In P. Magnusson and N. S. Endler (eds.), *Personality at the crossroads: Current issues in interactional psychology*. Hillsdale, N.J.: Erlbaum, 1977.

Epstein, S. The stability of behavior: II. Implications for psychological research. *American Psychologist*, 1980, *35*, 790–806.

Gentry, D., Foster, S., & Haney, T. Denial as a determinant of anxiety and perceived health in the cornary care unit. *Psychosom. Med.*, 1972, *34*, 39.

Glass, D. *Behavior patterns, stress and coronary disease*. Hillsdale, N.J.: Lawrence Erlbaum, 1977.

Goldsen, R. K., Gerhardt, P. T., & Handy, V. H. Some factors related to patient delay in seeking diagnosis for cancer symptoms. *Cancer*, 1957, *10*, 1–7.

Goldstein, M. J. The relationship between coping and avoiding behavior and response to fear-arousing propaganda. *Journal of Abnormal and Social Psychology*, 1959, *58*, 247–252.

Hackett, T. P. & Cassem, N. H. Factors contributing to delay in responding to the signs and symptoms of acute myocardial infarction. *Am. J. Cardiol.*, 1969, *24*, 651–658.

Hackett, T. P. & Cassem, N. H. Psychological management of the myocardial infarction patient. *Journal of Human Stress*, 1975, *1*, 25–38.

Hackett, T. P., Cassem, N. H., & Wishnie, H. A. The coronary care unit: An appraisal of its psychological hazards. *N. Engl. J. Med.*, 1968, *279*, 1365–1370.

Hamburg, D. A., Coelho, G. V., & Adams, J. E. Coping and adaptation: Steps toward a synthesis of biological and social perspectives. In G. V. Coelho, D. A. Hamburg, and J. E. Adams (eds.), *Coping and adaptation*. New York: Basic Books, 1974.

Horowitz, M. J. *Stress response syndromes*. New York: Aronson, 1976.

Janis, I. L. *Psychological stress: Psychoanalytic and behavioral studies of surgical patients*. New York: Wiley, 1958.

Janis, I. L. Effects of fear arousal on attitude change: Recent developments in theory and research. In L. Berkowitz (ed.), *Advances in experimental social psychology*, Vol. 3. New York: Academic Press, 1967.

Janis, I. L. *Stress and frustration*. New York: Harcourt Brace Jovanovich, 1971.

Janis, I. L. (ed.). *Counseling on personal decisions: Theory and research on short-term helping relationships.* New Haven, Conn.: Yale University Press, 1982.

Janis, I. L. & Mann, L. *Decision making: A psychological analysis of conflict, choice and commitment.* New York: Free Press, 1977.

Janis, I. L. & Quinlan, D. M. What disclosing means to the client: Comparative case studies. In I. L. Janis (ed.), *Counseling on personal decisions: Theory and research on short-term helping relationships.* New Haven, Conn.: Yale University Press, 1982.

Janis, I. L. & Rodin, J. R. Attribution, control, and decision-making: Social psychology and health care. In G. C. Stone, F. Cohen, & N. E. Adler (eds.), *Health psychology.* San Francisco: Jossey-Bass, 1979.

Kasl, S. V. Issues in patient adherence to health care regimens. *Journal of Human Stress*, 1975, *1*, 5–18.

Kasl, S. V. & Cobb, S. Health behavior, illness behavior, and sick role behavior. *Archives of Environmental Health*, 1966, *12*, 246–266, 531–541.

Kendall, P., Williams, L., Pechacek, T. F., Graham, L. E., Shisslak, C., & Herzoff, N. Cognitive-behavioral patient education interventions in catheterization procedures. Unpublished manuscript, University of Minnesota, 1977.

Kutner, B., Makover, H. B., & Oppenheim, A. Delay in the diagnosis and treatment of cancer: A critical analysis of the literature. *Journal of Chronic Diseases*, 1958, *7*, 95–120.

Langer, E. J., Janis, I. L., & Wolfer, J. A. Reduction of psychological stress in surgical patients. *Journal of Experimental Social Psychology*, 1975, *11*, 155–165.

McGill, A. M. Review of literature on cardiovascular rehabilitation. In S. M. Weiss (ed.), *Proceedings of the National Heart and Lung Institute Working Conference on Health Behavior.* Washington, D.C.: DHEW (Publication No. [NIH] 76-868), 1975.

McGuire, W. J. The nature of attitudes and attitude change. In G. Lindzey & E. Aronson (eds.), *The handbook of social psychology*, Vol. 3. Reading, Mass.: Addison-Wesley, 1969.

Mischel, W. *Personality and assessment.* New York: Wiley, 1968.

Moss, A. J., Wynar, B., & Goldstein, S. Delay in hospitalization during the acute coronary period. *Am. J. Cardiol.*, 1969, *24*, 659–665.

Olson, J. M. & Zanna, M. P. A new look at selective exposure. *Journal of Experimental Social Psychology*, 1979, *15*, 1–15.

Quinlan, D. M. & Janis, I. L. Unfavorable effects of high levels of self-disclosure. In I. L. Janis (ed.), *Counseling on personal decisions: Theory and research on short-term helping relationships.* New Haven, Conn.: Yale University Press, 1982.

Sarason, I. G. & Spielberger, C. D. (eds.). *Stress and anxiety*, vol. 2. Washington, D.C.: Hemisphere, 1975.

Sechrest, L. The psychologist as a program evaluator. In P. J. Woods (ed.), *Career opportunities for psychologists: Expanding and emerging areas.* Washington, D.C.: American Psychological Association, 1976.

Simon, A. B., Feinleib, M., & Thompson, H. K. Components of delay in the pre-hospital setting of acute myocardial infarction. *Am. J. Cardiol.*, 1972, *30*, 475–482.

Stone, G. C. Patient compliance and the role of the expert. *Journal of Social Issues*, 1979, *35*, 34–59.

Vernon, D. T. A. & Bigelow, D. A. Effect of information about a potentially stressful situation on responses to stress impact. *Journal of Personality and Social Psychology*, 1974, *29*, 50–59.

II

ENVIRONMENTAL STRESS
AND ANXIETY

5

Situational Factors in Research in Stress and Anxiety

Sex and Age Differences

David Magnusson
University of Stockholm

It is interesting to note how important issues in psychology can be raised and fundamental propositions made without any real impact on actual research. One of the best examples is the topic for my paper here; the role of situations in research on behavior. For decades, researchers from very different perspectives have stressed the evident fact that behavior cannot be understood in isolation from the situational conditions under which it occurs, and have advocated that situations and situational conditions must be considered in any effective model of personality. However, such formulations have only recently, and slowly at that, led to obvious consequences in empirical research: (a) systematic analyses of the lawfulness of person by situation interactions, and (b) systematic analysis of the situations, in which behavior is observed. When, in the middle of the sixties, I explored the literature to see which situational factors to vary systematically in studies of person situation interactions, I found almost nothing. In connection with the renewed interest in the old topic of personality consistency and the research on person situation interactions during the seventies, the need for systematic analyses of situations has been further emphasized. My purpose here is to draw attention to the potential of systematic studies on situations, and to the importance of incorporating knowledge about situations and situational conditions in research on stress and anxiety, in particular, and in the field of personality in general.

Situations play a central role in theorizing and empirical research on stress and anxiety. Stressors are identified in terms of situational factors and coping is often deferred as an individual's efforts to deal with stressful information from the environment. Test anxiety research is concerned with individuals' responses in a certain type of situation, as is research on social anxiety, etc. Schalling (1975) stated that there are "systematic differences, not only in the degree of anxiety (intensity and frequency), but also in the type of anxiety and the type of stressors (situations that evoke anxiety), and that these differences are related to personality dimensions" (p. 279). She empirically identified seven types of stressful situations, namely those involving criticism, anticipation, aggression, pain-medical, pain, thrill, and boredom. She reported empirical results on the relation between sensitivity to these types of situations and personality dimensions such as neuroticism, impulsivity, and anxiety. Spielberger's theoretical model for the construction and use of the STAI-T and STAI-S for measuring trait and state anxiety is closely bound to a certain type of situation, namely ego threatening situations (Spielberger, 1972). Endler (1975) in his interactional model of anxiety identified three types of anxiety provoking situations: interpersonal (closely similar to the ego threatening type of situations referred to by Spielberger), physical danger situations, and inanimate situations. Corresponding to these three types of anxiety-provoking situations, he distinguished three person trait-anxiety factors: interpersonal anxiety, physical danger anxiety, and inanimate anxiety. In order for state anxiety to occur in a person in a certain situation there must be congruence between the type of situational threat and the type of trait disposition in the individual. Persons high in interpersonal trait anxiety are assumed to react more strongly in interpersonal threatening situations than individuals low in interpersonal anxiety, etc.

Awareness of the importance of the role of situations in models of behavior in general, and in theorizing and empirical research on stress and anxiety, naturally suggests a need for systematic knowledge about situations and how they influence actual behavior. For understanding the individual in the situation we need (a) knowledge about the effective person variables and their interrelations, a recurrent theme during the history of personality and differential psychology, (b) knowledge about the effective situation variables and their interrelations, and (c) knowledge about the interplay between these two networks of factors (Magnusson, 1981). In the past most resources in the field of personality have been devoted to theorizing and research on the person side of the person-situation system. There is an obvious need at the present time for a psychology of situations.

Using this perspective, we have devoted some of our time in my research group in Stockholm to studies of situations, particularly to descriptions in terms of how situations are selected, perceived, reacted to, and acted in, and to interindividual and intergroup differences in these respects. Last year an international conference on the theme "The situation in psychological theory and research" was organized in Stockholm and a book "Toward a psychology of situations" will be published later this year. Shortly I will present two recent studies in our series of studies, concerned with sex and age differences in the way anxiety provoking situations are perceived and reacted to. My main purpose in discussing these studies is not to present conclusive or decisive results, but rather to illustrate the systematic and lawful nature of sex and age differences in individuals' perceptions of and reactions to various kinds of stressful situations. These studies show the importance of considering the character of the situations in which behavior is observed in planning, carrying through, and evaluating results of empirical studies on stress and anxiety.

SEX DIFFERENCES IN REACTIONS
TO ANXIETY–PROVOKING SITUATIONS

The first study is concerned with sex differences in reactions to anxiety provoking situations. Sarason and Smith (1971), in their review of personality research in Annual Review of Psychology, stated that sex perhaps is "the most frequently differentiating organismic variable" (p. 409). Numerous studies have been performed on sex differences in the area of interest in this conference on fear, anxiety, and stress. A review of the literature shows that the size and direction of sex differences observed in empirical research vary with (a) the type of variable that is under consideration, for example, whether it is emotions, cognitive worries, or physiological reactions, (b) the type of data that is used for analysis, for example, whether it is self reports or objective measures of physiological reactions, and (c) how the situations are presented to the subjects, for example, whether individuals' responses refer to real life situations or to hypothetical situations presented verbally or visually. A fourth and important factor, influencing the size and direction of sex differences and which is in the focus of our interest here, is the character of the situations in which behavior occurs.

The existence of important sex by situation interactions has often been demonstrated in empirical research. Let me use a few studies from our own department as examples. In a series of studies, Frankenhaeuser (1980) and her associates have consistently found stronger adrenaline reactions in males than in females in situations involving stress, while such differences have not been observed in neutral, everyday situations. A result in the same direction was presented by Bergman & Magnusson (1979). They found no significant correlation between relative achievement as a rather stable person characteristic and adrenaline excretion in a neutral school situation, but a strong significant correlation for boys and a negligible correlation for girls in a school situation involving demands for intellectual achievement. In these studies, males have consistently shown higher adrenaline excretion than females in stressful situations. However, it should be noted that the situations have been characterized by a demand for achievement of some sort. Of particular interest, then, is a recent study reported by Lundberg (1980), in which fathers' and mothers' physiological reactions to a situation involving a threat to their children were measured. In that situation the expected sex difference was not found; rather, a tendency in the reverse direction was observed. The present study was planned to investigate possible sex by situation interactions by a systematic variation of anxiety provoking situations (Magnusson & Törestad, 1980).

The situations were presented visually to 15-year-old boys and girls and the data were self-reported state anxiety reactions.

Situations

The situations were chosen to represent four different categories of anxiety provoking situations found to form distinct categories in earlier empirical research. In addition, neutral situations were included. Thus, five a priori groupings of situations were used. Each category was represented by four situations.

1. *Innocuous, nonprovocative situations.* These situations were included in order to determine whether there is a tendency for one sex to score higher than the other on anxiety in the absence of situational threat.

2. *Achievement-demanding situations.* Situation one is supposed to adapt to by accomplishing a goal or where one is to be evaluated along with peers and thus runs the risk of failure.

3. *Threat of punishment situations.* Situations involving a threat of punishment from someone higher in status or power, as a consequence of breaking norms.

4. *Physical danger situations.* Two situations ("Getting a shot from the doctor," and "Waiting in the dentist's waiting room") were supposed to induce anticipation of pain, and two situations ("Meeting a gang" and "A car accident") were supposed to involve anticipation of physical injury and destruction (violence).

5. *Inanimate situations.* Situations involving an undefined, possible danger (darkness, loneliness, fantasies, etc.).

Each of the twenty situations was presented in the form of a drawing. The pictures were shown to the subjects individually, one at a time, with a brief oral introduction to each drawing. It was emphasized in the instructions that this was not a test, and that there were no right or wrong answers.

Subjects

The subjects were randomly drawn from classes in grade 8 in a school within the undifferentiated, compulsory school system. Ten boys and ten girls with an average age of 14.9 served as subjects.

The study is now being replicated with a larger number of subjects.

Data

Reactions to the situations were measured by IRS 2 (Magnusson & Ekehammar, 1975). This instrument contains ten subscales covering feelings of psychic and somatic arousal ("I feel nervous"—"My stomach gets upset"). The scale ranges from 1 (= not at all) to 5 (= very much), which implies that intensity of reactions is measured. The total sum of reactions from the ten subscales was used as the measure of intensity of each individual's reaction to each situation.

Results and Conclusions

Means and standard deviations of reported anxiety reactions are reported in Table 1, for each type of situation. Figure 1 gives a summary picture of the results. It is based on mean reactions of boys and girls for types of situations, and the situation categories are ordered on the basis of their anxiety provocation, expressed in total means of reactions.

Figure 1 shows the two main results of interest here. First, there is a significant sex by situation type interaction in anxiety reactions ($p < 0.01$). Second, the interaction takes the general form of increasing sex difference with increasing level of mean anxiety reactions. The systematic relationship between anxiety provocation in situations and the size of sex difference in anxiety reaction is

Table 1 Means and standard deviations for each type of situations, sex difference scores

	Boys		Girls		
	Mean	Standard deviation	Mean	Standard deviation	Difference
Inanimate	107.2	29.3	140.7	23.5	33.5[*]
Threat of punishment	112.4	26.2	130.3	32.7	17.9
Physical threat	104.6	29.5	116.5	27.1	11.9
Achievement-demanding	97.3	32.3	95.5	28.8	−1.8
Innocuous	43.7	6.1	45.3	8.1	1.6

[*]$p < 0.02$.

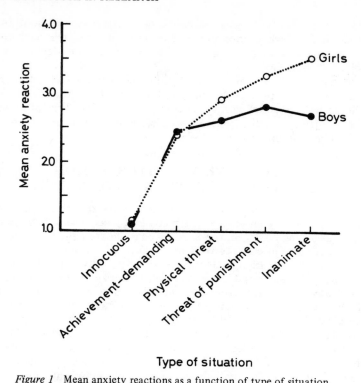

Type of situation

Figure 1 Mean anxiety reactions as a function of type of situation.

clearly visible for single situations. The correlation between the rank order of situations on the basis of mean anxiety reactions, on the one hand, and the rank order of sex differences in anxiety reaction for single situations, on the other is 0.76.

Figure 1 also reveals another interesting feature. For boys, mean reactions vary insignificantly and unsystematically across anxiety provoking situation types. For girls, in contrast, a one way analysis of variance for the differences between mean reaction in types of situations gave a significant result ($p < 0.02$).

The exact form of the curve in Fig. 1, representing intensity of anxiety reactions as a function of type of situation, should not be exaggerated. All inanimate situations do not provoke higher anxiety reactions than all other situations and so on. This means that the exact form of the curve will be dependent, to some extent, upon the sampling of situations to represent each category. However, the main result of a sex by situation interaction and that it takes the form summarized above has been demonstrated in two other studies in the project, one based on a reanalysis of data from an earlier study and one study that is a replication of the study presented here, but with a larger sample of boys and girls of the same age.

As stated above, the existence of sex by situation interactions has been demonstrated earlier. However, the systematic nature of this interaction, in the form that is showed in the present study, was not predicted. The result emphasizes the necessity of incorporating the character of the situations—in which behavior is observed—in planning, carrying through, and evaluating the results of research on stress and anxiety. However, this cannot be done effectively without knowledge about situations in relevant terms, obtained in systematic research. Such knowledge is sorely needed, so that situational conditions can be considered in a known, predictable, and controlled way.

The present study was characterized by the use of self-report data referring to hypothetical situations, presented visually to boys and girls at the age of 15. Similar studies should be conducted with systematic variation of the type of situations for other types of data, for other types of variables, with other procedures for presenting the situations, and for other age levels.

AGE DIFFERENCES IN PERCEPTION
OF ANXIETY–PROVOKING SITUATIONS

The second study is concerned with developmental trends in the perception and interpretation of anxiety provoking situations. In a recent study boys and girls for each of the age groups 12, 15, and 18 were asked to describe the three most anxiety provoking situations that came to their mind. For each of the situations they then described what in the situation made them anxious and why it did. The descriptions formed the basis for analyses of sex and age differences with respect to what causes anxiety and why. Some interesting and somewhat surprising results have been obtained. In the analyses of the youngsters' motives for anxiety a rather obvious age difference appeared. The preadolescent youngsters often referred to physical properties of the situations, to external bodily consequences and possible external sanctions; by contrast older teenagers referred to psychological consequences such as anticipated shame, guilt, separation, lack of personal integrity, etc. Where the young subjects spoke about spatially and temporally close sanctions, older ones referred to anticipated consequences in the future, in profiessional life, in marriage, etc. The preadolescent boys and girls even showed difficulties in conceptualizing the consequences for themselves. A preadolescent explanation in response to the described situation, "I am afraid when I ski down a steep hill" was "Because the hill is so steep" and did not refer to the possible physical injury that would be a common explanation given by older subjects.

The difference between preadolescents and older subjects with respect to experienced and expressed motives for situationally determined anxiety as indicated in the description above, is in accordance with the theory of cognitive development suggested by Piaget. According to Piaget during the period of concrete operations a child acquires the capacity to classify and interrelate objects in the environment and to give causal explanations based on spatial-temporal premises. However, the logic of the child is still mainly based on inferences from the immediately present situation, and relations are mainly based on physical properties of the objects. When formal operations begin, thought processes become progressively more independent of the immediate present, and the adolescent can go beyond the physical properties of the situation and base his judgment of relations on inferences and more subtle inherent qualities. There is a continuous "decentering" of thought processes from the given perceptual stimulus field.

Based on our observations, and with Piaget's theory as a background a study was performed to investigate age variations in perceptions and interpretations of anxiety provoking situations, from pre- to post-adolescence (Stattin, 1980). The basic assumption was that preadolescents would see relations between anxiety provoking situations in terms of manifest physical characteristics, while older subjects would conceptualize resemblances between such situations more and more in terms of latent psychological anticipated consequences.

Method

Data were obtained for three age groups, 11-12, 14-15, and 17-18, with about 60 boys and 60 girls for each age level. (For the age level 17-18 the number of boys was only 29.)

From a sample of nearly one thousand descriptions of anxiety provoking situations given by youngsters in the same age groups, eleven were selected for the present study. The criterion for the selection of situations was that they were reported by youngsters at all three age levels.

Our hypothesis was tested by the use of similarity ratings (Magnusson, 1971). For studying the present hypothesis this method was particularly adequate since, besides yielding quantitative, direct measures of subjective similarity between situations, it does not require verbal ability (which varies systematically with age).

All possible combinations of the eleven situations were reated on a four point scale, ranging from 0 ("Not at all similar") to 3 ("Very similar"). The order of presentation was randomized for the pairs of situations.

Situation similarity ratings were possible on two different grounds; on the basis of what can be designated manifest characteristics and on the basis of what can be designated latent characteristics. According to the first principle, situations could be judged as similar with reference to a common central object or person which was clearly visible and salient in the situations. In this respect, situations could have one of the following four elements in common: classmate, brother, relative, and dog. The first three appeared in three situations each and dog was the common element in two situations.

According to the second principle similarity could be judged on the basis of common anticipated consequences. Four types of latent characteristics were used: physical injury, separation, guilt, and shame. Physical injury was the anticipated consequence in two situations and the other three consequences appeared in three situations each. The categories were taken from content analysis of adolescents' own explanations of why they were anxious in various types of anxiety-provoking situations. The categories discriminated satisfactorily between consequences of this type.

An example will illustrate the way this procedure works. Two situations were described as follows: "An angry dog nips at you when you are out walking" and "Your dog is sick and has to be taken to the veterinary." According to the main hypothesis these two situations will be judged as similar among preadolescents because of the common element dog, but as different by postadolescents since the anticipated consequences are different (physical injury and separation).

Al possible combinations of situation pairs yield a matrix of 55 similarity ratings. Of these, 10 pertain to situation pairs with a common object, where similarity would be based on manifest characteristics. Ten cells refer to situation pairs with common anticipated consequences, where similarity would be based on latent characteristics. The remaining 35 cells represent similarity ratings for pairs that do not share common trigger objects or common anticipated consequences.

For each subject three mean similarity ratings were calculated:

1. Across situation pairs with common trigger object;
2. Across situation pairs with common anticipated consequences;
3. Across situation pairs without these common elements.

To analyze the relative weights of manifest and latent characteristics as the basis for similarity ratings, the mean of similarity ratings for situation pairs without a common element (3) was used as a base level, against which the mean similarity ratings for situation pairs with common objects and common anticipated consequences, respectively, were tested.

Results and Conclusions

The overall results are presented in Table 2 and Fig. 2. The results are clearly in line with the hypothesis for both boys and girls. In accordance with the hypothesis, with increasing age there is a gradual decrease in similarity ratings based on manifest characteristics, and a corresponding increase in similarity ratings based on latent characteristics. (Girls showed a slightly lower rating for situations with common manifest characteristics and somewhat higher ratings for situations with common latent characteristics. However, these differneces were not significant at any age level.)

The results thus support the assumption that the perception and interpretation of environmental threats change in nature from pre- to post-adolescence.

This is not the place to go into a detailed discussion and analysis of the results and of the consequences for theory and empirical research on stress and anxiety. (For a discussion see Stattin, 1980.) Let me only point out one implication, which is of more general interest for theory and research in the field of personality. During the seventies, the problem of personality consistency—both in cross-situational and in a longitudinal perspective—has been a central and controversial theme. As summarized above, our results indicated a clear change in the perception and interpretation of anxiety-provoking situations from pre- to postadolescence. To the extent that behavior is a function of how we perceive and construe the outer world as we encounter it in actual situations, the environmental conditions that determine cross-situational stability in actual behavior varies with age, i.e., what constitutes a stable environment as a prerequisite for behavioral consistency varies with age. For preadolescents a stable environment is characterized by similarity in physical, external properties. For postadolescents, on the other hand, it is charac-

Table 2 Difference scores for ratings of similarity based on manifest and latent characteristics, respectively

	Boys			Girls		
Characteristic	12 yrs	15 yrs	18 yrs	12 yrs	15 yrs	18 yrs
Manifest	0.164***	0.149***	0.80	0.160***	0.119*	0.095
Latent	0.179***	0.277***	0.421***	0.189***	0.342***	0.436***

*$p < 0.05$.
***$p < 0.001$.

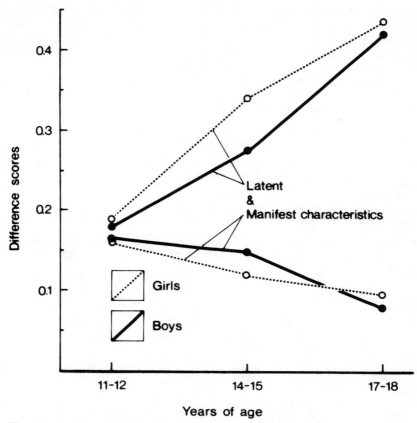

Figure 2 Developmental change in situation perception for boys (R) and girls (G), respectively.

terized by situations that are similar with respect to psychological, latent qualities. Age differences in the perception and interpretation of anxiety-provoking situations can also be assumed to imply age differences in actual behavior in the same kind of situations. These speculations open up a series of important and fruitful problems for systematic research not only in the area of stress and anxiety, but in the field of personality as a whole.

Final Comment

The results presented here show the systematic character of the interaction between person variables such as sex and age and type of anxiety-provoking situations. In a broader perspective, this demonstrates the systematic nature of the interaction between person and situation characteristics as emphasized especially by those advocating an interactional model of behavior. Again, this underlines the need for systematic research on situations. Systematic knowledge about situations is a prerequisite for more effective theory and empirical research in the field of personality. What seems to be a basis for confusion, when one looks at the diversity of empirical results in the field of personality, is actually often lawfulness, that has to be detected and understood. But the lawfulness of the person-situation interactions cannot be effectively investigated if we do not devote resources to the systematic study of the situations side of the person-situation system, as we have done on the person side for a hundred years (Magnusson, 1980). Descriptions and classifications of situations in relevant terms are needed to enable us to predict and explain why, when and how anxiety will occur in whom.

REFERENCES

Bergman, L. R. & Magnusson, D. Overachievement and catecholamine excretion in an achievement demanding situation. *Psychomatic Medicine*, 1979, *41*, 181–188.

Endler, N. S. A person-situation interaction model of anxiety. In C. D. Spielber & I. G. Sarason (eds.), *Stress and anxiety*, Vol. 1. Washington, D.C.: Hemisphere, 1975.

Frankenhaeuser, M. Psychoneuroendrocrine approaches in the study of stressful person-environment transactions. In H. Selye (ed.), *Selye's gyide to stress research. Volume 1.* New York: Van Nostrand Reinhold Company, 1980.

Lundberg, U. Catecholamine and cortisol excretion patterns in three-year-old children and their parents. Unpublished manuscript, Department of Psychology, University of Stockholm, 1980.

Magnusson, D. An analysis of situational dimensions. *Perceptual and Motor Skills*, 1971, *32*, 851–867.

Magnusson, D. Personality in an interactional paradigm of research. *Zeitschrift für Differentielle und Diagnostische Psychologie*, 1980, *1*, 17–34.

Magnusson, D. Wanted: A psychology of situations. In D. Magnusson (ed.), *Toward a psychology of situations: An interactional perspective.* Hillsdale, N.J.: Lawrence Erlbaum, 1981.

Magnusson, D. & Ekehammar, B. Perceptions of and reactions to stressful situations. *Journal of Personality and Social Psychology*, 1975, *31*, 1147–1154.

Magnusson, D. & Törestad B. Situational influences on sex differences. Unpublished manuscript. Department of Psychology, University of Stockholm, 1980.

Sarason, I. G. & Smith, R. E. Personality. *Annual Review of Psychology*, 1971, *22*, 393–446.

Schalling, D. Types of anxiety and types of stressors as related to personality. In C. D. Spielberger & I. G. Sarason (eds.), *Stress and anxiety*, Vol. 1. Washington, D.C.: Hemisphere, 1975.

Spielberger, C. D. Conceptual and methodological issues in research on anxiety. In C. D. Spielberger (ed.), *Anxiety: Current trends in theory and research*, Vol. 1. New York: Academic Press, 1972.

Stattin, H. The appraisal of relations between emotionally threatening situations: A developmental study. Unpublished manuscript, Department of Psychology, University of Stockholm, 1980.

6

Arousal, Affect, and Self-perception

The Role of the Physical Environment

Vernon L. Allen
University of Wisconsin

INTRODUCTION

The present chapter will present theory and empirical research focusing upon the relation between the physical environment and affective-cognitive states. In particular, we will examine the affective and cognitive experiences that are associated with destruction of objects in the physical environment. Our empirical research investigating the effects of destruction has taken two directions: (a) The psychological processes in destructive acts that help account for the level of intensity of an individual's hedonic response; and (b) consequences of destruction for an individual's perception about control. The present chapter will be concerned primarily with theory and research on the latter line of work—the impact of destruction on perceived control.

The first section of the paper calls attention to evidence indicating that stress, anxiety, and arousal often seem to produce positive or facilitative effects and that individuals often seek such experiences. An interpretation of the positive functions of stress and anxiety is advanced in the second section of the paper which discusses the relation between arousal and affect. Section three briefly considers the impact of the physical environment on affect and cognition. Presented in the fourth section is a discussion of the relation between destruction and perceived control and a brief description of methodological paradigms used in the research. The results of several empirical studies summarized in section five indicate that destruction does influence perceived control and success. Finally, the last section offers some interpretations of the findings and suggests a few implications.

POSITIVE FUNCTIONS OF AROUSAL, STRESS, AND ANXIETY

Stress and anxiety are usually thought to be aversive states that an individual tries to avoid and which result in damaging psychological and physiological consequences if they persist for a long period of time. That stress and anxiety do, in fact, frequently produce a wide range of detrimental consequences for the individual is well documented by an impressive body of empirical research (Spielberger &

This chapter was written while the author was a Fellow at the Netherlands Institute for Advanced Study in the Humanities and Social Sciences.

Sarason, 1975, 1978). Stress and anxiety have been implicated as contributing to negative outcomes across a variety of classes of behavior including motor performance, intellectual functioning, physiological responses, and interpersonal relationships. At the same time, other data indicate that stress and anxiety also appear to possess positive qualities in many instances. It seems that conditions of arousal, risk-taking, and excitement are often sought rather than avoided by people. Stress and anxiety thus seem to produce both negative and positive effects. Before offering an explanation for this apparent paradox, some of the positive functions of stress and anxiety should be discussed more fully.

One of the clearest instances of the facilitative effect of anxiety comes from research that has employed the Manifest Anxiety Scale (Taylor, 1953). Experiments have found that high levels of anxiety (as measured by the Taylor scale) serve to promote learning on simple tasks such as classical conditioning. Stating the finding in more general terms, it can be said that high (trait) anxiety facilitates learning and performance in the case of a dominant response (i.e., when alternative responses are not competing). Therefore, a simple learning task or a well-learned response will be improved by the presence of a high level of manifest anxiety (Taylor, 1956).

Beyond the experimental evidence concerning learning and performance, it is also abundantly clear that there exist a large number of situations and experiences that qualify as being "stressful" or "anxiety-provoking," but which produce positive consequences and are perceived by participants as being desirable, pleasant, and enjoyable. Certainly it is true that many people expend a considerable amount of time and effort in order to participate in activities that are dangerous (physically, psychologically, or financially—or all), frightening, physiologically arousing, and risky. Yet such occasions are experienced by participants as pleasurable and, perhaps, even as character-building. We would be well-advised in our research efforts to pay more attention to these positive functions of stress, anxiety, and arousal.

Goffman (1967), in a stimulating essay, uses the term "action" ("where the action is") to refer to those stimulation-enhancing characteristics of certain situations. "Action" is, according to Goffman (1967), ". . . to be found whenever the individual knowingly takes consequential chances perceived as avoidable" (p. 194). Gambling is the prototype of "action"—the willful undertaking of a risky behavior which carries important consequences. Dangerous, risky, or anxiety-arousing behavior is intrinsic to certain types of occupations and leisure-time pursuits. Real-estate or stock-market speculators, prospectors, salesmen, and entertainers are roles that are susceptible to large fluctuations in outcome. Other individuals choose occupations that are simply physically dangerous: test-pilots, soldiers, bull-fighters, race-car drivers, and criminals. For their leisure-time pursuits, many persons engage in activities such as parachute-jumping, gambling, taking rides in amusement parks, and driving too fast in automobiles. It has been observed in several amusement parks that on days immediately following a fatal accident on one of the rides there is a great increase in its popularity. As pointed out by Balint (1959), youngsters at amusement parks are clearly conscious of their fear and aware of the objective danger present, yet they still voluntarily expose themselves to danger and fear. Such arousal and excitement is experienced as pleasant, a "thrill," and is done for "kicks."

In addition to the pleasure and "fun" often associated with stressful and highly arousing conditions, such behavior may also serve positive functions for the individual's self-concept and social identity. Several investigators have emphasized the role of risk-taking, bravado, excitement, danger, and antisocial behavior in contributing to the social status ("reputation") of delinquents or members of youth gangs (Short & Strodtbeck, 1965; Thrasher, 1927). As Goffman (1967) has so aptly phrased this point: "The voluntary taking of serious chances is a means for the maintenance and acquisition of character . . ." (p. 235). Somewhat related are the positive consequences in the form of deeper "understanding" mentioned by persons who have been held as hostages under extremely stressful conditions (Bastiaans, 1980).*

Individuals differ widely, of course, in the extent to which they experience stressful and highly arousing conditions as being pleasurable. Persons can be differentiated on the basis of their level of sensation-seeking. Zuckerman (1978) notes that "fear, anger, and even pain can have some attractive aspects for a sensation-seeker" (p. 43). A scale has been developed by Zuckerman (1974) for measuring differences among persons in their "sensation-seeking" tendencies. Persons who score high on this scale seek excitement in a variety of ways, and prefer engaging in many risky activities; they would endorse an item on the scale such as "I sometimes do things that are a little frightening."

Thus, it appears that arousal and stress are sometimes pleasant and facilitative in various ways, and sometimes unpleasant and detrimental to psychological and physiological functioning. Several suggestions can be offered in an attempt to resolve this apparent paradox. First, the nature of the task is an important determinant of whether the outcome will be positive or negative. The clearest example is the relation between manifest anxiety and complexity of the task. As stated earlier, a high level of manifest anxiety (Taylor, 1953) facilitates the learning of a simple task—but it interfers with the acquisition of a complex learning task. Thus, task complexity explains why stress and anxiety ("drive") sometimes facilitate and sometimes interfere with learning and performance.

Second, the duration of stress and anxiety is an important determinant of the outcome. Experiences that might be pleasurable for a short period of time, or if they occurred intermittently, would become very noxious if they persisted for a long time. Likewise, transient physiological arousal that would produce only benign effects in the short-run, could have serious detrimental effects on health if continued over a long period of time. It is likely that negative outcomes for a person's physical and psychological health are the sequelae of chronic stress and anxiety.

Third, the difference in content between different kinds of stress and anxiety should be acknowledged as a crucial factor determining the nature of the outcome. Experiences such as loss of job, death in the family, and the like, are very different in cognitive content and in quality, as compared to experiences such as gambling, parachute jumping, riding on a roller coaster, and the like. Although common elements of arousal are present in both classes of events, it would be folly to ignore the real and significant differences between then in terms of the content of the experience and ramifications for other areas of life.

Fourth, the degree of personal control over the stress and anxiety may help

*Talk presented by J. Bastiaans at Conferences on Stress and Anxiety, Wassenaar, Netherlands, 7 February, 1980.

explain whether the experience has debilitating or facilitating consequences for the individual. A considerable degree of control by the individual seems to be a characteristic of many of the stressful situations that produce positive affective responses (e.g., dangerous sports, etc.); in particular, the person usually is afforded a great deal of freedom of choice about the initiation and termination of the experience as well as some degree of control during the experience itself. By contrast, the individual can exert very little control over many of the stressful and anxiety-provoking experiences that seem to create negative consequences. Usually, lack of personal control and chronicity of the experience will be correlated, of course.

Finally, the degree of arousal in relation to one's adaptation level will determine whether a positive or negative affective experience will result. A moderate discrepancy from adaptation level of the arousal is perceived as pleasant (Berlyne, 1971); too much or too little arousal is aversive. The experiences identified by the individual as constituting positive affect (enjoyment, pleasure, fun) seem to be based, at the physiological level, on a moderate increase or decrease in arousal (Berlyne, 1971). This is not to say that every instance of positive affect is due to the mechanism of optimal arousal in the organism. It is clear that there are other sources of positive affect, as suggested by evidence pointing to the existence of "pleasure" centers in the brain (Olds & Milner, 1954). Be that as it may, the available empirical evidence strongly supports the proposition that an optimal level of arousal (within the normal range) or de-arousal (with the extremely high range) in relation to adaptation level is sufficient to produce the experience of positive affect. The question of the source of positive affect can be reduced, then, to the conditions that produce a moderate discrepancy in arousal or de-arousal relative to adaptation level.

The sources of an increase in arousal (and, thereby, positive affect) are varied. One source is the class of events in the external world that holds important symbolic significance for one's self-identity, such as success or failure on the job and occurrences in the life of significant other persons. Another way is direct intervention at the level of the nervous system itself through the use of pharmaceutical agents familiar to members of the drug culture and much of bourgeois society. Another source of arousal can be found in experiences that are physically dangerous (e.g., parachuting) or which entail great risks to one's financial or social status, or in other ways. The items on the sensation-seeking scale devised by Zuckerman (1974) provide a representative sampling of the class of events considered to be "exciting." Another possible source of arousal, the physical environment, will be discussed in the next section.

ROLE OF THE PHYSICAL ENVIRONMENT

One of the sources of arousal that is often overlooked is the physical environment itself. Several variables that are involved in any stimulus array have been called "collative" variables by Berlyne (1971), because they involve the comparison ("collation") between two or more aspects of experience. The variables are complexity, novelty, uncertainty, surprisingness, and conflict. Research has shown that these variables can account for the degree of hedonic experience produced by a stimulus—including such complex aesthetic stimuli as art, music, and literature. These variables, along with some others (i.e., stimulus intensity, symmetry or balance) are capable of producing an increase in arousal which in turn is responsible for the pleasurable affect associated with "aesthetic" experiences. It has been proposed elsewhere (Allen & Greenberger, 1978) that these same variables can also account for the positive affect that an individual often experiences in connection with the destruction of a physical object.

Therefore, it is hypothesized that destruction is a pleasurable experience because it has the same underlying characteristics (i.e., the same psychological variables are involved) as an aesthetic experience. The degree of enjoyment derived from any act of destruction will depend upon the variables that determine the response of a person to any external stimulus situation, whether it is socially acceptable (e.g., art or music) or unacceptable (e.g., destruction or vandalism). The application of aesthetic theory to the problem of destruction leads to the prediction that the degree of enjoyment of destruction will be a function of the strength of variables such as complexity, novelty, unexpectedness, etc., which are involved in the process of destruction. This analysis of destruction is consistent with the anecdotal reports of youngsters who have stated that they engaged in vandalism because it was "fun" (Martin, 1961). We have obtained evidence supporting the aesthetic theory of destruction in a series of studies designed to investigate the several variables, including subjective and objective complexity, unexpectedness, and symmetry (Allen & Greenberger, 1978). Because the present chapter will concentrate on exploring the relation between destruction and perceived control, the research using aesthetic theory to explain the relation between destruction and affective experience will not be described.

Evidence cited above indicates that destruction is associated with a positive affective response. In addition to being involved in affective reactions, destruction may have an impact on an individual's cognitive responses as well. It is hypothesized that destruction will influence an individual's perception about certain cognitive aspects of self, viz., control or self-efficacy. Before discussing the conceptual rationale for expecting a relationship to exist between destruction and perceived control, the concept should be discussed briefly. Then, in the following section the theoretical basis for predicting that destruction will exert an impact on the individual's perception about control will be elaborated.

Modification of the physical environment has a strong potential for affecting an individual's perception about self. A set of interrelated concepts has been employed by several authors to indicate the extent to which a person believes he or she can produce an effect upon the external world. White (1959) maintained, in a well-known paper, that persons have a need to manipulate and control their surroundings—to produce an effective change in the environment. Several concepts which seem very similar, in spite of differences in emphasis, are the following: internal-external control (Rotter, 1966), competence (White, 1959), self-efficacy (Bandura, 1977), powerlessness or alienation (Seeman, 1959), and learned helplessness (Seligman, 1975). Perceived control is now recognized as being an extremely important concept in that it appears to have implications for behavior across many different areas of psychology. Recent research suggests that a person's belief about internal (ability or effort) versus external (luck, etc.) locus of control of outcomes may play a very central role in phenomena such as learned helplessness and depression.

The concept of perceived control can refer to the individual's beliefs about one's ability to influence any aspect of the world—physical, social, or cognitive. We shall restrict the present discussion of perceived control to the manipulation of some aspect of the physical environment (natural or man-made), since this type of behavior is one of the most direct means available to an individual for influencing the feeling of control (Piaget, 1952; White, 1959). The theoretical basis for making this assertion will be developed in the next section. For now, let us assume that as a result of a long history of personal experience of transactions with the physical environment, an individual has learned that the manipulation of the physical environment does result in an increase in feelings of success and control. It is assumed that when an individual is aware of a decrement in personal control, he or she will engage in instrumental responses directed toward the environment in an attempt to restore perceived control to its previous level. Efforts to influence or modify the physical environment may take the form of socially approved actions (e.g., personalization of space); but more drastic action may also be undertaken such as the purposeful destruction of an object. Successfully creating a change of some sort in the physical environment may be sufficient to produce an increase in the level of an individual's subjective control. Note that actions taken in an attempt to increase perceived control may be directed toward features of the physical environment that are completely unrelated to the original cause of the decrease in control.

DESTRUCTION AND PERCEIVED CONTROL: THEORY AND METHOD

It has been hypothesized that an individual will experience an increase in sense of control as a result of altering, modifying, or transforming the built environment in some way. Almost limitless are the ways available to an individual for affecting and modifying the physical environment or particular objects in the physical environment. The physical world is indeed malleable in a variety of ways, ranging from slight changes to a complete transformation of form and structure. Four broad categories of types of modification of the physical environment which are relevant to the present problem can be suggested: (1) transposition, (2) alteration, (3) construction, and (4) destruction.

The first category (transposition) refers to the restructuring or relocation of objects in the environment without any visible changes having been made in the nature of the objects themselves. Re-arranging the furniture in one's place of residence is an example. Selectively collecting certain types of objects or the particular placement of available objects can serve the function of marking territorial boundaries and also can express valued aspects of self to others. The latter function has been called "personalization" of space (e.g., changing the decorations inside a dwelling). One of the explanations offered for personalization of one's dwelling is that it contributes to a sense of competence and mastery (Becker, 1977). The second category (alteration) includes those actions directed toward objects which do not result in extensive change or damage. Remodeling a house would be an example. The slight defacement of the surface of objects by painting or writing on them (such as by graffiti) is another example. The last two categories involve more extensive transformations of the physical environment. The third category (construction) refers to the creation of new forms that did not exist before, e.g., building a house or other structure. In the fourth category (destruction) radical and drastic transformation also takes place, but in the opposite direction to that occurring in construction.

All four categories of types of modification of the physical environment may produce an impact on the individual's perception about important characteristics of self. It is the last category, though, destruction, that seems to hold especially great potential for affecting one's self-perception about control (competence or efficacy). The theoretical justification for this assertion will be presented later; but first it is necessary to specify the conditions under which the act of destruction is likely to be a particularly effective means for enhancing one's sense of control.

Certain distinctive features of the physical environment make destruction particularly attractive to an individual as a technique for demonstrating success in bringing about a change in the external world. First, it is very likely that an individual will be successful in an attempt to make a change in the environment by means of destruction. Destruction provides immediate and unequivocal feedback indicating that one has produced a noticeable impact on the environment; judgment about the success of the attempt is not ambiguous nor is it delayed until the future. Second, destruction produces an increase in level of arousal which is enjoyable, as our research has demonstrated (Allen & Greenberger, 1978). High arousal (and thus positive affect) can almost always be depended on to occur in an act of desstruction because, in addition to the operation of collative variables, an individual will also frequently experience excitement, fear, nervousness, and apprehension in connection with an act of destruction (especially if it is unacceptable). The experience of positive affect is likely to produce an increase in level of perceived control because in the individual's past experience positive affect and high control have frequently occurred simultaneously in connection with valued and favorable experiences (e.g., success). On the basis of this conjecture it could be predicted that the manipulation of mood would be sufficient to alter perceived control, i.e., positive mood would enhance the feeling of control.

Consistent with the foregoing analysis, existing evidence from several sources suggests that a very close relation exists between perceived control and destruction. For example, Taylor and Walton (1973) concluded that attempts by workers to assert control is one of the primary causes of acts of industrial sabotage. And destruction of windows, furniture, and equipment is quite common in living conditions in which individuals seem to have low control over their social and physical environment, such as children's residential institutions, mental hospitals, prisons, public housing, and public schools (Ward, 1973; Wenk & Harlow, 1978; Yancy, 1972). Likewise, the age group that is distinctive in terms of its marginality and powerlessness—that is, adolescents—accounts for a disproportionate number of the acts of "wanton" destruction or vandalism (Ward, 1973).

The hypothesis concerning the role of destruction in self-perception has been tested experimentally under controlled conditions in the laboratory. We conducted several studies that investigated various aspects of the relation between the destruction of physical objects and perceived control, success, and affect (Allen & Greenberger, 1980). Most of these studies employed, basically, the same general method and procedure; therefore, rather than present each experiment in detail only a general description of the paradigm used in all the studies need be given.

Typically, the procedure involved experimentally manipulating the affective experience of a subject (e.g., mood or success/failure), and then arranging for a subsequent experience of destruction by the subject under controlled conditions in the laboratory. To ensure comparability among subjects in their experience of destruction, it was desirable that the object to be destroyed should always break in a highly standard or consistent way. The objective degree of control that the subjects possessed over the outcome should be minimal and identical for all of them. After some pilot work the following method if implementing the destruction was adopted which satisfied these requirements. The destruction involved allowing the subjects to break a tower (constructed from small wooden blocks) by releasing a ball that rolled down a ramp and thence into the structure.

A tower was constructed from 12 square rings of wooden blocks placed on top of each other to a height of 72 cm. Each ring consisted of eight blocks (two on each of the four sides). The size of each block was $4.5 \times 6 \times 3.5$ cm. The appearance of the tower was identical for all subjects. The method used to break the tower involved an inclined ramp (2.8 m long). One end of the ramp was elevated (2.4 m) and the other end rested on the floor, thereby forming an angle of incline of 35 degrees. The lower end of the ramp was placed adjacent to the block tower. Subjects were instructed simply to place a volleyball at the top of the ramp and then release it—thereby permitting the ball to roll down the ramp and strike the tower. The velocity of the volleyball was always sufficient to result in breaking the tower in a realistic and interesting manner. After each instance of breaking by a subject the tower was reconstructed before the next subject appeared.

It should be noted that this procedure enabled the subjects to believe that they were responsible for the outcome (as they indeed were); but at the same time the degree of control over the outcome was sufficiently minor and ambiguous to allow the possibility of a considerable degree of variation in the reaction of subjects as a function of experimental conditions. The technique used to accomplish the destruction ensured that the tower would always break in a very similar manner for all subjects and that the same (minimal) amount of effort would be expended in all cases. Moreover, this technique provided subjects with the opportunity to observe the immediate consequences of their action.

Dependent measures used in the experiments consisted of bipolar scales designed to measure various aspects of perceived general control, control of outcome, general success, and mood or affect, among other measures (depending upon the purpose of a particular experiment). The findings summarized in the next section are based on four independent experiments, each experiment using more than 100 subjects. Both male and female college students served as subjects. It should be noted that all results reported in the following section are based on experimental manipulations, not correlational data. Also, many of the results below represent findings that have been replicated across two or more experiments.

RESULTS AND DISCUSSION

For ease of presentation (and to avoid duplicating proportions of findings that overlap across different studies) the results from the four experiments will be organized around four areas of impact on perceived control: mood, success and failure, active versus vicarious destruction, and different methods of modifying the environment.

Impact of Mood on Perceived Control

In one experiment mood was manipulated by using a technique developed by Velten (1968). The subject is required to read a sentence that appears on each of 50 cards. All the statements differ, and are designed to create a mood state of either elation or depression. The sentences either stress how well and energetic the person feels or refer to negative aspects of life (e.g., feeling depressed and tired). Immediately after the mood induction procedure was completed, a questionnaire was administered which included bipolar scales measuring mood, along with filler items.

Results showed that the two mood states did produce a significant difference in the subjects' feelings of general success/failure prior to the destruction. That is, subjects in the elation condition felt more successful (11.88, on the 15-point scale) than subjects in the depression condition (7.36). After breaking the tower, subjects received the following item (among other items) in a questionnaire: "How much control did you have over the outcome of the break?" The two mood states produced a significant difference in the subjects' perceived control over the outcome, with level of perceived control being greater for subjects in the elation than the depression condition. (Objectively, the outcome was identical in both mood conditions, of course.)

Thus, it appears that differential mood is sufficient to produce different levels of perception of success and of control over outcome. Note that the manipulation of mood, though effective, does not approach the level of intensity of elation and depression that often occurs in everyday life. In view of the modest intensity of the differences in mood produced in the experimental situation, the impact on perceived control and success is indeed very impressive. As an interpretation of the results it can be suggested that a close association has probably existed in a person's past experience between quality of affect (mood) and occurrences that involve different levels of control and success in everyday life experiences. Hence, on the basis of past conditioning, positive mood would tend to elicit an increase in the feeling of perceived control. In sum, then, sheer affect alone seems to be sufficient to produce a significant influence on the level of a person's perceived control and success. The relevance of this finding to destruction becomes clear when it is remembered that our previous research has found that destruction usually creates positive affect (Allen & Greenberger, 1978).

Success/Failure and Perceived Control

In one study subjects were led to believe that they had either succeeded or failed on a word-association task. Later, in one of the experimental conditions subjects were allowed to engage in destruction of the tower. Included among the dependent measures was an item measuring perception of general control ("In general, how much control do you feel you have over events in your life?"). It was predicted that the act of destruction would lead to an increase in the general feeling of control for subjects who had experienced failure, relative to subjects who had experienced failure but who did not participate in the destruction. Results supported the prediction: Perceived control increased after the destruction for subjects who had failed earlier, in comparison with subjects in the control condition (11.92 vs. 9.62, respectively). Destruction did not influence felt control for subjects in the success condition, relative to the control (11.64 vs. 11.15, respectively).

Two points should be made about these results. First, destruction was effective in increasing perceived general control for subjects in the failure condition to a level comparable to that obtained in the success condition. Second, destruction did not further increase felt control of the subjects who had experienced success earlier; the impact of destruction and earlier success was not multiplicative—it did not result in scores greater than the scores produced by successful task performance alone. It can be suggested, then, that destruction seems to exert its most powerful and direct effect on perceived (general) control when it occurs subsequent to the subject's having experienced a decrement in control produced by failure (and, perhaps, by other means). Destruction does seem to be very effective in restoring the level of control to the pre-failure level—or, to be more precise with reference to the present data, to the level that would have existed had success occurred instead of failure. The destruction used in the present experiment was, of course, rather mild; perhaps a more serious act of destruction would have enhanced felt control even for those persons who had experienced success.

Direct Versus Vicarious Destruction

In two experiments the impact of destruction on perceived control was compared when the subjects directly engaged in destruction or merely observed the same destruction being produced by someone else (the experimenter). It is possible that even vicarious destruction will increase the perception of control. To the extent that arousal contributes to felt control, vicarious destruction should also be effective since arousal and enjoyment are present. Our earlier research on aesthetic factors in destruction indicated that observing destruction does produce positive affect even when the observer is not personally responsible for producing the destruction. The opposite prediction can be made, however, on the basis of other components of destruction that may contribute to perceived control, such as attribution of success. This leads to the prediction that perhaps perceived control will be enhanced only when the person perceives a personal responsibility for producing the destruction; if so, observation of destruction should not influence perceived control.

An experiment was designed in which subjects in one condition were responsible personally for performing the destruction, and in another condition (different) subjects observed the experimenter produce destruction in the same standard manner. The effect on perceived control of direct and vicarious destruction was measured after all the subjects had experienced failure on a task. Results showed that the level of (general) perceived control was higher in the case of direct destruction (11.92) than with vicarious destruction (10.64); and, interestingly, scores for both direct and vicarious destruction were higher than the control (no-destruction) condition (9.62). Although these data suggest that vicarious destruction may have some influence on perceived control, the mean did not differ significantly from the control condition. Hence, only direct participation in destruction was effective in producing a significant increment in (general) perceived control. The direct and vicarious destruction conditions were replicated in another experiment with somewhat different experimental manipulations (success/failure was not used) and different dependent measures (felt success). Consistent with results from the earlier experiment, it was found that the level of perceived success was greater with direct than vicarious destruction (11.92 vs. 8.25, respectively). The difference between the two conditions was statistically significant. (This experiment did not include a no-destruction condition.) We should not completely dismiss the possibility that vicarious destruction may influence felt control somewhat through the mechanisms of general arousal, since it did produce a small (though insignificant) influence.

Type of Modification of the Environment

One study was designed to compare the effect on perceived control of destruction relative to other means of modifying the physical environment (Allen & Greenberger, 1980; Greenberger, 1980). Two conditions were created in addition to a destruction condition: (1) transposition (removing blocks from the floor and stacking them into a box); (2) construction (building a structure from the blocks). The number of blocks available was identical in all three experimental conditions (destruction, transposition, and construction). The experimental manipulations created initially a low level of perceived control for all subjects by reducing their freedom of choice on a task; afterwards, each subject was randomly assigned either to one of the three experimental conditions or to the control condition (rest). Results showed that the highest mean score for perceived control occurred in the destruction condition, with construction being next, and modification the lowest. It is important to notice, however, that with all three methods of modifying the environment the scores for perceived control were significantly greater than in the control condition. Hence, the greatest impact on perceived control was produced by destruction, but other methods of modifying the physical environment also seemed to exert some influence as well.

Before embarking upon a discussion of the present results and their implications, a few qualifications, cautions, and caveats should be raised. All the results presented above were derived from experimental studies conducted under laboratory conditions, and therefore partake of all the advantages and limitations of that method. The level of arousal of subjects who participated in the studies was at best moderate, that is, the destruction acts were not committed under a strong emotion such as anger or fear. Moreover, the destruction occurred with the approval of the experimenter, so it did not violate a societal prohibition as would likely be the case in everyday life. The amount of destruction was not extensive by any means. The subjects in the experiments were well-socialized college students behaving in isolation from social pressures of the sort that might exist when in the presence of a group of peers. Finally, the destruction was a very brief and transient experience; the duration of the influence of destruction on perceived control was not determined. The effect of all these characteristics on the generalizability of the results cannot be ascertained. On the other hand, it can be argued that the findings should be viewed as being very conservative. The data were obtained under well-controlled conditions and some of the findings were replicated across experiments. Moreover, it can be maintained that the results obtained in this research would be accentuated under conditions of everyday life, which often involve more intense arousal (e.g., anger or fear) and more serious destruction than present in the experimental situation.

INTERPRETATION AND IMPLICATIONS

Two sets of questions can be raised with reference to the results reported in this series of experiments. First, how can we explain the effects on perceived control of the destruction of a physical object? And, second, what are the practical implications of the findings?

First, why should the act of destruction be effective as a technique for enhancing an individual's perception of control or success? Several conjectures can be advanced which rest on an analysis of the elements inherent in the process of destruction of physical objects. Central among these are the psychological factors that have been alluded to earlier under the more general rubric of "collative" variables, which are responsible for the positive affect (enjoyment) produced by aesthetic stimuli (Berlyne, 1971). Destruction seems to activate variables such as complexity, novelty, uncertainty, etc., which in turn influence the degree of enjoyment experienced during the process of destruction. And it has been argued earlier that positive affect (enjoyment) will produce a concomitant increase in a person's perception of control. Thus, the set of aesthetic variables also contributes to the cognitive (perceived control) as well as to the affective consequences of destruction.

The sense of control may also be increased by the presence of certain perceptual and cognitive experiences that are associated with the rapid and extreme transformation in structure which occurs during destruction. Success in achieving any goal will contribute to an increase in one's sense of control; an act of destruction is simply one such instance, but one that provides a person with unambiguous evidence concerning the ability to achieve an outcome. A sense of power and success is involved in a destructive act just as in a creative act; a new form or structure is produced that did not exist before. And an act that reduces something to nothing cannot be evaluated as insignificant; it demands attention and respect.

As phenomenological accompaniments of destruction there are two factors which seem to influence the individual's self-attribution of control or efficacy; I shall use the labels "trigger effect" and "irreversibility" to identify them. An important characteristic of most destructive acts is the marked and dramatic discrepancy between the intensity of the stimulus and response (or cause and effect or input and outcome). This interesting aspect of destruction I shall refer to as the trigger effect. That is, it requires only a small action by an individual to bring about an outcome grossly disproportionate to the amount of effort expended in causing the destruction. Producing a large outcome by a small input may contribute strongly to the attribution of control to one's self. The strength of the self-attribution of control will be determined not by the absolute level of outcome nor by the absolute amount of effort (or time) expended, but by the ratio between the two. This is consistent with other analyses of the effect of input-outcome on perceptions about the self (Adams, 1965). Perhaps an even more important phenomenological component of control is the realization of the irreversibility of most acts of destruction. A person can attain a strong sense of control over the environment by taking an action that carries irrevocable consequences; the burning of a building is an example that should illustrate the point vividly. It is precisely this characteristic of irreversibility of the consequences of destruction—the irrevocability of the act—from which derives the sense of control or power experienced by the person responsible for the act.

I should now like to go considerably beyond available data and unabashedly engage in conjecture and speculation about aspects of destruction that may be even more basic or primitive than the psychological factors discussed above. First, intrinsic to destruction are interesting epistemological elements that deserve consideration. Destruction often conveys unique information about the nature of an object and, hence, about the nature of reality. Taking things apart to see "how they work" or "what they are made out of" is one of the ways that we learn about them. As part of their everyday play, children spend a great deal of time building and breaking structures, and in manipulating and altering objects in the physical world in a variety of apparently aimless ways—but which are actually very important for cognitive development, as the research by Piaget (1952) has so convincingly demonstrated. The process of destruction can accomplish the complete transformation of an object from its familiar "thingness" to an unrecognizable and formless state within an amazingly brief time period. Think of a large apartment building which is reduced to a nondescript pile of rubble in a few seconds by the strategic placement of a few sticks of dynamite. Destruction, then, goes to the "heart of the matter" by revealing the heart of matter—by laying bare the innermost properties of the object itself. Using a large machine designed to compress scrap metal into small bales, the artist Césare produced a new type of sculpture by the controlled use of "compression" to reduce large objects such as automobiles into a small mass. Analyzing this artistic effort, Restany (1976) stated: "We are in the presence of a new image, one that bears witness of the inner history of the object. It is no longer the metal that speaks to us, but the object itself that shows us what has happened to it." In a more general sense, the epistemological component of destruction is a special case of the general disposition of individuals toward curiosity about the secrets or hidden nature of the world, as evidenced in diverse activities (including scientific research). In short, destruction may reveal knowledge about the inner structure of an object that could not have been ascertained in any other way.

Finally, destruction may have even deeper roots in the basic functional relationship that exists between any organism and the world of "things" that surrounds it. Because objects in the external physical world are real and palpable, one can obtain a sense of accomplishment much more easily by creating changes in this domain than in more abstract or ephemeral areas such as the social and intellectual environment. Destruction is an act of extreme simplicity, par excellence, and the effect it produces on the outside world is immediately noticeable. Results produced by destruction can easily be seen and touched; and such tangible aspects of physical reality are a basic source of our sense of being in contact with reality. We even use terms derived from the manipulation of the external world in common parlance when discussing the non-physical world as well. Thus, we "destroy" or "build up" an organization or business, etc. Manipulation of the physical world, then, seems to be a very primitive and basic means by which a person can affirm a connection with external reality and assert a sense of control over a portion of this reality. All this is by way of saying that destruction seems to tap one of the very primitive and basic means by which a sense of control is manifested.

Turning to the second major question of this section, what are the practical implications of the results presented in this chapter? On the basis of theory and supporting empirical data it has been argued that arousal, stress, and anxiety often produce positive psychological effects for the individual. Further, it was argued that the destruction of a physical object will enhance one of the central components of the individual's self-organization, viz., perceived control. Thus, persons who have experienced failure or who are unhappy and depressed might find that the action of destruction is indeed an effective technique for ameliorating their aversive psychological state. In spite of the findings as reported in this chapter we certainly would not be prepared to advocate that persons suffering from a low sense of control should walk down the street and smash a window in a building. Feasible alternatives to the drastic remedy of destruction readily come to mind. As mentioned in an earlier section, there are ways of modifying the physical environment in addition to destruction. Though perhaps less effective and efficient than destruction, the techniques of transposition, modification, and construction offer viable psychological alternatives. At this stage of knowledge about this research area it would be prudent not to ignore the potentially positive effects on perceived control that might be derived from vicarious destruction (e.g., by observing films). Also, a situation that would permit an individual to engage in socially-approved destruction in a controlled setting (similar to the procedure used in the present laboratory experiments) might help increase one's perceived control. Furthermore, there are games available for children (e.g., leggo blocks, etc.) which allow one to build and then destroy a structure in a socially-acceptable fashion; perhaps similar "games" could be devised for adults. The Japanese have a special sculpture (small doll) that can be purchased and kept in the home specifically for the purpose of being smashed to bits by its owner if a psychologically propitious moment should arise. Furthermore, there are occupations (though not common) that allow a person to engage in destruction constructively, for example, house-wreckers and demolition experts.

It might also be possible to create a training program or therapeutic regime that would serve the same positive functions fulfilled by destruction; that is, that would mitigate the negative affective and cognitive states of an individual. Perhaps a program could be devised based on the psychological processes that seem to be involved in the act of destruction, as discussed above. Such a program would attempt to tap the same critical psychological components that are inherent in destruction (that is, those factors which are responsible for its positive cognitive and affective consequences), but in a form that would not entail the socially undesirable consequences that often accompany an act of destruction.

In summary, it has been maintained in the present chapter that the destruction of objects in the physical environment will produce positive consequences for an individual's self-perception in the form of increased positive affect (enjoyment) and an enhanced level of perceived control. Therefore, it can be concluded that destruction is an activity that (in the words of self-help advertisements) can be engaged in for both "fun" and "profit."

REFERENCES

Adams, J. S. Inequity in social exchange. In L. Berkowitz (ed.), *Advances in experimental social psychology*, Vol. 2. New York: Academic Press, 1965.

Allen, V. L. & Greenberger, D. B. An aesthetic theory of vandalism. *Crime and Delinquency*, 1978, *3*, 309–321.

Allen, V. L. & Greenberger, D. B. Destruction and perceived control. In A. Baum & J. Singer (eds.), *Advances in environmental psychology*, Vol. 2. New York: Academic Press, 1980.

Balint, M. *Thrills and regressions*. London: Hogarth Press and The Institute of Psycho-Analysis, 1959.

Bandura, A. Self-efficacy: Toward a unifying theory of behavioral change. *Psychological Review*, 1977, *84*, 191–215.

Becker, F. D. *Housing messages*. Stroudsbourg, Pa.: Dowden, Hutchinson & Ross, 1977.

Berlyne, D. E. *Aesthetics and psychobiology*. New York: Appleton-Century-Crofts, 1971.

Goffman, E. *Interaction ritual*. New York: Doubleday, 1967.

Greenberger, D. L. The effect of construction and destruction on self- and environmental-perception. Unpublished manuscript, University of Wisconsin, Madison, 1980.

Martin, J. M. *Juvenile vandalism: A study of its nature and prevention.* Springfield, Ill.: Thomas, 1961.

Olds, J. & Milner, P. Positive reinforcement produced by electrical stimulation of septal area and other regions of rat brain. *Journal of Comparative and Physiological Psychology*, 1954, *47*, 419–427.

Piaget, J. *The origins of intelligence in children* (trans. by M. Cook). New York: International University Press, 1952.

Restany, P. *Césare* (trans. by John Shepley). New York: Harry N. Abrams, 1976.

Rotter, J. B. Generalized expectancies for internal versus external control of reinforcement. *Psychological Monographs*, 1966, *80*(1, Whole No. 609).

Seeman, M. On the meaning of alienation. *American Sociological Review*, 1959, *24*, 783–791.

Seligman, M. E. P. *Helplessness.* San Francisco: Freeman, 1975.

Short, J. F. & Strodtbeck, F. L. *Group process and gang delinquency.* Chicago: University of Chicago Press, 1965.

Spielberger, C. D. & Sarason, I. G. (eds.). *Stress and anxiety*, vol. 1. Washington, D.C.: Hemisphere, 1975.

Spielberger, C. D. & Sarason, I. G. (eds.). *Stress and anxiety*, vol. 5. Washington, D.C.: Hemisphere, 1978.

Taylor, J. A. A personality scale of manifest anxiety. *Journal of Abnormal and Social Psychology*, 1953, *48*, 285–290.

Taylor, J. A. Drive theory and manifest anxiety. *Psychological Bulletin*, 1956, *53*, 303–320.

Taylor, L. & Walton, P. Industrial sabotage: Motives and meanings. In S. Cohen (ed.), *Images of deviance.* London: Penguin Books, 1971.

Thrasher, F. *The gang.* Chicago: University of Chicago Press, 1927.

Velten, E. A laboratory task for induction of mood states. *Behavioral Research and Therapy*, 1968, *6*, 473–482.

Ward, C. (ed.). *Vandalism.* London: Architectural Press, 1973.

Wenk, E. & Harlow, N. (eds.). *School crime and disruption.* Davis, Calif.: Responsible Action, 1978.

White, R. W. Motivation reconsidered: The concept of competence. *Psychological Review*, 1959, *66*, 297–333.

Yancy, W. L. Architecture, interaction, and social control: The case of a large-scale housing project. In J. F. Wohlwill & D. H. Carson (eds.), *Environment and the social sciences: Perspectives and applications.* Washington, D.C.: American Psychological Association, 1972.

Zuckerman, M. The search for high sensation. *Psychology Today*, 1978, *11*, 38–46, 96–97.

Zuckerman, M. The sensation-seeking motive. In B. Maher (ed.), *Progress in experimental personality research.* New York: Academic Press, 1974.

7

Stress, Anxiety, and the Air Traffic Control Specialist

Some Surprising Conclusions from a Decade of Research

Roger C. Smith

INTRODUCTION

When stressful occupations are discussed, particularly in the popular press, it is common for the air traffic control specialist (ATCS) to be identified as belonging to a professional group under intense stress. As one author put it: "The job of juggling airliners and making snap decisions on which lives depend exacts a steep toll in stress-related diseases, nightmares, and acute anxiety" (Martindale, 1977). In a recent book on occupational stress, Kasl (1978) notes that air traffic control work is one of those vocations that seems intuitively to be stressful.

This paper reviews a series of field studies conducted with ATCSs to assess possible stress effects in their work. The studies are presented in chronological order to provide some indication of how results from one investigation influenced the conduct of the next one. The presentation is also designed to show the development of the perspectives needed to assess most properly the presence or absence of work stress in this occupation.

Attempts to document the presence of unusual stress in the air traffic setting date from the middle 1960s (Dougherty, Trites, & Dille, 1965; Hauty, Trites, & Berkley, 1965; Dougherty, 1967); however, concerted efforts to study this issue did not get underway until the last part of that decade. The Civil Aeromedical Institute (CAMI) began its program of stress research in 1968, an effort which continued throughout the 1970s.

Most of the CAMI studies were multidisciplinary in scope and involved psychological, physiological, and biochemical assessments of the state of the ATCS. The format of these studies followed the same general pattern in each investigation. Volunteers were solicited from the crews working at each facility with the under-

EDITOR'S NOTE: This posthumously published chapter is based on the paper presented by Dr. Smith, formerly of the FAA Civil Aeromedical Institute, at the 1980 Conference on Stress and Anxiety in The Netherlands. Dr. Smith died in an automobile accident on returning from the trip. This paper was edited and revised for publication by his colleagues at the FAA Aeronautical Center in Oklahoma City. We are especially indebted to Dr. William Collins, Chief, Aviation Psychology Laboratory, Civil Aeromedical Institute, for his work in preparing it for publication. Information about Dr. Smith's work can be obtained from Dr. Collins, P.O. Box 25082, Oklahoma City, OK 73125.

standing that they would be involved with the project for up to 10 days. For the psychological portion of the studies, each participant filled out one or more assessment questionnaires at the beginning and again at the end of each work shift under consideration. The questionnaires varied across studies and each will be discussed in the context of the specific study in which it was used. The major physiological measure, heart rate, was recorded throughout the work shifts under investigation by the use of miniature tape recorders. These instruments permitted the participants to remain ambulatory throughout the work shift while providing continuous electrocardiographic (ECG) recordings. On occasion blood pressure and the galvanic skin response were also measured. The biochemical measures were derived primarily from urine samples collected before, during, and after the work shifts under consideration. In some of the earlier CAMI studies there was also collection of blood samples after at least one work shift. Since my concern in these studies was with the psychological domain, that will be the main focus of this paper; however, the physiological findings from the studies will be highlighted as well.

CHICAGO'S O'HARE TOWER: AN "ULCER FACTORY"?

Our first study was undertaken at the control tower and radar room for Chicago's O'Hare International Airport, the world's busiest airport (Smith, Melton, & McKenzie, 1971). Twenty-two ATCSs agreed to participate in the study although we were limited to assessing them only on the evening (1600-2400) and night (0000-0800) shifts. In this study we used Malmstrom's Composite Mood Adjective Check List (CMACL) (Malmstrom, 1968) which was basically a collection of items from the Zuckerman (1960), Clyde (1963), and Nowlis (1965) checklists. It consisted of 80 adjectives, each rated on a 9-point scale of "not at all" to "definitely" descriptive of one's current feelings. Each participant completed the CMACL immediately before and after five evening and five night shifts. Since limited normative data and no control subjects for the CMACL were available, the only meaningful comparisons that could be drawn from this part of the study were between evening and night shifts and from the beginning to the end of the work periods. Not surprisingly, the CMACL factors related to fatigue (concentration, fatigue, vigor, and sleepiness) showed significant increases across work shifts and were higher on night than on evening shifts. On the other hand, there was the rather surprising finding that the mean scores on every indicator of anxiety (the Nowlis Anxiety Scale, the single word "anxious," and the Zuckerman Affect Adjective Check List) were all very low on the scale. The mean on the 9-point scale was between the second and third points, where the first point indicated "not at all" descriptive and the ninth point indicated "definitely" descriptive of one's current feelings. It was also found that the anxiety scores tended to be higher after than before work, a finding to be repeated in every study we have conducted.

The physiological measures from the O'Hare subjects (Hale, Williams, Smith, & Melton, 1971) showed that heart rates were generally somewhat above those expected in the general population and were higher during the busier evening shift than the slower night shift. Galvanic skin response and blood pressure measures were generally not remarkable.

The biochemical assessment revealed that phospholipid concentrations were apparently somewhat elevated. The findings from the analysis of urinary metabolites were quite complicated. In comparison to control subjects (biomedical technicians simply observing the ATCSs work), the ATCSs had higher levels of physiological arousal, particularly during heavy work periods. Taken together, these findings were not entirely consistent with what had been expected. While there probably was some notable physiological arousal, psychologically, there was no evidence of reaction to significant stress.

A COMPARISON OF ATCS STRESS AT CHICAGO'S O'HARE AND AT HOUSTON

Our next study was conducted at the tower and radar facilities for Houston Intercontinental Airport (Smith, Melton, & McKenzie, 1971; Melton, McKenzie, Polis, Hoffman, & Saldivar, 1972). The volume of air traffic at this facility was about 60 percent of that for O'Hare International Airport. Test procedures were much the same as those followed in the previous study except that day shifts (0800–1600) were studied instead of evening shifts. For the psychological measures the CMACL was used again, and the State-Trait Anxiety Inventory (STAI: Spielberger, Gorsuch, & Lushene, 1970) and a questionnaire on shift-difficulty were added. The STAI is a standardized measure of both A-Trait, the propensity to experience anxiety, and A-State, the moment-to-moment level of anxiety. Physiological measurements were restricted to ECGs and biochemical analyses were conducted on urine and blood. In this study the control subjects (again biomedical observers) contributed both psychological and physiological/biochemical measurements.

A total of 16 ATCSs and 4 biomedical observers completed the research tasks. The data from the CMACL indicated that, as a group, the Houston ATCSs showed the same general pattern as the O'Hare controllers. Scores related to fatigue were higher at the end of shifts than at the beginning and were higher for night than day shifts. The trend for anxiety indicators in the CMACL to be higher at the end of work shifts than at the beginning was also found but was not as pronounced as in the O'Hare study.

Compared to the control subjects who had observed them, Houston ATCSs were less fatigued, more vigorous, and less anxious. The comparisons with ATCSs at Chicago's O'Hare International Airport showed the overall degree of positive affect to be somewhat higher in Houston. However, most of this effect was due to the difference in scores between the day shift measures at Houston and the evening shift measures at O'Hare, especially on scales related to fatigue. On the night shifts, the situation was reversed, with the O'Hare ATCSs showing the lesser feelings of fatigue even though they were considerably busier during this shift than were the Houston ATCSs.

The STAI scores followed the trend of the CMACL data in that scores on the A-State scale increased significantly from before to after work on both day and night shifts. The use of the STAI also permitted comparison to normative groups, whereas this was not possible with the CMACL. The normative group most closely matching our air traffic sample was that of college undergraduates who had the lowest mean score of any of the available normative groups (high school students, surgical patients, prisoners). According to the college student norms, the mean A-State score for the Houston ATCSs was at the 42nd percentile. The A-Trait scale (anxiety proneness) was at the 24th percentile. These findings tend to affirm the CMACL results that the expressed levels of anxiety reported by ATCSs are certainly within normal limits and are at relatively low levels. These data are inconsistent with the presence of any unusual emotional stressors.

Physiological measures showed that heart rates were generally higher during the day shift than during the night shift for the Houston ATCSs. The heart rates of Houston ATCSs during the day shift were lower than the heart rates obtained from evening shifts at O'Hare. The night shifts did not differ. Preshift measures of heart rate also showed that the ATCSs at O'Hare had the higher mean rate. This suggests that some of the differences observed between these two facilities may relate to different baseline levels of physiological arousal rather than to differences in the work situation itself.

The urine analyses for Houston ATCSs showed epinephrine and norepinephrine to be higher during day shifts than during night shifts. The comparison with O'Hare ATCSs showed that the two facilities differed primarily on night shift measures where the greater workload at O'Hare is reflected in the higher level of catecholamine excretion. Plasma phosolipids were also found to be higher for O'Hare than for Houston ATCSs.

These findings, taken with those from O'Hare, suggested that the belief that ATCSs are typically under intense stress was at least questionable. In fact, from the psychological perspective, the most notable finding was the lack of evidence indicating the presence of emotional stress.

ATCS JOB ATTITUDES AS POSSIBLE INDICATORS OF STRESS

During this time we also conducted some attitude research that further increased doubts about the presence of any unusual psychological or emotional stressors in air traffic work. One study (Smith, Cobb, & Collins, 1972) asked 614 ATCSs at 17 busy towers what they liked and disliked about their work. Stress was never specifically mentioned as a negative feature of air traffic work, nor was it implied. These ATCSs complained about management, shift schedules, equipment, and noncontrol tasks, but not about stress. To the contrary, as a group they found the challenging, fast-paced, constantly changing nature of air traffic work much to their liking. Interestingly, these data were collected just about the time (1968) of the first major labor conflict between ATCSs and management in the Federal Aviation Administration (FAA), a time when concern over stress in ATCSs was becoming well publicized.

A FOLLOWUP OF ATCS JOB ATTITUDES

A second attitude study (Smith, 1973) was conducted 4 years later and again was coincidentally in sequence with a second major labor upheaval in the air traffic system. In this study, 792 ATCSs from 18 large facilities answered an extensive questionnaire about their work. The findings were essentially the same as those for the first study: Most of the dislikes concerned management and various aspects of working conditions, while various aspects of job challenge and the work itself were most often mentioned as positive features. Over 92 percent of the respondents reported that they were satisfied with their work as air traffic controllers, a percentage well above the usual value of 80 percent found in most other occupations.

Furthermore, when asked to specifically rate their liking for various aspects of their work, these ATCSs generally reported that they liked heavy and moderate density traffic, the difficulty of the work, and the constant traffic change. They did not like night shifts, light traffic, and management. Again the data seemed inconsistent with the notion that these people were exceedingly stressed.

HOUSTON REVISITED: A COMPARISON OF DIFFERENT SHIFT SCHEDULES

Our next stress study (Melton, McKenzie, Smith, Polis, Higgins, Hoffman, Funkhouser, & Saldivar, 1973) again took place at Houston, 1 year after the first study at that facility. The reason for returning was that the facility changed from a straight 5-day rotation of shifts (5 day shifts followed by 5 evening shifts followed by 5 night shifts with 2 days between each change) to a short rotation schedule called the 2-2-1 (2 days shifts followed by 2 evening shifts followed by 1 night shift and then 2 days off).

The type of shift schedule employed had relatively little effect on the scores from the psychological measures. The CMACL measures related to fatigue showed a modest tendency to increase with the shorter turnaround schedule, while other measures, including the STAI, were unchanged; otherwise, the findings were the same as in the first Houston study. Physiological biochemical measures either showed no difference between the two shift schedules or slightly favored the shorter schedule.

AIR TRAFFIC WORK DEMANDS AND STAI SCORES: A SENSITIVE MEASURE

At this point the psychological data seemed clearly to contradict the notion that significant psychological or emotional stress was a factor in air traffic work. However, limitations in the design of the previous studies, often due to real-world situational and administrative constraints, left many questions unanswered. One of these was the question of the sensitivity of the measures, particularly the STAI, to stress in the air traffic situation. To answer this question we compared the STAI data from the Houston ATCSs with data from a total of 62 additional ATCSs from (i) an extremely busy general aviation tower (Opa Locka, Florida, a nonradar tower primarily serving light and business aircraft) and (ii) an air route traffic control center (ARTCC), a radar facility controlling high-altitude cross-country traffic (Smith & Melton, 1975). Ratings of the difficulty of each day or night of work were also obtained. The A-State score was found to increase over twice as much across shifts rated "difficult" as for shifts rated "easy." Thus, it appears that the STAI was in fact sensitive to variaitions in arousal associated with perceived changes in demand or difficulty.

The physiological and biochemical measures showed personnel at the general aviation tower to be under greater physiological arousal during work than were personnel at the ARTCC or the Houston tower, and at about an equal level of arousal with the O'Hare ATCSs (Melton, McKenzie, Saldivar, and Hoffman, 1974).

VALIDATION OF FINDINGS FROM HOUSTON

The next study was designed to replicate and clarify findings from the two studies comparing shift rotation schedules at the Houston tower (Melton, Smith,

McKenzie, Saldivar, Hoffmann, & Fowler, 1975). The earlier comparisons of the two schedules, the 5-day and 2-2-1, at the Houston facility had been hampered by a variety of problems, including the fact that no assessment of evening shifts was available for the 5-day schedule. This new study was conducted at two large ARTCCs, one on the 5-day and the other on the 2-2-1 schedule, and covered all shifts at each facility.

The findings from the STAI in this study again showed (i) no difference in shift schedules, (ii) low A-Trait and A-State scores compared to scores of college students, and (iii) the significant increase in A-State from the beginning to the end of work. The biochemical assessment (only biochemical measures were taken in this study) appeared to favor the 2-2-1 schedule to some degree, although no impressive differences were found.

SOME EFFECTS OF AUTOMATION
ON ATCS STRESS INDICATORS

About this time, the middle 1970s, computer assistance for ATCSs was beginning to be a factor in the air traffic work situation. The system being brought on-line was designed to enhance radar targets and to handle information concerning aircraft that up until then was either committed to memory or noted by hand. The ATCS remained the decision maker but now possessed a rather sophisticated memory aid. In order to assess the impact of the introduction of the new computer systems on ATCSs, we visited two busy terminal radar facilities (Los Angeles and Oakland, California) on the west coast of the United States (Melton, Smith, McKenzie, Hoffman, & Saldivar, 1976). Data were first collected before the installation of the new computer systems, then again some 5 months after the systems were in full operation. There were no differences in the psychological measures (STAI) taken before and after installation of the computers. Surprisingly, the biochemical indices showed several statistically significant increases after the installation of the computer systems, primarily in catecholamine excretion. However, baseline (resting) levels of these metabolites also increased significantly between the two assessments. This suggests that the observed increases in catecholamine excretion cannot be clearly attributed to the addition of the new equipment but may have been due to other unspecified factors outside the purview of this review.

Up to this point, no concerned effort had been made to relate the psychological and physiological measures obtained from ATCSs, primarily because most other investigators had been unable to show correspondence between these types of data (Levitt, 1967). However, the development of a new biochemical stress index (Melton, McKenzie, Saldivar, & Hoffmann, 1974) provided a new opportunity to integrate the two sets of data. This was attempted with the records from Los Angeles and Oakland. Unfortunately the index, which integrates catecholamines and steroid secretion into a single index adjusted for baseline values of each metabolite, was not related in any way to the psychological measures.

STRESS DATA FROM ATCSs AT FACILITIES
WITH LOW WORKLOADS

The last multidisciplinary assessment of stress was conducted at several smaller facilities with relatively low levels of activity (Melton, Smith, McKenzie, Wicks, &

Saldivar, 1978). The by-now often-replicated finding that A-State increases significantly across work shifts was again confirmed, as were the relatively low scores of ATCSs (compared to STAI norms) on both scales of the STAI. The mean STAI scores for these ATCSs did not differ from the overall mean for the ATCSs from busier facilities; however, the levels of the biochemical indices were generally lower than for most other facilities. An analysis of the level of epinephrine excretion at the various tower facilities studied to this point as a function of traffic volume yielded a straight linear relationship and a correlation of 0.96 (Spearman rank-order). Measures of norepinephrine and steroids showed no such relationship to traffic volume. This makes it rather clear that epinephrine excretion is a workload, rather than an emotional, indicator in these studies (Melton et al., 1978).

STAI SCORES FOR ATCSs VERSUS WORKERS–IN–GENERAL

An issue that continued to be of concern was the proper perspective in which to place the data from the psychological assessments. There is some evidence that reported anxiety levels may diminish across age (Cattell, 1962). If so, then the apparently low scores of ATCSs compared to scores of college students may have only been an artifact of a developmental process. One piece of information was available to suggest that this possibility did not explain our data. A study of anxiety in 15 student pilots showed that the 7 ATCSs in the course scored significantly lower on A-Trait than did a group of 8 noncontroller professionals, all as old as or older than the ATCSs (Smith & Melton, 1978). However, the small number of participants in that study makes the comparison less than conclusive.

What was needed was (i) normative data from the STAI on adults and (ii) knowledge as to whether the increase in A-State from the beginning to the end of work was a function of air traffic work in particular or of work-in-general. To meet these needs, we gave the STAI to approximately 1900 men and women of varying ages employed in a wide variety of non-air-traffic occupations. Over 1800 of these participants provided useable data to permit the establishment of age-related norms (see Table 1). The mean A-Trait and A-State levels are lower for this sample than for college undergraduates. However, these mean scores are still significantly higher than the mean scores obtained in our several studies of ATCSs. It can now be confidently stated that ATCSs do indeed score below the population-in-general on the STAI.

STAI scores from a major portion (1303 men) of the people who provided data for the normative sample in Table 1 were used in a comparison with (i) 198 ATCSs from whom we had obtained both A-Trait and A-State data in our field studies and (ii) an additional sample of 92 former ATCSs who had become instructors in the air traffic training program (Smith & Hutto, 1980). The mean scores for these instructors on both the A-Trait and A-State scales of the STAI fell at an intermediate level between the ATCS and the non-ATCS groups. All the differences in A-Trait and A-State between the instructors and ATCSs were statistically significant; however, the differences between instructors and non-ATCSs were significant only for the A-Trait scale. In other words the instructors reported higher levels of psychological arousal than did active ATCSs but lower-to-equal levels with non-ATCSs. Similarly, a biochemical study (McKenzie, Fowler, Moses, & Burr, 1977) of instructors also showed elevated excretion of epinephrine (but not norepinephrine

Table 1 STAI (Form Y) Means and Standard Deviations for Normal Adults

Age:	25–29		30–34		35–39		40–44		45–49		50–54		55–59		60–69	
Sex:	M	F	M	F	M	F	M	F	M	F	M	F	M	F	M	F
A-Trait																
Mean	36.6	39.4	34.8	35.7	35.2	34.8	34.9	36.0	35.3	33.7	34.2	32.4	34.0	32.0	33.0	30.7
SD	10.3	11.4	9.2	8.9	9.3	9.1	8.7	8.7	9.2	9.4	9.0	7.5	8.8	9.0	8.5	7.5
N	57	46	147	61	192	68	260	80	307	55	197	50	131	38	53	19
A-State																
Mean	36.8	39.5	36.1	35.0	36.2	36.4	35.6	36.3	36.5	35.9	34.6	32.6	35.0	31.5	32.1	32.4
SD	9.6	12.1	10.5	10.0	9.7	11.7	9.9	10.5	11.0	11.9	10.1	7.3	11.0	9.4	8.9	10.4
N	57	46	147	62	193	69	259	80	305	55	199	50	131	38	53	22

Table 2 STAI A-Trait and A-State scale means and standard deviations (SD) for ATCSs, ATCS instructors, non-ATCS adult men, and male college undergraduates

Group	N	A-Trait		A-State	
		Mean	SD	Mean	SD
ATCSs	198	30.3	6.6	31.1	7.5
Instructors	92	32.8	8.9	33.8	10.1
Non-ATCSs	1303	35.8	10.4	35.1	9.2
College undergraduates[a]	253	37.7	9.7	36.4	9.7

[a]Taken from Spielberger et al. (1970).

or steroids) for instructors in comparison with ATCSs. These studies, taken together, further support the conclusion that working air traffic has no unusual arousal value as an occupation, since those away from actual air traffic had higher indices of arousal, both psychological and physiological, than did active ATCSs. The difference in arousal levels between ATCSs and instructors may reflect a higher degree of competitiveness in those ATCSs chosen to be instructors. Since these positions were seen at that time as important opportunities to open avenues for advancement, there was often considerable competition for them. This suggests the possibility that those who applied for instructor positions might be more of the Type A personality (more ambitious, striving, hard-driving, and competitive; cf. Friedman & Rosenman, 1959; Jenkins, Zyanski, & Rosenman, 1978) than is true of most ATCSs.

Finally, the increase in A-State from the beginning to the end of work that had been found in virtually all of the studies of ATCSs was also found for 88 non-air-traffic employees (from the sample in Table 1) who had completed A-State scales at the beginning and end of from 1–3 workdays (see Table 3). Although the size of the increment was somewhat greater for ATCSs than for non-ATCSs, scores for the former included more variable working shifts and more replications per subject (and scores at both the beginning and end of work were clearly lower for ATCSs). In any event, these comparisons indicate that the increment in arousal during work is more of a general characteristic of work itself than the result of stressors unique to a particular work setting.

RELATED RESEARCH

There are several other researchers who have conducted similar investigations with ATCS. Grandjean, Wotzka, and Kretzschmar (1968) obtained reports of fatigue and mood from Swiss ATCSs. They found response patterns similar to those in our O'Hare and Houston studies (Smith et al., 1971): Self-ratings of fatigue were

Table 3 STAI A-State scale means at the beginning and end of work for ATCSs and non-ATCSs (scores are based on several replications for each subject)

Group	N	Beginning	End
ATCSs	210	30.2	35.0
Non-ATCSs	88	33.1	37.0

higher, and mood self-ratings were lower, at the end than at the beginning of work. Hibler (1978) expanded upon our study of shift difficulty and anxiety (Smith & Melton, 1975) to include ratings by military ATCSs of difficulty and anxiety during shifts, and confirmed that A-State levels were higher for difficult shifts and that A-State scores generally increased across shifts. The mean A-Trait and A-State scores for the military ATCSs were similar to those obtained in our studies of civilian ATCSs. In another study, Caplan, Cobb, French, Harrison, and Pinneau (1975) found anxiety levels among a group of midwestern ATCSs to be intermediate in comparison to 22 other occupations. Rose, Jenkins, and Hurst (1978) reported that more than 80 percent of a group of ATCSs participating in an evaluation of health change scored low (over 1 standard deviation below the mean for college students) on the Tension/Anxiety Scale of the Profile of Mood States (McNair, Lorr, & Droppleman, 1971). Thus, those researchers who have made comparable measures of psychological states have obtained results highly consistent with our own.

Related work in the physiological area has been limited to two main studies. Schad, Gilgen, and Grandjean (1969) found that six Swiss ATCSs excreted higher levels of catecholamines while doing air traffic work than when providing general supervision or doing clerical work. Rose et al. (1978) considered heart rate and blood pressure in their health change study. The heart rate values they obtained from ATCSs in the northeastern region of the United States tended to be lower than the rates obtained from both the O'Hare (Melton, McKenzie, Polis, Funkhouser, & Iampietro, 1971) and Houston (Melton et al., 1973) studies. On the other hand, the mean blood pressures obtained by Rose et al. were considerably higher than those obtained at O'Hare. The meaning of these differences in physiological/biochemical findings is not readily apparent.

Though not directly comparable to our research, there have been other investigations of the health consequences of air traffic work that have implications for the assessment of stress in ATCSs. The findings from these studies have been mixed. Two studies, by Cobb and Rose (1973) and Rose et al. (1978), suggest that ATCSs are at higher risk than man-in-general for hypertension; however, Booze (1978) found hypertensive diagnoses to be well below expectancy in a review of health records for 25,000 ATCSs. Dougherty (1967) found no difference between ATCSs and non-ATCSs in the prevalence of ECG abnormality. The evidence that the air traffic system is an "ulcer factory" (Martindale, 1977) is also equivocal. Dougherty, Trites, and Dille (1965) and Hauty, Trites, and Berkley (1965) found a higher incidence of self-reported gastrointestinal symptoms by ATCSs than by non-ATCS personnel. The Cobb and Rose (1973) and Rose et al. (1978) studies both reported higher than expected incidence of ulcers in their samples of ATCSs. However, Singal, Smith, Hurrell, Bender, Kramkowski, and Salisbury (1977) found no evidence that ulcers were above expectancy at the O'Hare facility, nor did Booze (1978) in his survey of medical records from ATCSs. Neuropsychiatric problems were commonly reported in both the Rose et al. (1978) and Booze (1978) studies. However, it was not possible to determine (i) if the rates were above expectancy in the Rose et al. study because of the lack of comparable norms, or (ii) if the high rate in the survey by Booze occurred only after introduction of a special benefits program for ATCSs who were separated from their work for medical or administrative reasons. Reaching a general conclusion about these diverse results is difficult; perhaps they are best summarized as suggesting that some

ATCSs at some air traffic facilities may be at higher risk for health change, particularly cardiovascular problems, but this is probably not true for the ATCS work force in general.

CONCLUSIONS AND METHODOLOGICAL PROBLEMS

In coming to conclusions about the entire body of data just reviewed, it must be kept in mind that a number of questions are still unresolved. One important issue concerns the use of volunteers in these kinds of stress studies. As Singal et al. (1977) point out, "This . . . is a particularly crucial methodologic problem in studies of psychiatric and psychosomatic disorders since the psychologic and sociologic characteristics associated with the disorders in question may be among the very determinants of whether someone volunteers for the study." These characteristics may influence physiological responsiveness as well (Frankenhaeuser & Patkai, 1965). Unfortunately, there is no clear resolution to the volunteer problem; physiological and biochemical measurements involve various degrees of inconvenience or discomfort and cannot be routinely required of employees for research purposes. Psychological measurements cannot be effectively demanded of employees since they usually require the cooperation of the respondent. The best resolution at this time consists in obtaining as many participants as possible at a variety of facilities and gathering as many unobtrusive measures as possible through medical records and the like.

A problem unique to the psychological aspects of these investigations is that of response sets. Since self-report data are sensitive to the approach taken by the participant to the research, we must rely on the participant's cooperation to obtain reasonably veridical reports of their psychological states. When programs and benefits may depend on research findings, the probability that dissimulation will occur may be increased. Because of the potential for this problem, screening procedures for "fake bad" response sets were developed for both the CMACL (Smith, 1971) and for the STAI (Smith, 1974). When these scoring procedures were applied to the records of participants in our research, we found that all but one of the ATCSs scored within the valid range. This was also the experience in the Rose et al. (1978) study, in that the validity indicators on the California Personality Inventory were generally within acceptable limits. A few of their participants were found to be more defensive than expected, but on the whole it was concluded that the respondents answered openly and honestly.

Another issue that presents some problems for the clear-cut interpretation of these various findings is that of the rotation of work shifts. The research literature on shift work suggests that there may be a variety of negative psychological, social, and health consequences associated with working rotating shift schedules (Mott, Mann, McLoughlin, & Warwick, 1965; Harrington, 1978). Since the busier air traffic facilities require 24-hour coverage, while smaller facilities generally do not, shift work and workload are confounded to some degree. Furthermore, comparisons of data from ATCSs with data from normative populations generally do not take work schedule into account. Thus, for example, symptomatic differences between ATCSs and non-ATCS airmen in the Cobb and Rose (1973) study may have been partly a function of a lower percentage of shift workers in the non-ATCS group. At the present time, our laboratory is engaged in an extensive research project designed to explore this issue as it applies to the well-being of ATCSs and other personnel.

Finally, there is the problem of uncontrolled personological variables. We have a considerable amount of information about the kinds of people who choose air traffic work. As a group, they have been found to score in the upper 20 percent of the population on intellectual assessments (Trites, 1965; Cobb & Mathews, 1973) but are usually not collegiately educated (Cobb, Mathews, & Lay, 1972). On the 16PF test, ATCSs tend to be average on most of the factors. They differ substantially from men-in-general on only 4 of the 16 factors: intelligence, group-conformity, tough-mindedness, and compulsivity (Smith, 1974; Karson & O'Dell, 1974; Rose et al., 1978). In comparison, airline pilots differ substantially from men-in-general on 11 of the 16PF scales. ATCSs score within the normal range on all scales of the California Personality Inventory with relative elevations on the factors associated with dominance and relatively lower scores on factors measuring mature socialization and respect for authority (Trites, Kurek, & Cobb, 1967; Rose et al., 1978). On the Strong Vocational Inventory Blank (Campbell, 1966), ATCSs score like men-in-general on all but a few scales mostly concerned with technical supervisors (Smith, 1975). These findings suggest that ATCSs form a unique occupational group only on a few personality dimensions. However, it is possible that those dimensions may be related to their psychological and physiological responses to air traffic work. Rose et al. (1978) did find that ATCSs who were Type B personalities seemed at higher risk for hypertension than were those who were more competitive, an interesting reversal of the usual sort of findings (Jenkins et al., 1978). The problem is to discern to what extent the incidence of hypertension or other physical or psychological problems results from the work, not the person. In other words, it is quite possible that ATCSs who contract hypertension or other problems may be likely to do so in any work circumstance. Only the development of carefully matched control groups can resolve this question.

Although the problems just discussed require further research, it is clear from presently available evidence that the ATCSs appear remarkably free of emotional distress. According to Spielberger's (1972) process theory of anxiety, this means that ATCSs perceive little, if any, threat in their work or the responsbilities associated with that work. The physiological data obtained in ATCS research suggest normal physiological responses to varied workloads. The extent to which high workloads are related to negative consequences for ATCSs is uncertain. There is some evidence (Higgins, Lategola, & Melton, 1978) linking increased physiological responsiveness with cardiovascular and gastrointestinal problems; however, the extent to which this correlation is a function of the individual's response style as opposed to the effects of workload or other aspects of the work itself has not yet been determined. According to Rose et al. (1978), the types of health change data that they obtained are suggestive of an interaction between individual predispositions to certain disorders and characteristics of the work setting. They suggest that it is not the work itself, but the context in which the work is conducted, that is the important factor interacting with predisposing factors in the individual ATCS.

In conclusion, there is little evidence to support the notion that ATCSs are engaged in an unusually stressful occupation. This is not to say that ATCSs never encounter unusual stress on the job; however, it does appear that this is the exception rather than the rule. ATCSs appear both well qualified and well suited for air traffic work. The demands of air traffic work do not appear to place unusual stress on ATCSs; this professional group appears quite capable of handling requirements of the job without distress. The notion that this occupational group is being pressed to the psyhological and physiological limit is clearly unjustified.

REFERENCES

Booze, C. F. *The moribidity experience of air traffic control personnel* (FAA-AM-78-21). Federal Aviation Administration, Washington, D.C.: Civil Aeromedical Institute, April 1978. (NTIS No. AD A056 053/2GI)

Campbell, D. P. *Manual for the Strong Vocational Interest Blank.* Stanford, Calif.: Stanford University Press, 1966.

Caplan, R. D., Cobb, S., French, J. R. P., Harrison, R. V., & Pinneau, S. R. *Job demands and worker health* (NIOSH 75-160). Rockville, Md.: Department of Health, Education, and Welfare; National Institute for Occupational Safety and Health, 1975.

Cattell, R. B. *Manual for the Sixteen Personality Factor Questionnaire* (Forms A and B). Champaign, Ill.: Institute for Personality and Ability Testing, 1962.

Clyde, D. J. *Manual for the Clyde mood scale.* Coral Gables, Fla.: Biometric Laboratory, University of Miami, 1963.

Cobb, B. B. & Mathews, J. J. New screening test for air traffic controller applicants. *Aerospace Medicine*, 1973, *44*, 184–189.

Cobb, B. B., Mathews, J. J., & Lay, C. D. *A comparative study of female and male air traffic controller trainees* (FAA-AM-72-22). Federal Aviation Administration, Washington, D.C.: Civil Aeromedical Institute, May 1972. (NTIS No. AD-751 312)

Cobb, S. & Rose, R. M. Hypertension, peptic ulcer and diabetes in air traffic controllers. *Journal of the American Medical Association*, 1973, *224*, 489–492.

Dougherty, J. D. Cardiovascular findings in air traffic controllers. *Aerospace Medicine*, 1967, *38*, 26–30.

Dougherty, J. D., Trites, D. K., & Dille, J. R. Self-reported stress-related symptoms among air traffic control specialists (ATCS) and non-ATCS personnel. *Aerospace Medicine*, 1965, *36*, 956–960.

Frankenhaeuser, M. & Patkai, P. Interindividual differences in catecholamine excretion during stress. *Scandinavian Journal of Psychology*, 1965, *6*, 117–123.

Friedman, M. & Rosenman, R. H. Association of specific overt behavior pattern with blood and cardiovascular findings. *Journal of the American Medical Association*, 1959, *169*, 1289–1296.

Grandjean, E., Wotzka, G., & Kretzschmar, H. *Psychophysiologic investigations into professional stress on air traffic control officers at the Zurich-Kloten, and Geneva-Cointrin airports*, unpublished manuscript, Swiss Confederate College of Technology, 1968.

Hale, H. B., Williams, E. W., Smith, B. N., & Melton, C. E., Jr. Excretion patterns of air traffic controllers. *Aerospace Medicine*, 1971, *42*, 127–138.

Harrington, J. M. *Shift work and health.* London: University of London, London School of Hygiene and Tropical Medicine, 1978.

Hauty, G. T., Trites, D. K., & Berkley, W. J. *Biomedical survey of ATC facilities. 2. Experience and age* (FAA-AM-65-6). Washington, D.C.: Federal Aviation Administration, March 1965.

Hibler, N. S. The effects of stress on state anxiety in air traffic controllers (Doctoral dissertation, University of South Florida, 1977). *Dissertation Abstracts International*, 1978, *38*, 6155-B. (University Microfilms No. 7809323)

Higgins, E. A., Lategola, M. T., & Melton, C. E. *Three reports relevant to stress in aviation personnel* (FAA-AM-78-5). Federal Aviation Administration, Washington, D.C.: Civil Aeromedical Institute, February 1978. (NTIS No. AD A051 690/6GI)

Jenkins, C. D., Zyanski, S. J., & Rosenman, R. H. Coronary-prone behavior: One pattern or several? *Psychosomatic Medicine*, 1978, *40*, 25--43.

Karson, S. & O'Dell, J. W. Personality makeup of the American air traffic controller. *Aerospace Medicine*, 1974, *45*, 1001–1007.

Kasl, S. V. Epidemiological contributions to the study of work stress. In C. L. Cooper & R. Payne (eds.), *Stress at work.* New York: Wiley & Sons, 1978.

Levitt, E. E. *The psychology of anxiety.* New York: Brooks-Merrill, 1967.

Malmstrom, E. J. *Composite mood adjective check list*, unpublished manuscript. Los Angeles: Department of Psychology, University of California, 1968.

Martindale, D. Sweaty palms in the control tower. *Psychology Today*, 1977, *10*, 71–75.

McKenzie, J. M., Fowler, P. R., Moses, R., & Burr, M. J. Evaluation of stress in air traffic controllers: FAA Academy instructors. *Preprints of the 1977 Annual Scientific Meeting of the Aerospace Medical Association*. Washington, D.C.: 1977, 99–100. (Summary)

McNair, D. M., Lorr, M., & Droppleman, L. F. *Profile of mood-states: Manual*. San Diego, Calif.: Educational and Industrial Testing Service, 1971.

Melton, C. E., McKenzie, J. M., Smith, R. C., Polis, B. D., Higgins, E. A., Hoffmann, S. M., Funkhouser, G. G., & Saldivar, J. T. *Physiological, biochemical, and psychological responses in air traffic control personnel: Comparison of the 5-day and 2-2-1 shift rotation patterns* (FAA-AM-73-22). Federal Aviation Administration, Washington, D.C.: Civil Aeromedical Institute, December 1973. (NTIS No. AD 778 214/7GI)

Melton, C. E., Smith, R. C., McKenzie, J. M., Hoffmann, S. M., & Saldivar, J. T. Stress in air traffic controllers: Effects of ARTS-III. *Aviation, Space, and Environmental Medicine*, 1976, *47*, 925–930.

Melton, C. E., Smith, R. C., McKenzie, J. M., Saldivar, J. T., Hoffmann, J. M., & Fowler, P. R. *Stress in air traffic controllers: Comparison of two air route traffic control centers on different shift rotation patterns* (FAA-AM-75-7). Federal Aviation Administration, Washington, D.C.: Civil Aeromedical Institute, September 1975. (NTIS No. AD A020 679/8GI)

Melton, C. E., Smith, R. C., McKenzie, J. M., Wicks, S. M., & Saldivar, J. T. Stress in air traffic personnel: Low-density towers and flight service stations. *Aviation, Space, and Environmental Medicine*, 1978, *49*, 724–728.

Melton, C. E., Jr., McKenzie, J. M., Polis, B. D., Funkhouser, G. E., & Iampietro, P. F. *Physiological responses in air traffic control personnel: O'Hare tower* (FAA-AM-72-1). Federal Aviation Administration, Washington, D.C.: Civil Aeromedical Institute, January 1971. (NTIS No. AD 723 4GI)

Melton, C. E., McKenzie, J. M., Polis, B. D., Hoffmann, J. M., & Saldivar, J. T. *Physiological responses in air traffic control personnel: Houston Intercontinental tower* (FAA-AM-73-21). Federal Aviation Administration, Washington, D.C.: Civil Aeromedical Institute, December 1972. (NTIS No. AD 777 838/4GI)

Melton, C. E., McKenzie, J. M., Saldivar, J. T., & Hoffmann, S. M. *Comparison of Opa Locka tower with other ATC facilities by means of a stress index* (FAA-AM-74-11). Federal Aviation Administration, Washington, D.C.: Civil Aeromedical Institute, December 1974. (NTIS No. AD A008 378/2GI)

Mott, P. E., Mann, F. C., McLoughlin, Q., & Warwick, D. P. *Shift work*. Ann Arbor, Mich.: University of Michigan Press, 1965.

Nowlis, V. Research with the mood adjective check list. In S. S. Tomkins & C. E. Izard (eds.), *Affect, cognition and personality*. New York: Springer, 1965.

Rose, R. M., Jenkins, C. D., & Hurst, M. W. *Air traffic controller health change study* (FAA-AM-78-39). Federal Aviation Administration, Washington, D.C.: Boston University School of Medicine, December 1978. (NTIS No. AD A063 709/0GA)

Schad, R., Gilgen, A., & Grandjean, E. Excretion of catecholamines in air traffic personnel. *Schweizerische Medizinische Wochenschrift*, 1969, *99*, 889–892.

Singal, M., Smith, M. J., Hurrell, J. J., Bender, J., Kramkowski, R. S., & Salisbury, S. A. *Hazard evaluation and technical assistance report: O'Hare International Airport* (Report No. TA 77-67). Cincannati, Oh.: National Institute for Occupational Safety and Health, August 1977.

Smith, R. C. *Assessment of a "stress" response-set in the composite mood adjective check list* (FAA-AM-71-14). Federal Aviation Administration, Washington, D.C.: Civil Aeromedical Institute, April 1971. (NTIS No. AD 727 020)

Smith, R. C. Comparison of the job attitudes of personnel in three air traffic control specialties. *Aerospace Medicine*, 1973, *44*, 918–927.

Smith, R. C. Response bias in the state-trait anxiety inventory: Detecting the exaggeration of stress. *Journal of Psychology*, 1974, *86*, 241–246.

Smith, R. C. *A realistic view of the people in air traffic control* (FAA-AM-74-12). Federal Aviation Administration, Washington, D.C.: Civil Aeromedical Institute, December 1974. (NTIS No. AD A006 789/2GI)

Smith, R. C. Vocational interests of air traffic control personnel. *Aerospace Medicine*, 1975, *46*, 871–877.

Smith, R. C., Cobb, B. B., & Collins, W. E. Attitudes and motivations of air traffic controllers in terminal areas. *Aerospace Medicine*, 1972, *43*, 1–5.

Smith, R. C. & Hutto, G. L. Does air traffic control work lead to psychological arousal? A comparison of air traffic and non-air-traffic employees within the FAA. *Preprints of the 1980 Annual Meeting of the Aerospace Medical Association.* Washington, D.C.: 1980, 50–51. (Summary)

Smith, R. C. & Melton, C. E. Susceptibility to anxiety and shift difficulty as determinants of state anxiety in air traffic controllers. Aerospace Medicine, 1975, *45*, 599–601.

Smith, R. C. & Melton, C. E. Effects of ground trainer use on the anxiety of students in private pilot training. *Aviation, Space, and Environmental Medicine*, 1978, *49*, 406–408.

Smith, R. C., Melton, C. E., & McKenzie, J. M. Affect adjective check list assessment of mood variations in air traffic controllers. *Aerospace Medicine*, 1971, *42*, 1060–1064.

Spielberger, C. D., Gorsuch, R. L., & Lushene, R. E. *Manual for the state-trait anxiety inventory.* Palo Alto, Calif.: Consulting Psychologists Press, 1970.

Spielberger, C. D. Anxiety as an emotional state. In C. D. Spielberger (ed.), *Anxiety: Current trends in theory and research.* New York: Academic Press, 1972.

Trites, D. K. *Problems in air traffic management: VI. Interaction of training entry age with intellectual and personality characteristics of air traffic control specialists* (FAA-AM-65-21). Federal Aviation Administration, Washington, D.C.: Civil Aeromedical Institute, July 1969. (NTIS No. AD 620 721)

Trites, D. K., Kurek, A., & Cobb, B. B. Personality and achievement of air traffic controllers. *Aerospace Medicine*, 1967, *38*, 1145–1150.

Zuckerman, M. The development of an affect adjective checklist for the measurement of anxiety. *Journal of Consulting Psychology*, 1960, *24*, 457–462.

8

Life Against Life

The Psychosomatic Consequences of Man-Made Disasters

J. Bastiaans
University of Leyden, The Netherlands

Throughout human history life on earth has been threatened by all kinds of man-made disasters. In our time, man seems to have exceeded himself in creating actual and potential disasters, the greatest of which have resulted from his ability to wage technologically powerful and totally destructive warfare. The instruments of man, when turned against mankind, set off an almost inevitable chain of effects and events, of which not the least are psychological in nature. It is, however, only comparatively recently that we have developed the concepts and frameworks that make it possible to interpret and predict the psychic consequences of man-made disasters.

In the post-war period much attention has been devoted to the psychological, psychiatric, and psychosomatic consequences of the stress of war and concentration camps; of late, the human consequences resulting from the hostile actions of terrorists, hijackers, and other persons taking hostages have added new dimensions to the problem of stress related to man-made disasters. This field of research has been largely a byproduct of World War II, since it was in the aftermath of that great catastrophic event that the urgency and dimensions of the problem became visible. Even then, we did not expect the effects to be either so long-lasting or so intense as we now know them to be; and today we have no reason to believe that as traumatic events recede into the historical past, so will their psychological consequences.

Bastiaans (1957) described the psychosomatic consequences of war stress. Based on observations of hundreds of survivors of World War II, many of whom were former members of underground resistance movements, Bastiaans placed his empirical findings within the general frameworks of Selye's (1951, 1974) stress theory together with other relevant frameworks and concepts from the psycho-dynamic and psychobiological thinking of the time. In this early research the concepts which we now accept—namely, the KZ-syndrome (concentration camp), the survivor-syndrome, and the post-concentration camp syndrome—were not recognized. Psychosomatic syndrome formation did appear to be one aspect of the so-called delayed reactions to traumatizing stress, usually found in those highly

---

The term "man-made," as used in this paper, refers to disasters of human origin such as terrorist activities and nuclear warfare.

self-controlled personalities who had expended considerable willpower and energy in trying to control, suppress, or repress the painful traumatic experiences of the war. To illustrate these points, let us look more closely at the dynamics of the psychological processes that contribute to the development of the psychosomatic symptoms associated with the KZ-syndrome.

KZ–PATHOLOGY AND PSYCHOSOMATIC SYNDROMES

The KZ-syndrome is not a syndrome in the traditional sense of a combined formation of symptoms. In essence, it is a process comprising four distinct phases, each of which is marked by the presence of different conventional syndromes. These phases are shown in Table 1.

Phase 1: The Shock Phase

The Shock Phase usually begins at the time of arrest, severe interrogation, ill treatment, or the first experience of life in prison or in a concentration camp. Extreme shock involves loss of consciousness; somewhat less extreme shock may imply extreme depersonalization and ego-paralysis. In this phase of shock the self-defense mechanisms cannot be utilized. In instances when consciousness has not been significantly lowered, extreme feelings of powerlessness tend to dominate.

Table 1 Symptomatology in the traumatic situation; reactions to traumatizing stress[a]

Phases of adaptation syndrome	Emotional	Intellectual
Shock	Fainting, no emotions	Paralysis of intellectual functioning in dream or coma
Alarm	Alarm emotions and feelings; affects, anxiety, pain, terror, panic, extreme insecurity and nervousness, hyperaesthesia, agitation, hesitation, doubt	Hyperactivity in perception and thinking
Adaptation with accent on fight	Overactivity, destruction vs. construction, ranging from hostile action to protest, sadism, and overproduction	Intellectual overactivity
Adaptation with accent on fight and flight	Depression, masochism, disappointment; manifest or masked mourning	Insufficient investment of intellectual capacities in action, production, communication; everything lacks sense
Adaptation with accent on flight	Indifference, dislike or disgust of action, work, contact; feeling lonely; emotional autism and apathy	Failing functioning in orientation, perception, memory, conceptualization, thinking
Exhaustion	Feelings of weakness, asthenia, sleep paralysis, feeling of impotence	Chronic asthenia of intellectual functions; narrowing of mental horizon

[a]From "Fixation Points in the Regulation of Aggression and Their Meaning for Syndrome Formation" by J. Bastiaans, *Psychiatry, Proceedings of Fifth World Congress of Psychiatry*, 1971. Copyright 1971 by Excerpta Medica, Amsterdam. Used with permission.

These feelings may be so overwhelming that, at later stages, they give rise to fixations in conscious or unconscious states of powerlessness.

Phase 2: The Alarm Phase

The Alarm Phase, or contra-shock phase, is a condition of intra-psychic lability marked by all the signs and symptoms of psychophysiological arousal, usually expressed in such symptoms as neurasthenia and extreme nervousness in combination with fear, sleeplessness, and restlessness. The main feelings in the Alarm Phase are pain, guilt, and shame. These emotions have a feedback as well as a warning function, insofar as they prepare the individual for his task of finding solutions to problems of adaptation and coping.

Phase 3: The Adaptation Phase

The Adaptation Phase can go in either of two directions: it may lead to a healthy adaptation, but it may also end in pathological mechanisms that prevent adaptation to reality and to the environment. The primary biological reactions are fight or flight mechanisms. Excessive flight may lead to states of depression, while excessive fight may lead to overt hostility or psychopathic agressiveness. Controlled fight can also result in over-controlled and coping behavior, which leads in turn to psychosomatic syndrome formation. Psychiatric and psychomatic syndromes are usually the consequences of forced adaptation.

Phase 4: The Exhaustion Phase

Phase 4, characterized by exhaustion, is usually reached when adaptation or coping procedures have succeeded. In this phase the subject experiences symptoms of asthenia, tiredness, and general weakness, in combination with a diversity of phenomena common to psychological and psychosomatic regression.

Under conditions of war stress, soldiers and former inmates of prisons and concentration camps usually come home in a state of complete exhaustion. While some of these persons try to resume work and normal activities as soon as possible after an initial period of physical recovery, many others require more time for readjustment. The second group is psychologically less endangered than the first group because the excessively early hyperactivity of the first group frequently gives rise to psychic and psychosomatic decompensation in later years.

Between Phase 2 and Phase 3 there is usually a symptom-free interval that is seldom present between phases 3 and 4. This interval has been described as the "deciving" latent period that successfully hides the causal relationship between the initial and the later phases of the KZ-syndrome.

The Netherlands has had a great deal of experience in dealing with the problems of war victims, and especially with the victims of World War II, of whom more than 100,000 are still alive. Of this number there are many who have been disabled for a considerable length of time. Only the strongest, most of whom are now between the ages of 50 and 70 years, have managed to survive without serious impairment. During the last few years the members of this group have been decompensating both mentally and physically.

Morbidity is higher in war victims as compared to other groups who have not been exposed to the stresses of man-made disasters. It has not been established, however, that their mortality rate is any higher than that of other groups unaffected by such disasters. This is an amazing fact that can probably be explained by the relatively protected and isolated environments in which such victims spend their lives. In their efforts to avoid the bombardment and intense stimulation of the welfare state, they cope with the actual stresses of life by living a so-called *vita minima*. The precise circumstances of their social isolation are determined by many cultural factors that differ from one country to another. If social systems support these survivors by offering attention, safety, and security, it is easier for them to communicate with their environment than it is in those systems which implicitly threaten survivors with unsafety and insecurity (see Bastiaans, 1979).

The safety principle, diagrammed in Fig. 1, helps to explain the essence of KZ-pathology, since the feelings of safety is the best indicator of optimal homeo-stasis and psychosomatic equilibrium. Under healthy conditions, safety is pri-marily derived from pleasurable experiences within the context of human inter-action. Victims of the stresses of man-made disasters have, for shorter or longer periods, been isolated from such vital contacts. And fixed as they are in their traumatic experiences, their only possibility of deriving feelings of safety in their environment lies in an increase of their own power (as subjectively perceived)— power derived from status, possessions, sheltered isolation—in other words, the power derived from a psychological defense structure.

Such an increase in power may protect the individual or the group from the more unpleasant feelings or experiences associated with powerlessness. Unfor-tunately, however, this increase in power—usually a pathological power status— implies a strong motivation to bring about a potential decrease in the power status of any person or group considered an enemy of the power system. Victims of the power system can be killed. They can be thrown into jails or concentration camps. They may be subjected to torture or other forms of ill-treatment intended to place the individual back in a state of extreme powerlessness.

This dependence on enhanced power might explain the tragic fact that many victims of disasters tend to be regarded as "difficult" for their environment, espe-cially in the later periods of adaptation. Psychosomatic syndrome formation may be based on a pathological increase in the power status of the individual, otherwise blocked from participating in more flexible interactions. Psychosomatic patients

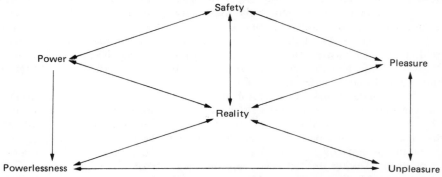

Figure 1 A schematic representation of the safety principle which indicates the reciprocal effects of reality, pleasure, and subjective power on feelings of safety and security.

pretend to be normal and mentally healthy; but due to their over-adaptive behavior and inner inability to express their feelings of aggression, sooner or later they fall ill (see Bastiaans, 1972).

The essence of the KZ-syndrome has also been described as the master-slave syndrome, a concept developed by Hoppe (1971). This comparison implies that the main roles preferred by the victims, especially in the post-stress periods, are those of either master or slave. Some victims behave as if they are masters, others as if they are slaves; but the behavior of most of them is characterized by some combination of both roles.

In view of what is known about KZ-pathology, it could be predicted that victims of such terroristic acts as hijacking would suffer, in the post-stress period, from symptoms or syndromes related to those recognized in KZ-pathology. Even though these stressful events were usually of shorter duration than those associated with war or concentration camp internment, the difficulties in adaptation to normal life are predictable.

CONSEQUENCES OF TERRORIST AND HOSTAGE–TAKING ACTS: THE DUTCH EXPERIENCE

The Netherlands was confronted during the 1970s with an alarming series of terrorist and hostage-taking acts, each stemming from a different political motivation. Some victims were killed, others were taken hostage. Most of the latter gained their freedom after some hours, days, or weeks. But the experience of having been taken hostage proved so stressful and threatening that many of the victims continue to suffer long-lasting negative effects.

In order to improve the organization of care and assistance to the victims of these violent actions, the Ministry of Health of The Netherlands established a Central Steering and Guidance Committee in 1976. A scientific research program was initiated, and the final report was presented to the Ministry in July 1979. One of the main objectives of this project was to identify all psychic or psychosomatic changes manifested in the victims as a result of their experiences. To determine whether such changes occurred, whether they were positive or negative, and whether they had been caused by the stress of man-made disasters presented a challenge to the researchers.

Invitations to cooperate in the research program were given to 283 former hostages affected by seven acts of terrorism in The Netherlands. Of this number, 168 persons agreed to cooperate in procedures comprising both free and structured psychological interviews. In addition, interviews were also conducted with family members, social workers, general practitioners (GPs), and other persons involved in the care and aftercare of victims.

During the short-term—that is to say, during the first four weeks immediately following termination of the event—the negative effects were mainly tenseness, fears and phobias, and insomnia. Long-term negative effects appearing after the first four weeks were observed in two-thirds of the former hostages. These effects were predominantly the following: irritability, increased lability, the presence of fears and phobias, feelings of unsafety, feelings of being misunderstood, preoccupations with the experience of captivity, insomnia, and vague physical complaints that were sometimes of an organ-neurotic nature.

The intensity of the above effects was different for various groups. Women experienced negative effects of greater intensity than men. Further, intensity of negative feelings showed a clear correlation with the duration of captivity (the longer the situation lasted, the greater the intensity of effects). Younger persons and those with less education experienced more intensely the effects of their ordeal than did older and more educated persons. Moreover, there was a clear connection between the intensity of negative effects in the short term and in the long term.

Two-thirds of the former hostages reported positive effects over the short term, while half of the subjects reported positive effects in the long run. The enhanced ability to see the relativity of things was the main positive effect reported by subjects. The implications of these so-called positive effects over longer periods of time are not yet clear, but it may be expected that they will disappear after some time. It is of course possible that in some cases the stressful events will stimulate the process of mental growth.

For family members of former hostages, the intensity of negative effects was rather low over the short term. Over the long term, two-thirds of the family members suffered from negative effects of the same nature, but not the same intensity, as the negative effects experienced by the former hostages. New acts of terrorism had negative effects on former hostages as well as on members of their families. Half of the persons who were interviewed experienced vicariously the fears and stresses characteristic of their own captivity whenever new acts of terrorism occurred.

Over the long term, psychosomatic syndrome formation could be observed in 12 percent of the cases experiencing negative consequences. States of depression were found in 7 percent of the cases. These percentages, however, were far lower than were those for fears and phobias (29 percent). We may interpret this discrepancy as evidence that, in the first months or years after captivity, the majority of former hostages were predominantly fixated on the symptomatology of the Alarm Phase of the survivor syndrome. This usually gives rise to well-defined clinical syndromes on the psychiatric and psychosomatic levels.

Many details of the related symptomatology of the Alarm Phase have been described. It is not yet known whether, in the future, there will be a syndrome shift in the direction of more flexible adaptation to reality or in the direction of more pronounced pathology. Repeated interview procedures will be needed to discover to what extent psychosomatic syndrome formation will occur in those former hostages and their family members who have already suffered from neurasthenic and organ-neurotic complaints during the first months or years following captivity.

A special chapter of the Report of the Central Steering and Guidance Committee was devoted to recommendations for immediate and aftercare of former hostages. The findings of the investigation revealed that a situation of terrorism must be regarded as a state of crisis. In such a state, there is a need for immediate crisis-intervention, marked by intensive and active therapeutic activities. In relatively normal situations of mental distress therapists tend to postpone therapy until the person involved either needs or asks for help. In states of crisis, more active therapeutic intervention is required since the former hostages are partially fixated in states of powerlessness; they have neither the motivation nor the initiative to seek guidance, support, or treatment; and consequently such support should be offered to victims of stress in a flexible manner and on a voluntary basis.

The importance of the general practitioner's function in these circumstances soon become clear. If guidance is not offered, there is a danger that the processes of denial, suppression, and repression of negative effects will be progressively activated during the coming days and weeks, thereby creating conditions favorable to the development of psychosomatic symptoms. On the other hand, it has become clear that some former hostages may become even more unstable if their need for support and treatment is too strongly emphasized. They do not want to be stigmatized as patients and, especially, not as psychiatric patients. This finding indicates the importance of the manner in which therapeutic services are offered to former hostages and their family members.

Further research into the psychosomatic consequences of man-made disasters will help to illuminate and clarify some of the procedures and issues now confronting researchers in this field. For example, we know that unless a psychological interview procedure is combined with a proper physical examination of the patient at the outset of the investigation, it is seldom clear in a later phase whether reported bodily complaints are the expression of a psychosomatic disease or a genuine physical disturbance. The Dutch research project will attempt to guide its investigations in such a manner, so as to improve procedures aimed at diminishing the uncertainties in this area.

Comparable studies on the victims of stress related to man-made disasters have been conducted by in Germany by a group of psychiatrists led for many years by Ploeger; results were published in 1966. Subjects were ten miners who were trapped in a mine disaster in Lengede, completely isolated from the outer world for two weeks and successfully rescued in the final moments before the total collapse of the mine shaft. During the period of the investigation, nearly all the victims suffered from irritability, fears, phobias, and some had nightmares and hallucinations related to their traumatic experience.

Other comparable studies have been undertaken in Ireland, where suspects accused of having taken part in IRA activities were subjected to severe in-depth interrogation. After their release from prison in 1971, it was predicted which persons would suffer afterwards from fears, phobias, depression, and psychosomatic diseases. Those who tried to control themselves as much as possible after the traumatic event, and who were inclined to repress memories and emotions related to this event, suffered predominantly from psychosomatic disease. The less controlled group suffered from other symptoms and syndromes for at least two years after their interrogation.

STRESS AND PSYCHOSOMATIC SPECIFICITY

Psychosomatic specificity refers to the hypothesis that psychosomatic syndromes are the outcome of the interaction between specific situations involving stress and specific personality traits. Although this specificity theory and all its modifications—i.e., complete specificity, relative response specificity, and multi- and unidimensional specificity—have been criticized and rejected by many researchers in the field, it is striking how few of the researchers have had the opportunity to observe the psychological differences between psychiatric and psychosomatic patients and between different groups of psychosomatic patients in a clinical setting (see Bastiaans, 1977).

In The Netherlands, much research has been conducted along these lines. While there is not yet a definitive answer to the question of specificity, it is clear that if survivors of man-made disasters suffer from a well-known psychosomatic disease, they are very seldom suffering from only one psychosomatic syndrome. The examiner is much more likely to be confronted with a whole set of psychiatric and psychosomatic syndromes—that is, with a combination of essential hypertension and general nervousness, tenseness, and nightmares of reliving the terrifying aspects of their traumatic experiences.

At the present time, the victims of World War II in Holland suffer predominantly from the combination of involutional depression and more or less outspoken psychosomatic phenomena. These syndromes are the result of a long and continuous effort to adapt themselves to the post-war demands imposed by society, work, and family. Years ago, when attention was first directed to these victims, we had no way of knowing—nor did we suspect—that the delayed consequences of war stress would be so intensive, pervasive, and outspoken.

One must ask whether there will be similar effects over the long term for the victims of terrorist acts, for the civilians taken hostage in a country not engaged in warfare. The stress to which these peace-time victims have been subjected was admittedly shorter in duration than the stress undergone by war survivors; and today many more psychotherapeutic facilities are available than there were 30 years ago. But these facts should not seduce the researcher into thinking that this makes it easier on today's victims than it was for those suffering from the negative effects of World War II.

We must remember that those victims who appear to be the strongest, those who pretend that they successfully coped with traumas of stress, may also be those who will experience delayed psychosomatic reactions. Therefore, much more research must be done. It is especially important to be able to predict at the right moment who among us is endangered by his own strategies of adaptation, coping, and defense. We must be prepared and ready to assist the victims of man-made disasters of the past, and just as prepared to aid the victims of the all too uncertain future.

REFERENCES

Bastiaans, J. Psychosomatische gevolgen van onderdrukking en verzet. *Thesis*, Amsterdam, 1957.

Bastiaans, J. General comments on the role of aggression in human psychopathology. *Psychother. Psychosom.*, 1972, *20*, 300–311.

Bastiaans, J. The implications of the specificity concept for the treatment of psychosomatic patients. *Psychother. Psychosom.*, 1977, *28*, 285–293.

Bastiaans, J. Models of teaching psychobiological medicine to medical students. *Biblthca Psychiat.*, 1979, *159*, 48–61.

Bastiaans, J. De behandeling van oorlogsslachtoffers. *Journal of Drug Research*, 1979, *4*, 352–358.

European Commission of Human Rights, Council of Europe; Report Ireland against the United Kingdom of Great Britain and Northern Ireland (adopted 25 January 1976). Application No.: 5310/71.

Hoppe, K. D. The master-slave-see-saw relationship in psychotherapy. *Reiss Davis Clin. Bull.*, *8*(2), 117–125.

Netherlands Ministry of Health: Report on Psychological investigations into the consequences of hostage-taking situations in The Netherlands (1974–1977). The Hague, 1977.

Ploeger, A. Zeiterleben in einer Extremsituation: Untersuchungen an den Bergleuten von Lengede. *Psychotherapie und medizinische Psychologie*, 1966, *16*, 13–19.

Selye, H. The story of the adaptation syndrome. In *Annual reports on stress*. Montreal, 1952.

Selye, H. *Stress*. New York: 1974.

III

STATE AND TRAIT ANXIETY

9

General vs. Situation-specific Traits as Related to Anxiety in Ego-threatening Situations

Lothar Laux
University of Bamberg

Peter Glanzmann and Paul Schaffner
Johannes Gutenberg University

In the 1960s the trait model in personality research came under serious attack by proponents of situationism and interactionism. In the subsequent debates it turned out that the situationist approach of rejecting traits as determinants of behavior was not tenable and the interactionism model was regarded as an alternative to the trait and the situationism models (Bowers, 1973; Endler & Magnusson, 1976; Magnusson & Endler, 1977; Mischel, 1977).

Recently, Herrmann (1980) has argued that a simple division of personality psychology into the trait, situationism, and interactionism models does not account for the enormous complexity of personality theories. In particular, he points out that many trait conceptions deal explicitly with person by situation interactions. Even proponents of interactional psychology now seem to agree that most modern trait theory formulations are compatible with the interaction model (see Magnusson, 1980).

Whether the interactional model is regarded as a new theory or only as a refinement of trait theory, it has undoubtedly contributed to the development of tests that incorporate situational variables in the test design. In the area of anxiety research such tests have been classified as situation-specific trait anxiety tests. They focus on a person's disposition to be anxious in selected stressful situations or classes of situations, e.g., examinations or speech situations (Spielberger, 1972; Spielberger, Anton, & Bedell, 1976). Mellstrom, Zuckerman, and Cicala (1978) suggest that specific traits can be conceived of as a redefinition of the trait concept to take into consideration the situation and the person by situation interaction.

In contrast to situation-specific tests, general trait anxiety tests such as the Taylor (1953) Manifest Anxiety Scale (MAS) and the A-Trait scale of the State-Trait Anxiety Inventory (STAI) (Spielberger, Gorsuch, & Lushene, 1970) do not specify situations in the instructions or the test items. A considerable body of research evidence nevertheless suggests that these general trait anxiety scales actually measure individual differences in anxiety proneness in *ego-involving* situations. Accordingly, they might also be classified as situation-specific although the situations are rather broadly defined (see Spielberger, 1977). In the research literature, however, the term "situation-specific" is restricted to tests that include the description of the situation explicitly either in the instructions or the items (Mellstrom et al., 1978; Spielberger, 1980).

The predictive validity of situation-specific trait anxiety scales has been compared to that of general tests of trait anxiety in a number of studies (Lamb, 1973, 1976; Mellstrom, Cicala, & Zuckerman, 1976; Mellstrom et al., 1978; Paul, 1966). While the results in most of these studies demonstrated the predictive superiority of the situation-specific tests, surprisingly, in two studies these measures did not yield better predictions of elevations in state anxiety than did general A-trait measures (Mellstrom et al., 1976, 1978). In both studies, the situation-specific A-trait tests were better predictors of behavioral and subjective anxiety in the corresponding criterion situation than the general tests. The latter, however, equaled the predictive accuracy of the specific tests for the specific anxiety-arousing situations that contained ego-threat.

The implications of these findings draws attention to the theoretical and practical importance of identifying the particular conditions that contribute to the relative predictive power of general and situation-specific anxiety tests. Therefore, the findings in the Mellstrom et al. (1978) study will be examined in detail in the present chapter, and a possible explanation of these results will be suggested. The results of a study that compared the predictive power of general and situation-specific A-trait measures in an ego-threat situation will then be described.

EXPERIMENTAL CONDITIONS THAT INFLUENCE THE VALIDITY OF GENERAL AND SITUATION–SPECIFIC TRAIT ANXIETY MEASURES

In the Mellstrom et al. (1978) study, 114 subjects (56 male, 58 female undergraduates) were pretested with general and specific trait anxiety measures and later exposed to three experimental situations, described as a *rat*, a *test*, and a *social* anxiety situation. The following predictors were used:

1. A *neurotic trait anxiety composite* which consisted of the summed standard scores on the A-Trait scale of the STAI (Spielberger et al., 1970) and the Neuroticism scale of the Eysenck Personality Inventory (Eysenck & Eysenck, 1964). The rationale for combining the scores of both scales was the high correlation between them (see Zuckerman, 1979).

2. An *omnibus measure of trait anxiety* which consisted of the summed standard scores of the total scores on the Geer (1965) Fear Survey Schedule (FSS) and the Zuckerman Inventory of Personal Reactions (ZIPERS; Zuckerman, 1977). The FSS lists a variety of objects, situations, and concepts and asks subjects to indicate how fearful they feel in response to each. Subjects' total fear scores across all 51 items were used as a general A-trait measure. The ZIPERS consists of 12 situations in which subjects rate the degree to which these situations elicit in them each of the 13 reactions. By summing a subject's scores across all situations on the responses comprising the fear factor, a measure of general A-trait was derived.

3. *Situation-specific trait anxiety measures* which consisted of the summed standard scores of the particular items (rat, test, social situation) of the FSS and the ZIPERS. In addition to the 12 standard situations of the ZIPERS, a rat, a test,

and a social anxiety situation were included because these situations matched the real situations in the study.

Six weeks after pretesting, the subjects were exposed to the *rat, test,* and *social* situation, in which they were asked (1) to approach a rat and to pick it up, (2) perform on a difficult memory task introduced as an indicator of one's intelligence, and (3) participate in a stressful interview used to create social anxiety. In addition to obtaining behavioral measures and observational ratings, three scales were administered to assess subjective (state) anxiety in each situation: The STAI A-State scale, the A-state form of the ZIPERS, and the fear thermometer of Walk (1956). These three scales comprised the "self-report" composite.

The interpretation of the Mellstrom et al. (1978) data will be restricted to the correlations of the "self-report" composite with the three classes of predictors. For the rat situation, the specific composite clearly surpasses the general scales. In the test situation, the general measures equaled the predictive accuracy of the specific ones. In the social situation, the specific measure was a better predictor of state anxiety than the general measure, but only for females; there was no difference for males.

As to the test situation, Mellstrom et al. (1978) argue that the predictive power of the specific predictors may have been limited by two factors: (a) subjects' lack of experience with anything similar to the test situations, making it difficult for them to imagine how they would react on the predictor test, and (b) lack of correspondence between the situation described in the predictor test and the actual situation. While such arguments concern peculiarities of the Mellstrom et al. study, these authors suggest another explanation that is of prime importance for the current debate on the predictive validity of general and specific A-trait measures:

The specific predictors did not surpass the general ones in predicting the self-report criteria of the test situation, because the general ones achieved relatively high levels of predictive accuracy for this situation. It may be that the ego threat pressure in such situations is the main cause of anxiety, permitting the neuroticism composite to be predictive of these self-reports. (Mellstrom et al., 1978, p. 429)

Despite Mellstrom et al.'s advocacy of situation-specific trait measures, this explanation clearly emphasizes the importance of using general A-trait measures in most ego-threatening situations. If situation-specific tests do not surpass the general ones in these situations, it would seem more parsimonious to use general tests that cover a wide range of such situations instead of developing specific trait tests for each particular situation. A more logical explanation might be in terms of the advantages of the situation-specific tests being overshadowed by the disadvantages such as relative brevity and the fact that they focus on one unique situation. The ZIPERS situation, for example, is described as follows: "You are asked to perform a difficult memory task that is an indicator of your intelligence." Subjects report, on a 5-point scale, the degree to which the situation elicits each of 13 reactions. Summing the subject's scores on the following three "fear" reactions yields the specific test A-trait measure: Your heart beats faster; you feel fearful; you get out of the situation or avoid it. The rationale for the selection of these three responses was the assumption that each represents one of three basic human response channels: physiological, phenomenal, and behavioral. In contrast, the general A-trait tests are based on a much larger number of items, for example, the A-Trait scale of the STAI consists of 20 items.

While the brevity and specificity of the situational description and the reaction mode in the ZIPERS have obvious advantages, the shortness of the test, might restrict its value. A comparison of the differential predictive power of general and specific A-trait tests should therefore be based on tests of comparable length.

COMPARATIVE VALIDITY OF GENERAL AND TEST TRAIT ANXIETY

In the present study it was hypothesized that a test A-trait scale would be more strongly related to self-reports of state anxiety in a test situation than a general A-trait scale. This hypothesis was tested by administering the STAI A-Trait scale (Spielberger et al., 1970) and the Test Anxiety Inventory (TAI, Spielberger, 1980), which have similar formal characteristics. The TAI was developed to measure individual differences in test anxiety as a situation-specific personality trait. It is similar in structure to the A-Trait scale of the STAI. Both tests consist of 20 items and utilize the same rating-scale format. Furthermore, subjects are instructed in both tests to indicate how they *generally* feel.

In contrast to the A-Trait scale of the STAI, the items of the TAI refer to anxiety reactions in examination situations. Subjects are asked to report how frequently they experience specific symptoms of anxiety before, during, and after examinations. The TAI provides subscales for measuring worry and emotionality which appear to be the major components of test anxiety. Worry is defined as cognitive concerns about the consequences of failure and emotionality as self-perceived feelings of tension and apprehension, and autonomic reactions evoked by evaluative stress (Liebert & Morris, 1967).

The subjects were 73 undergraduate psychology students enrolled in a statistics program at the University of Mainz, West Germany. All subjects were volunteers and received credit for serving as subjects in psychological investigations. Complete data were available for 60 subjects, 29 males (mean age = 22.0 years) and 31 females (mean age = 22.2 years).

Several anxiety tests were repeatedly administered during the course of a single term. Trait tests were the A-Trait scale of the German form of the STAI (Laux, Glanzmann, Schaffner, & Spielberger, 1981) and a preliminary version of the German adaptation of the TAI (Hodapp, Laux, & Spielberger, 1982). The coefficients of internal consistency computed from a larger sample of the same population were greater than 0.90 for both scales. Retest reliabilities for an interval of seven weeks were 0.86 (TAI; males), 0.85 (TAI; females), 0.89 (STAI, A-Trait scale; males), and 0.85 (STAI, A-Trait scale; females). The trait tests were administered at the beginning of a regular statistics lecture one week prior to the final of a series of three examinations. The first two examinations took place seven weeks and one week prior to trait assessment. Therefore, statements about the *prediction* of state anxiety from the trait measures are only applicable to the third examination. Passing the examinations, each lasting for two hours, was a necessary requirement for admittance to courses the following term.

State anxiety was assessed by the A-State scale of the German version of the STAI (Laux et al., 1981), which was administered immediately after the termination of each of the three examinations, with instructions to indicate how subjects felt while working on the tests. In addition, the Cognitive Interference Questionnaire (CIQ) (Sarason, 1978) was given. This questionnaire contains 10 items referring to worry cognitions, for example, thinking about one's level of ability, consequences of doing poorly, etc. Subjects respond by indicating on a 5-point scale how often each thought occurred to them while they were working on the tests.

Table 1 shows the correlations of the general and situation-specific A-trait scales with the state anxiety measures in the exam situation. In every instance the situation-specific test yielded higher correlations than the general A-Trait scale. The results may be taken as evidence that the situation-specific A-trait test bears a stronger relationship to the state anxiety measures than the general A-trait test.

Table 1 also shows the correlations between the TAI/Worry and the TAI/Emotionality subscales with the state anxiety measures in the exam situation. Each subscale yielded generally higher correlations with the state anxiety measures than the general A-trait scale.

DISCUSSION AND CONCLUSIONS

The results of the present investigation demonstrate that even under ego-threat conditions, situation-specific tests are superior to general A-Trait scales provided that both tests possess similar formal characteristics. A prerequisite for these results, however, might have been the subjects' prior experience with examinations, facilitating responses to the subsequent TAI items. It should be emphasized that neither the instructions nor the content of the TAI items make reference to any specific kind of test situation. The items describe tests or examinations in general, e.g., "While taking examinations I have an uneasy, upset feeling"; "I worry a great deal before taking an important examination."

Future research should be addressed to the question of whether a detailed description of the criterion situation in individual test anxiety scale items would lead to better predictions with these scales. But such descriptions of specific test situations would not necessarily result in a stronger relationship with anxiety in the actual situation because subjects' responses to TAI items, which refer to examinations without any precise situational referent, may actually be determined by the experience of specific test situations. In other words, subjects may not report how they "generally feel" in test situations, but may respond in terms of specific test situations experienced during the near past. Such a strategy would reduce the difference between broad and narrow definitions of examination situations in test anxiety scales. From a practical point of view, very narrowly defined situation-specific trait tests would not be desirable because such tests would be highly limited in applicability.

If situation-specific trait measures prove to be better predictors of state anxiety than general A-trait tests such as the MAS or the STAI A-Trait scale, one might conclude that the latter type of tests are obsolete. But this view ignores the fact that general A-trait tests show moderate positive correlations with A-state reactions in a wide range of ego threat situations. While situation-specific test anxiety measures are better predictors of A-state elevations in trait-congruent situations, general A-trait scales are better predictors of A-state reactions in many different ego-threat situations, which are not trait-congruent (see Spielberger, 1977). For example, general A-trait scales are likely to be better predictors of elevations in A-state in a speech situation than test A-trait scales. Since general A-trait scales

Table 1 Correlations of the general and the situation-specific A-trait scales with the anxiety measures in the exam situation

	Males						Females					
	A-State exams			CIQ exams			A-State exams			CIQ exams		
	1	2	3	1	2	3	1	2	3	1	2	3
A-Trait	0.61	0.49	0.47	0.47	0.52	0.58	0.59	0.27	0.33	0.55	0.31	0.38
TAI (total)	0.83	0.72	0.70	0.56	0.64	0.64	0.67	0.67	0.44	0.74	0.71	0.55
Worry	0.72	0.70	0.65	0.33	0.45	0.40	0.57	0.64	0.40	0.56	0.54	0.39
Emotionality	0.73	0.52	0.45	0.74	0.70	0.68	0.60	0.68	0.41	0.67	0.82	0.59

combine pertinence to a great variety of ego-threatening situations with brevity, they are most useful in ego-threat situations for which situation-specific anxiety measures are not available.

REFERENCES

Bowers, K. S. Situationism in psychology: An analysis and a critique. *Psychological Review*, 1973, *80*, 307–336.

Endler, N. S. & Magnusson, D. Toward an interactional psychology of personality. *Psychological Bulletin*, 1976, *83*, 956–974.

Eysenck, H. J. & Eysenck, S. B. An improved short questionnaire for the measurement of extraversion and neuroticism. *Life Sciences*, 1964, *3*(10), 1103–1109.

Geer, J. H. The development of a scale to measure fear. *Behavior Research and Therapy*, 1965, *3*, 45–53.

Herrmann, T. Die Eigenschaftskonzeption als Heterosterotyp. Kritik eines persönlichkeits-psychologischen Geschichtsklischees. *Zeitschrift für Differentielle und Diagnostische Psychologie*, 1980, *1*, 7–16.

Hodapp, V., Laux, L., & Spielberger, C. D. Theorie und Messung der emotionalen und kognitiven Komponente der Prüfungsangst. *Zeitschrift für Differentielle und Diagnostische Psychologie*, 1982, *3*, 169–184.

Lamb, D. H. The effect of two stressors on state anxiety for students who differ in trait anxiety. *Journal of Research in Personality*, 1973, *7*, 116–126.

Lamb, D. H. Usefulness of situation-specific trait and state measures of anxiety. *Psychological Reports*, 1976, *38*, 188–190.

Laux, L., Glanzmann, P., Schaffner, P., & Spielberger, C. D. *Strait-Trait-Angstinventar (STAI). Theoretische Grundlagen und Handanweisung*. Weinheim: Beltz, 1981.

Liebert, R. M. & Morris, L. W. Cognitive and emotional components of test anxiety: A distinction and some initial data. *Psychological Reports*, 1967, *20*, 975–978.

Magnusson, D. Personality in an interactional paradigm of research. *Zeitschrift für Differentielle und Diagnostische Psychologie*, 1980, *1*, 17–34.

Magnusson, D. & Endler, N. S. Interactional psychology: Present status and future prospects. In D. Magnusson & N. S. Endler (eds.), *Personality at the crossroads: Current issues in interactional psychology*. Hillsdale, N.J.: Erlbaum, 1977.

Mellstrom, M., Cicala, G. A., & Zuckerman, M. General versus specific trait anxiety measures in the prediction of fear of snakes, heights, and darkness. *Journal of Consulting and Clinical Psychology*, 1976, *44*, 83–91.

Mellstrom, M., Zuckerman, M., & Cicala, G. A. General versus specific tests in the assessment of anxiety. *Journal of Consulting and Clinical Psychology*, 1978, *46*, 423–431.

Mischel, W. The interaction of person and situation. In D. Magnusson & N. S. Endler (eds.), *Personality at the crossroads: Current issues in interactional psychology*. Hillsdale, N.J.: Erlbaum, 1977.

Paul, G. *Insight vs. desensitization in psychotherapy*. Stanford, Calif.: Stanford University Press, 1966.

Sarason, I. G. The Test Anxiety Scale: Concept and research. In C. D. Spielberger & I. G. Sarason (eds.), *Stress and anxiety*, vol. 5. Washington, D.C.: Hemisphere, 1978.

Spielberger, C. D. Conceptual and methodological issues in research on anxiety. In C. D. Spielberger (ed.), *Anxiety: Current trends in theory and research*, Vol. 2. New York: Academic Press, 1972.

Spielberger, C. D. State-trait anxiety and interactional psychology. In D. Magnusson & N. S. Endler (eds.), *Personality at the crossroads: Current issues in interactional psychology*. Hillsdale, N.J.: Erlbaum, 1977.

Spielberger, C. D. *Test Anxiety Inventory ("Test Attitude Inventory")*. Palo Alto, Calif.: Consulting Psychologists Press, 1980.

Spielberger, C. D., Anton, W. D., & Bedell, J. The nature and treatment of test anxiety. In M. Zuckerman & C. D. Spielberger (eds.), *Emotions and anxiety: New concepts, methods, and applications*. New York: LEA/Wiley, 1976.

Spielberger, C. D., Gorsuch, R. L., & Lushene, R. E. *Manual for the State-Trait Anxiety Inventory*. Palo Alto, Calif.: Consulting Psychologists Press, 1970.

Taylor, J. A. A personality scale of manifest anxiety. *Journal of Abnormal and Social Psychology*, 1953, *48*, 285–290.

Walk, R. D. Self-ratings of fear in a fear-invoking situation. *Journal of Abnormal and Social Psychology*, 1956, *52*, 171–178.

Zuckerman, M. Development of a situation-specific trait-state test for the prediction and measurement of affective responses. *Journal of Consulting and Clinical Psychology*, 1977, *45*, 513–523.

Zuckerman, M. Traits, states, situations, and uncertainty. *Journal of Behavioral Assessment*, 1979, *1*, 43–54.

10

The Development and Validation of the Dutch State-Trait Anxiety Inventory

"Zelf-Beoordelings Vragenlijst"

Henk M. van der Ploeg
University of Leyden, The Netherlands

INTRODUCTION

During the last decade, psychologists and psychiatrists in The Netherlands have become more involved in understanding the phenomena of stress and anxiety. They have also developed new and more effective methods for treating patients with anxiety symptoms or anxious behavior patterns. In these research programs and in clinical and diagnostic work, the question is often posed: what is the level of anxiety of this person? In order to answer this question, reliable and valid questionnaires for the measurement of anxiety were required. *Documentation of Tests and Test Research in The Netherlands—1974* mentions only three anxiety inventories: the Test Anxiety Scale for Children (Cuppens, 1967), a Dutch version of Wolpe and Lang's Fear Survey (Bremer, 1968), and the Social Anxiety Scale developed by Willems, Tuender-de Haan, and Defares (1973).

In 1976, we began to investigate the relation between a woman's level of anxiety and her decision to participate in a breast cancer screening project (Spruit, Van Kampen-Donker, Van der Ploeg, De Lezenne Coulander, Obermann-de Boer, & Van Nieuwenhuijzen, 1979). No Dutch questionnaire purporting to measure general anxiety level was available at that time. Therefore, after an intensive search of the literature, we decided to translate and adapt Spielberger's State-Trait Anxiety Inventory (STAI, Spielberger, Gorsuch, & Lushene, 1970), and to use this scale to study the relationship between trait anxiety (T-Anxiety) and participation in the cancer screening project. The development and validation of the Dutch STAI: the "Zelf-Beoordelings Vragenlijst" (ZBV), will be described in this chapter.

THE DEVELOPMENT OF THE DUTCH STAI–D

The STAI measures two anxiety constructs: state and trait anxiety. State anxiety (S-Anxiety) is defined as a transitory emotional state characterized by consciously perceived feelings of tension and apprehension; trait anxiety refers to relatively stable individual differences in anxiety proneness (Spielberger et al., 1970). Spielberger's Trait-State theory of anxiety provides a conceptual framework which specifies the relationship between the two anxiety concepts and other variables related to stress and anxiety. Depending upon the characteristics of stressful stim-

129

ulus conditions, individuals experience differential levels of S-Anxiety as a function
of their level of T-Anxiety (Spielberger, 1966). For example, situations which
evaluate personal adequacy are likely to be perceived as more threatening by
high T-Anxiety individuals than by persons who are low in T-Anxiety (Spielberger,
1972).

Work on translating and adapting the STAI (Form X) in the Dutch language was
begun in 1976 in the context of the above-mentioned screening project. This early
form of the Dutch STAI was also used to measure anxiety in projects with Dutch
medical students, psychiatric out-patients and general practice patients (see respectively Van der Ploeg, 1979, 1980a, 1980b). During this process of testing, our
attention was drawn to a publication by Eijkman and Orlebeke (1975) in which
they used a Dutch translation of the STAI (Form X) in their research on dental
anxiety. They found their Dutch STAI S-Anxiety scale to be particularly useful
in measuring the anxiety experienced just prior to a dental treatment. Thus, in
1976, two Dutch inventories for measuring state and trait anxiety, both adaptations of the STAI, were available.

The two Dutch versions of the STAI showed some similarities e.g., the adaptation of several items ("I feel calm"—"Ik voel me kalm") were exactly the same.
But there were also differences with regard to item-translations (e.g., "I am
worried"—"Ik ben ergens bezorgd over" by Eijkman and Orlebeke, and "Ik maak
me zorgen" by Van der Ploeg). There were also differences in format and instructions, and in the translations of the response categories for the S-Anxiety scale.

On the basis of developments in the field of personality research and research
with the original English form of the STAI-X, Spielberger (1980) developed in the
U.S. a revised version of the STAI, called Form Y. The difference between the X-
and Y-versions of the STAI is that 30 percent of the original items were replaced.
The Form-X items that were eliminated were depression-oriented or had poor
psychometric properties for high school students. A better balance between the
number of anxiety-present and anxiety-absent items was also achieved in the STAI
Form Y Trait scale.

Although the psychometric properties of the earlier Dutch versions of the STAI
(Form X) were quite satisfactory, Form DY (Dutch Y) of the STAI was developed
in The Netherlands to incorporate the recent revisions in the English STAI and to
avoid the simultaneous use of different translations in the same country. The use
of different Dutch adaptations of the same scale can give rise to confusion in the
interpretation of results and makes the comparison of results more difficult.

The development of the STAI-DY will be described hereafter in more detail.
In constructing the Dutch Y version we endeavored to benefit from the advantages
and experience with earlier Dutch versions of the scale. Therefore, jointly with
Spielberger and Defares, items were selected from: (a) the Eijkman and Orlebeke
version; (b) Van der Ploeg's earlier versions; and (c) Spielberger's newly developed
English Form Y.

The first step in constructing the STAI-DY was to develop an itempool, consisting of several translations of each English item. Next, in the light of the compo-
sition of the Y version, a number of new items were written for the state and
trait scales. The preliminary versions consisting of a larger number of items than
was ultimately desired, was then administered to medical and psychology students
at the University of Leyden. This scale was also administered to psychiatric out-
patients at the Leyden University Hospital. On the basis of item-remainder correla-

tions and the content of the translated items, the most satisfactory items were selected for the revised STAI-DY.

It was observed that some items with poor internal consistency reliability for non-anxious students yielded highly satisfactory results with patients of varying degrees of anxiety. For example, the S-Anxiety item 7: "Ik pieker over nare dingen die kunnen gebeuren" ("I am presently worrying over possible misfortunes") and item 18: "Ik voel me gejaagd" ("I feel confused") worked well for the patient groups. We also observed this in the trait anxiety subscale, for example, item 28: "Ik voel dat de moeilijkheden zich opstapelen, zodat ik er niet meer tegenop kan" ("I feel that difficulties are piling up so that I cannot overcome them") and item 39: "Ik ben een rustig iemand" ("I am a steady person").

It was also found that a literal translation sometimes produced somewhat poorer results compared to a more ideomatic translation. An example of this was item 11 of the state anxiety scale: "I feel self-confident." This was translated literally: "Ik voel me vol zelfvertrouwen," but the more free translation or adaptation, "Ik voel me zeker" was more adequate because it described the absence of anxiety more accurately.

In the trait anxiety scale, examples of such adaptation peculiarities were item 27: "I am calm, cool, and collected"; the free translation "Ik voel me rustig en beheerst" works better than the literal translation "Ik ben rustig, kalm en heb mezelf in de hand." Another example is item 37: "Some unimportant thought runs through my mind and bothers me." The literal translation, "Een onbelangrijke gedachte gaat door mijn hoofd en zit me dwars," is inferior to the free adaptation "Er zijn gedachten die ik heel moeilijk los kan laten." The latter works better with both students and patients. These examples demonstrate that, in the process of translating an inventory into another language, we have to be aware of cultural differences. Because of these differences it is not accurate to speak of a "translation" of the STAI; we should say that the STAI has been adapted for use in another language in a manner that cultural differences have also been considered.

In this way, 20 S-Anxiety and 20 T-Anxiety items were selected. In the selection procedure, we made use of statistics like item-remainder correlations, Cronbach's alpha reliability coefficients and also the probability values of answers to the four response categories in each subscale. Computations were done with SPSS (Nie, Hull, Jenkins, Steinbrenner, & Bent, 1975). This set of 40 items (two 20-item subscales) that form the Y version of the Dutch STAI, the "Zelf-Beoordelings Vragenlijst" (Van der Ploeg, Defares, & Spielberger, 1979, 1980). It should be pointed out that the Dutch T-Anxiety scale is perfectly balanced, containing 10 anxiety-absent (e.g., "I am a steady person") and 10 anxiety-present (e.g., "Some unimportant thought runs through my mind and bothers me") items. Its English counterpart (Form Y), has 11 anxiety present and 9 anxiety absent items.

Given the replacement of some items which had depressive connotations (e.g., "I feel like crying") rather than an anxiety connotation, and the process of selecting items on the basis of clearer conceptions of state and trait anxiety, the newly developed STAI-DY yielded higher Cronbach alpha coefficients than the earlier Dutch versions; the item-remainder correlations were also higher. Although the validity of the earlier scale was satisfactory, evidence of the validity of the revised STAI-DY was also stronger. In evaluating the validity of the Y-version, results previously obtained with regard to the validity of the X-version can also be considered because the two versions are highly correlated and contain a number of identical items.

On completing the construction of the Dutch STAI-DY, the Dutch and English versions (STAI-Y) were administered to a group of (bilingual) doctoral students at the University of Leyden with a high degree of proficiency in both the English and Dutch language. Spearman correlations between the Dutch and English subscales were 0.97 for state anxiety and 0.99 for trait anxiety. Thus the two questionnaires are essentially equivalent for Dutch-English bilinguals.

PSYCHOMETRIC PROPERTIES OF THE STAI–DY

In gathering normative data for the STAI-DY, we tested large groups of university students, psychiatric out-patients and in-patients, and male draftees. The norms for students are based on three different samples: first year psychology students, and first and second year medical students. The test was administered at the beginning of the academic year during or just after a lecture (a non-stressful testing condition). The means, standard deviations, and alpha coefficients for the three samples of students are summarized in Table 1.

As can be seen in Table 1, the T-Anxiety scores of women were, on the average, slightly higher than for the comparable group of men. The mean anxiety scores of first year psychology and medical students are comparable, but the mean T-Anxiety scores of second year medical students were lower than those of first year medical students. We may assume that relatively more anxious first year medical students are, to some extent, less successful in examinations, and thus more likely to fail and not be able to proceed with their second year.

The draftees, 17–18 years of age, were tested in a selection situation on the same day they were screened for the army. They were informed that their responses to the test would be anonymous. It was also stressed that their answers would have no influence on their being selected or not selected for military service in The Netherlands. Of the sample of 547 draftees, 56 percent had a relatively low level of education (mostly elementary school), 24 percent had a middle level (secondary school), and 20 percent had a high level of education (secondary school, advanced-

Table 1 STAI-DY means, standard deviations, and Cronbach's alpha reliabilities for university students

	All students		First year psychology		First year medical		Second year medical	
	M	F	M	F	M	F	M	F
S-Anxiety								
N	205	202	67	105	71	42	67	55
Mean	34.3	35.2	36.0	35.5	36.5	39.2	30.5	31.5
SD	8.3	8.4	8.5	8.7	7.9	7.4	7.2	7.1
Alpha	0.90	0.91	0.89	0.92	0.89	0.87	0.92	0.91
T-Anxiety								
N	205	202	67	105	71	42	67	55
Mean	36.1	37.7	38.2	38.6	37.2	40.0	32.8	34.3
SD	8.4	8.4	8.9	8.4	7.5	8.6	7.9	7.4
Alpha	0.91	0.90	0.92	0.90	0.87	0.90	0.91	0.90

Table 2 STAI-DY means, standard deviations, and alpha reliabilities for male draftees at the time of selection

	All draftees	Level of education			All male students
		Lower	Middle	Higher	
S-Anxiety					
N	547	302	135	108	205
Mean	39.8	41.0	38.9	37.4	34.3
SD	8.6	8.2	8.7	9.0	8.3
Alpha	0.87	0.85	0.88	0.91	0.90
T-Anxiety					
N	538	298	135	103	205
Mean	37.9	39.0	36.3	36.9	36.1
SD	8.2	7.9	8.3	8.8	8.4
Alpha	0.87	0.84	0.89	0.90	0.91

level). The means, standard deviations and alpha coefficients for the draftees are summarized in Table 2 as a function of level of education.

In the group of draftees, the level of education was negatively correlated with state and trait anxiety scores. This finding that men who have more education were lower in anxiety was consistent with results published for the STAI-X (Spielberger et al., 1970). It is also noteworthy that the S-Anxiety scores of the draftees were higher than their T-Anxiety scores, whereas the T-Anxiety scores for the students were slightly higher than their S-Anxiety scores. Although the draftees were informed that their STAI-scores had no influence on the selection procedure, their test situation was undoubtedly far more stressful than the student test situation. As a result of these differences in the stressfulness of the testing conditions, the S-Anxiety for the draftees was much higher than the S-Anxiety for the male students ($t = 7.87$, $p < 0.0001$). Although there was less difference in T-Anxiety, the draftees scored significantly higher than the students ($t = 2.65$, $p < 0.005$). When draftees with higher levels of education were compared with the male students difference in T-Anxiety scores was not significant ($t = 0.77$). But the S-Anxiety scores of the better educated draftees in the selection condition were still much higher than the S-Anxiety of the students in the non-stressful classroom condition ($t = 3.04$, $p < 0.0025$).

The norms for the psychiatric patients were obtained by individual administration of the STAI-DY just before, or just after, their consultation with a psychiatrist or a psychotherapist. The samples consisted of 151 psychiatric outpatients and 39 in-patients. Presumably the condition of the patient, as well as the testing conditions, predisposed these patients to higher levels of state and trait anxiety. The statistics for the psychiatric samples are summarized in Table 3.

The mean anxiety scores for the psychiatric patients were substantially higher on T-Anxiety than for the students and the draftees. The anxiety scores of the in-patients were higher on the average than for the out-patients. It is also interesting to note that the mean S-Anxiety scores of the in-patients decreased more on re-testing than those for the out-patients, which was consistent with the hypothesis that state anxiety decreases during a period of hospitalization suggesting that the in-patients experienced anxiety more frequently and more intensely in the past than the out-patients. The fact that patients with anxiety diagnoses scored higher

Table 3 STAI-DY means, standard deviations, and alpha reliabilities
for psychiatric patients

	Psychiatric out-patients		Psychiatric in-patients	
	M	F	M	F
S-Anxiety				
N	65	86	18	21
Mean	50.6	50.5	57.6	56.2
SD	12.9	12.5	10.7	13.0
Alpha	0.93	0.93	0.90	0.95
T-Anxiety				
N	65	86	18	21
Mean	52.0	51.3	60.4	57.3
SD	12.4	11.0	7.0	13.1
Alpha	0.93	0.91	0.73	0.95

on T-Anxiety than those without this diagnosis provides additional evidence of the
construct validity of the Dutch STAI-DY.

RELIABILITY OF THE STAI–DY

Given the fact that state anxiety is influenced by situational-stress, S-Anxiety
scores are expected to fluctuate over time, whereas T-Anxiety scores are relatively
stable and impervious to situational-stress (Spielberger, 1972). The test-retest
reliabilities are less useful for S-Anxiety measures than statistics that assess internal
consistency, such as Cronbach's alpha (α). The alpha-reliabilities for the Dutch
STAI-DY S-Anxiety, reported in Tables 1, 2, and 3, for the normative groups
varied between 0.87 and 0.92 in the student groups, between 0.85 and 0.91 in the
draftees groups, and between 0.90 and 0.95 in patient groups and were considered
satisfactory for all groups. The internal consistency for the trait anxiety subscale
varied from 0.87 to 0.92 (students), from 0.84 to 0.90 (draftees), and from 0.73
to 0.95 (patients), and were also satisfactory.

The item-remainder correlations for the individual Dutch STAI-DY items (not
reported in this paper, but summarized in the test manual) provide evidence that
each individual S-Anxiety and T-Anxiety item was correlated highly with the total
score for the subscale. For both samples (students and patients), all item-remainder
correlations were 0.30 and above, and most correlations were 0.50 and above.
Although the median item-remainder correlations for the draftees were somewhat
lower than for the student or patient groups, the item-remainders for draftees with
an average level of education were similar to those of the students.

The differences that were found in the item-remainder correlations for the
"anxiety-present" items were of particular interest, demonstrating that some items
were more adequate in the lower range of anxiety, while others were better in the
higher range. Spielberger et al. (1970) have referred to this phenomenon as "item-
intensity specificity." They emphasize the need to include items that cover the
entire range of anxiety in order to be able to use the same with diverse groups such
as students and patients.

Due to the fact that the STAI-DY was developed so recently, no test-retest

Table 6 Effects of examination stress in state and trait anxiety for medical students

	State anxiety		Trait anxiety	
	Lecture situation "nonstress"	Examination situation "stress"	Lecture situation "nonstress"	Examination situation "stress"
Males ($N = 85$)				
Mean	34.3	43.4	33.9	33.6
SD	7.5	9.9	7.5	7.9
Females ($N = 45$)				
Mean	33.3	45.6	36.6	35.6
SD	6.4	12.4	6.9	7.3
Total group ($N = 130$)				
Mean	34.0	44.2	34.8	34.3
SD	7.1	10.8	7.3	7.7

results are presented in Table 6, in which it can be noted that the mean trait anxiety scores were about the same in both conditions. In contrast the mean state anxiety scores during the examination were substantially higher than at the time of the lecture.

In a comparable group of 85 male medical students, 76 (89 percent) had higher state anxiety scores during an examination, 2 remained at the same level, and 7 students had lower scores. For a group of 45 female medical students, 37 (82 percent) had higher state anxiety scores, 6 had lower scores, and 2 remained unchanged. The mean trait anxiety scores for females was somewhat higher than for the males, and the increase in state anxiety was also slightly greater for the females. The differences between groups (males vs. females) and conditions (stress vs. non-stress) were tested by means of analysis of variance (ANOVA, mixed design with repeated measures). The ANOVA for S-Anxiety resulted in a highly significant main effect for conditions ($F(1, 130) = 107.2, p < 0.001$); there were no other statistically significant effects. For T-Anxiety there was no sex difference, nor did conditions influence the T-Anxiety scores.

Additional evidence for the validity of the STAI-D was obtained by Van der Ploeg (1980b) in a study of two groups of general practice patients. One group had regular contact with their G.P. family doctor; the other group consulted the G.P. less frequently. The group of patients that had the higher consultation rate also had higher mean trait ($t = 3.3, p < 0.01$) and state ($t = 2.4, p < 0.05$) anxiety scores than patients with relatively low or zero consultation rate (see Table 7).

In order to evaluate the concurrent validity of the Dutch STAI, Pearson corre-

Table 7 STAI scores of general practice patients related to consultation rate

	State anxiety		Trait anxiety	
	Infrequent consultation	Frequent consultation	Infrequent consultation	Frequent consultation
N	206	178	201	172
Mean	34.8	37.3	34.0	36.7
SD	9.8	10.4	8.5	8.9

lations were computed with other Dutch inventories that could be regarded as measures of trait anxiety. These correlations have been presented in the STAI-DY Test Manual and will not be reported in this paper. The STAI-DY T-Anxiety scale was more highly correlated with other trait anxiety measures than the S-Anxiety scale. The correlations with other personality measures provide evidence of concurrent and discriminant validity of the STAI-DY State and Trait anxiety scales.

CURRENT RESEARCH WITH THE DUTCH STAI

Several research projects have been initiated in which the Dutch STAI-DY was utilized. One of these involves research with the Dutch STAI in the field of test anxiety and the relationship between anxiety and academic performance. In a study carried out with medical students in their second year at the University of Leyden, a significant negative correlation was found between trait anxiety and grades for the eight courses taken by these students.

In a second study with another group of medical students, described in more detail by Van der Ploeg (1979), students with high trait anxiety had lower grades than low anxiety students. For the females, the mean grades for students with lower and higher trait anxiety were 53.0 and 48.6, respectively; for the males these means were 51.6 and 47.8, respectively, for students with low and high trait anxiety.

In another project, described in detail in the STAI-DY Test Manual, a negative correlation was found between trait anxiety and level of education. It has also been found that Dutch females have higher anxiety scores than males, and that older people (41 years and above) have higher anxiety scores than younger persons. From these results, it may be concluded that less educated women have the highest anxiety scores and younger, more educated men have the lowest scores. Such findings demonstrate the importance of consulting the proper age and sex-reference groups, and reporting the exact number of male and female subjects under study, their approximate levels of education, and their ages. Otherwise, differences in research outcomes may stem from population differences with regard to sex, age, and level of education.

REFERENCES

Bremer, J. J. C. B. *Vreesvragenlijst van Wolpe en Lang* (adaptation of the by Wolpe and Lazarus in 1966 published scale) (unpublished), 1968.
Cuppens, I. W. Th. *Test Anxiety Scale for Children* (adaptation of the by Sarason designed scale) (unpublished), 1967.
Documentatie van Tests en Testresearch in Nederland—1974. N.I.P., Amsterdam, 1974.
Eijkman, M. A. J. & Orlebeke, J. F., De factor "angst" in de tandheelkundige situatie. *Nederlands Tijdschrift voor Tandheelkunde*, 1975, *82*, 114–123.
Nie, N. H., Hull, C. H., Jenkins, J. G., Steinbrenner, K., & Bent, D. H., *SPSS, Statistical Package for the Social Sciences*, New York: McGraw-Hill, 1975.
Ploeg, H. M. van der, Relationship of state-trait anxiety to academic performance in Dutch medical students. *Psychological Reports*, 1975, *45*, 223–227.
Ploeg, H. M. van der, Validatie van de Zelf-Beoordelings Vragenlijst (een nederlandstalige bewerking van de Spielberger State-Trait Anxiety Inventory). *Nederlands Tijdschrift voor de Psychologie*, 1980, *35*, 243–249. (a)
Ploeg, H. M. van der, *Persoonlijkheid en medische consumptie. Een onderzoek naar de relatie van persoonlijkheidsfactoren en de frequentie van huisartsbezoek.* Academisch proefschrift Universiteit van Amsterdam. Lisse: Swets en Zeitlinger, 1980. (b)

Ploeg, H. M. van der, Defares, P. B., & Spielberger, C. D., *Zelf-Beoordelings Vragenlijst. STAI-versie DY-1 en versie DY-2*. Lisse: Swets en Zeitlinger, 1979.

Ploeg, H. M. van der, Defares, P. B., & Spielberger, C. D., *Handleiding bij de Zelf-Beoordelings Vragenlijst, ZBV. Een Nederlandstalige Bewerking van de Spielberger State-Trait Anxiety Inventory, STAI-DY*. Lisse: Swets en Zeitlinger, 1980.

Spielberger, C. D., Theory and research on anxiety. In C. D. Spielberger (ed.), *Anxiety and Behavior*. New York: Academic Press, 1966, pp. 3-20.

Spielberger, C. D., Anxiety as an emotional state. In C. D. Spielberger (ed.), *Anxiety, Current Trends in Theory and Research*, vol. 1. New York: Academic Press, 1972, pp. 23-49.

Spielberger, C. D., *The State-Trait Anxiety Inventory—Form Y* (publication in preparation), 1980.

Spielberger, C. D., Gorsuch, R. L., & Lushene, R. E., *Manual for the State-Trait Anxiety Inventory*. Palo Alto, Calif.: Consulting Psychologists Press, 1970.

Spruit, I. P., Van Kampen-Donker, M., Ploeg, H. M. van der, De Lezenne Coulander, C., Obermann-de Boer, G. L., & Van Nieuwenhuijzen, M. G., Opkomstgedrag bij bevolkingsonderzoek op borstkanker in Leiden. *Tijdschrift voor Sociale Geneeskunde*, 1979, *57*, 784-795.

Willems, L. F. M., Tuender-de Haan, H. A., & Defares, P. B., Een schaal om sociale angst te meten. *Nederlands Tijdschrift voor de Psychologie*, 1973, *28*, 415-422.

11

Anxiety Induced by Ego- and Physical Threat

Preliminary Validation of a Dutch Adaptation of Spielberger's State-Trait Anxiety Inventory for Children (STAIC)

F. C. Bakker and P. C. W. van Wieringen
Vrije Universiteit, Amsterdam

INTRODUCTION

The present study was designed to validate a Dutch adaptation of the State-Trait Anxiety Inventory for Children (STAIC) (Spielberger, Edwards, Lushene, Montouri, & Platzek, 1973). The STAIC consists of two 20-item scales for measuring state and trait anxiety. State anxiety (A-State) refers to the emotional reactions that are evoked in individuals who interpret specific situations as personally threatening. These reactions are characterized by "feelings of tension and apprehension, and by heightened autonomic nervous system activity" (Spielberger, 1972, pp. 30–31).

Trait anxiety (A-Trait) refers to relatively stable individual differences in anxiety proneness. Persons who are high in A-Trait are more disposed, ". . . to perceive a wide range of stimulus situations as dangerous or threatening, and to respond to such threats with A-State reactions" (Spielberger, 1972, p. 39). Spielberger's (1966, 1972, 1977) theory of anxiety assumes that the level of A-State is determined by the interaction of trait anxiety and situational characteristics. According to Endler, Magnusson, Ekehammar, and Okada (1976) and Spielberger (1966, 1977), trait-anxiety scales are especially suited for the prediction of state anxiety in ego-threatening circumstances.

In order to obtain information on the reliability and validity of a newly developed Dutch adaptation of the STAIC, this scale was administered in several different situations. The Dutch STAIC A-Trait and A-State scales were given in two neutral situations, and the A-State scale was also administered during ego-threat and physically threatening situations. This procedure permitted the computation of test-retest correlations under neutral conditions and trait-state correlations under two types of stress conditions. Trait anxiety was also assessed by two existing Dutch tests, Wilde's (1967) ABV-K and Hermans' (1969) PMT-K, which were administered to evaluate the concurrent validity of the STAIC.

METHOD

The subjects were 55 male pupils from two Dutch primary schools. They were 11 or 12 years old at the time they participated in the study. It was not possible for all of the children to be present during all four testing situations. Therefore, the computations are based on different subsamples of the total group.

The children completed the following three questionnaires: (a) The Dutch adaptation of Spielberger et al.'s (1973) State-Trait Anxiety Inventory for Children, which was developed by the authors in cooperation with two Anglists; (b) A Dutch test for debilitating fear of failure, viz. the F⁻ scale of Hermans' (1969) PMT-K; and (c) A Dutch test for neuroticism, viz. the N scale of Wilde's (1967) ABV-K.

The children were tested under four different conditions. In the first testing session ("Neutral 1"), the children were given the STAIC State and Trait Anxiety scales, the F⁻ scale of the PMT-K, and the N scale of the ABV-K in this order in their own classroom. The STAIC was readministered in the same locality, four weeks later ("Neutral 2").

During the third testing session ("Jump"), which occurred two weeks after the second session, the State Anxiety scale was administered just before the subjects had to jump from a 3-meter diving board into a swimming pool. This requirement was meant to pose a physical threat to the children, who were asked to report if they had previously jumped either more or less than five times before they participated in the present experiment. Of the 55 subjects, 48 participated in this condition.

The fourth testing session took place one week after the third session. The State Anxiety scale was administered to the 41 subjects who participated in this condition just before starting a written "school test paper." This condition was intended to be a threat to the students' self-esteem (ego-threat).

RESULTS

Reliability of the STAIC

The test-retest reliability for the Dutch STAIC A-Trait scale obtained over a four-week period in the two neutral conditions was 0.71 ($n = 54$). This coefficient was of the same order of magnitude as the test-retest stability coefficients reported by Spielberger et al. (1973). viz. 0.65, the latter being based on a group of 132 boys and a test-retest interval of six weeks.

The homogeneity indices (alpha coefficients) for the A-Trait and A-State scales in the "Neutral" conditions are reported in Table 1, along with the alpha coefficients obtained by Spielberger et al. (1973). It may be concluded that the test-

Table 1 Alpha-coefficients for the STAIC A-Trait and A-State scales in neutral conditions

	Neutral 1	Neutral 2	Spielberger[a]
Trait	0.80	0.81	0.78
State	0.74	0.74	0.82

[a]Reported by Spielberger et al. (1973).

Table 2 Means and standard deviations for the STAIC A-State scores in four testing situations and for the A-Trait scores in two neutral conditions

	A-State		A-Trait	
	Mean	SD	Mean	SD
Neutral 1	29.2	3.07	30.7	5.56
Neutral 2	28.9	2.95	29.9	5.19
"Exam"	31.5	4.34		
"Jump"	29.8	5.85		

retest reliability and the homogeneity of the Dutch A-Trait scale was very close to the values reported for the English Form by Spielberger et al. in the STAIC Test Manual.

The test-retest correlation for the Dutch STAIC A-State scale in the neutral conditions was 0.54 ($n = 54$) as compared to a test-retest correlation of 0.31 reported by Spielberger et al. (1973). Since A-State scores are expected to fluctuate from situation to situation, test-retest correlations are not useful as a reliability index; the alpha coefficient is more suited for this purpose. The alpha coefficients for the A-State scales during "Neutral 1," "Neutral 2," "Jump," and "Exam" were 0.74, 0.74, 0.87, and 0.92, respectively. During "Neutral 2," items 2 and 11 were non-discriminating: therefore, for this condition, computation of alpha was based on 18 of the 20 items. Spielberger et al. (1973) report an alpha of 0.82 for a neutral condition. The finding of greater homogeneity (higher alphas) for A-State in threatening situations as compared with neutral situations was also reported by Spielberger et al. (1970) for the STAI. It may be concluded that the reliability indices for both the A-Trait and A-State scale are acceptable and similar in magnitude to those reported by Spielberger et al. (1973).

Validity of the STAIC

Evidence for the construct validity of the STAIC A-State scale may be derived from comparisons of the scores obtained in the stressful and non-stressful situations of the present study. Means and standard deviations for the A-State and A-Trait scores in the two neutral conditions, the "Exam" condition and the "Jump" condition are reported in Table 2.

A one-way analysis of variance of the data for the A-State scale indicated that the differences between the means were statistically significant ($F = 3.52$, $df = 3/194$, $p < 0.05$). A Student Newman-Keuls post hoc analysis demonstrated that the A-State scores during the "Exam" condition were significantly higher ($p < 0.05$) than during the two neutral conditions. There were no significant differences, however, between the A-State means for the "Jump" condition and the neutral conditions.

In the "Jump" condition, it is important to distinguish between subjects with more experience (five or more jumps from the diving board) and those with less experience (fewer than five jumps). It might be expected that less experienced subjects ($n = 26$) would be higher in A-State in the "Jump" condition than the more experienced subjects ($n = 22$). This expectation was supported by the finding that the

A-State mean of 31.7 for the less experienced subjects in the "Jump" condition was significantly higher than the mean of 27.6 for the more experienced subjects in this condition ($t = 2.53$, $df = 46$, $p < 0.01$). The mean A-Trait scores for the experienced and inexperienced subjects were 31.5 and 30.2 in the Neutral 1 condition, and 30.4 and 29.2 in Neutral 2. Thus, the differences in the A-State scores cannot be attributed to differences in A-Trait.

Correlations between scores on the A-Trait scale, the F^- scale and the N scale that provide evidence of the concurrent validity of the Dutch STAIC are reported in Table 3. The correlations between the A-Trait and Neuroticism scales were approximately the same as the test-retest reliability of the A-Trait scale. The moderately high correlations between these scales and the comparability of item-content suggest that both scales measure the same construct. Although the correlations between A-Trait and F^- are somewhat lower, these correlations are of the same magnitude as those reported by Sarason et al. (1960) between a general trait anxiety measure and debilitating anxiety, and somewhat higher than the relationships reported by Hermans (1971).

Correlations between STAIC A-State scores and scores on the A-Trait, N, and F^- scales for the 35 children who participated in all four experimental conditions are reported in Table 4. The following conclusions may be drawn from these correlations:

1. The A-State scores were positively correlated with the A-Trait, N, and F^- scores.

2. In the "Exam" condition, the strongest relationship was between A-State and F^- ($r = 0.42$). This finding was compatible with Hermans' (1971) interpretation of high F^- scores as reflecting anxiety reactions in typical test situations.

3. The correlations between the A-State and A-Trait scores in the "Exam" condition were lower than in the Neutral conditions. A similar result was published by Spielberger et al. (1970) without interpretation. These findings are contrary to Spielberger's (1972, 1977) and Endler et al.'s (1976) hypothesis that A-Trait scales are especially suited for predicting anxiety reactions in ego-threatening situations.

As previously noted, the mean A-State score for inexperienced subjects in the "Jump" condition was significantly higher than for the experienced subjects, suggesting that only the inexperienced subjects showed increased anxiety. For the "Jump" condition, correlates between the A-State scores and scores on the A-Trait, N, and F^- scales for the experienced and inexperienced subjects are reported in Table 5, in which it can be noted that these correlations were only significant for the inexperienced subjects. These findings appear to contradict Spielberger et al.'s

Table 3 Correlations between the A-Trait scores the F^- scores and the Neuroticism scores for 54 children

	A-Trait (neutral 2)	N	F^-
A-Trait (neutral 1)	0.71***	0.72***	0.60***
A-Trait (neutral 2)		0.71***	0.59***
N			0.45***

***$p < 0.001$.

Table 4 Correlations between STAIC A-State scores and A-Trait, F^- and N scores in the four testing situations

	Trait (neutral 1)	Trait (neutral 2)	F^-	N
A-State scores				
Neutral 1	0.53***	0.35*	0.13	0.43**
Neutral 2	0.31*	0.24	0.24	0.27
"Exam"	0.23	0.26	0.42**	0.16
"Jump"	0.20	0.37*	0.29	0.36*

*$p < 0.05$.
**$p < 0.01$.
***$p < 0.001$.

(1970) hypothesis that changes in A-State evoked by threats of physical danger are unrelated to level of A-Trait. However, the results would be consistent with Spielberger's theory if the "Jump" situation constitutes a threat to self-esteem for the inexperienced subjects who are more likely to be afraid to jump and to feel shame and ridicule from their peers if they fail to jump.

DISCUSSION

The results concerning the reliability and construct validity of the preliminary Dutch adaptation of the STAIC are encouraging, especially when one takes note of the many problems that may arise when testing children by means of self-ratings. Not only are children inclined to respond in a socially desirable way (Sarason et al., 1960), but there is also the possibility that "the child's linguistic skills have not developed to a point where they could serve adequately in the role of observer of his own behavior" (Lang, 1976, p. 17).

The satisfying results of the present study notwithstanding, it would seem that changes in the preliminary form of the Dutch STAIC are necessary. First, the power of the A-State scale in discriminating between different situations seems rather weak and has to be improved. Secondly, in the "Neutral 2" condition, two of the A-State items did not discriminate and will have to be replaced by more sensitive items.

Interpreting the present findings in the framework of Spielberger's Trait-State Anxiety Theory leads to two difficulties: Whereas Spielberger predicts that A-Trait measures predict state anxiety in response to ego-threat and not to physical threat, the results of the present study show an opposite trend. This was especially true

Table 5 Correlations between STAIC A-State scores and A-Trait, F^- and N scores in the "Jump" condition, for the inexperienced ($n = 26$) and the experienced group ($n = 22$)

	Trait (neutral 1)	Trait (neutral 2)	F^-	N
A-State ("Jump")				
Inexperienced	0.36*	0.48**	0.40*	0.56***
Experienced	0.26	0.22	0.32	0.08

*$p < 0.05$.
**$p < 0.01$.
***$p < 0.001$.

for subjects inexperienced in jumping from the diving board, who might therefore be expected to be more afraid than the experienced subjects. The correlations between A-Trait and A-State for these subjects were higher for the physically threatening "Jump" condition than for the "Exam" condition (see Tables 4 and 5). It might be argued, however, that that jump situation was ego-threatening ("shame" about one's fear) as well as a physical danger. A greater elevation in A-State would then be expected for the high A-Trait subjects and the results would be consistent with Spielberger's theory.

The second difficulty arises in connection with Spielberger's suggestion that A-Trait predicts the *intensity* of anxiety states in ego-threatening situations. Accordingly, higher correlations between trait and state anxiety scores would be expected for the "Exam" situation than for the Neutral situations, an expectation which was not confirmed by our data. It is perhaps worth noting that Spielberger himself presented results on adult subjects which are compatible with those in the present study, viz. correlations for males varying from 0.51 to 0.67 during neutral, and from 0.37 to 0.67 during threatening conditions, while the figures for women vary between 0.44 and 0.55, and 0.11 and 0.53, respectively (Spielberger et al., 1970).

While only very tentative conclusions can be based on results of a small validation study, these findings might have important implications for Spielberger's anxiety theory if future research bears them out. In this respect, we might note that it is not logically compelling to expect that *frequency* of anxiety experiences (as measured by A-Trait) should predict *intensity* of state anxiety in threatening situations.

REFERENCES

Endler, N. S., Magnusson, D., Ekehammar, B., & Okada, M. The multi-dimensionality of state and trait-anxiety. *Scandinavian Journal of Psychology*, 1976, *17*, 81–96.

Hermans, H. J. M. *Prestatie Motivatie Test voor Kinderen* (test-boekje). Amsterdam: Swets & Zeitlinger, 1969.

Hermans, H. J. M. *Prestatiemotief en faalangst in gezin en onderwijs.* Amsterdam: Swets & Zeitlinger, 1971.

Lang, P. J. The psychophysiology of anxiety. Paper presented at Studiedagen Post Academisch Onderwijs, Psychologie, NIP, Amersfoort, 1976.

Sarason, S. B., Davidson, K. S., Lighthall, F. F., Waite, R. R., & Ruebush, B. K. *Anxiety in elementary school children.* New York: Wiley, 1960.

Spielberger, C. D. Theory and research on anxiety. In C. D. Spielberger (ed.), *Anxiety and behavior.* New York: Academic Press, 1966.

Spielberger, C. D. Anxiety as an emotional state. In C. D. Spielberger (ed.), *Anxiety, current trends in theory and research*, vol. 1. London: Academic Press, 1972.

Spielberger, C. D. State-trait anxiety and interactional psychology. In D. Magnusson & N. S. Endler (eds.), *Personality at the crossroads: Current issues in interactional psychology.* Hillsdale, N.J.: Lawrence Erlbaum Associates, 1977.

Spielberger, C. D., Gorsuch, R. L., & Lushene, R. E. *The State-trait anxiety inventory* (test manual). Palo Alto, Calif.: Consulting Psychologists Press, 1970.

Spielberger, C. D., Edwards, C. D., Lushene, R. E., Montouri, J., & Platzek, D. *Preliminary manual for the state-trait anxiety inventory for children.* Palo Alto, Calif.: Consulting Psychologists Press, 1973.

Wilde, G. J. & Dijl, H. van. *Handleiding bij de ABV-K.* Amsterdam: Van Rossum, 1967.

IV

STRESS AND THE CARDIOVASCULAR SYSTEM

12

Breathing to the Heart of the Matter

Effects of Respiratory Influences upon Cardiovascular Phenomena

P. Grossman
Institute for Stress Research,
Wageningen, The Netherlands

P. B. Defares
University of Wageningen, The Netherlands

INTRODUCTION

The cardiovascular system has long attracted the attention of psychologists and psychophysiologists. Various cardiovascular measures, such as heart rate, blood pressure, and regional blood flow have been utilized in attempts to index psychological arousal, emotional states and cognitive processes, and certain investigators have focused upon the operant control of these cardiovascular response systems (Hassett, 1978). Most recently, much interest has been generated concerning the roles that psychological stressors and anxiety may play in the development of hypertension and heart disease (Glass, 1977). With few exceptions, the great majority of psychophysiological investigations in these areas have largely refrained from exploring cardiac interactions and relationships with the respiratory system which forms a crucial interdependent link with cardiovascular phenomena.

This paper will attempt to show that consideration of respiratory parameters may shed new light on current issues in cardiovascular psychophysiology. Specifically, we will consider the interplay of respiratory and cardiovascular processes with regard to two different but possibly related concerns of the area: Cardiac attentional responses and stress-related cardiovascular disease.

RESPIRATORY INFLUENCES UPON CARDIOVASCULAR PHYSIOLOGICAL FUNCTIONING

In order to better understand the close connection between respiratory and cardiovascular processes, one need only glance at a diagram of the two systems (Fig. 1): The heart and lungs, in fact, could easily be thought of as one higher order system represented by a knot directly tying the left and right chambers of the heart firmly to the lungs via the pulmonary vessels. In its journey from the right to the left chambers of the heart, the body's blood must perfuse the capillary system of the lungs where wastes are removed and oxygen is replaced. It would

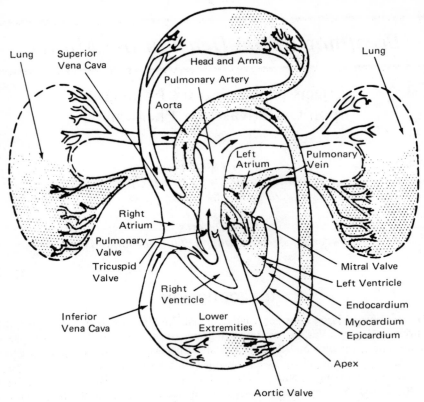

Figure 1   Diagram of the respiratory and cardiovascular systems.

seem inevitable in such closely intertwined structures that mechanical and chemical alterations in one system would affect those of the other. Indeed, physiologists have discovered special relationships between lung inflation, intrathoracic pressure, and cardiovascular hemodynamics, and it is one of the oldest doctrines of physiology that the pumping action of respiration forces the blood into and out of the chest (Richards, 1965). Yet, typically, either the respiratory system has been entirely ignored in cardiovascular psychophysiological studies, or has been relegated to the status of a control variable. In the latter case a cursory measure of respiration rate is usually used to reflect the functioning of the entire respiratory system (Lacey, 1967; Lang, 1974).

The historical reasons for the exclusion of respiration from the empirical repertoire of contemporary psychophysiology are not entirely clear, and a discussion of this topic is well beyond the scope of this presentation. However, it is our point of view that in order to understand the psychophysiology of the cardiovascular system, it is essential to investigate cardiovascular-respiratory interactions, with a specific emphasis upon the influences that different respiratory parameters may have upon cardiovascular function. There is evidence, for example, to suggest that certain cardiovascular patterns used to index psychological processes, such as the cardiac orienting response, may be epiphenomenal to respiratory alterations.

Likewise, there are other lines of evidence indicating that specific respiratory processes may play a mediating role between psychological stressors and particular kinds of stress-related cardiovascular disease.

Before attempting to deal with specific issues, it may be useful to review what is known about the effects of respiration and respiratory acts upon cardiovascular function (Richards, 1965; Sharpey-Schafer, 1965). In reviewing the literature in this area, it becomes clear that, despite large gaps of knowledge, there are certain well-established phenomena that may be of interest to cardiovascular researchers. These relate to both tonic and phasic alterations in cardiovascular processes that accompany the carrying out of particular respiratory patterns and maneuvers.

First, hyperventilation is a pattern of respiratory activity characterized by an increased ventilatory response which has the affect of both lowering the arterial level of pressure of carbon dioxide in the blood and altering pH. This, in turn, brings about a constriction of cerebral and skin blood vessels and dilatation of muscle vessels, while increasing heart rate, cardiac output, and the probability of cardiac dysrhythmias.

Another respiratory pattern marked by very deep inspirations, but not necessarily hyperventilatory in nature, is known to increase both heart rate and heart rate variability. Blood flow to the hands and feet is diminished while there is also an increase in blood flow to the skeletal muscles and forehead (Abramson, 1967; Royer, 1966; Stern & Anschel, 1968).

Several studies have reported another pattern of breathing, characterized by a both slow and deep diaphragmatic style of ventilation that reduces peripheral systolic blood pressure (Datey, Deshmukh, Dalvi, & Vinekar, 1969; Goldman & Lee, 1978; Tirala, 1952). It is also well-established that this slow, deep respiration pattern increases heart rate variability and the relative level of parasympathetic control of the cardiovascular system; we will return to this point later. Furthermore, deep diaphragmatic breathing appears to decrease cardiac output, while a more shallow thoracic mode of breathing seems to increase it (Krogh & Lindhard, 1912).

There are also several respiratory maneuvers which bring about dramatic cardiovascular changes, and these maneuvers may often form an integral part of specific breathing patterns. Breathholding, for example, has been found to induce large, rapid heart rate decelerations: a 20-beat-per-minute decrease has been observed in different studies to occur within one or two beats of breathholding, most of the deceleration taking place between pairs of beats (Furedy & Poulos, 1975; Laird & Fenz, 1971). Many individuals take substantial pauses during most breathing cycles, and such pauses may bring about large fluctuations in heart rate. Other frequently occurring respiratory maneuvers with more or less well-known effects upon the cardiovascular system include gasping, coughing, sighing, and the Valsalva response (Sharpey-Schafer, 1965).

Perhaps the best known of respiratory effects upon cardiovascular function is the phenomenon of respiratory sinus arrhythmia in which heart rate varies with phase of respiration (Clynes, 1960). Simply stated, heart rate is typically observed to accelerate during inspiratory phase and decelerate during expiratory phase (although this relationship is not invariant and depends on specific parameters of the breathing pattern). These respiratory linked variations in heart rate have been tied to parasympathetic autonomic control and seem to diminish with increasing age and infirmity (Hellman & Stacy, 1976; Johnston, 1980).

Various authors present evidence supporting the position that respiratory sinus arrhythmia reflects the level of balance in the autonomic nervous system between sympathetic and parasympathetic components. It has also been suggested that sinus arrhythmia may be used as a noninvasive quantitative measure of parasympathetic cardiac control and that the degree of sinus arrhythmia is negatively correlated with the occurrence and risk of cardiovascular disease (Johnston, 1980; Katona & Jih, 1975). Sinus arrhythmic heart rate variation is a frequency- dependent phenomenon, and seems to be maximized at a respiratory frequency of approximately six breathing cycles per minute among adults (Hellman & Stacy, 1976). Shallow and/or rapid breathing, on the other hand, induces a response of decreased cardiac signal variability (Sroufe, 1971; Sroufe & Morris, 1973), which is likely to be indicative of increased sympathetic dominance.

On the basis of our brief review of the literature, it can be seen that various respiratory parameters—including rate and depth of respiration, phase of cycle, alterations in arterial CO_2 pressure and breathholding—have been substantially implicated as significant influences upon cardiovascular function. These effects are produced by three general mechanisms (Richards, 1965): The first involves effects due to altered pulmonary, thoracic, and abdominal mechanics, mainly resulting from changes of pressure, position, and movement. The second includes chemical changes taking place in the blood and tissue due to such factors as alterations in blood levels of respiratory gases, i.e., O_2, CO_2, and altered blood concentrations of epinephrine, norepinephrine, and other hormonal substances. The third mechanism involves reflex effects on the heart and circulation produced by the first two mechanisms.

What all this then demonstrates is that the cardiovascular system is indeed quite responsive to a host of respiratory alterations. And because this area of concern has been to date inadequately researched—that is to say, research has not addressed many of the effects of respiratory parameters upon cardiovascular function nor various respiratory-cardiovascular interactions—there is a possibility that even more profound and probably more complex linkages between the two systems may yet be discovered. There is already sufficient information, however, to entertain seriously the manner in which respiratory mechanisms might be involved in phenomena traditionally investigated in cardiovascular psychophysiology. Let us take attentional responses as our first example.

RESPIRATION AND CARDIAC INDICES OF COGNITIVE PROCESSING

It is common knowledge that an unexpected stimulus suddenly entering one's sensory field may "take our breath away," that is, may cause us momentarily to cease breathing. The actual nature of the stimulus, its modality, intensity, and temporal patterning—and our affective ties to it—are all likely to influence the manner by which we respond respiratorily and "catch our breath." A beautiful landscape just happened upon is likely to produce a more profound respiratory alteration than a mild but novel auditory stimulus. A frightening, unexpected, abrupt burst of light might make one gasp while a display of anticipated fireworks will usually evoke a more gentle cessation of breathing. Each one of us is at least crudely aware of the more dramatic of these respiratory changes that occur from time to time. However, we are remarkably unaware of the more subtle respiratory shifts that take place in our everyday lives, both in terms of a subjective conscious experience of them and an empirical knowledge of their significance for cognitive functioning. Moreover, there has been relatively little research on how respiratory alterations in response to environmental stimuli may influence and interact with other physiological parameters, such as cardiac measures.

There is substantial evidence from the psychological and physiological literature to indicate that phasic alterations in respiratory pattern to environmental stimuli may contribute to the cardiac orienting response (see Fig. 2). This cardiac orienting response is characterized by a brief but marked heart rate deceleration to a novel stimulus. Several studies have reported immediate respiratory inhibition followed by increased respiratory amplitude and decreased respiratory frequency to simple visual and auditory stimuli. It has also been noted that phasic respiratory pauses to novel stimuli habituate with stimulus repetition (Barry, 1978; Davis, 1957; Davis, Buchwald, & Frankmann, 1955; Rousey, 1979). These respiratory shifts closely parallel heart rate changes to similar stimuli and suggest that phasic alterations in breathing may at least partially account for the cardiac decelerative phenomenon, since, as previously noted, cessation of breathing produces rapid and substantial heart rate deceleration. Respiration has received very little interest in orienting-response studies in the past (Barry, 1977), and would seem to provide an exciting new avenue for exploration.

Another related subject, perhaps more directly connected to the notion of psychological stress, concerns the effects of sustained attentional tasks and informational loads upon the respiratory and cardiovascular systems. Skaggs (1930) was one of the first investigators to study the effects of mental activity on respiratory pattern. He found that subjects during a mental multiplication task breathed more rapidly and shallowly than during quiet relaxation. Consistent with these early findings, more recent research has reported that there is partial or complete inhibition of respiration during momentary attention, but with continuous mental work, breathing quickens and becomes more shallow (Porges & Raskin, 1969; Woodworth & Schlossberg, 1954). Other studies have found that, with increasing informational load and task difficulty, respiration rate also increased (e.g., Coles, 1972; Mulder, 1980).

Respiratory changes in response to tasks that require sustained mental effort seem to parallel cardiac responses, as diagrammed in Fig. 3. With increasing mental load and sustained attentional tasks, it has been consistently found that heart rate

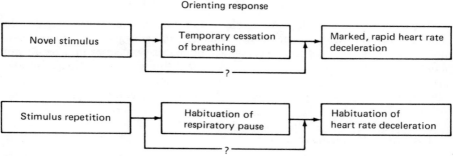

Figure 2   Orienting responses.

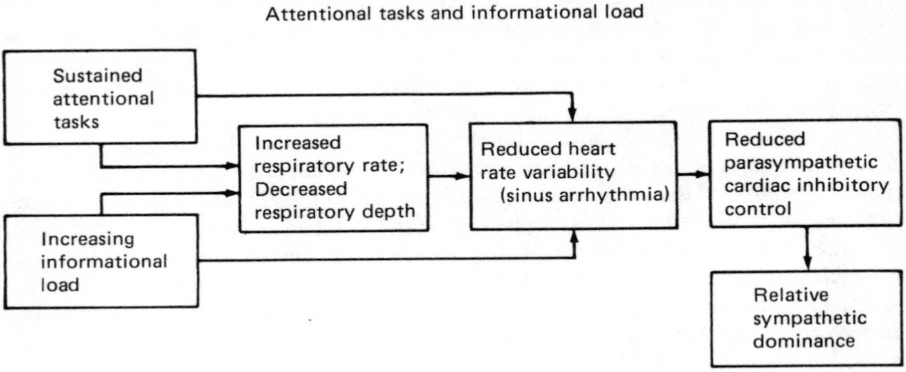

Attentional tasks and informational load

Figure 3 Attentional tasks and informational level.

variability decreased (see Mulder, 1980). Given the evidence we have concerning reductions in cardiac signal variability resulting from increases in respiratory rate and decreases in depth of respiration, it seems reasonable to suggest that the decrease in heart rate variability under these circumstances might be secondary to respiratory changes. Several studies provide empirical support for this position (Kalsbeek, 1967; Mulder, 1980; Sayers, 1975). We would also like to emphasize that we are not suggesting that all cardiac responses to attentional tasks are epiphenomenal to shifts in breathing pattern. The recent study by Mulder (1980) in The Netherlands points to the important role other factors also play. Nevertheless, our review clearly indicates the importance of respiratory influences upon the cardiac signal.

A decreased level of sinus arrhythmia thus seems to result from sustained attention and increasing informational load. This implies that the balance between parasympathetic and sympathetic autonomic systems is disturbed in such a manner that there is a loss of parasympathetic inhibitory control and a preponderance of sympathetic activity. Such physiological responses to mental effort will also be specifically dealt with later in our discussion of the Type A coronary prone behavior pattern.

BREATHING AND STRESS–RELATED
CARDIOVASCULAR DISEASE

The other main topic that we would like to deal with in this chapter pertains more directly to the main topic of this volume. What emerges from our review of the literature is the strong impression that respiratory processes may be directly implicated in the etiology of certain stress-related forms of cardiovascular disease. Here we will discuss respiration in relation to the development of essential hypertension and Friedman and Rosenman's (1974) Type A coronary prone behavior pattern.

Essential Hypertension

Hypertension is a chronic condition in which blood pressure is consistently elevated well above normal. In approximately 80 to 95 percent of the patients clinically diagnosed as hypertensive, there is no known cause for the disease; hence the classification "essential hypertension." It appears likely, however, that there are predisposing genetic and environmental factors. Furthermore, it is generally believed by many investigators that psychological stressors contribute to the development of at least some subset of cases of essential hypertension (Forsyth, 1974).

The consequences of this disease are by no means insignificant; they include substantially increased risks of cerebrovascular accidents, heart failure, coronary heart disease, and renal damage. Hypertension is progressive and long-term in nature. In early stages, a person's resting blood pressure may only sometimes be elevated above normal, and this condition is termed early labile hypertension. One must mention that such early labile blood pressure responses do not necessarily predestine an individual for later essential hypertension. However, they do significantly increase the probability of development of essential hypertension (Johnston, 1980).

The abnormal physiological patterning of early labile hypertension and the changes in that pattern among individuals who develop into essential hypertensives is both interesting and pertinent to our discussion. Early labile hypertensives as compared to normotensive controls exhibit increased O_2 consumption and a raised cardiac output (mainly due to an elevated heart rate), while their total peripheral resistance is normal (Eich, Cuddy, Smulyan, & Lyons, 1966; Lund-Johansen, 1967). A recent study (Johnston, 1980) provides strong evidence that early labile hypertensives show a much reduced respiratory sinus arrhythmia response, indicating abnormal reduction of parasympathetic control and increased sympathetic dominance. The transitional course to essential hypertension is one in which cardiac output, heart rate, and O_2 consumption gradually become more normal, but the peripheral resistance permanently increases to a dangerous level.

The atypical physiological patterning of the early labile hypertensive has only rarely been directly tied to respiratory function, but there are several reasons to believe that respiratory processes may play an important mediating role in the development of this syndrome. First, it is well established that there is a direct relation between oxygen consumption and minute ventilation (Bouhuys, 1974; Otis, 1964), thus implying that labile hypertensives, who show increased O_2 consumption, may be breathing at a faster rate and/or depth than normotensives. Secondly, the normal coupling of heart rate to respiratory phase, as seen with respiratory sinus arrhythmia, is substantially disturbed: Early labile hypertensives exhibit less heart rate variability tied to respiratory phase (Johnston, 1980). This fact, in combination with the increased oxygen consumption, further suggests that these individuals may be chronic rapid breathers since increased respiratory rate has repeatedly been shown to produce decreased variability of heart rate response (Clynes, 1960; Sroufe, 1971; Sroufe & Morris, 1973). It is also interesting to note that prolonged excessive breathing leads to a similar pattern of physiological responding as that seen with early labile hypertensives, i.e., increases in oxygen consumption, heart rate, and cardiac output (Richards, 1965; Sharpey-Schafer, 1965).

Another issue that needs to be considered is the contributory influence of psychological and environmental stressors to hypertension and how these tie in with breathing. If respiratory function represents one component of the total physiological patterning of early labile hypertension, it could be a major mediating physiological response system in the development of the syndrome. Both stress responses and anxiety have been associated with increased respiration rate (Lum, 1975; Matsumoto, 1977; Pfeffer, 1978; Skarbek, 1969; also see the last section of this chapter). Since increased respiration rate is known independently to induce rapid heart rate, increased cardiac output and decreased sinus arrhythmia, it seems plausible that respiratory processes may at least partially mediate the relationship between stress and hypertension in predisposed individuals.

The model that we are proposing suggests that respiratory processes play an important contributory role in the development of early labile and later essential hypertension among susceptible persons. Figure 4 attempts to clarify the model: Environmental and psychological stressors alter the respiratory pattern such that there is an increase in respiratory rate and minute ventilation volume. This increased respiratory response, probably in combination with other physiological processes, induces increased oxygen consumption, heart rate, and cardiac output. Respiratory sinus arrhythmia is diminished, causing decreased heart rate variability, a deficit in parasympathetic inhibitory cardiac control and, consequently, heightened sympathetic dominance and increased catecholamine production. The model also provides for the possibility that there are other physiological disturbances that interact with respiratory function so that each may contribute to the other. There may also be feedback loops from other components of the pattern that help to maintain disturbed respiratory function. Furthermore, we should like to stress that the model may hold only among susceptible individuals.

A final source of support for the central involvement of respiration in the etiology of essential hypertension comes from several studies which report that decreasing respiratory rate and increasing depth of respiration serve to reduce systolic blood pressure among both normo- and hypertensives (Datey et al., 1969; Goldman & Lee, 1978; Patel, 1973; Tirala, 1952). This evidence hence suggests that the respiratory process somehow fits into the total physiological pattern of

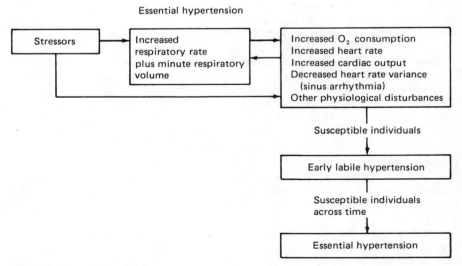

Figure 4 Essential hypertension.

early labile and essential hypertension in such a manner that respiratory alterations can effectively diminish the aberrant physiological responses producing high blood pressure.

In summary, we have presented a provocative and admittedly speculative hypothesis concerning the role of respiratory processes in the etiology of early labile and essential hypertension. We certainly recognize that there are many other factors besides respiration to consider. Our model is put forth as a heuristic device for considering ways in which respiratory phenomena can be investigated and integrated into a theoretical analysis of cardiovascular psychophysiology. Since our propositions can be subjected to empirical test, we shall be striving in our own research program to verify them.

Type A Behavior Pattern

It appears that there may be a link between chronic excessive ventilation and the Type A behavior pattern observed by Friedman and Rosenmann (1974) among individuals with an increased risk of coronary heart disease: Such individuals tend to be hostile or aggressive, are always worried about time, constantly engage in compulsive behaviors to ward off what they perceive to be threats, continually feel as though outside pressures are bearing down on them, and feel guilty about relaxing. In sum the Type A behavior pattern is one of perpetual restlessness, impatience, time consciousness, and compulsive striving.

In an early investigation, Friedman (1969) found that individuals generally exhibiting the Type A coronary-prone behavior pattern tended to sigh frequently, and this was included as one of the important evaluative criteria in a standard interview developed by Friedman and Rosenman to assess Type A behavior (Sparacino, 1979). Other central criteria used for the classification of subjects include speech that is clipped, staccato, and overly rapid and explosive.

Relating these speech peculiarities to respiratory variables is not difficult. There is in fact convergent evidence from both the physiological and psychological literature. First of all, frequent sighing is considered to be a hallmark of the chronic hyperventilation syndrome (Lum, 1975), which is characterized by an extremely rapid rate of breathing, often induced by psychological and environmental stressors. Several authors have reported frequent sighing among chronically and situationally anxious individuals who *also* display an increased respiratory rate (Finesinger, 1944; Heim, Knapp, Vachon, Globus, & Nemetz, 1968). Furthermore, it becomes apparent from the physiological literature that restricted, shallow breathing exhibited by these individuals leads to a decreased compliance of the lungs that is corrected for by an increased tidal volume of air produced by sighing. People who normally breathe deeply do not, it seems, often need to sigh (Massaro, 1979).

Other paralinguistic characteristics that seem to be associated with the Type A pattern have also been related to an anxiety-associated high respiration rate (Goldman-Eisler, 1955; Goldman-Eisler et al., 1966; Heim et al., 1968). Rapid breathing has been found to be associated with speech that is rapid and lacking in smoothness, hence choppy and clipped. What this evidence seems to indicate is that Type A individuals may habitually display a rapid, shallow breathing pattern that, though perhaps not as extreme in form as the hyperventilation syndrome, may at least approximate it.

The physiological effects of hyperventilation also seem to correspond to the serious cardiovascular risks seemingly inherent in the Type A behavior pattern and could conceivably contribute to them. The arterial depletion of carbon dioxide occurring with hyperventilatory breathing, together with the resultant arterial pH changes, seems to produce specific symptoms that closely resemble those observed in cardiac disease (Lum, 1975; Pfeffer, 1978). Chest pains, heart palpitations, and distinct alterations in cardiac activity, including increased heart rate, ischemia and dysrhythmias, have all been reported among hyperventilators and are considered to be danger signs in their own right. Additionally, this rapid, shallow mode of respiration that is apparently seen with both hyperventilators and Type A individuals also induces a decrease in sinus arrhythmia, as previously mentioned. This in turn reduces cardiac parasympathetic inhibitory control and sympathetic activity dominates, probably resulting in enhanced catecholamine production.

One explanation for the rapid, shallow style of breathing that seems to be associated with the Type A behavior pattern may lie in the nature of activities that Type A individuals engage in (Friedman & Rosenman, 1974; Glass, 1977). Type A's seem to be preoccupied with attentional tasks and under persistent pressure to carry them out, as reflected in striving for achievement and time-consciousness. On the other hand, there is little attempt to relax or to divert attention to more quiet leisure-time activities. Hence Type A individuals may be characterized by a mental overload and an attentional perseverance. It may be recalled from the previous discussion that sustained attention and increasing mental load seem to result in a reduction in sinus arrhythmia and a shift in autonomic balance toward sympathetic dominance. This may be displayed in the Type A individual in a most exaggerated, persisting manner, resulting in a substantial autonomic imbalance.

The possibility that the Type A behavior pattern is in some way related to chronic hyperventilatory responses raises a number of interesting questions that, to our knowledge, have not as yet been investigated: Do hyperventilation syndrome patients have an increased risk of heart disease? Is there a significant subset of Type A individuals who are habitual hyperventilators, or are Type A individuals, in fact, rapid shallow breathers but characteristically less extreme in their ventilatory pattern than clinically diagnosed hyperventilators?

RESPIRATION AS MEDIATOR BETWEEN STRESS AND DISEASE

The fact that breathing seems to provide an additional link between mental effort, stress, and anxiety, on the one hand, and cardiovascular disease on the other, seems to provide tangible evidence to support the concept of "stress-induced cardiovascular disease." The breathing patterns associated with stress, anxiety, and mental effort produce relatively clearcut cardiovascular effects consistent with those observed in certain cardiovascular diseases. A persistent problem in the literature (Rachman, 1978), however, has been the failure to find consistent and stable relationships between the subjective experience of anxiety and psychophysiological measurements used as indices of anxiety. This lack of correspondence has made it difficult to substantiate the possibility that psychological stressors induce physical disease states. Closer examination of respiratory parameters may provide some resolution for this problem, since several investigations clearly indicate that respiration may be consistently related to the subjective perception of anxiety.

Mathews and Gelder (1969) reported that breathing rate was positively correlated with subjective anxiety among phobic patients, and strongly negatively correlated with a subjective sense of relaxation. These associations between respiration rate and subjective ratings of anxiety were more frequent than associations between self-ratings of anxiety and other physiological variables.

Another study (Oken, Grinker, Heath, Herz, Korchin, Sabshin, & Schwartz, 1967) found that respiration rate was the only autonomic measure that discriminated between male students at the two ends of a continuum of self-reported anxiety. These differences also held up across different conditions of psychological stress, heat stress, and a neutral control day. The hypothesis that respiratory rate is more closely and consistently correlated with the subjective perception of anxiety than other physiological measures has been borne out in numerous studies (Paul, 1969; Gatchel, Korman, Weis, Smith, & Clark, 1978; Clark, 1978; McCaul, Solomon, & Holmes, 1979).

More illuminating than research merely correlating respiration rate with subjective anxiety are investigations that have experimentally manipulated breathing rate under anxiety-provoking conditions by using pacing procedures (Foss, 1975; Harris et al., 1976; Jung & Klapsing-Hessenbruch, 1978; Clark, 1978; McCaul et al., 1979). These studies uniformly indicate that voluntary changes in respiration rate by subjects under threatening conditions served to modify the subjective perception of anxiety. In one experiment (Clark, 1978), for example, a paced respiration procedure was used with female subjects who were highly anxious in dental situations. Subjects were randomly assigned to one of 5 conditions: 3 groups with paced respiration at 8, 16, or 24 cycles per minute, one group merely tracking a visual display of lights used with the former groups to pace breathing (attention group), and one no-treatment control group. All groups were shown a filmed dental sequence and administered a scale designed to measure subjective level of anxiety.

Clark's results showed that the pacing technique was effective in altering each group's respiration rate. Furthermore, the eight-cycle-per-minute subjects reported less anxiety than all other groups, while the 24-cycle-per-minute group reported the greatest unease. There were no differences between the control groups and the 16-cycle-per-minute group. Additionally, the correlations between anxiety ratings and respiration rate were highly positive and significant. In contrast, the correlations between self-reports and other autonomic measures (cardiac and electrodermal) were low and nonsignificant. Whether the primary respiratory parameter influencing the perception of anxiety is breathing rate itself, or the accompanying changes in depth of respiration, which apparently occur under such pacing manipulations (McCaul et al., 1979), it seems that a respiratory pattern that maximizes sinus arrhythmic variation can effectively quell anxious feelings.

Evidence was presented in the foregoing discussion that physical and psychological states of well-being are mediated, at least in part, by relatively simple respiratory maneuvers. Our analysis suggested some interesting possibilities for interventional strategies to reduce coronary risk among Type A individuals. A breathing therapy oriented toward slowing down the respiratory pattern and increasing the depth of respiration might prove an effective means of treatment. Numerous approaches, including cardiovascular exercise, yogic and meditational practices, and various techniques used with the hyperventilation syndrome indicate that it is possible to alter the breathing pattern in a relatively stable manner. Such therapies might simultaneously reduce both psychological and coronary risk.

REFERENCES

Abramson, D. I. *Circulation in the Extremities.* New York: Academic Press, 1967.

Barry, R. J. Failure to find evidence of the unitary OR concept with different low-intensity auditory stimuli. *Physiological Psychology,* 1977, *5*, 89–96.

Barry, R. J. Physiological changes in a RT task: Further problems with Sokolov's dimension of stimulus significance. *Physiological Psychology,* 1978, *6*, 438–446.

Bouhuys, A. *Breathing: Physiology, environment and lung disease.* New York: Grune & Stratton, 1974.

Clark, M. E. Therapeutic applications of physiological control: The effectiveness of respiratory pacing in reducing autonomic and subjective distress. Unpublished dissertation, Kentucky State University, 1978.

Clynes, M. Respiratory sinus arrhythmia: Laws derived from computer simulation. *Journal of Applied Physiology,* 1960, *15*, 863–874.

Coles, M. G. H. Cardiac and respiratory activity during visual search. *Journal of Experimental Psychology,* 1972, *96*, 371–379.

Datey, K. K., Deshmukh, W. S., Dalvi, C. P., & Vinekar, S. L. Shavasan: A yogic exercise in the management of hypertension. *Angiology,* 1969, *20*, 325–333.

Davis, R. C. Response patterns. *Transactions of the New York Academy of Science,* 1957, *19*, 731–739.

Eich, R. H., Cuddy, R. P., Smulyan, H., & Lyons, R. H. Hemodynamics in labile hypertension: A follow-up study. *Circulation,* 1966, *34*, 299–307.

Finesinger, J. E. The effect of pleasant and unpleasant ideas on the respiration pattern (spirogram) in psychoneurotic patients. *American Journal of Psychiatry,* 1944, *100*, 659–667.

Forsyth, R. P. Mechanisms of the cardiovascular responses to environmental stressors. In P. A. Obrist, A. H. Black, J. Brener, & L. V. DiCara (eds.), *Cardiovascular psychophysiology—Current issues in response mechanisms, biofeedback and methodology.* Chicago: Aldine, 1974.

Foss, T. P. Effectiveness of a breathing therapy treatment program on the reduction and management of anxiety. Unpublished dissertation, University of Maryland, 1975.

Friedman, M. *Pathogenesis of coronary artery disease.* New York: McGraw-Hill, 1969.

Friedman, M. & Rosenman, R. F. *Type A behavior and your heart.* New York: Knopf, 1974.

Furedy, J. J. & Poulos, C. X. Human Pavlovian decelerative cardiac conditioning based on a respiratory-induced cardiac deceleration as an unconditioned reflex. *Biological Psychology,* 1975, *2*, 165–173.

Gatchel, R. J., Korman, M., Weis, C. B., Smith, D., & Clark, L. A. A multiple-response evaluation of EMG biofeedback performances during training and stress induction conditions. *Psychophysiology,* 1978, *15*, 253–261.

Glass, D. C. *Behavior patterns, stress, and coronary disease.* Hillsdale, N.J.: Lawrence Erlbaum Associates, 1977.

Goldman, M. S. & Lee, R. M. Operant conditioning of blood pressure: Effects of mediators. *Psychophysiology,* 1978, *15*, 531–537.

Goldman-Eisler, F. Speech-breathing activity—A measure of tension and affect during interviews. *British Journal of Psychology,* 1955, *46*, 53–63.

Goldman-Eisler, F., Skarbek, A., & Henderson, A. Breath rate and selective action of chlorpromazine on speech behavior. *Psychopharmacologie* (Berlin), 1966, *8*, 415–427.

Harris, V., Katlick, E., Lick, J., & Habberfield, T. Paced respiration as a technique for modification of autonomic response to stress. *Psychophysiology,* 1976, *13*, 386–391.

Hassett, J. *A primer of psychophysiology.* San Francisco: W. H. Freeman, 1978.

Heim, E., Knapp, P. H., Vachon, L., Globus, G. G., & Nemetz, S. J. Emotion, breathing and speech. *Journal of Psychosomatical Research,* 1968, *12*, 261–274.

Hellman, J. B. & Stacy, R. W. Variations of respiratory sinus arrhythmia with age. *Journal of Applied Physiology,* 1976, *41*, 734–738.

Johnston, L. C. The abnormal heart rate response to a deep breath in borderline labile hypertension: A sign of autonomic nervous system dysfunction. *American Heart Journal,* 1980, *99*, 487–493.

Jung, F. & Klapsing-Hessenbruch, A. A comparative study with a placebo group. *Zeitschrift für Psychosomatische Medizin und Psychoanalyse,* 1978, *24*, 36–55.

Kalsbeek, J. W. H. *Mentale belasting* (Mental effort) (Dutch). Assen: Van Gorcum, 1967.

Katona, P. G. & Jih, R. Respiratory sinus arrhythmia: A noninvasive measure of sympathetic cardiac control. *Journal of Applied Physiology,* 1975, *39*, 801–805.

Krogh, A. & Lindhard, J. Measurements of the blood flow through the lungs of man. *Skandinavian Archives of Physiology*, 1912, *27*, 100–114.

Lacey, J. Somatic response patterning and stress: Some revisions of activation theory. In M. H. Appley & R. Trumbull (eds.), *Psychological stress*. New York: Appleton-Century-Crofts, 1967.

Laird, G. S. & Fenz, W. O. Effects of respiration on heart rate in an aversive classical conditioning situation. *Canadian Journal of Psychology*, 1971, *25*, 395–411.

Lang, P. J. Learned control of human heart rate in a computer directed environment. In P. A. Obrist, A. H. Black, J. Brener, & L. V. DiCara (eds.), *Cardiovascular psychophysiology*. Chicago: Aldine, 1974.

Lum, L. C. Hyperventilation: The tip of the iceberg. *Journal of Psychosomatic Research*, 1975, *19*, 375–383.

Lund-Johansen, P. Hemodynamics in early essential hypertension. *Acta Medica Skandinavia*, Supplement, 1967, *482*, 1–101.

Massaro, D. Clinical implications of the effect of breathing pattern on the lung. *Basics of RD*, 1979, 8, No. 2. New York: American Thoraric Society.

Mathews, A. M. & Gelder, M. G. Psychophysiological investigations of brief relaxation training. *Journal of Psychosomatical Research*, 1969, *13*, 1–12.

Matsumoto, H. A psychological study of the relation between respiratory function and emotion. In V. Akishige (ed.), *Psychology of Zen*. Tokyo: Komazawa University, 1977.

McCaul, K., Solomon, S., & Holmes, D. Effects of paced respiration on physiological and psychological responses to threat. *Journal of Personality and Social Psychology*, 1979, *37*, 564–571.

Mulder, G. *The heart of mental effort. Studies on the cardiovascular psychophysiology of mental work.* University of Groningen, Groningen, The Netherlands, 1980.

Oken, D., Grinker, R. R., Heath, H. A., Herz, M., Korchin, S. J., Sabshin, M., & Schwartz, N. B. Relation of physiological response to affect expression. *Archives of General Psychiatry*, 1967, *6*, 336–351.

Otis, A. B. The work of breathing. In W. O. Fenn & H. Rahn (eds.), *Handbook of physiology*. Section 3, Respiration, Vol. 1. Washington, D.C.: American Physiological Society, 1964.

Patel, C. Yoga and biofeedback in the management of hypertension. *Lancet*, 1973, *10*, 1053–1055.

Paul, G. L. Physiological effects of relaxation training and hypnotic suggestion. *Journal of Abnormal Psychology*, 1969, *74*, 425–437.

Pfeffer, J. M. Etiology of the hyperventilation syndrome: A review of the literature. *Psychotherapy and Psychosomatics*, 1978, *30*, 47–55.

Porges, S. W. & Raskin, D. C. Respiratory and heart rate components of attention. *Journal of Experimental Psychology*, 1969, *81*, 497–503.

Rachman, S. *Fear and lovrage*. San Francisco: Freeman, 1978.

Richards, D. W. Circulatory effects of hyperventilation and hypoventilation. In W. F. Hamilton & P. Dow (eds.), *Handbook of physiology*. Section 2, Circulation. Washington, D.C.: American Physiological Society, 1965.

Rousey, C. L. Auditory acuity during sleep. *Psychophysiology*, 1979, *16*, 363–366.

Royer, F. L. 'Respiratory vasomotor reflex' in the forehead and finger. *Psychophysiology*, 1966, *3*, 258–261.

Sayers, B. McA. Psychological consequences of informational load and overload. In P. N. Venables & M. J. Christie (eds.), *Research in psychophysiology*. New York: Wiley, 1975.

Sharpey-Shafer, E. P. Effects of respiratory acts upon the circulation. In W. F. Hamilton & P. Dow (eds.), *Handbook of physiology*. Section 2, Circulation. Washington, D.C.: American Physiological Society, 1965.

Skaggs, E. B. Studies in attention and emotion. *Journal of Comparative Psychology*, 1930, *10*, 373–419.

Skarbek, A. A psychophysiological study of breathing behavior. *British Journal of Psychiatry*, 1969, *116*, 637–641.

Sparacino, J. The type A behavior pattern: A critical assessment. *Journal of Human Stress*, 1979, *5*, 37–51.

Sroufe, L. A. Effects of rate and depth of breathing on heart rate and heart rate variability. *Psychophysiology*, 1971, *8*, 648–655.

Sroufe, L. A. & Morris, D. Respiratory-cardiac relationships in children. *Psychophysiology*, 1973, *10*, 377–382.

Stern, R. M. & Anschel, C. Deep inspirations as stimuli for response of the ANS. *Psychophysiology*, 1968, *5*, 132–141.

Tirala, L. G. *Ademhalingstherapie* (Breathing therapy) (Dutch). Amsterdam: De Driehoek, 1969.

Woodworth, R. S. & Schlossberg, H. *Experimental psychology*. New York: Holt, Rinehart & Winston, 1954.

13

Individual Response Specificity in Phasic Cardiac Activity

Implications for Stress Research

J. F. Orlebeke, M. W. van der Molen,
R. J. M. Somsen, and L. J. P. van Doornen
Vrije Universiteit, Amsterdam

INTRODUCTION

During the fifties and sixties the concept of *autonomic response specificity* enjoyed great popularity in psychophysiology and in psychosomatic medicine. The concept was first used by Lacey, Bateman, and Van Lehn (1953). They continued the research line of Malmo and Shagass (1949), who used the term "symptom-specificity" in their research on psychosomatic diseases. The latter authors demonstrated that patients with tension-headache complaints were hyperreactive with the muscles of the neck and the forehead in response to a stressor as compared to hypertension patients, whose cardiovascular system was more reactive in response to the same stressor.

Lacey et al. (1953) demonstrated that nonpatients too reacted to stress in a stereotyped way. Using four different stressors and three autonomic response variables, they demonstrated that each subject showed a more or less consistent preference for the order in which maximum, medium, and minimum activity in the three autonomic variables was expressed (i.e., irrespective of the type of stressor, the subjects' autonomic reactions were similar). This hierarchy appeared to be individual-specific, i.e., consistent over stressors *within* subjects, but different *between* subjects.

Engel and Bickford (1961) exposed 18 hypertension patients and 17 normal control subjects to five different stressors. They measured reactive changes in systolic and diastolic blood pressure, skin conductance, skin-temperature, heart rate, heart rate variability, and respiration frequency. A finding of special interest was that 14 hypertension patients showed maximum reactivity in either systolic or diastolic blood pressure to all stressors, whereas this was true for only five subjects in the control group. Moreover, the controls were generally less specific in their autonomic reactions. Other experimenters reported similar findings (e.g., Moos & Engel, 1962; Schacter, 1957). The main message that these studies seem to convey is: (a) people differ in the "choice" of the response system in which they express maximal autonomic activity and they differ in the degree of rigidity of this "choice"; and (b) people tend to develop diseases in response systems in which they are maximally reactive to stressors.

Interest in the specificity phenomenon has gradually waned because the phenomenon could only be demonstrated in groups. It has proved to be difficult to establish individually unique patterns that were stable over time, which is a necessary prerequisite for the use of the phenomenon for diagnostic purposes. However, a form of individual response specificity which seems to meet this criterion has been recently demonstrated by Van der Molen and Orlebeke (1980). This experiment will be described below and the findings will be examined in the context of current theoretical views about the components of the coronary response.

HEART RATE CHANGES IN A BINARY
CHOICE REACTION TIME EXPERIMENT

Subjects received 8×40 binary choice RT trials. A trial consisted of a visual warning signal (S_1.) followed by an auditory "lead" after 2.5 sec and an auditory imperative signal (S_2), 0.5 sec after the start of the "lead." This paradigm is presented schematically in Fig. 1.

The subject was instructed to press, as fast as possible, either a left-hand button or a right-hand button, depending on the pitch of S_2 when it appeared. The intensity of S_2 varied randomly: eight intensities were presented, each 40 times. Heart rate, from S_1 until 5 sec after S_2, was recorded and averaged per S_2-intensity. The intensity effect as such will be discussed in the next section, but for the moment, we will consider the 8×40 trials as eight replications.

The results showed that each individual subject had an idiosyncratic and specific heart rate response. These responses are presented for three different subjects (A, B, and C) in Fig. 2. Figure 3 gives the heart rate responses for the same subjects measured under the same conditions six months later. Comparing Figs. 2 and 3 gives a reasonably valid impression of the reliability of this specificity phenomenon as well as the individual assessibility.

Figure 4 presents the general cardiac response form across subjects ("go" trials) and the response when the subject was instructed (by the color of S_1) not to respond to S_2 ("no go" trials). The difference between these two cardiac response forms provides some indication for the (partial) psychological origin of the response.

With regard to the meaning of this cardiac waveform, there is no consensus. It is almost certain, however, that the whole waveform is caused primarily by vagal activity. Obrist, Lawler, Howard, Smithson, Martin, and Manning (1974) have demonstrated that short latency cardiac changes remain unchanged when the sympathetic innervation of the heart is blocked. Tonic cardiac response effects, however, are significantly reduced under such a condition.

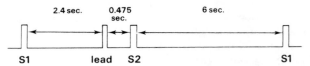

Figure 1 Schematic representation of the fixed foreperiod binary choice paradigm. S_1 is a 100 msec visual warning signal; the lead is a click of 25 msec duration of 80 dB and 2000 Hz. S_2 is a 250 msec tone of either 1000 or 3000 Hz and intensities of 50, 60, 70, 80, 90, 100, and 110 dB.

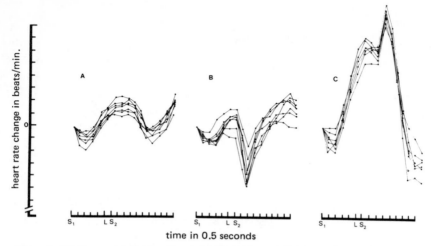

Figure 2 Cardiac responses for three subjects (A, B, and C) in a S_1–S_2 choice of RT situation. A single line in each graph represents the averaged heart rate response to 40 trials of one stimulus intensity.

With regard to the possible psychological meaning of the components of the cardiac response, several viewpoints have been nicely reviewed by Bohlin and Kjellberg (1979). According to Gatchel and Lang (1973), the response is subdivided into three components: the short latency deceleration after S_1 (D_1), the subsequent acceleration (A), and the second deceleration (D_2), which is maximal at or just beyond S_2 when the S_1–S_2 ISI is long (i.e., 4 sec or longer) or a bit earlier when the ISI is shorter.

Most authors (e.g., Walter & Porges, 1976; Coles & Duncan-Johnson, 1975)

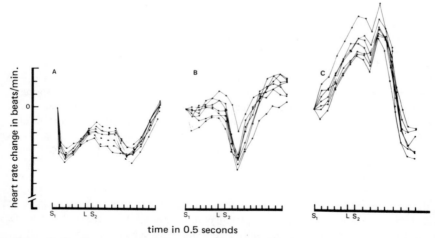

Figure 3 Cardiac responses of the same subjects as in Fig. 2, measured six months later under the same conditions.

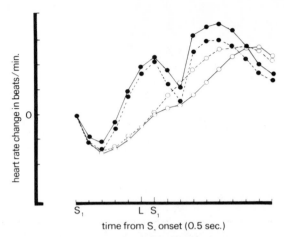

Figure 4 Mean heart rate changes for loud tones, averaged over 100 and 110 dB (solid lines), and soft tones, averaged over 50 and 60 dB (dashed lines), in the "go" (filled dots) and the "no go" condition (open dots). After van der Molen and Orlebeke (1980).

agree that D_1 is the OR to the nonsignal aspect of S_2. The A-component is supposed to be a response to the significance of S_1 (e.g., Walter & Porges, 1976), but also to the response or energy requirements at S_2 (e.g., Bower & Tate, 1976; Montgomery, 1977). Coles and Duncan-Johnson (1975) have suggested that A reflects the information processing demands during S_1. These options, of course, are not independent of one another. For example, the significance of S_1 is determined by what has to be done at S_2. In any event, A seems to disappear when the subject knows (100 percent certain) that no response is required at S_2. So A has something to do with anticipated effort. On the other hand, uncertainty about the response to be given at S_2 is a factor that enhances A.

The third component, D_2, is considered to reflect either response, preparation and expectance (Lawler, Obrist, & Lawler, 1976), or sensory facilitation (Lacey & Lacey, 1974). These two viewpoints are a constant source of dispute in psychophysiology. There are arguments for both positions. A well established fact seems that D_2 —other than A—increases with an increase in response certainty.

Despite the ambiguity regarding the interpretation of the response components, there is one thing that seems clear, viz., the fact that the distinction between D_1, A, and D_2 (and a post-S_2 component A_2, which is not considered in most studies) is useful and that these components reflect (at least partly) different processes because the magnitude of the components are uncorrelated (Jennings, Averill, Opton, & Lazarus, 1970).

The difference in heart rate response between the "go" and the "no go" condition in the Van der Molen/Orlebeke study (see Fig. 4) is compatible with the "certainty" interpretation. The presence of a marked A-component in a *simple* RT task, however, does not fit the certainty hypothesis. With regard to the D_2-component, the data of Van der Molen and Orlebeke are absolutely in contradiction with the above-mentioned D_2-speed relationship: D_2 is smallest when speed (= RT) is highest.

An interesting interpretation of phasic heart rate changes, which seems to apply also to the mostly neglected post-S_2 acceleration, has been proposed by Graham (1979). She argues that stimulation results either in input facilitation or in output facilitation. The former is the case during orienting activity, manifesting itself in cardiac deceleration; the latter is the case during defensive activity, as manifested in cardiac acceleration. According to this viewpoint, the A component can be considered as reflecting a *response set* and the D_2 as a *stimulus set*, whereas the post-S_2 acceleration (A_2) is also a motor-output (response-set) phenomenon.

Before proceeding further in formulation some hypotheses concerning the possible meaning of the *individual* responses, as depicted in Figs. 2 and 3, we will discuss some of the findings of the Van der Molen and Orlebeke study that might be relevant for a clarification of the previously indicated phenomenon. This experiment departs from the information processing model of Sternberg (1969). According to this model, three information processing stages in simple decision tasks (such as in a choice of RT situation), can be distinguished, viz. *stimulus encoding, response choice,* and *motor adjustment.* The model assumes that these stages are independent from one another, that each stage receives its input from the preceding stage, and that the total processing time equals the sum of the times of each separate stage. Further, it is assumed (based on experimental evidence) that some stimulus parameters predominantly affect one stage and some, another stage (or other stages).

Within this framework, stimulus intensity is assumed, for example, to affect exclusively the stimulus encoding stage. Several authors, however, (e.g., Sanders, 1977; Van der Molen & Keuss, 1979) have reported evidence that auditory stimulus intensity affects the motor adjustment stage. Thus auditory intensity is assumed to produce an immediate so-called arousal effect, which influences directly the motor adjustment stage. In the choice RT paradigm, presented schematically in Fig. 1, the data are compatible with this viewpoint. These data are presented in Fig. 5. Panel b shows the binary choice RT as a function of stimulus intensity. This is a U-shaped function. Panel c gives the RT's of error responses (pressing the wrong button). This function is the same as the ordinary simple RT function, i.e., decreasing RT with increasing intensity. Obviously intensity facilitates motor-output. The inhibition of that facilitation—necessary for the choice stage to take place— consumes time (more with high intensities than with lower intensities) and this lengthens RT. Because half of the errors are illegitimately scored as correct, one may expect a relatively high variance at higher intensities. This is what we see in panel a. Panel d gives the proportions of errors as a function of stimulus intensity. This picture is consistent with panel b. Intensity increases motor readiness and it is difficult to inhibit that readiness.

The question that was now put forward was whether the increase in RT at higher intensities is paralleled by a defensive reflex (DR). According to Sokolov (1963), an OR facilitates input, a DR inhibits input, and the transition from OR to DR is mainly determined by the intensity of the stimulation, with weak stimuli evoking OR's and strong stimuli, DR's. Thus, in Sokolov's view, the OR and DR have exclusively *input*-modulating functions. As was previously noted, Graham (1979) has proposed a somewhat different interpretation of the functions of OR and DR. She states that stimulation facilitates either input or output, depending on the intensity; the OR is assumed to enhance sensory intake, and the DR to enhance motor output.

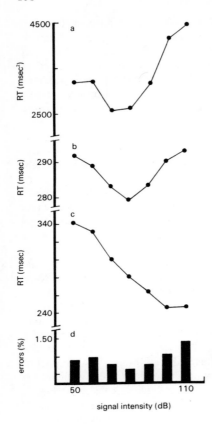

Figure 5 The effect of auditory stimulus intensity on various aspects of the choice reaction process: Choice RT variance of correct responses (panel a); mean RT of correct responses (panel b); mean RT of incorrect responses (panel c) and proportion of incorrect responses as a function of the intensity of the imperative signal (panel d). After Van der Molen and Orlebeke (1980).

Our conclusion, based on the data reported in Fig. 5 that high stimulus intensities facilitate the output system, is compatible with Graham's conception. Since the OR and DR can be differentiated on the basis of phasic heart rate (HR) changes, the intensity effect should be present in the HR-response to the imperative stimulus, i.e., the higher the stimulus intensity, the stronger the HR-acceleration to that stimulus. The averaged HR response to stimulu of low (50 and 60 dB) and high intensity (100 and 110 dB) was shown in Fig. 5. The high intensity stimulation produced an earlier shift from anticipatory deceleration to acceleration. This and other information will be utilized in the next section, in which we will endeavour to formulate some ideas with regard to the psychophysiological meaning of the individual cardiac response, such as presented in Figs. 2 and 3.

THE PSYCHOPHYSIOLOGICAL RELEVANCE
OF THE SPECIFICITY PHENOMENON

Does the morphology of the individual HR-responses carry psychologically relevant information? Or, in other words, once we assess a highly reliable individual physiological feature, is there a particular psychological feature (trait) that is related to it? Or from a psychophysical viewpoint, is the relative contribution of the sympathetic and parasympathetic branch of the ANS to the innervation of an organ (the heart) related to one or more psychological features?

Although we have not yet found a clear-cut answer to these questions, we would like to present two preliminary hypotheses at this time. The first of these can be formulated as follows: The shift from deceleration to acceleration *after* S_2 is related to a component of the personality trait "impulsiveness," which can be labeled as "impatience" or "hurry" (Eysenck & Eysenck, 1977). This hypothesis is based on the assumption that hurry is actually a chronic pressure on motor output. As can be seen in Fig. 6, the high intensity stimuli evoke a stronger accelerative response, or perhaps it is better to say that these stimuli produce an earlier shift from deceleration to acceleration; Fig. 2 showed that high intensity stimuli facilitate motor output.

Since motor output is *always* associated with cardiac acceleration, it is not surprising that the low intensity stimuli also produce an accelerative cardiac response; however, it occurs *later* and/or is of less magnitude. The shift from deceleration to acceleration is produced by response *initiation* (i.e., the central triggering of the motor system) rather than response *completion* (= RT), as Jennings and Wood (1977) found. This is so because reactions to both low and high intensity stimuli are completed at the same moment, but the cardiac shifts associated with these reactions are different (see also Fig. 5, panel b).

Figure 6 (right panel) presents the results of a best-worst analysis: The averaged response to the 25 percent of trials at each intensity with the fastest reactions, and to the 25 percent of trials with the slowest reactions. Given the striking resemblance with the left panel of Fig. 6, one may conclude that variations in RT may be ascribed to fluctuations in the subjects' response criterion. When this criterion is experimentally manipulated (Van der Molen, Orlebeke, & Somsen, 1980), the deceleration-acceleration switch is shifted in time in the predicted direction. It seems plausible that the shift—*as a group effect*—from post-S_2 deceleration to acceleration, is some form of a "motor-readiness" index. It might be expected that

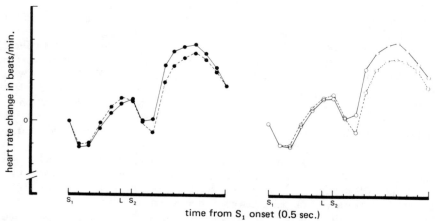

Figure 6 Mean HR changes for strong tones averaged over 100 and 110 dB (left panel, solid line), weak tones averaged over 50 and 60 dB (left panel, dashed line), fast reactions (right panel, solid line), and slow reactions (right panel, dashed line). After Van der Molen and Orlebeke (1980).

differences *between* individuals with regard to this shift would be correlated with a psychological or behavioral trait such as "hurry." This "hurry"-hypothesis might also be relevant for psychosomatic theorizing on cardiovascular diseases since hurry is considered a component of the well known Type A coronary-prone behavior pattern (Friedman & Rosenman, 1974).

The second hypothesis, which has some empirical basis, can be formulated as follows: The amplitude of the cardiac acceleration during the S_1-S_2 interval is an indication of what may be called "stress tolerance." The higher this amplitude, the higher the tolerance for stress. For the legitimacy of this hypothesis, we have a set of arguments that will be presented in most of the remainder of this paper.

1. Lykken, Macindoe, and Tellegen (1972) have investigated what they call *negative perception*. This is defined as a reduction in response amplitude to an aversive stimulus when the latter is preceded by a warning signal. Lykken et al. believe the warning signal initiates an inhibitory process as a consequence of which the impact of the aversive stimulus is reduced. The most essential prerequisite for the occurrence of negative perception is, according to Lykken et al., the predictability of the aversive stimulus. This is the case only when the interstimulus interval (ISI) between the warning signal and the aversive stimulus is relatively short or when additional cues improve the predictability.

Lykken et al. (1972) have demonstrated that the existence of the negative perception phenomenon for several responses such as GSR, phasic heart rate acceleration, and the P300. Assuming that optimal functioning of such an input reduction mechanism has adaptive value for the organism, Lykken et al. hypothesized that input reduction would be less effective for high anxious subjects for whom there would be a relatively smaller reduction in response amplitude than for low anxious subjects. Cardiac responses in anticipation of, and in response to, an aversive stimulus (electric shock) are presented in Fig. 7 for high and low anxious subjects. Two differences deserve careful attention. First, the cardiac accelerative response to S_2 is smaller for the low anxious group than for the high anxious group. A second difference was that the acceleration in anticipation of S_2 was considerably smaller for the high anxious group than for the low anxious subjects.

Since the morphology of the cardiac response in the situation used by Lykken et al. (actually a classical aversive conditioning paradigm) is not essentially different from that of the S_1-S_2 RT paradigm, as has been noted by Bohlin and Kjellberg (1979), it seems justifiable to consider Lykken et al.'s results in interpreting the individual heart rate patterns described above. More specifically, the group with the best ability to tolerate stress, i.e., presumably the low anxious group, displays the strongest cardiac anticipatory acceleration. While it is an open question in what way this anticipatory response component is related to the post-S_2 response reduction, it should be noted that low-anxiety and relatively large cardiac anticipatory acceleration go together.

2. Orlebeke and Van Doornen (1977) have carried out a modified replication of the Lykken et al. study, replacing the S_2-electric shock with an aversive noise. Three groups of subjects, viz., low trait anxious (LA), high trait anxious (HA), and neurotic patients (PAT), participated in the experiment. These groups did not differ with regard to reduction in the cardiac response amplitude to S_2 when warned, but differed with respect to the amplitude of the anticipatory cardiac acceleration. The LA group showed the strongest acceleration; the PAT group the weakest, whereas the HA group took an intermediate position. Figure 8 presents the anticipatory cardiac responses for the three groups. These results are compatible

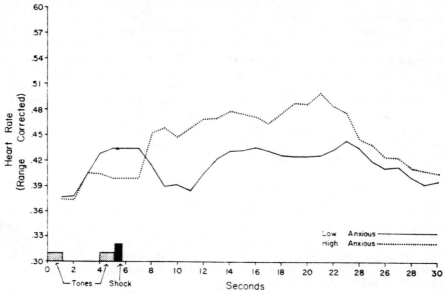

Figure 7 Pre and post shock cardiac responses for low and high trait anxious groups. After Lykken et al. (1972).

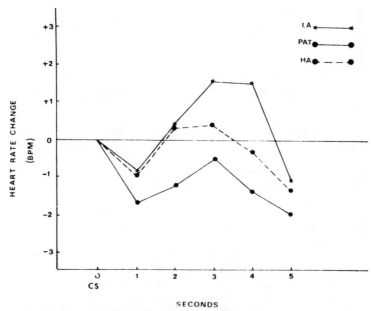

Figure 8 Cardiac responses in anticipation of an aversive tone for high and low trait anxious subjects and neurotic patients. After Orlebeke and Van Doornen (1977).

with those of Lykken et al., in that the LA group, which probably has the best stress-coping capacities, shows the strongest anticipatory acceleration.

3. Van Doornen, Orlebeke, and Somsen (1980) compared a group of cardiac infarction patients with two groups of health controls, one of the latter groups having a low medical infarction risk and the other having a relatively high infarction risk. All subjects received a random series of warned and unwarned tones. The ISI between warning signal (S_1) and aversive tone (S_2) was 12 sec. To optimize exact predictability, according to Lykken, a necessary prerequisite for perception of the event to take place, the subject saw the pointer of a clock move over a known distance during the S_1-S_2 interval. The reduction in GSR amplitude in the warned condition relative to the unwarned condition was significant, and this reduction was stronger in the low risk group than in the high risk and patient groups.

As far as the heart rate response is concerned, no differences were found between groups in the magnitude of the reduction in response to S_2, but the groups differed considerably with regard to the anticipatory cardiac acceleration. This response was significantly greater in the low risk group as compared to the high risk group and patient groups. Figure 9 depicts the cardiac anticipatory responses for the three groups. Again, it is the group which supposedly had the highest tolerance for stress (or the best coping capacities) that showed the strongest cardiac acceleration in anticipation of S_2.

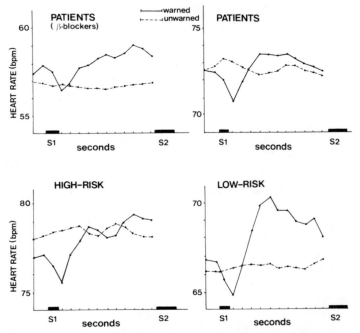

Figure 9 HR responses in a 12 sec S_1-S_2 interval (S_2 being an aversive tone) for infarction patients using β-blockers (not considered here), non-mediated patients and high and low risk controls. The dashed lines give the HR responses to trials when S_1 was omitted. After Van Doornen, Orlebeke, and Somsen (1980).

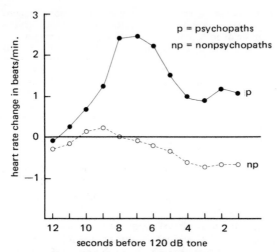

Figure 10   Cardiac response in anticipation of a 120
dB tone in a group psychopathic subjects and a normal
control group. Adapted from Hare, Frazelle, and Cox
(1978).

4. Hare, Frazelle, and Cox (1978) measured heart rate in a group of prison inmates while they were awaiting the delivery of a 120 dB tone during a 12 sec
"count-down" procedure. Twelve of the subjects had high ratings of psychopathy,
according to the criteria of Cleckley (1976), whereas 20 subjects had low ratings.
The former group showed larger increases in heart rate in anticipation of the
aversive tone than the latter group. This finding was interpreted by Hare et al. as
providing evidence that psychopathic subjects have more efficient mechanisms for
coping with threat. Figure 10 presents an adapted version of Hare et al.'s Fig. 1.
     So far we have presented evidence consistent with the hypothesis that the
amplitude of cardiac anticipatory acceleration might be an index of stress-tolerance.
Now we present some recent pilot data from a larger study designed for testing
the two above-mentioned hypotheses. A major assumption in this study was that
the experience of stress is reflected in (or correlated with) the excretion of catecholamines (see, among others, Frankenhaeuser, 1975). Twelve subjects were run
in an experimental stress condition, a difficult tracking task in which there was
immediate punishment for errors in the form of white noise bursts. Two of the
measures taken were adrenaline (A) and noradrenaline (NA) in urine (collected
after the stress). On a *different* day, these subjects participated in exactly the same
RT task as in the Van der Molen and Orlebeke study.
     The A and NA concentrations in urine correlated (Spearman rank correlation)
with two parameters of the heart rate response, viz.: (a) Amplitude of anticipatory
acceleration (AA), measured from rough of first deceleration to peak; and (b)
maximal difference (Max Dif.) in total response (i.e., including also the post-S_2
part). These correlations are reported in Table 1, in which it can be seen that
when the hypothesis is restricted to the AA-component, it gets some support;
but only with regard to NA for which the relationship between NA and Max. Dif.
is much stronger than for NA. This finding suggests the more general idea that a

Table 1 Correlations between adrenaline (A) and noradrenaline
(NA) at the one hand and two parameters of phasic cardiac activity,
viz. amplitude of anticipatory acceleration (AA) and maximal
difference in the total response (maximum difference) at the other

	A	NA
AA	+0.14	−0.38*
Maximum difference	−0.02	−0.62**

*p < 0.10.
**p < 0.02.

crucial feature (correlate) of stress tolerance is a high vagal reactivity. The short-latency type of responses we are speaking about are very probably vagally mediated (Obrist et al., 1974), though the amplitude of such vagal effects can be influenced by the level of sympathetic activity.

In conclusion, the individual heart rate patterns described in this paper may be regarded as a form of individual response specificity. These HR response patterns appear to fulfill the scientific requirements of objectivity and reproducibility and provide tentative supporting evidence for two hypotheses: (a) The post-S_2 shift from deceleration to acceleration seems to be related to a personality trait which may be labeled "impatience" or "hurry"; and (b) The amplitude of anticipatory cardiac acceleration may be correlated with a personality trait labeled "stress tolerance."

At the present time, we are carrying out a series of three experiments aimed at providing a better understanding of the individual heart rate response. First, since high sympathetic reactivity seems to be an important risk factor in the development of cardiovascular disease as well as other types of psychosomatic disorders, the effects of sympathetic blocking on the morphology of the heart rate response are being investigated. Second, the heritability of the heart rate response is being evaluated in a twin study. Finally, the relationship between cardiac response and personality traits, such as "hurry" and "stress tolerance," will be further investigated.

REFERENCES

Bohlin, G. & Kjellberg, A. Orienting activity in two-stimulus paradigms as reflected in heart rate. In H. D. Kimmel, E. H. van Olst, & J. F. Orlebeke (eds.), *The orienting reflex in humans.* Hillsdale: Erlbaum, 1979.

Bower, A. C. & Tate, D. L. Cardiovascular and skin conductance correlates of a fixed foreperiod reaction time task in retarded and non-retarded youth. *Psychophysiology*, 1976, *13*, 1–9.

Cleckley, H. *The mask of sanity.* St. Louis: Mosby, 1976.

Coles, M. G. H. & Duncan-Johnson, A. C. Cardiac activity and information processing: The effects of stimulus significance and detection and response requirements. *Journal of Experimental Psychology: Human Perception and Performance*, 1975, *104*, 418–428.

Engel, B. T. & Bickford, A. F. Response specificity. *Archives of General Psychiatry*, 1961, *5*, 478–489.

Eysenck, S. B. G. & Eysenck, H. J. The place of impulsiveness in a dimensional system of personality description. *British Journal of Social and Clinical Psychology*, 1977, *16*, 57–68.

Frankenhaeuser, M. Experimental approaches to the study of catecholamines and emotion. In L. Levi (ed.), *Emotions. Their parameters and measurement.* Amsterdam, North Holland, 1975, pp. 209–234.

Friedman, M. & Rosenman, R. H. The central nervous system and coronary heart disease. In Braunwald (ed.), *The myocardium: Failure and infarction.* New York: HP Publishing, Inc., 1974.

Gatchel, R. J. & Lang, P. J. Accuracy of psychophysical judgments and physiological response amplitude. *Journal of Experimental Psychology*, 1973, *98*, 175-183.

Hare, R. D., Frazelle, J., & Cox, D. N. Psychopathy and physiological responses to threat of an aversive stimulus. *Psychophysiology*, 1978, *15*, 165-172.

Graham, F. K. Distinguishing among orienting, defensive and startle reflexes. In H. D. Kimmel, E. H. van Olst, & J. F. Orlebeke (eds.), *The orienting reflex in humans*. Hillsdale: Erlbaum, 1979.

Jennings, J. R., Averill, J. R., Opton, E. R., & Lazarus, R. S. Some parameters of heart rate change: Perceptual versus motor task requirements, noxiousness and uncertainty. *Psychophysiology*, 1970, *7*, 194-212.

Jennings, J. R. & Wood, C. C. Cardiac cycle time effects on performance, phase cardiac responses and their intercorrelation in choice reaction time. *Psychophysiology*, 1977, *14*, 297-307.

Lacey, B. C. & Lacey, J. I. Studies of heart rate and bodily processes in sensory-motor behavior. In P. A. Obrist, A. H. Black, J. Brener, & L. V. DiCara (eds.), *Cardiovascular Psychophysiology*. Chicago: Aldine, 1974.

Lacey, J. I., Bateman, D. E., & Van Lehn, R. Autonomic response specificity an experimental study. *Psychosomatic Medicine*, 1953, *15*, 8-21.

Lawler, K. A., Obrist, P. A., & Lawler, J. E. Cardiac and somatic response patterns during a reaction time task in children and adults. *Psychophysiology*, 1976, *13*, 448-455.

Lykken, D. T., Macindoe, J., & Tellegen, A. Preception: Autonomic response to shocks as a function of predictability in time and locus. *Psychophysiology*, 1972, *9*, 318-333.

Malmo, R. B. & Shagass, C. Physiologic study of symptom mechanisms in psychiatric patients under stress. *Psychosomatic Medicine*, 1949, *11*, 25-29.

Montgomery, G. K. Effects of performance evaluation and anxiety on cardiac response in anticipation of difficult problem solving. *Psychophysiology*, 1977, *14*, 251-257.

Moos, R. H. & Engel, B. T. Psychophysiological reactions in hypertensive and arthritic patients. *Journal of Psychosomatic Research*, 1962, *6*, 227-241.

Obrist, P. A., Lawler, J. E., Howard, J. L., Smithson, K. W., Martin, P. L., & Manning, J. Sympathetic influences on cardiac rate and contractility during acute stress in humans. *Psychophysiology*, 1974, *11*, 405-427.

Orlebeke, J. F. & Van Doornen, L. J. P. Preception (UCR diminution) in normal and neurotic subjects. *Biological Psychology*, 1977, *5*, 15-22.

Sanders, A. F. Structural and functional aspects of the reaction process. In S. Dornic (ed.), *Attention and performance, VI*. New York: Wiley, 1977, pp. 3-25.

Schacter, J. Pain, fear and anger in hypertensives and normotensives. *Psychosomatic Medicine*, 1957, *19*, 17-29.

Sokolov, E. N. *Perception and the conditioned reflex*. Oxford: Pergamon, 1963.

Sternberg, S. The discovery of processing stages: Extensions of Donder's method. In W. G. Koster (ed.), *Attention and performance II*, Acta Psychologica, 1969, *30*, 276-315.

Van der Molen, M. W. & Keuss, P. J. G. The relationship between reaction time and intensity in discrete auditory tasks. *Quarterly Journal of Experimental Psychology*, 1979, *31*, 95-102.

Van der Molen, M. W. & Orlebeke, J. F. Phasic heart rate and the U-shaped relationship between choice reaction time and auditory signal intensity. *Psychophysiology*, 1980, *17*, 471-481.

Van Doornen, L. J. P., Orlebeke, J. F., & Somsen, R. J. M. Coronary risk and coping with aversive stimuli. *Psychophysiology*, 1980, *17*.

Walter, G. F. & Porges, S. W. Heart rate and respiratory responses as a function of task difficulty: The use of discriminant analysis in the selections of psychologically sensitive physiological responses. *Psychophysiology*, 1976, *13*, 563-571.

14

A Social-Psychophysiological Model of Biobehavioral Factors and Coronary Heart Disease

Theodore M. Dembroski and James M. MacDougall
Eckerd College Stress and Cardiovascular Research Center

Robert S. Eliot and James C. Buell
University of Nebraska Medical Center

THE PROBLEM

In the industrialized world, the major contributors to death are myocardial infarction, sudden cardiac death, and hypertension. Explaining the current "pandemic" of coronary heart disease (CHD) that exists in most developed societies is one of the most difficult tasks facing modern medicine. Examination of data from studies in the United States indicates that the best combination of risk factors, including age, serum cholesterol, blood pressure, cigarette smoking, and obesity, does not predict most new cases of CHD (Jenkins, 1971, 1976, 1978; Keys, Aravanis, Blackburn, et al., 1972). In addition, the same levels of these risk factors that result in greater probability of CHD in the Framingham study, for example, do not show the same result when applied to other countries such as Yugoslavia or even other ethnically different populations in the United States (Kozarevic, Pirk, Dawber, et al., 1976; Gordon, Garcia-Palmieri, Kagan et al., 1974). Moreover, the rapid rise in the incidence of CHD during the past few decades cannot readily be attributed to age increases, improved diagnosis, alteration of genetic factors, changes in diet, or decreased physical activity (Keys et al., 1972; Michaels, 1966; White, 1974; Yudkin, 1957; Trulson, 1959; Keys, Karvonen, & Fidanza, 1958).

Since less than 50 percent of the variance in CHD can be explained by traditional risk factors, the search has continued for additional risk factors in the multiple risk factor approach to understanding, predicting, and controlling CHD. One assumption is that over the past few decades changes in the social environment and related compensatory behavioral and physiological adjustments might be implicated in the increase in the incidence of CHD. Thus, the search for additional risk factors has included psychosocial factors. Psychosocial factors such as anxiety, depression, sleep disturbance, neuroticism, psychological denial, Type A coronary-prone behavior pattern, cultural setting, social mobility, status incongruity, and various types of job, interpersonal, and life stresses have been correlated with CHD. (See Jenkins (1971, 1976) for an extensive review of this research.)

In fact, the relationship between emotions and CHD events has been recognized throughout history in a series of anecdotes that describe people dying suddenly in the throes of fear, rage, grief, humiliation, or joy. However, until specific patho-physiologic mechanisms linking the central nervous system with the cardiovascular system are clearly identified, these observations can be expected to hold little sway with the scientific community. Clearly, there is a strong correlation between psychosocial conflict, emotions, behavioral patterns, and the pathogenesis of coronary heart disease, sudden death, cardiac arrhythmias, and hypertension (Buell & Eliot, 1979). Even the traditional risk factors for coronary heart disease demonstrate strong behavioral components.

While it is clear that psychosocial variables are importantly related to the incidence of CHD, the mechanisms through which such factors exert their physiological effects are not well understood. Human behavior reflects ongoing complex interactions between a person and an environment in which demands and resources fluctuate. Many of the person-environment interactions produce a variety of autonomic nervous and biochemical responses which directly affect cardiovascular functioning. Ultimately, a complete understanding of the behavioral components involved in the etiology of CHD will require systematic investigation of these processes. More specifically, the following types of research questions must be systematically addressed in order to understand the relationship between any psychosocial factor and CHD.

1. Is there a correlation between the psychosocial factor and CHD?

2. Is there a correlation between the psychosocial and standard risk factors; i.e., how does the psychosocial factor affect standard risk factors and vice versa?

3. Does the psychosocial factor predict CHD independent of the standard risk factors; i.e., does the psychosocial factor reduce unexplained variance in CHD?

4. What is the relationship of the psychosocial factor to other psychosocial factors; i.e., how well is the nature of the psychosocial factor understood?

5. What is the relationship of the psychosocial factor to physiological factors, and how well are the relationships understood?

6. How does the psychosocial factor dispose someone to behave in response to day-to-day environmental demands in a manner conducive to the development of CHD; i.e., what are the behavioral and/or inherent physiologic processes that excite physiological reactions pathogenetic to CHD?

7. How does the progressive development of CHD affect behavior and their reactions?

8. Does alteration of the psychosocial risk factor result in reduced risk of CHD? (Although answers to questions like the ones advanced above would be necessary before consideration of grand scale intervention strategies, it would be useful to explore intervention tactics as part of the research designed to understand the relationship of the psychosocial factor to CHD.)

9. Can animal models be created which allow closer examination of the processes likely to be occurring in human behavior?

10. What are the pathophysiological mechanisms responsible for CHD in humans?

A BIOBEHAVIORAL MODEL

The structural components of a preliminary biobehavioral model of the environmental-behavioral interactions that require examination to clarify the relationship between a psychosocial variable and CHD are presented in Fig. 1 (Dembroski, 1978). The model attempts to account not only for static relationships between psychosocial and physiological variables, but also for psychological and physiological compensatory adjustments to environmental demands. It is hoped that the model can be used as an heuristic device to organize extant knowledge and suggest future research directions involving a psychosocial factor with CHD.

Point I in the Model

The upper portion of the model at point I reflects the bulk of research in the area of psychosocial precursors to CHD, which typically is correlational with the aim of establishing a link between a particular psychosocial "risk factor" and the major manifestations of CHD. Intimately related is more correlational research, which attempts to establish a relationship between a psychosocial factor and such standard risk factors as smoking, serum cholesterol, and hypertension. An aim here, however, should be to determine whether the psychosocial factor predicts CHD independent of standard risk factors, thus reducing unexplained variance in CHD.

If a correlation between a psychosocial factor and CHD is established it is then necessary to understand the nature of the psychosocial factor in order to derive hypotheses concerning the processes that mediate the relationship between the psychosocial factor and CHD. An initial procedure useful to this purpose is to systematically examine the psychosocial and physiological variables, including standard risk factors, that correlate with the psychosocial factor in an effort to construct patterns of interrelated variables that may dispose an individual to develop CHD. Some of the factors or patterns, for instance, may correlate more strongly with CHD than others. When such relationships have been formulated, it is then necessary to examine how a psychosocial factor and/or its correlates dispose an individual to respond to his environment.

In sum, combinations of factors in point I represent psychological and physiological dispositions to respond to certain environmental events in particular ways. For example, high levels relative to low levels of depression, anxiety, or achievement need and their physiological correlates dispose an individual to respond to work demands, interpersonal interactions, or other life events in different ways. The key assumption is that certain levels of psychosocial-physiological dispositions

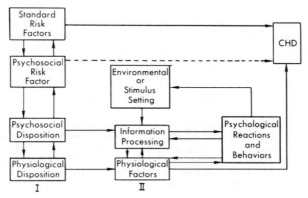

Figure 1 Model of the relationship between psychosocial-physiological variables and coronary heart disease.

in interaction with certain kinds of environmental events produce psychological, behavioral, and physiological reactions that play a role in the pathogenesis of CHD.

Point II in the Model

Point II in the model represents interactions between variables that can be examined using experimental and correlational techniques. The aim of research at this point is to explore ongoing behavioral and physiological processes in an effort to isolate those which are damaging to the cardiovascular system.

The *environmental or stimulus setting* in which an individual operates includes, among other things, a large variety of demands and resources.* In fact, description of environmental demands is one way in which stress has been defined in past research, e.g., work requirements, job loss, divorce, death of spouse, etc. (Glass, 1977; Jenkins, 1976). In considering demands, equal attention should be devoted to environmental resources, e.g., financial condition, number of friends, access to professional help, etc. (Kaplan, Cassel, & Gore, in press).

When environmental events occur, they stimulate *information processing*, that is, an individual perceives and evaluates the situation at one or more levels of awareness. At one end of the awareness continuum, information-processing may occur automatically and with great rapidity as when one reacts almost instantaneously to avoid a traffic accident. At the other end, it can occur with more deliberate intent as when one actively decides to work more hours or launch a new project in order to enhance one's career. In other words, the process may be relatively habitual in some instances and in other instances may be a more complex conscious effort to evolve a coping strategy. This may include evaluation of possible control of and resources in the situation and consideration of the probability and consequences of certain outcomes associated with one or more courses of action. The manner in which an individual interprets, evaluates, and plans action in response to environmental events is a second way in which stress has been customarily defined in past research, e.g., subjective evaluation of job pressure, life satisfaction, etc.

Evaluation of environmental events affects psychological reactions and behaviors. These reactions in turn can alter the environment and subsequent information processing, and so on. For example, the consequences of working longer hours may be a promotion to a more responsible position and a higher level of anxiety which, when evaluated, may lead to different work habits, and so on (Matthews & Brunson, 1979). Thus, the present conceptualization places emphasis on ongoing acting and reacting dimensions of human behavior (Dembroski & MacDougall, 1978).

Human actions and reactions affect and are affected by physiological factors. For example, physiological arousal can affect and be affected by evaluation of the actual or imagined consequences of working harder. It has been demonstrated, for instance, that levels of catecholamines and serum cholesterol are elevated in ac-

---

*The present model focuses primarily on environmental stimuli of a social-behavioral nature rather than environmental physical stimuli or substances such as food constituents, drugs, chemicals, and pollutants. To incorporate such stimuli and substances into the model would only require the addition of a direct connection between environment and physiological factors in Fig. 1. It is hoped that the present model can be used in conjunction with separate models, which illustrate how environmental substances and physical stimuli affect the development of CHD.

countants and medical students during periods in which heavier workloads are required (Friedman, Rosenman, & Carroll, 1958; Dreyfuss & Czazckes, 1959). The effects of such events on the cardiovascular system might be more severe in individuals who possess certain types of psychosocial-physiological dispositions. Thus, the task of research is to systematically examine how particular psychosocial and physiological attributes chronically dispose an individual to respond to his environment in a manner that excites physiological processes instrumental in the development of CHD (Dembroski, MacDougall, & Shields, 1977; Dembroski, Mac-Dougall, Shields, Petitto, & Lushene, 1978).

For example, the Type A pattern characterized by excessive vigor, hard-driving competitiveness, hostility, impatience, and time urgency (Rosenman, Friedman, Straus et al., 1964) has been prospectively linked with clinical CHD (Brand, 1978). In our laboratory, we have been testing the hypothesis that Type A subjects relative to their less intense Type B counterparts are prone to respond to environmental challenges with excessive and potentially damaging physiologic reactions (also see Glass, Krakoff, Contrada et al., in press). To give the reader some idea of this work, the results of several studies will be summarized briefly.

(a) Heart rate (HR) and blood pressure (BP) changes were significantly higher in Type A relative to B subjects in both the cold pressor test and a reaction time task under instructional conditions that emphasized the challenging nature of the tasks. Under low challenge instruction, little difference in physiologic response between the Types was observed. Component analyses revealed that the high hostile Type A's tended to respond with excessive arousal regardless of instructional condition (Dembroski, MacDougall, Herd, & Shields, 1979a).

(b) Both Type A coronary patients and controls evidenced significantly greater BP reactions during the course of a challenging interview and during a history quiz. Case and control Type A's and the Type B cases showed larger quiz-induced increases in systolic BP (SBP) than Type B controls despite beta blocking medication present in the cases (Dembroski, MacDougall, & Lushene, 1979b).

(c) No A/B difference was observed on any physiologic parameter in females ($n = 60$) subjected to the same paradigm as were the males in (a) above. However, high hostile Type A females showed significantly greater SBP and HR reactions than low hostile females (MacDougall, Dembroski, & Krantz, in press). A new sample of females ($n = 60$) showed a significant A/B difference in SBP reactions during verbal competition with another woman, during a challenging interview and a history quiz. However, as in the previous study, no A/B difference was observed during a challenging reaction time task (MacDougall et al., in press).

(d) In a study in collaboration with Krantz and associates, a significant A/B difference was observed during a challenging interview in HR reactions and in SBP changes of patients scheduled for angiography. The lowest SBP reactions of all were shown by Type B's with low levels of coronary artery disease (Krantz, Schaeffer, Davia et al., in press).

It is emphasized, however, that excessive physiologic response is simply not characteristic of many Type A's and, in fact, some Type B's are quite reactive. In this connection, we have argued previously that many factors other than Type A must be considered (Dembroski et al., 1979a). For example, factors directly associated with propensity for exaggerated physiologic reactivity should be studied directly as well as behavioral factors such as smoking, exercise, diet, etc. In other words, CHD has multiple etiologic pathways involving many factors.

INTERVENTION RESEARCH

If such factors can be identified, it is then possible to examine the effectiveness of various techniques in altering them. For example, suppose an individual evidences significantly higher levels of plasma catecholamines during the working day than at night (Friedman, St. George, Byers et al., 1960). This reaction may be due to certain challenges encountered in the work situation which result in enhanced sympathetic autonomic nervous system (ANS) arousal (Friedman, Byers, Diamant, & Rosenman, 1975; Dembroski, MacDougall, & Shields, 1977). If such is the case, interventions aimed at any of a variety of factors in Fig. 1 may succeed in reducing physiologic arousal (Suinn, 1975).

A change in the environment, for example, such as altering time deadlines or the work load in the work setting, might produce the desired result. It also is possible to leave the work situation unaltered, but train the individual to perceive the situation differently; i.e., process the information in a manner that will not produce physiologic arousal. However, if the individual's psychological reaction is such that physiologic arousal is produced, then training the individual to reduce physiologic arousal may be efficacious, e.g., through relaxation training (Benson, 1975). Yet another possibility is to teach the individual to behave in a manner that alters the environment and eliminates or diminishes the environmental stimuli that trigger enhanced physiologic arousal. If, for instance, an individual interacts with his or her work associates in a different way the result might be a change in the behaviors of the associates that excite the physiologic arousal in the individual. Finally, it is possible to intervene directly on the physiologic state with pharmacological agents (Rosenman, 1978).

Any one or combination of the above strategies can be applied in controlled studies aimed at reducing risk factors or CHD. A particularly fertile area for research of this kind is with coronary patients using recurring myocardial infarction as the major dependent variable. Apart from its practical value, such research would be critical to establishing a causal role of a psychosocial factor in CHD. In other words, if alteration of a psychosocial factor in controlled experiments results in a reduction in CHD, then its role as a causal factor in CHD is strengthened (Roskies, Kearney, Spevack et al., 1979).

ANIMAL RESEARCH

Abundant research already exists which demonstrates that animals are also susceptible to many of the same stress-related diseases seen in humans. As such, research with infrahuman subjects can play a significant role in clarifying certain neuro-behavioral and physiological processes which are suggested by the variables in Fig. 1, but which are not easily subject to experimental test in human subjects. It is appropriate to review the current state of understanding with regard to the pathophysiology of these conditions and the manner in which psychosocial and behavioral factors appear to operate in animals.

The prevalence of coronary artery disease and hypertension generally parallels the increasing complexity and ambiguity of social systems and social hierarchies whether we are speaking of animals or mankind. Obviously, it is easier to develop controlled experiments in the less cognitively complex members of the animal kingdom. For example, Mason (1968) has reviewed the research that found that psychosocial stimuli can elicit either of two neuroendocrine responses. One neuro-endocrine response involves arousal of the pituitary adrenal cortical system; the other involves arousal of the sympathetic adrenal medullary system. Social inter-actions resulting in downward displacement in the social hierarchy result in stimu-lation of the pituitary adrenal cortical system which is attended by mental depres-sion, decreased gonadotropin levels, enhanced vagal activity, gluconeogenesis, and pepsin production. By contrast, sympathetic adrenal medullary responses are called into play when agonistic or competitive behavior is invoked to prevent threatened loss of esteem and/or related objects of attachment.

The behavioral paradigms employed to challenge cardiovascular response in animals include classical conditioning, avoidance conditioning, avoidance yoke procedure, pre-avoidance experience, and psychosocial stress. In classical condi-tioning, electrical shock stimulation of monkeys gives rise to heart rate changes as long as the conditioned stimulus (light or tone) remains novel. Chronic habitua-tion results in a loss of the physiological response (Schneiderman, 1978). Thus, the novelty in classical conditioning appears to be important with regard to cardio-vascular response. In avoidance conditioning, the animal must make a designated response to avoid being shocked. A variety of animal species in this setting demon-strate increased arterial pressure, heart rate, and cardiac output with variable changes in peripheral systemic resistance (Anderson & Tosheff, 1973; Forsyth, 1971). Changes have also been noted in cardiac electrophysiologic properties during avoidance conditioning (Lown, Verrier, & Corbalan, 1973; Lawler & Lown, 1974; DeSilva, Verrier, & Lown, 1978). These alterations have been implicated in diverse cardiac arrhythmias, including ventricular fibrillation. Changes in coro-nary blood flow have also been demonstrated in other avoidance conditioning experiments (Ernst, Kordenat, & Sandman, 1979).

In the avoidance yoke procedure, an animal is trained to manipulate a level to avoid a shock and both animals are shocked if the "avoidance" animal fails. Ob-viously, the "yoked" partner has no control over the outcome. These "yoked" monkeys rapidly develop physical deterioration, bradycardia and ventricular arrest without significant myocardial necrosis (Corley, Mauck, & Shiel, 1975). In contrast, the "avoidance" monkeys develop electrocardiographic abnormalities and myocardial degenerative lesions. Thus, apparently distinct cardiovascular physiologic responses occur in avoidance animals relative to yoked, helpless ani-mals. The former appears to be a sympathetic autonomic response whereas the latter appears to be a vagally mediated response. Even in monkeys, the perception of control or no control has physiologically distinct consequences that are asso-ciated with overt behavioral patterns. Preavoidance experience is gained by sub-jecting animals to repeated sessions of avoidance conditioning. Eventually such animals demonstrate changes in their baseline cardiovascular physiology during the periods immediately preceding the session. These experiences can clearly influence the behavioral, physiological, and biochemical responses of the organism. Antici-pation of a daily sessions of unsignalled avoidance is frequently attended by a progressive decrease in heart rate and cardiac output, and a progressive increase in peripheral resistance in dogs (Anderson & Tosheff, 1973).

The experimental designs which most closely approximate those conditions experienced by humans occur in experiments involving manipulation of the social hierarchy in animal colonies. Among the cardiovascular conditions demonstrated by these experimental psychosocial and behavioral designs are fixed hypertension, myocardial hypertrophy, progressive arteriosclerosis, myocardial fibrosis, and renal failure (Henry & Ely, 1979). These conditions were induced by subjecting socially deprived mice to social interaction. At least some of these changes were apparently mediated by increases in the adrenal enzymes, tyrosine hydroxylase and phenyl-ethanolamine N-methyltransferase (Henry & Ely, 1979). Basically, the increases observed appeared to reflect a situation in which brief sympathetic discharges elicited by discontinuous emotional stimulus were transformed into sustained sympathetic arousal.

There are many examples similar to those referred to above that amplify the evidence that environmental novelty and/or adversity (particularly when sustained) are capable of eliciting physiologic responses. When these conditions are unabated, they may lead to pathologic consequences. In addition, psychosocial interactions are powerful and important influences in eliciting such responses. It is important to remember that social stimuli do not act directly on the individual (Henry & Ely, 1979). Rather, perception of the social environment, as mediated by personality, role, and status variables, arouses emotions which induce physiologic responses.

PATHOPHYSIOLOGY OF CARDIOVASCULAR DISEASE IN HUMANS

If we review what is known and suspected concerning the pathophysiology of the standard coronary risk factors, it is obvious that each represents a single mani-festation of a more complex underlying process. What constitutes the fundamental pathophysiology remains conjectural, but the orchestration of such factors occurs in a living, emotional, reacting organism attempting to adapt to its environment in the interest of maintaining its own integrity.

Coronary Heart Disease

A variety of psychosocial and conditioning experiments in animals point clearly to mechanisms attending the development of accelerated atherosclerosis, and the neuroendocrine system is undoubtedly of pivotal importance in orchestrating the pathophysiologic mechanisms culminating in atherosclerosis. Among the standard risk factors, dietary fat intake appears to be statistically important. However, the documented observations that dietary cholesterol is limited in absorption and that most cholesterol is manufactured in the liver suggests that other factors might be importantly involved. It is curious that Friedman et al.'s (1958) studies of ac-countants, mentioned earlier, demonstrated that their highest serum cholesterol levels consistently occurred during periods of severe occupational and emotional stress. Conversely, minimal values occurred during periods of minimal stress despite unchanged levels of dietary fat intake. While fat feeding rabbits to produce athero-sclerosis has been carried out as a reliable animal model for the last sixty years, Nerem (1979) reports that if the animals are fondled or given daily doses of diazepam, the extent of atherosclerosis is significantly reduced despite comparable levels of attained hypercholesterolemia. Thus, the association between dietary intake of fat and atherosclerosis is incomplete.

Cigarette smoking is another risk factor with definite physiologic consequences resulting from nicotine and carbon monoxide exposure. Nicotine is a stimulator of both sympathetic and parasympathetic ganglia and increases the arterial epinephrine concentrations in man. Nicotine also induced ADH secretion, liberates catecholamines from the heart, increases heart rate and cardiac output, lowers the threshold for ventricular fibrillation, and causes peripheral vessel constriction. Nicotine increases free fatty acids in serum through its catecholamine release and usually promotes the development of atherosclerotic lesions in fat-fed animals (Astrup & Kjeldsen, 1974). Necrosis and calcification of the medial layers of the aorta were often seen in these animals, and this might be explained by an effect of catecholamines since their administration to animals has a similar effect. The effect, if any, of smoking on blood coagulation and platelet function is probably related to an action of nicotine. Carbon monoxide does induce arterial hypoxia which accelerates atherosclerosis in cholesterol-fed rabbits (Astrup & Kjeldsen, 1974). However, there is no qualitative difference between lesions in animals exposed to carbon monoxide and animals exposed to hypoxia.

At the present state of our understanding, it appears that the atheroslcerotic process involves injury and proliferation of intimal smooth cells with subsequent alteration in permeability and/or metabolism and tends to occur at bifurcating or originating sites of vessel branches. With the progressive insudation of lipid material, hemodynamic impairment to flow eventually results. The site of lesion formation suggests that hydrodynamic stress and shear forces participate in the process. A second factor having obvious face validity is that enhanced lipid availability is an integral part of the atherosclerotic process. Here also psychosocial and behavioral factors appear to be involved. An additional link to be considered in the atherosclerotic chain of events is the role of platelets and thrombosis. This phenomenon appears to be distinctive for atherogenic sequelae in man as compared to the rest of the animal kingdom. If smooth muscle cell proliferation, lipid accumulation, and thrombosis are parts of the atherosclerotic mosaic, clotting and platelet function must be suspected as potentially culpable agents in the process. A variety of studies have demonstrated the ability of catecholamines to enhance platelet stickiness and aggregation while other studies have demonstrated increased platelet aggregation and consumption under a variety of situations, both emotional and physical, broadly referred to as "stress" (Haft & Arkel, 1976; Fleischman, Bierenbaum, & Stier, 1976).

The mechanisms through which Type A behavior operates as a risk factor and how it facilitates the progression of coronary heart disease remains conjectural, a weakness shared with all risk factors until the pathogenesis of coronary atherosclerosis is fully understood. However, the prevalence of certain biochemical and physiological phenomena is highly associated with fully developed Type A behavior. These include elevated serum cholesterol levels, elevated pre- and post-prandial serum triglycerides, enhanced platelet aggregation, faster clotting time, higher excretion of norepinephrine particularly when provoked by emotional challenge, a higher average serum level of corticotropin, a greater insulinemic resonse to glucose, a decreased growth hormone response to arginine and greater lability and magnitude of blood pressure response under time demand tasks (Freidman, 1977, 1978; Dembroski et al., 1977, 1978, 1979a, b; Glass et al., in press; Rosenman & Freidman, 1974).

Many of the incriminated mechanisms appear to work through or are activated by catecholamines in concert with hyperlipemia. Catecholamines are probably the most important factors promoting lipid mobilization. They are effective in mobilizing lipid from adipose tissue both by their liberation from non-adrenergic nerve terminals in adipose tissue and by their secretion from the adrenal medulla into the blood. The free fatty acids not stored or utilized in the production of energy are eventually taken up by the adipose tissues or by the liver. Free fatty acids taken up by the liver are formed into triglycerides and secreted as components of very low density lipoproteins. The rate at which the liver secretes very low density lipoproteins is determined partly by the rate it synthesizes free fatty acids from carbohydrates and partly by the rate it receives free fatty acids in the blood. In the fasting state, the secretion of very low density lipoproteins by the liver is determined principally by the levels of free fatty acids in the blood. These levels in turn are determined principally by the effects of catecholamines on adipose tissue and the rates of energy production. Catecholamines promote platelet adhesiveness and aggregation, promote arrhythmias and lower the threshold to arrhythmia generation, and increase secretion of glucagon, thyroxin, calcitonin, parathormone, renin, erythropoietin, and gastrin while diminishing insulin secretion.

Glucocorticoids convert protein into carbohydrate and fat, have a minor antagonistic effect on insulin, promote the development of diabetes, foster hyperlipidemia and hypercholesterolemia, enhance water diuresis, diminish circulating lymphocytes, reduce leukocytosis and polycythemia, increase platelet counts with an enhancement of clotting tendencies, lower the electrical excitation threshold of the brain, increase gastric acidity and pepsin production, block growth hormone secretion, decrease calcium absorption, enhance angiotensinogen production, sensitize arterioles to the pressor effect of catecholamines, and decrease the inflammatory response. Accelerated atherosclerosis is one of the main cuases of death in Cushing's Syndrome, whereas the sequelae of pheochromocytoma include hypertensive crisis, myocardial infarction with or without coronary disease, arrhythmias, and catecholamine myocarditis. Both of these endocrine excesses have been demonstrated to occur in reactions to various psychosocial circumstances mediated by cognitive perception (also see Herd, 1978; Williams, 1978).

Sudden Cardiac Death

The influences of psychosocial and behavioral factors is becoming increasingly well substantiated in the clinical areas of arrhythmogenesis and sudden death. A variety of physiologic mechanisms contributing to these clinical phenomena are being discovered and examined. The aspects of cognitive integration eliciting such responses remain an important frontier for further investigation. Several reports have recently appeared in the literature documenting the effects of psychological stress in lowering the threshold for ventricular fibrillation and sudden death both in animals and in man (Lynch, Paskewitz, Gimbel, & Thomas, 1977; Engel, 1978; Lown, DeSilva, & Lenson, 1978). The combination of arousal with enforced helplessness and extreme conflicting stimulation has been demonstrated by Gelhorn (1967) to result in breakdown of the reciprocity between the fight or flight reaction and the playing dead reaction. Under overwhelming stress, both systems become active simultaneously or in rapid alternation with each other. This constitutes the neurophysiologic basis for the behavioral disorganization typically exhibited by animals under extreme stress: the dog that startles, crouches, trembles, moves about aimlessly, barks, whines, salivates, urinates, defecates, pants, piloerects and sometimes momentarily dozes. All these activities indicate simultaneous or rapidly alternating sympathetic parasympathetic activation.

Although it is difficult to conduct controlled human studies comparable to those readily obtained in animals, electrocardiographic monitoring during a variety of psychologically stressful tasks in humans has documented significant and potentially fatal rhythm disturbances in direct association with episodes of emotional stress (DeSilva & Lown, 1979).

Sudden cardiac death is a rare event in histologically normal hearts and one of the most frequent histologic abnormalities found is that of coagulative myocytolysis. The fact that this form of tissue necrosis, consisting of anomalous contraction bands as a characteristic feature, can be found in central nervous system lesions and produced by catecholamine injections suggests that neurohumoral excess and the creation of metabolic imbalances render the myocardium more vulnerable to a final electrical catastrophe. The hyperfunctional form of necrosis has been well described in cases of pheochromocytoma and in association with a variety of examples of so-called stress-induced sudden death.

The results of catecholamine (isoproterenol) administration to dogs showed a marked increase in the rate of development of tension in the left ventricle and significant reductions in the level of total high-energy phosphates with preferential depletion of the inner layer (Pieper, Clayton, Todd, & Eliot, 1979a, b; Eliot, Todd, Clayton, & Pieper, 1978). As compared to coronary artery ligation, the metabolic derangements from catecholamine administration were found to be similar, although myocardial contractility was increased by catecholamine administration and decreased during coronary artery ligation (Pieper et al., 1979a; Eliot et al., 1978). In addition to mimicking the contraction band lesions, these studies also point toward severe mechanical overdrive as a fundamental factor in contraction band formation since these lesions occur in large numbers only following isoproterenol infusion (Eliot, Clayton, Pieper, & Todd, 1977; 1978). The metabolic, histologic and hemodynamic abnormalities of isoproterenol infusion could be largely ameliorated by beta blockade pretreatment (Eliot et al., 1978; Pieper et al., 1979a). The favorable response to beta blocking agents in the prevention of sudden death together with the histologic similarity between sudden cardiac death and catecholamine administration suggests that neurohumoral mechanisms participate in the pathogenesis.

Hypertension

A wide variety of experimental and clinical observations implicates psychosocial and behavioral factors in the phenomenon of essential hypertension. The interaction between mind and environment engrafted upon a genetic substrate is a complex topic for study. Yet, the foregoing discussions of neuroendocrine mechanisms and consideration of the concept that essential hypertension represents specific disturbances or shifts in the bias of physiologic regulatory mechanisms are consistent with observations of epidemiologic, experimental, and clinical data. Since either adrenal medullary or adrenal cortical systems can lead to hypertension and are known to be activated by psychosocial stimuli with concomitant behavioral phenomena, it is not too difficult to see that repeated exposure to such stimuli can lead to structural vascular thickening and mechanically increased resistance. Whereas initially the imbalance is probably reversible, chronically repeated and sustained arousals are likely to result in a permanent disregulatory state with fixed hypertension. Whether these observations linking personality, behavior and neuroendocrine mechanisms with hypertension or a protective response to genetic vulnerability or even a functional defect as a consequence of the disease process remains to be elucidated.

It would appear that a social structure which positively reinforces competition, aggression and time urgent performance would result in a perpetual dynamic struggle for status and dominance so characteristic of the Type A behavioral pattern. Such behavior, reinforced and rewarded by agonistic societies, is attended by all the previously discussed physiologic mechanisms implicated in the pathogenesis of coronary heart disease. These include large fluctuations in blood pressure, excessive catecholamine and ACTH production, enhanced lipid mobilization and increased platelet aggregation.

Such observations do not deny the importance of innate physiologic reactivity, nor should we minimize the important influence of heredity. Nevertheless, if we are to talk about phenomena which may accelerate or foster the biologic time clock of a degenerative process, the psychosocial and behavioral factors discussed provide a unifying link between epidemiologic and pathophysiologic mechanisms in the study of coronary heart disease, hypertension, and sudden cardiac death.

REFERENCES

Anderson, D. E. & Tosheff, J. Cardiac output and total peripheral resistance changes during preavoidance periods in the dog. *Journal of Applied Physiology*, 1973, *34*, 650–654.

Astrup, P. & Kjeldsen, K. Carbon monoxide, smoking and atherosclerosis, Symposium on Atherosclerosis, Ed. M. D. Altschule, *Medical Clinics of North America*, vol. 58, Philadelphia: W. B. Saunders Co., 1974, pp. 323–350.

Benson, H. *The Relaxation Response*. New York: Morrow, 1975.

Brand, R. J. Coronary-prone behavior as an independent risk factor for coronary heart disease. In T. M. Dembroski, S. M. Weiss, J. L. Shields, et al. (eds.), *Coronary-Prone Behavior*. New York: Springer-Verlag, 1978.

Buell, J. C. & Eliot, R. S. Stress and cardiovascular disease. *Modern Concepts of Cardiovascular Disease*, 1979, *48*, 19–24.

Corley, K. C., Mauck, H. P., & Shiel, F. O. M. Cardiac responses associated with "yoked-chair" shock avoidance in squirrel monkeys. *Psychophysiology*, 1975, *12*, 439–444.

Dembroski, T. M. Reliability and validity of methods used to assess coronary-prone behavior. In T. M. Dembroski, S. M. Weiss, J. L. Shields et al. (eds.), *Coronary-Prone Behavior*. New York: Springer-Verlag, 1978.

Dembroski, T. M. & MacDougall, J. M. Stress effects on affiliation preferences among subjects possessing the Type A coronary-prone behavior pattern. *Journal of Personality and Social Psychology*, 1978, *36*, 23–33.

Dembroski, T. M., MacDougall, J. M., Herd, J. A., & Shields, J. L. Effects of level of challenge on pressor and heart rate responses in Type A and B subjects. *Journal of Applied Social Psychology*, 1979, *9*, 209–228. (a)

Dembroski, T. M., MacDougall, J. M., & Lushene, R. Interpersonal interaction and cardiovascular response in Type A subjects and coronary patients. *Journal of Human Stress*, 1979, *5*, 28–36. (b)

Dembroski, T. M., MacDougall, J. M., & Shields, J. L. Physiologic reactions to social challenge in persons evidence the Type A coronary-prone behavior pattern. *Journal of Human Stress*, 1977, *3*, 2–9.

Dembroski, T. M., MacDougall, J. M., Shields, J. L., Pettito, J., & Lushene, R. Components of the Type A coronary-prone behavior pattern and cardiovascular responses to psychomotor challanges. *Journal of Behavioral Medicine*, 1978, *1*, 159–166.

DeSilva, R. A. & Lown, B. The role of the central nervous system in fatal arrhythmias. *Journal of South Carolina Medical Association*, 1979, *75*, 567–571.

DeSilva, R. A., Verrier, R. L., & Lown, B. Effects of psychological stress and vagal stimulation with morphine in the conscious dog. *American Heart Journal*, 1978, *95*, 197.

Dreyfuss, F. & Czazckes, J. W. Blood cholesterol and uric acid of healthy medical students under the stress of an examination. *Archives of Internal Medicine*, 1959, *103*, 708–711.

Eliot, R. S., Clayton, F. C., Pieper, G. M., & Todd, G. L. Influence of environmental stress on the pathogenesis of sudden cardiac death. *Federation Proceedings*, 1977, *36*, 1719–1724.

Eliot, R. S., Todd, G. L., Clayton, F. C., & Pieper, G. M. Experimental catecholamine-induced acute myocardial necrosis. in V. Manninen & P. I. Halonen (eds.), *Sudden Coronary Death, Advances in Cardiology*, vol. 25. Basel: S. Karger AG, 1978, pp. 107–118.

Engel, G. L. Psychologic stress, vasodepressor (vasovagal) syncope and sudden death. *Annals of Internal Medicine*, 1978, *89*, 403–412.

Ernst, F. A., Kordenat, R. K., & Sandman, C. A. Learned control of coronary blood flow. *Psychosomatic Medicine*, 1979, *41*, 79–85.

Fleischman, A. I., Bierenbaum, M. L., & Stier, A. Effect of stress due to anticipated minor surgery upon in vivo platelet aggregation in humans. *Journal of Human Stress*, 1976, *2*, 33–37.

Forsyth, R. P. Regional blood flow changes during 72 hour avoidance schedules in the monkey. *Science*, 1971, *173*, 546–548.

Friedman, M. Type A beahvior: Its possible relationship to pathogenetic processes responsible for coronary heart disease. In T. M. Dembroski, S. M. Weiss, J. L. Shields et al. (eds.), *Coronary-Prone Behavior*. New York: Springer-Verlag, 1978.

Friedman, M. Type A behavior pattern: Some of its pathophysiological components. *Bulletin of the New York Academy of Medicine*, 1977, *53*, 593–604.

Friedman, M., Byers, S. O., Diamant, J., & Rosenman, R. H. The plasma norepinephrine response of coronary-prone subjects (Type A) to a specific challenge. *Metabolism*, 1975, *24*, 205–210.

Friedman, M., Rosenman, R. H., & Carroll, V. Changes in the serum cholesterol and blood-clotting time in men subjected to cyclic variation of occupational stress. *Circulation*, 1958, *17*, 852–861.

Friedman, M., St. George, S., Byers, S. O. et al. Excretion of catecholamines, 17-ketosteroids, 17-hydroxycorticoids and 5-hydroxyindole in men exhibiting a particular behavior pattern (A) associated with high incidence of clinical coronary artery disease. *Journal of Clinical Investigation*, 1960, *39*, 758–764.

Gelhorn, E. *Principles of Autonomic Somatic Integrations*. Minneapolis: University of Minnesota Press, 1967.

Glass, D. C. *Behavior Patterns, Stress and Coronary Disease*. Hillsdale, N.J.: Lawrence Erlbaum, 1977.

Glass, D. C., Krakoff, L. R., Contrada, R. et al. Effect of harassment and competition upon cardiovascular and catecholaminic responses in Type A and B individuals. *Psychophysiology*, in press.

Gordon, T., Garcia-Palmieri, M. R., Kagan, A. et al. Differences in coronary heart disease in Framingham, Honolulu and Puerto Rico. *Journal of Chronic Diseases*, 1974, *27*, 329–337.

Haft, J. I. & Arkel, Y. S. Effect of emotional stress on platelet aggregation in humans. *Chest*, 1976, *70*, 501–505.

Henry, J. P. & Ely, D. L. Physiology of emotional stress. Specific responses. *Journal of South Carolina Medical Association*, 1979, *75*, 501–509.

Herd, J. A. Physiological correlates of coronary prone behavior. In T. M. Dembroski, S. M. Weiss, J. L. Shields et al. (eds.), *Coronary-Prone Behavior*. New York: Springer-Verlag, 1978.

Jenkins, C. D. Behavioral risk factors in coronary artery disease. *Annual Review of Medicine*, 1978, *29*, 543–562.

Jenkins, C. D. Psychologic and social precursors of coronary disease. *New England Journal of Medicine*, 1971, *284*, 244–255, 307–317.

Jenkins, C. D. Recent evidence supporting psychologic and social risk factors for coronary disease. *New England Journal of Medicine*, 1976, *294*, 987–994, 1033–1038.

Kaplan, B. H., Cassel, J., & Gore, S. Social support and health. *Medical Care*, in press.

Keys, A., Aravanis, C., Blackburn, H. et al. Probability of middle-aged men developing coronary heart disease in five years. *Circulation*, 1972, *45*, 815–828.

Keys, A., Karvonen, M. J., & Fidanza, F. Serum cholesterol studies in Finland. *Lancet*, 1958, *2*, 175–178.

Kozarevic, D., Pirk, B., Dawber, T. R. et al. The Yugoslavia Cardiovascular Disease Study–1. The incidence of coronary heart disease by area. *Journal of Chronic Diseases*, 1976, *29*, 405–414.

Krantz, D. S., Schaeffer, M. A., Davia, J. et al. Investigation of extent of coronary atherosclerosis, Type A behavior, and cardiovascular respone to social interaction. *Psychophysiology*, in press.
Lown, B., DeSilva, R. A., & Lenson, R. Roles of psychologic stress and autonomic nervous
system changes in provocation of ventricular premature complexes. *American Journal of
Cardiology*, 1978, *41*, 979–985.
Lown, B., Verrier, R. L., & Corbalan, R. Psychologic stress and threshold for repetitive ventri-
cular response. *Science*, 1973, *182*, 834.
Lynch, J. J., Paskewitz, D. A., Gimbel, K. S., & Thomas, S. A. Psychological aspects of cardiac
arrhythmia. *American Heart Journal*, 1977, *93*, 645–657.
MacDougall, J. M., Dembroski, T. M., & Krantz, D. S. Effects of physical and psychomotor
performance challenge on pressor and heart rate responses in Type A and B female subjects.
Psychophysiology, in press.
Mason, J. W. A review of psychoendocrine research on the pituitary adrenal cortical system.
Psychosomatic Medicine, 1968, *30*, 576–607.
Matta, R. J., Lawler, J. E., & Lown, B. Ventricular electrical instability in the conscious dog.
Effects of psychologic stress and beta-adrenergic blockade. *American Journal of Cardiology*,
1974, *34*, 692.
Matthews, K. A. & Brunson, B. I. The attentional style of Type A coronary-prone individuals.
Implications for symptom reporting. *Journal of Personality and Social Psychology*, 1979,
37, 2081–2090.
Michaels, L. Etiology of coronary artery disease: An historical approach. *British Heart Journal*,
1966, *28*, 258–264.
Nerem, R. Social environment as a factor in diet induced aortic atherosclerosis in rabbits.
Hugh Lofland Conference on Arterial Wall Metabolism, May 1979, Boston, Mass.
Pieper, G. M., Clayton, F. C., Todd, G. L., & Eliot, R. S. Temporal changes in endocardial
energy metabolism following propranolol and the metabolic basis for protection against
isoprenaline cardiotoxicity. *Cardiovascular Research*, 1979, *13*, 207–214. (a)
Pieper, G. M., Clayton, F. C., Todd, G. L., & Eliot, R. S. Transmural distribution of metabolites
and blood flow in the canine left ventricle following isoproterenol infusions. *Journal of
Pharmacology and Experimental Therapeutics*, 1979, *209*, 334–341. (b)
Rosenman, R. H. The role of the Type A behavior pattern in ischaemic heart disease: Modifica-
tion of its effects by beta-blocking agents. *British Journal of Clinical Practice*, 1978, *32*
(Suppl. 1), 58–65.
Rosenman, R. H. & Friedman, M. Neurogenic factors in pathogenesis of coronary heart disease.
Medical Clinics of North America, 1974, *58*, 269–279.
Rosenman, R. H., Friedman, M., Straus, R. et al. A predictive study of coronary heart disease.
The Western Collaborative Group Study. *Journal of the American Medical Association*,
1964, *189*, 15–22.
Roskies, E., Kearney, H., Spevack, M. et al. Generalizability and durability of the treatment
effects in an intervention program for coronary-prone (Type A) managers. *Journal of
Behavioral Medicine*, 1979, *2*, 195–207.
Schneiderman, N. Animal models relating behavioral stress and cardiovascular pathology. In
T. M. Dembroski, S. M. Weiss, J. L. Shields et al. (eds.), *Coronary-Prone Behavior*. New
York: Springer-Verlag, 1978, p. 157.
Suinn, R. The cardiac stress management program for Type A patients. *Cardiac Rehabilitation*,
1975, *5*, 13–15.
Trulson, M. F. The American diet: Past and present. *American Journal of Clinical Nutrition*,
1959, *7*, 91–97.
White, P. D. The historical background of angina pectoris. *Modern Concepts of Cardiovascular
Disease*, 1974, *43*, 109–112.
Williams, R. B. Psychophysiological processes, the coronary-prone behavior pattern, and coro-
nary heart disease. In T. M. Dembroski, S. M. Weiss, J. L. Shields et al. (eds.), *Coronary-
Prone Behavior*. New York: Springer-Verlag, 1978.
Yudkin, J. Diet and coronary thrombosis, hypothesis and fact. *Lancet*, 1957, *2*, 155–162.

15

Differential Effects of Work-related Stressors on Cardiovascular Responsivity

Siegfried Streufert, Susan C. Streufert, Ann L. Denson,
Janet Lewis, and Rugh Henderson
The Pennsylvania State University College of Medicine

Jim L. Shields
National Institutes of Health, NHLBI

INTRODUCTION

It has been widely recognized that stress, particularly at excessive levels, may contribute to decrements in human task performance (e.g., Cohen, 1980; Crump, 1979; Evans, 1978; Kubala & Warnick, 1979; Sarkesian, 1980). Stress effects on performance appear to occur specifically or more severely in more complex tasks (c.f., Evans, 1978; Frankenhauser, 1971) and as long range after effects (c.f., Crump, 1979; Baum, Singer, & Baum, 1981; Cohen, 1980). Unfortunately, detrimental stressor levels (i.e., levels of external stimuli which have undesirable effects) frequently do exist in work environments (Cooper & Payne, 1978).

Improving performance and satisfaction of the work force are linked to the development of environments which do not contain excessive stressor conditions. To develop better, more pleasant and more effective work environments, we need to learn more about stressors and their effects as they occur in work-like settings. It is especially necessary to recognize whether different forms of stressors in the work environment (e.g., social stressors vs. task related stressors) operate in the same or in differential fashion to produce important physiological responses (strain) and subsequent changes in performance and satisfaction.

While earlier work made few, if any, distinctions between the effects of different kinds of stressors (e.g., Selye, 1956, 1976), more recent theory and research have considered diverse kinds of stressors, differential coping responses and specific stressor effects on behavioral outcome (c.f., the review of Baum et al., 1981). For example, the distinction between (perceived) stressors as threatening, harmful or challenging (c.f., Lazarus, 1966) is a likely cause of differential stressor impact. Differences in the level of physiological response to stressors have been described. Yet few distinctions in the kind of physiological responsivity to the different kinds of stressors have been observed.

This research was supported by contract N00014-80-C-0581, NR 170-909 between the Office of Naval Research and Pennsylvania State University. Requests for reprints should be sent to Dr. Siegfried Streufert, Department of Behavioral Science, Pennsylvania State University, Hershey, PA 17033.

Can one expect such different stressors as cataclysmic phenomena and powerful events, requiring adaptive responding vs. daily hassles (descriptions used by Lazarus & Cohen, 1977), to produce identical physiological activity? Would the *magnitude* of adjustment required, the *kind* of adjustment, perceptions of control (c.f., the reviews of Baum et al., 1981; Miller, 1979; Thompson, 1981) and valence (terms used by Kiretz & Moos, 1974) result in the same level and kind of catecholamine response as well as the same magnitude and kind of cardiovascular reactivity? Thus far there is relatively little evidence for any differentiation of physiological response to stressor impact (c.f., Selye, 1956, 1976). Nonetheless, the argument for specific patterning of physiological responses to specific stressors has been made (e.g., Mason, 1975). Some relevant research data are discussed below.

The question whether stressors differ only in the level of strain and stress experience (and performance change) which they produce, or whether they differ in the *characteristic kind* of physiological response and the type of performance change as well, then, remains open. If we wish to generate an overall theory of stress, if we wish to make relatively simple predictions about the stressor to performance relationship, then a single stress response in working human beings would certainly be welcome. If, on the other hand, stressors occurring in work environments differ not only in the level but also in the kind of effect they have on physiological responses and subsequent performance (assuming some meaningful and consistent impact of arousal upon performance), or if different stressors interact with specific tasks in unique ways to modify physiological status and subsequent response, then we will have to engage in considerably more effort to learn when and where we need to intervene to optimize task performance and satisfaction. In the present paper, the relationship between various stressor conditions and physiological activity (strain), as measured via increases and decreases of blood pressure and heart rate, will be considered. The employed stressor conditions will vary in level and will be both social and nonsocial. The selected stressor conditions will be manipulated in an experimental setting and will be somewhat similar to stressors experienced in work environments. Stressors of "cataclysmic" nature will not be considered in this research.

CARDIOVASCULAR EFFECTS OF STRESSORS

We know that stressors that impinge upon persons act upon their cardiovascular systems causing increases in diastolic blood pressure and heart rate. Simultaneous increases in blood pressure (particularly systolic) and heart rate are typically interpreted as indicants of sympathetic arousal due to stress conditions. Diastolic blood pressure increases (without parallel systolic elevation), in the presence of relatively constant or decreasing heart rate are believed to be caused by increased peripheral resistance (vasomotor tone), representing a somewhat different *kind* of strain reaction to different kinds of stressors. If this is so, then the measurement of heart rate and pressor responses provides convenient non-invasive indicators of both *kind* and *level* of experienced stress. This form of measurement may be quite useful to determine whether different levels and kinds of stressor conditions have similar or diverse effects on human physiological status and, potentially, on subsequent work performance.

It would be particularly useful to determine whether different work related stressors merely produce different levels of physiological strain or result in diverse kinds of strain responses as well. If there is little commonality in the hemodynamic responses to work-related stressors and tasks, then little commonality of subsequent performance across the various stressor conditions would be expected, and diverse procedures for reducing stressor conditions in the work environment may be required.

Previous research concerned with the effects of stressor conditions on hemodynamic responsivity has not been very systematic in nature. Tasks, environments and/or cardiovascular response measures have varied widely from one researcher to the next which makes comparisons among the results obtained by the various researchers difficult. In other words, from previous research efforts, it is difficult to determine whether physiological reactivity to various stressor conditions is different in kind, as well as in level. The majority of research reports appear to suggest that both blood pressure and heart rate become simultaneously elevated with stress experience (e.g., Andrien & Hansson, 1981; Bassan, Marcus, & Ganz, 1980; Bonelli, Hortnagl, Brucke, Magometschnigg, Lochs, & Kaik, 1979; Roscoe, 1978; Rush, Shepherd, Webb, & Vanhoutte, 1981; Sime, Buel, & Eliot, 1980). Such data are based on diverse stressor tasks, ranging from landing aircraft to performing mental arithmetic. Yet, despite the number of studies reporting similar or equivalent results, some researchers report data that appear to be inconsistent with findings of similar degrees of physiological response to diverse stressors. Danner, Endert, Koster, and Dunning (1981), for example, found that students about to take a medical school examination had elevated diastolic blood pressure, unchanged systolic blood pressure, and decreased heart rate.

INDIVIDUAL DIFFERENCES IN CARDIOVASCULAR RESPONSES TO TASK STRESSORS

Differences in cardiovascular reactivity may interact with tasks, environments, and social settings to produce specific responses. Such differences suggest that differential physiological responses (e.g., peripheral vascular resistance vs. increase in heart rate or output) may be due to specific stressor types which would need to be identified. But such divergent data might also be due, for example, to individual differences in cognitive style i.e., Vossel and Laux (1978) have shown that some persons adapt to stressors and subsequently show less physiological arousal (cardiovascular responsivity) even if stressors are now presented in a different mode. Other researchers have demonstrated that cognitive styles affect the degree to which altered cardiovascular hemodynamics are obtained (e.g., Gaines, Smith, & Skolnik, 1977; Kelsall & Strongman, 1978; Streufert, Streufert, Dembroski, & MacDougall, 1979; Woods, 1977). Still other researchers have looked at natural expressive tendencies and their relationship to autonomic arousal.

Notarius and Levinson (1979) investigated subjects who were less facially expressive in response to stress, and found them to be more physiologically reactive in terms of heart rate than their more expressive counterparts. Research by Newlin (1981) investigated both expressive tendencies and hemispheric dominance. Subjects with right hemisphericity had higher heart rates, while subjects who were left hemisphere dominant or highly expressive tended to have larger autonomic responses. A combination of both characteristics (expressiveness and left dominance) showed particularly heightened responses.

Attempts have also been made to relate certain personality and stylistic variables to cardiovascular arousal (e.g., Hinton & Craske, 1977; VanImschoot, Liesse, Mertens, & Lauwers, 1978). The large volume of research on the Type A coronary prone behavior individual and his/her reactivity is now very well known (e.g., Dembroski, Weiss, & Shields, 1978). Elevated cardiovascular responsivity to certain stressors may also be aggravated by specific work or job characteristics. Sime et al. (1980), for example, reported data indicating that blood pressure was considerably higher for the executives in their sample as compared to non-executives.

Finally, cardiovascular hemodynamics may be affected by medication, particularly beta blockers, and other drugs used to decrease autonomic neural effects on the cardiovascular system. Specifically, heart rate elevations in response to stress appear to be diminished or eliminated while elevations in blood pressure often persist (e.g., Bonelli et al., 1979; Dunn, Lorimer, & Lawrie, 1979; Heidbrenner, Pagel, Rockel, & Heidland, 1978; Nakano, Gillespie, & Hollister, 1978; Pritchard, 1981).

The results of studies in which discrepant types of responsivity to diverse stressor conditions are found are suggestive, but hardly conclusive because the data were obtained with different subject populations, diverse tasks and experimental settings, and varying measurement techniques. Therefore, one cannot be certain that studies reporting different types of physiologic responsivity are reliable and valid, especially, given the larger number of studies that have reported differences in level, but not in kind of responsivity. A reliable test of whether different stressor conditions will produce physiological (here, cardiovascular) responsivity which varies not only in level, but also in kind, requires that responsivity to a number of different stressors be obtained with similar measurement methods and with the external research environment held constant. Moreover, the measures should be obtained for the same subjects while performing tasks sufficiently similar to work environments to allow for generalization. Ideally, the subjects should perform on a number of tasks which occur (or have parallels) in the work environment.

CARDIOVASCULAR RESPONSES TO MULTIPLE TASKS

Only few studies in which the same subjects performed on more than one task have been reported. Andrien and Hansson (1981) exposed subjects to cold pressor and arithmetic tasks and obtained increases in blood pressure in both tasks, but heart rate increased only in the arithmetic task. Rush et al. (1981) measured cardiovascular reactivity during physical exercise and during mental stress with essentially similar results. On the other hand, Light and Obrist (1980) found that persons reacting with specific arousal values in one task reacted quite similarly in another different task. Cacioppo and Sandman (1978) obtained different arousal levels in unpleasant visual tasks as compared to unpleasant cognitive tasks. Such discrepancies have led some researchers to conclude that the obtained effects are highly specific to the kind of stressor and the type of task (Lulofs, Wennekens, & VanHoutem, 1981), and that diverse stressor exposures may be reflected in totally different hemodynamic mechanisms (Andrien & Hansson, 1981).[*] Considering

---

[*]Researchers concerned with hormonal responses (e.g., Frankenhäuser, 1975; Frankenhäuser, vonWright, Collins, vonWright, Sedvall, & Swahn, 1976) have obtained data that would argue, at least in part, for nonuniformity of the human stress reaction as well (c.f. also Singer, 1980).

the large number of researchers reporting rather similar results, specificity of the effects of both stressors and tasks on hemodynamic response seems unlikely. With the wide variety of tasks employed, however, differences in either level or kind of response may have generated the apparent discrepancies in observed data.

From the inconclusive findings in previous research, especially in studies where comparisons among responses to more than one task environment have been made, what appears to be needed is research which systematically compares several stressor types that are potentially relevant to work environments across the same subjects, holding all other variables constant. The present investigation was designed to approach these problems in a systematic fashion. Subjects were exposed to a pleasant social interaction, a stressful social interaction, a (social) rest period in the presence of another person, and (non-social) task performance and rest periods while alone. Pressor (i.e. systolic and diastolic blood pressure measured via a self-inflating cuff operated by a Vitastat 900D) and heart rate responses to these conditions were measured for the same persons across stressor conditions and compared to baseline measures.

METHOD

Stressor Conditions

Five different stressor conditions were employed. These conditions were designed to differ in (a) the degree of potential stress, (b) the social vs. non-social environment in which they occurred, and (c) the kind of behavior/performance that was required. The stressors were selected to allow for precise control of the experimental manipulations, yet to have sufficient similarity to the work environments with which they might be compared. The following stressor conditions were utilized:

Non-Social Baseline

This baseline measure was taken while the subject rested alone, as in a break taken in a private setting. The four conditions described below were compared to this condition; differences are expressed as delta values which are used as the basis for the data analysis.

Social Baseline

This baseline measure was taken while the subject rested in the presence of another person, as in a break taken with others present, but without interaction with them.

Complexity Interview

This interview represented a task in which a social interchange on non-self selected topics occurs, yet in a pleasant and open interpersonal atmosphere. The complexity interview is based on the sentence completion task developed by Schroder and Streufert (1963), for which extensive validity and reliability data (Schroder, Driver, & Streufert, 1967) are available.

Type A Interview

This interview represented a task in which social interchange on non-self selected topics occurs, yet in a somewhat unpleasant, challenging interpersonal atmosphere, not unlike the interaction with a moderately hostile demanding boss. Again, extensive reliability and validity data, as well as administration requirements, are available (c.f., Rosenman, 1978).

Visual-Motor Task

The visual motor task was a non-social, task-oriented setting in which the person is working alone against different levels of experimentally scaled and controlled challenges, experiencing both potential success and failure in the task setting. The task is similar to many visual-motor tasks found in work environments (c.f., Streufert, Streufert, & Denson, 1982).

Procedure

The subjects were 26 adult male paid volunteers, with a median age of 50.5 (range 24 to 71). Each subject participated individually in the series of tasks which required approximately four hours. Upon arrival at the laboratory, subjects were individually briefed about the forthcoming events and signed a consent form. Subjects were then taken to one of two identical experimental rooms. For half of the subjects, the experimenter attached a blood pressure cuff to the dominant arm. The cuff allowed the experimenter to measure systolic blood pressure, diastolic blood pressure and heart rate at two-minute intervals. The experimenter then sat at a desk across from the subject and asked a number of biographic questions. Subjects' responses to these questions were recorded by the experimenter on a data sheet. Upon completion of the questionnaire, the subject was asked to sit back and relax for a few minutes. The experimenter remained in the room and quietly worked on organizing a set of papers.

Complexity Interview

After approximately six minutes, the experimenter handed the subject a set of 12 cards, each containing the stem of a sentence (e.g., When someone competes with me . . .). The subject was asked to complete the sentence and add several additional sentences on the same topic. After the subject completed his responses to the card, the experimenter asked several non-leading, non-directive questions, encouraging the subject to continue his statements on the topic at hand. When the subject's repertoire of responses to each topic was exhausted, he was asked to go on to the next card. This procedure was, essentially, an interview version of the sentence completion task developed by Schroder and Streufert (1963) (c.f. also, Schroder et al., 1967). The experimenter interacted with the subject in a warm and cooperative fashion. The behavior and responsiveness of the experimenter allowed the subjects to "open up" and report their significant thoughts and feelings to another person. Responses were recorded on videotape. Physiological measurement procedures during this and other parts of the research are described below.

Type A Interview

Following the complexity interview, the original experimenter left the room and a second experimenter entered to administer the Type A Structured Interview developed by Rosenman and Friedman to measure coronary prone behavior (c.f., Rosenman, 1978). This interview represents a standardized social challenge situation considered by many to exemplify severe social stress. Respones of the subjects were again videotaped. After completion of the interview, the blood pressure cuff was removed from the subject's arm to allow him the freedom to write. The subject was then asked to respond to a paper-and-pencil questionnaire (of no relevance to the research presented here).

Visual-Motor Task

Upon completion of the questionnaire, the subject was escorted to another identical experimental room. The blood pressure/heart rate cuff was attached to the non-dominant arm and the subject was instructed to watch a video screen. After the experimenter left the room, videotaped instructions were displayed on the screen which presented a visual-motor task in the form of a video game (similar to Pac Man). The task was generated by Apple II+ Computer using a program specifically developed for this research program by Mr. Clifford Schafer of the Wise Owl Workship, 1168 Avenida de Las Palmas, Livermore, CA 94550. The instructions were sufficiently detailed to allow all subjects, including those who had no previous experience with video games, to understand the task. The specific task was selected on the basis of its general interest across divergent groups of potential subjects and because it did not rely on previous visual-motor and/or video game experience. Once the subject had completed watching the instructions, he was asked to sit back and relax for a few minutes, while a kaleidoscopic display of colors slowly unfolded on the video screen in front of him. Subjects spent several minutes watching the kaleidoscope.

The task employed in this research has been described in detail by Streufert et al. (1982). Subjects are asked to use a control lever on their desk to move a horseshoe shaped scoop through concentric passageways on a video screen. The passageways were occupied by squares which were to be collected with the scoop. Points are obtained for collecting squares and avoiding movement through unoccupied passageways. In addition, from one to nine differently colored dots move through the passageways. Collision with the dots costs a large number of points, reducing subjects' obtained scores to values below zero when repeated collisions occur.

Subjects were presented with a continuous read-out of their current score as they performed on the visual-motor task. Collision with a dot resulted in a loud noise and vibrations of the video screen, in addition to an immediate drop in the subjects' current score. Further, upon their first try subjects were presented (on the screen) with the "average" initial score of previous subjects. All but two subjects did better than that score. During subsequent games, "the highest score achieved by any player so far" was presented. None of the subjects reached that score level on any of their tries.

During the first (practice) task period, subjects were confronted by only one dot in the passageways. Movement of both dot and scoop were relatively slow. For the subsequent four task periods, movement was increased to a moderate speed and either 2, 4, 6, or 8 dots (in random sequence) appeared during any one period. The presence of only 2 dots represents low stressor levels; 8 dots represents moderately high stressor conditions (c.f., Streufert et al., 1982). Following each task period, subjects rated the difficulty level of that task. On completing the rating they were asked to sit back and relax for a few minutes before the beginning of their next try. Perceptions of difficulty matched the experimentally induced difficulty levels (numbers of dots in the passageways).

After the subject completed all task periods and the subsequent relaxation periods, the experimenter re-entered the room, removed the blood pressure/heart rate cuff, and instructed the subject to complete another paper-and-pencil questionnaire (again, of no relevance to this research). Following the completion of the questionnaire, each subject was debriefed, paid and released.

The task sequence described above held for half ($n = 13$) of the subjects. The remaining 13 subjects were exposed to the experimental procedures in the inverse order (paper-and-pencil questionnaire, followed by visual-motor task instructions, kaleidoscope, visual-motor task, questionnaire, Type A interview, complexity interview, and biographic questions, with rest periods appropriately interspersed).

Measurement of Blood Pressure and Heart Rate

Measurement of systolic blood pressure, diastolic blood pressure, and heart rate were taken throughout the sequence of tasks at two minute intervals except when subjects were working on questionnaires. For the present research, measurements during the Type A interview, the Complexity interview, the rest period between the biographical and Complexity interview (social baseline), the rest period with presentation of a kaleidoscope (non-social baseline), and during the visual-motor task periods are of interest. Multiple measurements were obtained during each segment to increase reliability, but were limited to four measures for each segment to avoid excessive compression of subjects' arms. For the purpose of data analysis, multiple measures for any one segment were averaged to obtain single (mean) values.

RESULTS AND DISCUSSION

Delta values for mean systolic blood pressure, diastolic blood pressure and heart discrepancies from non-social baseline values were calculated for the measures obtained during the Complexity interview, the Type A interview, the visual-motor task, and the social baseline measure. The non-social baseline was used in all calculations of delta values for the following reasons: (1) Establishing common and consequently comparable delta scores across the social and non-social measures; (2) equivalence, i.e. comparability to delta measures used by other researchers; and (3) potential for comparing social and non-social baselines in terms of delta values. Data analysis was based on these delta values. Primary data analysis used Analysis of Variance techniques for overall and partial comparison among the measures. Secondary data analysis employed correlations to relate blood pressure to heart rate (see below).

The main concern in the analysis and interpretation of the data was with elevations of systolic and diastolic blood pressure measurements since these two measures may respond differently to different stressors and may indicate differential response tendencies (as discussed above). Parallel elevations of systolic and diastolic blood pressure will be considered evidence for similar responsivity to stressors across different stressor environments. Parallel elevations (delta values) of different magnitudes in response to different stressors will be viewed as reflections of diverse levels of strain. Interactions of the four stressor environments with the two measures of blood pressure will be considered evidence for differential *kinds* of strain responses to different stressor conditions.

An Analysis of Variance (2 X 4, entirely within) for systolic and diastolic blood pressure deltas comparing the effects of four stressor conditions [(1) social baseline, (2) Complexity interview, (3) Type A interview, and (4) four levels of the visual-motor task] resulted in a highly significant F ratio for stressor conditions ($F = 26.52$, $3/75$ df, $p < 0.01$). The significant main effect for stressor conditions reflects the diverse increases in blood pressure produced by the four experimental treatments. The absence of a significant main effect for blood pressure delta ($F < 1.0$) suggested that the elevations in systolic and diastolic blood pressure were, in general, quite similar.

The significant interaction between blood pressure and stressor conditions was especially interesting. While individual comparisons among the three measures that were obtained in the social settings (social baseline, Type A interview, and Complexity interview) did not produce significant interaction terms, all three produced significant interaction F ratios when singly compared with blood pressure elevations during the visual-motor task. As shown in Fig. 1, systolic and diastolic blood pressure elevations differed only slightly for the three measures taken in social settings, but quite different values were obtained during the visual-motor task, the only non-social stressor condition. Delta systolic blood pressure with a mean elevation of

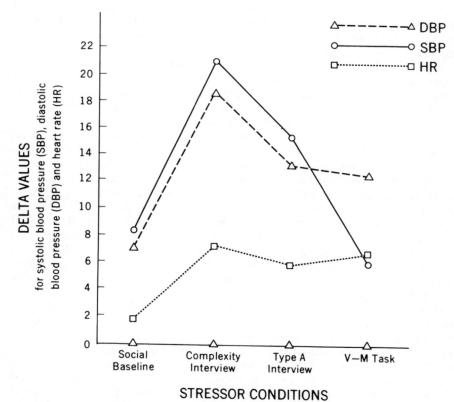

Figure 1 Effects of four stressor conditions on delta systolic blood pressure, delta diastolic blood pressure, and delta heart rate.

6.4 mm Hg was relatively low during the visual-motor task, while delta diastolic blood pressure, with a mean elevation of 12.7 mm Hg, was relatively high and quite similar to the level obtained for that measure during the Type A interview (13.4 mm Hg).

While the greater elevation of diastolic blood pressure for the visual-motor task was typical for the majority of subjects, a minority showed the inverse physiological response: for these persons delta systolic blood pressure exceeded diastolic blood pressure, again specifically and only for the non-social task setting. Both findings clearly suggest that there is a difference in the kind of physiological response when social and non-social conditions are compared. Future research should attempt to establish the underlying differences between those persons who show greater systolic vs. those who show greater diastolic arousal in response to a non-social visual-motor task. The effects of specific kinds of stressors on both levels *and* kinds of physiological response appear to be an even more important area of investigation for subsequent researchers.

Another finding of interest was the discrepancy between blood pressure elevations obtained during the Complexity interview as compared to the measures from the Type A interview. On first consideration, one might expect that higher arousal levels should be obtained in the Type A interview which involved confrontation from a challenging and apparently hostile experimenter—not unlike a somewhat unpleasant interaction with a demanding and hostile boss. Thus, the Type A interview could be viewed as more stressful than the pleasant, non-directive interaction with the interviewer in the Complexity interview.

A closer look at the topics discussed in the Complexity interview, however, may suggest why significantly higher arousal levels were obtained in that interview as compared to the Type A interview ($p < 0.02$ for systolic blood pressure; $p < 0.002$ for diastolic blood pressure). The sentence stems employed in the Complexity interview suggested problems, uncertainties, and challenges of the past to which subjects responded in a permissive atmosphere. Apparently, many of the subjects had never been able to express their feelings about some of the past (and some present) problems they had experienced. In the Complexity interview, they not only cognitively re-experienced these problems, some of them seemed to experience the difficulties and problems for the first time. An example may be a subject who emphasized, after completion of the Complexity interview, that he had never told anyone about any of the thoughts he expressed during the interview. He followed that statement with the concern that his wife or anyone else he knew might find out what he said. He was, of course, assured that no one would. In other words, while there was no externally induced stressor present at the time of the Complexity interview, subjects apparently responded to the stems in the permissive environment, by generating their own internal stressors.

If an increase in systolic blood pressure associated with an increase in heart rate reflects sympathetic arousal, then correlations of some size should be expected between those two measures, and between their delta values. But correlations depend on the distributions of the samples. The fact that we are dealing with comparisons between mean values, and the fact that a few subjects were taking beta blockers should diminish the expected correlations somewhat. Further, individual differences are potentially quite influenced on obtained correlations: some persons apparently experience a decrease in heart rate in some of the stressor conditions (see above, e.g. Danner et al., 1981).

A check on the sample distributions showed that delta values for systolic and diastolic blood pressure were distributed around a single median across the various stressor conditions, while heart rate deltas produced a bimodal distribution. Slightly less than half of the subjects fit well into a distribution ranging from a decrease in heart rate of -8 to an increase of $+3$, while the remainder of the subjects distributed themselves in the range of $+4$ to $+25$ beats per minute. Such a bimodal distribution would make a high correlation between systolic blood pressure and heart rate quite unlikely. In fact, the correlations between systolic blood pressure and heart rate were only $+0.23$ in the Complexity interview, $+0.20$ for the Type A interview, and $+0.16$ for the visual-motor task, and heart rate and systolic blood pressure appeared uncorrelated for the social baseline condition.

Diastolic blood pressure correlated positively with heart rate for the Complexity interview ($+0.23$) and the Type A interview ($+0.36$), but negatively for the visual-motor task (-0.21). While the correlations were generally quite low and positive, the striking departure from the typical results occurred again on the visual-motor task. This negative correlation, together with the parallel increases in blood pressure measures and heart rate for the social stressor conditions, (while elevations in heart rate and diastolic blood pressure were associated with generally lower levels of systolic blood pressure in the non-social task), suggested that the different stressor conditions did indeed produce physiological strain of different level and different kind.

While the hemodynamic changes on the reaction to the social stressor conditions can be primarily related to differentially elevated cardiac functioning, the strain produced by the visual-motor task may be more general in nature: vasomotor tone (peripheral resistance) was likely affected as well. It is quite possible that other measures of the more general response, e.g., measures of perspiration, had they been employed in this research, may also have distinguished between the social and the non-social stressor conditions.

The results obtained in this study are consistent with suggestions made by investigators who view different stressor conditions as productive of not only diverse levels, but also diverse kinds of physiological arousal. Since the stressor conditions utilized in this research were selected to be situations which persons tend to experience in normal work environments, the task of developing a general theory of stressor effects on physiological arousal in work environments has become more complicated.

The present research demonstrates the different effects of diverse (social vs. non-social) stressor environments on physiological arousal. Clearly, different stressors not only produce differential levels but also different kinds of responses. In addition, individual difference variables may determine the kind of response discrepancies that are obtained. The findings would tend to support those investigators that have argued for differential responses to diverse task conditions (e.g., Andrien & Hansson, 1981; Cacioppo & Sandman, 1978; Rush et al., 1981). Future research will have to establish both the kind of strain (diverse arousal levels to task conditions on, for example, cardiovascular parameters) and the level of arousal on each of the measures before meaningful predictions of stress effects can be made.

The research reported in this paper has been concerned with stress experience in work-like environments. This research did not investigate performance or satisfaction with the work environment which may be related to arousal levels. It would seem likely that different work stressor environments and their physiological counterparts have diverse effects on satisfaction and performance in the work setting. Future research should explore relationships among the variables in these realms.

REFERENCES

Andrien, L. & Hansson, L. Circulatory effects of stress in essential hypertension. *Acta Medica Scandinavia*, 1981, *646*, 69–72.

Bassan, M. M., Marcus, H. S., & Ganz, W. The effect of mild-to-moderate mental stress on coronary hemodynamics in patients with coronary artery disease. *Circulation*, 1980, *62*, 933–935.

Baum, A., Singer, J. E., & Baum, C. S. Stress and the environment. *Journal of Social Issues*, 1981, *37*, 4–35.

Bonelli, J., Hortnagl, H., Brucke, T., Magometschnigg, D., Lochs, H., & Kaik, G. Effect of calculation stress on hemodynamics and plasma catecholamines before and after beta-blockade with propranolol and mepindolol sulfate. *European Journal of Clinical Pharmacology*, 1979, *19*, 1–8.

Cacioppo, J. T. & Sandman, C. A. Psychological differentiation of sensory and cognitive tasks as a function of warning, processing demands and reported unpleasantness. *Biological Psychology*, 1978, *6*, 193–201.

Cohen, S. Aftereffects of stress on human performance and social behavior: A review of research and theory. *Psychological Bulletin*, 1980, *88*, 82–108.

Cooper, C. L. & Payne, R. *Stress at work*. New York: Wiley, 1978.

Crump, J. H. Review of stress in air traffic control: It's measurement and effects. *Aviation, Space and Environmental Medicine*, 1979, *50*, 243–248.

Danner, S. A., Endert, E., Koster, R. W., & Dunning, A. J. Biomedical and circulatory parameters during purely mental stress. *Acta Medica Scandinavia*, 1981, *209*, 304–308.

Dembroski, T. M., Weiss, S. M., & Shields, J. L. *Coronary-prone behavior*. New York: Springer-Verlag, 1978.

Dunn, F. G., Lorimer, A. R., & Lawrie, T. D. Objective measurement of performance during acute stress in patients with essential hypertension: Assessment of the effects of propranolol and metotrolol. *Clinical Science*, 1979, *57*, 413–415.

Evans, G. W. Human spatial behavior: The arousal model. In A. Baum & Y. Epstein (eds.), *Human response to crowding*. Hillsdale, N.J.: Erlbaum Associates, 1978.

Frankenhauser, M. Behavior and circulating catecholamines. *Brain Research*, 1971, *31*, 241–262.

Frankenhauser, M. Experimental approaches to the study of catecholamines and emotions. In L. Levi (ed.), *Emotions: Their parameters and measurement*. New York: Raven, 1975.

Frankenhauser, M., vonWright, M., Collins, A., vonWright, J., Sedvall, G., & Swahn, C. G. Sex differences in psycho-endocrine reactions to examination stress. Report 489, University of Stockholm, Department of Psychology, 1976.

Gaines, L. S., Smith, B. D., & Skolnik, B. E. Psychological differentiation, event uncertainty and heart rate. *Journal of Human Stress*, 1977, *3*, 11–25.

Heidbrenner, E., Pagel, G., Rockel, A., & Heidland, A. Beta-adrenergic blockade in stress protection. *European Journal of Clinical Pharmacology*, 1978, *14*, 391–398.

Hinton, J. W. & Craske, B. Differential effects of test stress and the heart rates of extraverts and introverts. *Biological Psychology*, 1977, *5*, 23–28.

Kelsall, P. N. & Strongman, K. T. Emotional experience and the implication grid. *British Journal of Medical Psychology*, 1978, *51*, 243–251.

Kiretz, S. & Moos, R. H. Physiological effects of social environments. *Psychosomatic Medicine*, 1974, *36*, 96–114.

Kubala, A. L. & Warnick, W. L. A review of selected literature on stresses affecting soldiers in combat. U.S. Army Research Institute for the Behavioral and Social Sciences, Technical Report TR79-A14, 1979.

Lazarus, R. S. *Psychological stress and the coping process*. New York: McGraw-Hill, 1966.

Lazarus, R. S. & Cohen, J. B. Environmental stress. In I. Altman & J. F. Wohlwill (eds.), *Human behavior and environment*, vol. 1. New York: Plenum, 1977.

Light, K. C. & Obrist, P. A. Cardiovascular reactivity to behavioral stress in young males with and without marginally elevated casual systolic pressures. *Hypertension*, 1980, *2*, 802–808.

Lulofs, R., Wennekens, R., & VanHoutem, J. Effects of physical stress and time pressure on performance. *Perceptual and Motor Skills*, 1981, *52*, 787–793.

Mason, J. W. A historical view of the stress field. *Journal of Human Stress*, 1975, *1*, 6–12, 22–36.

Miller, S. M. Controllability and human stress: Method, evidence and theory. *Behavioral Research and Therapy*, 1979, *17*, 287–304.

Nakano, S., Gillespie, H. K., & Hollister, L. E. Propranolol in experimentally induced stress. *Psychopharmacology* (Berlin), 1978, *59*, 279–284.

Newlin, D. B. Hemisphericity, expressivity and autonomic arousal. *Biological Psychology*, 1981, *12*, 13–23.

Notarius, C. I. & Levinson, R. W. Expressive tendencies and physiological responses to stress. *Journal of Personality and Social Psychology*, 1979, *37*, 1204–1210.

Pritchard, B. N. C. Beta blockade and the effects of stress on the normal and ischaemic heart. *Aviation, Space and Environmental Medicine*, 1981, *52*, S9–S18.

Roscoe, A. H. Stress and workload in pilots. *Aviation, Space and Environmental Medicine*, 1978, *49*, 630–633.

Rosenman, R. H. The interview method of assessment of the coronary-prone behavior pattern. In T. M. Dembroski, S. M. Weiss, & J. L. Shields (eds.), *Coronary-prone behavior.* New York: Springer-Verlag, 1978.

Rush, N. J., Shepherd, J. T., Webb, R. C., & Vanhoutte, P. M. Different behavior of the resistance vessels of the human calf and forearm during contralateral isometric exercise, mental stress and abnormal respiratory movements. *Circulation Research*, 1981, *48*, 118–130.

Sarkesian, S. C. (ed.). *Combat effectiveness.* Beverly Hills: Sage, 1980.

Schroder, H. M., Driver, M. J., & Streufert, S. *Human information processing.* New York: Holt, Rinehart & Winston, 1967.

Schroder, H. M. & Streufert, S. The measurement of four systems of personality structure varying in level of abstractness: Sentence completion method. Princeton University: ONR Technical Report No. 11, 1963.

Selye, H. *The stress of life.* New York: McGraw-Hill, 1956/1976.

Sime, W. E., Buel, J. C., & Eliot, R. S. Cardiovascular response to emotional stress in post-myocardial infarction patients and matched control subjects. *Journal of Human Stress*, 1980, *6*, 39–46.

Singer, J. E. Traditions of stress research: Integrative comments. *Stress and Anxiety*, 1980, *7*, 3–11.

Streufert, S., Streufert, S. C., Dembroski, T. M., & MacDougall, J. M. Complexity, coronary prone behavior and physiological response. In D. J. Oborne, M. M. Gruneberg, & J. R. Eiser (eds.), *Research in psychology and medicine*, vol. I. London: Academic Press, 1979, pp. 206–218.

Streufert, S., Streufert, S. C., & Denson, A. L. Information load stress, risk taking and physiological responsivity in a visual-motor task. Pennsylvania State University College of Medicine: Technical Report ONR No. 8, 1982.

Thompson, S. C. Will it hurt less if I can control it? A complex answer to a simple question. *Psychological Bulletin*, 1981, *90*, 89–101.

VanImschoot, K., Liesse, M., Mertens, C., & Lauwers, P. Psychological links and coronary diseases. *Acta Psychiatrica Belgica*, 1978, *78*, 321–326.

Vossel, G. & Laux, L. The impact of stress experience on heart rate and task performance in the presence of a novel stressor. *Biological Psychology*, 1978, *6*, 193–201.

Woods, D. J. The repression-sensitization variable and self-reported emotional arousal: Effects of stress and instructional set. *Journal of Consulting and Clinical Psychology*, 1977, *45*, 173–183.

V

STRESS AND HEART
DISEASE

16

Type A Behavior and Coronary Heart Disease

Review of Theory and Findings

R. H. Rosenman and M. A. Chesney
Stanford Research Institute

INTRODUCTION

The 20th century witnessed the marked increase of coronary heart disease (CHD) that has occurred in most industrialized societies (Michaels, 1966; White, 1974), but which cannot be ascribed simply to improved longevity, better diagnostic methods, or altered genetic predisposition (White, 1974).

There are many reasons to believe that environmental factors play a dominant causal role in the coronary epidemic, which doubtless has a multifactorial etiology (Epstein, 1965) whose pathogenetic linkage is still unclear. They probably include dietary habits, physical activity, and risk factors such as the blood pressure, serum lipids and lipoproteins, and cigarette smoking. However, these factors fail to explain individual or societal prevalence and incidence (Gordon & Verter, 1969). Many patients do not exhibit either high levels of these factors or differences of diet or physical activity (Kannel, 1970; Mann, 1977), and various risk factors are at high levels in populations with low CHD rates (Bruhn & Wolf, 1970). Framingham subjects exhibit much higher CHD rates than do Europeans at similar levels of standard risk factors (Keys, Aravnis, Blackburn, Vanvuchem, Buzina, Djordjenic, Fidanza, Karvonen, Menotti, Puddy, & Taylor, 1972), and similar inconsistencies occur in CHD rates in Framingham compared to Honolulu, Puerto Rico (Gordon, Garcia-Palmieri, Kagan, Kannel, & Schiffman, 1974), and Yugoslavia (Kozarevic, Pire, Ravic, Dawber, Gordon, & Zukel, 1976). Given these inconsistencies, it is not surprising that CHD risk factors considered together account for less than half of the numerical incidence of CHD in epidemiological studies (Kozarevic et al., 1976). Increased CHD rates of the 20th century cannot be ascribed to changes of diet, physical activity or risk factors (Michaels, 1966; Yudkin, 1957; Trulson, 1959; Froelicher, Longo, & McIver, 1976). Finally, altered diet, physical activity or decrease of standard risk factors have not been shown to significantly diminish either the rates of primary or recurring coronary morbidity, despite "the remarkable aura of faith in such treatment" (Can I avoid, 1974; Corday & Corday, 1975; Werko, 1976; Sparrow, Dawber, & Colton, 1978; Gordon, Kannel, & McGee, 1974; Seltzer, 1977).

Supported by Grant No. MH-31269 of the National Institute of Mental Health, Rockville, Md.

Critical reviews (Can I avoid, 1974; Corday et al., 1975; Werko, 1976; Rosenman & Friedman, 1971) lead to the conclusion that the classical factors are far from providing a total explanation of either the 20th century epidemic or the occurrence of CHD in specific individuals. There must be a continued search for the causes as well as prediction and prevention of CHD (Gordon et al., 1974; Corday et al., 1975).

Many studies of the possible role of various psychosocial factors have been critically reviewed (Keith, 1966; Syme, 1968; Caffrey, 1967; Lehman, 1967; Antanovsky, 1968; Mai, 1968; Jenkins, 1971, 1976). Various demographic, social, psychological, and emotional factors have been investigated, including social class and status, educational level, religion, ethnic background, marital status, occupation, work overload, social and geographic mobility, status incongruity, anxiety, neuroticism, life events and change, life satisfactions and dissatisfactions, emotional loss and deprivation, and others. These studies suggest that certain factors do put subjects at higher risk for CHD (Jenkins, 1971, 1976).

HISTORY OF THE ASSOCIATION OF CHD WITH PERSONALITY ATTRIBUTES AND BEHAVIOR PATTERNS

The most consistent evidence relating psychological factors to CHD appears associated with personality and behavioral traits. Historical findings are sparse but consistent. In 1868, Von Dusch observed that person with loud vocal stylistics and excessive work involvement were predisposed to CHD (Van Dusch, 1868). Osler strongly implicated stress and hard-driving behavior (Osler, 1910). Many years passed before the Menningers noted strongly aggressive behavior in CHD patients (Menninger & Menninger, 1936). Dunbar found them to be hard-driving and goal-directed (Dunbar, 1943), and Kemple perceived them to be ambitious and compulsively striving to achieve goals that incorporated power and prestige (Kemple, 1945). Arlow (1945) and Gildea (1949) observed similar behavior, and in 1950 Stewart correlated new conditions of stress in England with increased CHD rates (Stewart, 1950).

These investigators observed a remarkably similar psychological facade in CHD patients, but most failed to consider the environmental milieu in the genesis of the behavior they found so characteristic. It now appears that such behavior is typical of CHD patients, and that this specific pattern of overt behavior, termed the *Type A Behavior Pattern* (TABP), clearly antedates the CHD.

DEFINITION OF TYPE A BEHAVIOR PATTERN (TABP)

TABP is a particular action-emotion complex exhibited by those individuals who are engaged in a relatively *chronic* struggle to obtain a usually unlimited number of things from their environment in the shortest period of time, or against the opposing efforts of other things and other persons in the same environment. This chronic "struggle" is an attempt to do and to achieve more and more in less and less time, often in competition with others (Rosenman, 1978). Type A persons seldom despair, despite the intensity or duration of the struggle, and thus differ from subjects with classic anxiety states who, finding or believing challenges or afflictions to be overwhelming, either withdraw or seek therapeutic counsel. Type As confidently grapple with challenges while subjects with anxiety retreat from similar situations.

Contemporary Western environment has increased the prevalence of TABP by offering special rewards to those who can communicate and perform more rapidly and aggressively than others. Urbanization and technological progress of Western Society, with densification of population and necessity for finely timed synchronization of interdependent human services, present uniquely new challenges not experienced by earlier generations. TABP does not stem *solely* from behavioral attributes, but emerges when the milieu's challenges or conditions elicit a particular set of responses in susceptible individuals. This requisite inclusion of the milieu implies that if the challenges are *severe enough*, regardless of basic personality or behavior, almost any person might so react that TABP emerges. Thus, there frequently is an environmental as well as intrinsic psychological component in the TABP.

TABP is a characteristic style of response to salient environmental stressors that threaten this individual's sense of control over the environment, and is an enhanced performance to maintain control whenever this is challenged. The high drive and pace of Type As may reflect the need for command over their environment, with deep commitment to vocation and relative neglect of other life aspects in favor of an impatient drive to achieve ever-expanding but often poorly defined goals.

TABP is not a personality type but is rather a syndrome of behaviors that can be operationally defined and correlated with neurohormonal and physiological responses. It includes behavioral dispositions such as ambitiousness, aggressiveness, competitiveness, and impatience; specific behaviors such as muscle tenseness, alertness, rapid and emphatic speech stylistics; and emotional reactions such as irritation, anger, and hostility that is often covert.

Persons without such attributes are called Type B, with an overt behavior pattern that is more relaxed, easygoing, satisfied, and unhurried. Type Bs are rarely harried by desires to obtain increasing numbers of things and rarely participate in an endlessly growing series of events in ever decreasing amount of time.

It is important to distinguish TABP from the ill-defined concept of "stress," since it is neither a stressor situation nor a distressed response, but is rather a style of overt behavior to confront life situations. TABP may be elicited by pleasant or troubling situations, but is particularly triggered by situations that are perceived as relevant challenges. TABP is manifested by characteristic values, thought, and approach to interpersonal relationships as well as by characteristic gestures, facial expressions, respiratory movements, motor activity and pace, stylistics of speech, and other mannerisms. It is prevalent in industrialized societies and is readily recognized by the behavioral facade that we have described in considerable detail (Rosenman, 1978; Friedman & Rosenman, 1959; Rosenman & Friedman, 1961, 1974).

Other investigators have confirmed these earlier observations about the behavior, traits, and emotional reactions of Type A individuals. They too have observed that Type As are orderly and well-planned (Barry, 1967), self-controlled (Russek, 1967), self-confident (Howard, Cunningham, & Rechnitzer, 1977), prefer to work alone when challenged (Dembroski & MacDougall, 1978), are not easily distracted from task performance (Matthews & Brunson, in press), are outgoing (Matthews et al., in press), hyperalert (Matthews et al., in press; Bortner & Rosenman, 1967), fast-paced, competitive (Howard et al., 1977; Van Egeren, 1979), tense and unrelaxed (Lovell & Verghese, 1967), impatient (Burnam, Pennebaker & Glass, 1975), aggressive (Van der Valk & Groen, 1967), time-conscious (Burnam et al., 1975; Carver & Glass, 1978; Glass, Snyder, & Hollis, 1974), deeply involved in their vocation and unable to relax away from work (Russek, 1967; Lovell et al., 1967), with excessive striving, and exhibit hostility which is often suppressed but more overt when they are frustrated (Carver et al., 1978; Glass et al., 1974). Achievement-orientation in Type As is strong enough to lead to denial of failure (Weidner & Matthews, 1978), suppression of symptoms and fatigue (Matthews et al., in press; Weidner et al., 1978), and denial of illness, including CHD. Type As exhibit enhanced desire to control their environment (Glass, 1977; Krantz, Glass, & Snyder, 1974) and greater job conflicts and dissatisfaction (Howard et al., 1977; Theorell & Rahe, 1971; Kavanagh & Shephard, 1973; Sales & House, 1971; Howard et al., in press).

ASSESSMENT OF TYPE A BEHAVIOR PATTERN

In order to assess the TABP an interview was designed (Rosenman, 1978; Rosenman, Friedman, Straus, Würm, Kositchek, Hahn, & Werthessen, 1964) and structured to provide a suitable challenge setting to study an indivual's response style. The intensity of TABP represents the reaction when such persons are challenged or aroused by relevant environmental stressors. These responses may not be felt or exhibited by Type As when confronted by an environment that presents no salient challenge. For example, a usually rushed and hard-driving person might not exhibit TABP when relaxing on vacation. In order for TABP, with its characteristic verbal reports, voice stylistics (loudness, rapid, emphatic and explosive speech), and psychomotor behaviors (Rosenman, 1978; Rosenman et al., 1964), to become manifest, relevant, perceived, environmental challenge must usually serve as a fuse (Rosenman, 1978). The Structured Interview (S.I.) (Rosenman, 1978) was designed to provide a suitable challenge to assess the response style of the individual. It requires 15 minutes to administer and is audio- or video-taped for subsequent rating. Both interviewers and raters must be specifically trained to provide a standardized, valid assessment.

Rating by the S.I. takes into account stylistics of speech (i.e., the *way* something is said by the subject), the content of answers to the questions (i.e., what is said), and the overt psychomotor, nonverbal behaviors exhibited during the interview. While all three factors are taken into account, the content of responses is not weighted heavily, since Type As often have little insight into their behavior. Instead, emphasis is placed on the speech stylistics shown in the course of responding to the S.I. situation.

Methodological studies have shown high degree of interrater agreement (Jenkins, Rosenman, & Friedman, 1968; Caffrey, 1968; Dembroski, MacDougall, Shields, Petitto, & Lushene, 1978; NIH, 1979) and stability of the respective behavior patterns over time (Jenkins et al., 1968). The value of speech stylistics for assessment of TABP has been confirmed (Scherwitz, Berton, & Leventhal, 1977; Schucker & Jacobs, 1977).

Over a period of 15 years there has been a search for other methods of assessment since the S.I. (Rosenman, 1978; Rosenman et al., 1964) is relatively subjective, and requires training for proper administration and rating. Bortner developed a performance test battery that sampled components of TABP to successfully delineate the behavior patterns (Bortner & Rosenman, 1967). Type A and B subjects have been given an array of psychometric questionnaires such as the Adjective Checklist of Gough and Heilbrun, Thurstone Temperament Schedule, Eysenck Personality Inventory, Symptom Distress Checklist, State-Trait Anxiety Inventory (STAI), Work Environment Scale, California Psychological Inventory, Minnesota Multiphasic Personality Inventory, Cattell 16-Personality Factors Test, and Barrett Impulsiveness Scale. However, while strong construct validity of TABP is supported by findings with these scales, they are influenced by the subject's insight and response bias. The hurry, poor insight and self-appraisal of many Type As lead to inaccuracy that limits the ability of questionnaires to serve as measures of TABP.

A second approach is development of questionnaires to duplicate assessment made by the S.I. Bortner's short scale correctly classified 70 percent of our subjects (Bortner, 1969) and 75 percent in the Belgian study (Rustin, Dramaiz, Kittle, Degre, Kornitzor, Thilly, & de Backer, 1976), but other scales have not been adequately validated.

The best studied questionnaire is the Jenkins Activity Survey (JAS), now available for clinical use (Jenkins, Rosenman, & Friedman, 1967; Jenkins, Rosenman, & Zyzanski, 1979). It provides a composite Type A scale and three subscales: Speed and Impatience, Job Involvement and, and Hard-Driving. TABP assessed by the JAS is significantly related to CHD prevalence in populations in Houston (Glass, 1977), San Francisco (Kannel, 1970), Bridgeport (Kenigsberg, Zyzanski, Jenkins, Wardwell, & Licciardello, 1974), Chicago (Shekelle, Schoenberger, & Stamler, 1976), St. Petersberg, Durham, Poland, and Hawaii (Cohen, Syme, Jenkins, Dagan, & Zyzanski, 1975). JAS scores for TABP are predictive of new cases of CHD (Jenkins, Rosenman, & Zyzanski, 1974), risk of reinfarction (Jenkins et al., 1971), and the degree of basic coronary atherosclerosis (Zyzanski, Jenkins, Ryan, Flessas, & Everest, 1976), although the latter was not found by two other groups (Blumenthal, Williams, Kong, Schanberg, & Thompson, 1978; Dimsdale, Hackett, Hutter, Block, & Catanzo, 1978). Compared to the S.I., the JAS is a much weaker predictor of CHD incidence (Brand, Rosenman, Jenkins, Sholtz, & Zyzanski, in press), severity of coronary atherosclerosis (Blumenthal et al., 1978), and of challenge-induced physiological arousal that characterizes TABP (Dembroski et al., 1978; MacDougall, Dembroski, & Musante, 1979). The strength of the S.I. resides in an assessment based far more upon direct observation of the behavior pattern than upon content of answers to questions (Rosenman, 1978; Rosenman et al., 1964). The JAS depends upon self-report and unfortunately fails to include items for assessing the very important hostility emotional response of Type A subjects that appears to be of major relevance for its association with CHD.

RELATIONSHIP OF TYPE A BEHAVIOR PATTERN TO PREVALENCE OF CHD

A significant association of TABP with CHD prevalence was found in both sexes, that could not be ascribed to differences of diet or other risk factors (Friedman & Rosenman, 1959; Rosenman et al., 1961). Other investigators have confirmed this association whether TABP was assessed by the S.I. (Caffrey, 1969; Howard, Cunningham, & Rechnitzer, 1976), the JAS, the Bortner Scale (Heller, 1979), the Framingham Type A Questionnaire (Haynes, Feinleib, Levine, Scotch, & Kannel,

1978), other scales of TABP (Wardwell, Hyman, & Bahnson, 1968), or the major facets of TABP. As recently pointed out, "since response bias and sample selection can in many ways influence the results and interpretations in case-control studies these replications take on added meaning. They assume greater significance in that they speak to the following issues; (1) random phenomena rarely replicate; (2) a variety of population groups were studied, and not simply narrowly defined and selected cases vs. controls; and (3) epidemiological studies have often found that replicated associations based on prevalence data are prospectively related as well" (Feinleib, Brand, Remington, & Zyzanski, 1978).

Differences of TABP may in part explain considerably higher CHD rates in the densely populated, industrialized regions of the U.S. and England (Can I avoid, 1974; Sigler, 1958; Enterline & Stewart, 1959) compared to farm belts where consumption of animal and dairy fats is probably high, as well as apparent low rates in closely-knit religious groups (Groen, Tjiong, Karmminger, & Willegrands, 1962). It may in part also explain higher rates in the U.S. compared to Europe (Keys et al., 1972) and in Framingham compared to Yugoslavia (Kozarevic et al., 1976), Puerto Rico and Hawaii (Gordon et al., 1974).

RELATIONSHIP OF TYPE A BEHAVIOR PATTERN TO INCIDENCE OF CHD

Epidemiological studies often find that replicated associations based on prevalence data are prospectively related as well (Feinleib et al., 1978). This prevails for TABP since it is also strongly related to the CHD incidence in prospective studies. The Western Collaborative Group Study (WCGS) is a prospective epidemiological study of 3154 initially well men, aged 39 to 59 years at intake in 1960–61, who were employed by 10 participating California companies (Rosenman et al., 1964). The subjects were comprehensively studied for all risk factors. The population and methodology are described elsewhere (Rosenman et al., 1964), as are findings at follow-up.

CHD occurred in 257 men by 8.5 year follow-up. Final results showed that intake Type A men were 2.37 times as likely to develop CHD as Type B subjects (Rosenman et al., 1975). When statistical multivariate adjustment for other risk factors was made, the relative Type A/B risk of CHD decreased to 1.97, the small difference (0.40) between adjusted and nonadjusted relative risk being the amount of risk conferred by other standard risk factors that showed small correlations with the TABP (Rosenman et al., 1976; Brand et al., 1976). The significant adjusted remainder (1.97) is the relative risk for TABP that is independent of other risk factors. The observed associations cannot be attributed to chance fluctuation since both adjusted and non-adjusted relative risk ratios achieve high statistical significance ($p < 0.001$) and are closely similar to those later found at Framingham (Haynes, Feinleib, & Kannel, 1980).

The Framingham study provided the basis for a multivariate risk equation for prediction of CHD, based on standard risk factors. The predicted risk levels in the WCGS are highly correlated with those using Framingham equations (Brahd et al., 1976). Multiple logistic analysis of the direct association between CHD incidence and behavior pattern gives an approximate relative risk of 1.9 ($p < 0.0006$) and 2.1 ($p < 0.0015$) for Type A to Type B men, aged 39–40 and 50–59 years, respectively. Thus substantial risk is associated directly with TABP and does not diminish in older compared to younger men.

In the WCGS the association of TABP with CHD incidence prevailed for initial myocardial infarction, whether symptomatic or silent, as well as for angina pectoris (Rosenman et al., 1966, 1970, 1975, 1976; Brand et al., 1976; Haynes et al., 1980; Rosenman, Friedman, & Jenkins et al., 1967). Although significant CHD incidence occurred in Type A men even at low risk factors. Type B subjects at similar levels exhibited relative CHD immunity (Rosenman, Friedman, Jenkins, Straus, Wurm, & Kositcheck, 1966). TABP also was associated with recurring and fatal CHD events in the WCGS (Jenkins et al., 1971, 1974; Rosenman, Friedman, Jenkins, Straus, Wurm, & Kositcheck, 1967).

Multivariate statistical evaluations show associations between TABP and CHD incidence to be independent of interrelationships with other risk factors (Rosenman et al., 1975, 1976; Brand et al., 1976). The findings indicate a synergistic pattern for CHD risk in which TABP operates with nearly a constant multiplicative effect applied to whatever background level results from other risk factors (Brand et al., 1976). It seems clear that TABP appears to double the risk of CHD at all levels of other risk factors (Rosenman et al., 1975, 1976), in a relationship that cannot be explained by chance fluctuation (Brand, 1978).

In the WCGS, standard risk factors were confirmed as being significantly associated with CHD risk, including serum cholesterol, blood pressure, and cigarette smoking (Rosenman et al., 1976). As in most prospective studies, systolic was a relatively stronger predictor than diastolic blood pressure (Rosenman, Sholtz, & Brand, 1976). Although associated with serum cholesterol levels, corneal arcus was independently related to CHD risk in men under age 50 (Rosenman, Brand, Sholtz, & Jenkins, 1974). Reported parental CHD history also was an independent risk factor in WCGS subjects under age 50 (Sholtz, Rosenman, & Brand, 1975). As in the Framingham (Kannel, 1970) and most other prospective studies, diet did not predict either serum lipid levels or CHD risk in the WCGS.

There are other reports studying relationships between TABP and CHD incidence. As part of the collaborative study of CHD among Japanese in Japan, Hawaii, and California, 2437 men in Hawaii were administered the JAS questionnaire in 1967-68. Only 15 percent were classified as Type A, but CHD rates were associated with hard-driving and competitive behavior. Japanese men in Hawaii who had undergone cultural change were more prone to CHD, and those who were both culturally mobile and Type A had two to three times the CHD risk during follow-up (Cohen et al., 1975). The results support the initial TABP construct as being an interplay of specific behaviors and the environmental milieu that challenges the susceptible individual. The Thurstone Temperament Schedule was given in the Minnesota study of businessmen, in which the Activity Scale is concerned with the pace of daily activities such as eating, talking, walking, driving, etc. Subjects who score high on this scale enjoy rapid psychomotor pace, even when they do *not* have to function at this accelerated pace. This is an excellent description of this TABP facet and this scale shows the highest correlations with TABP of any psychometric questionnaire (Rosenman et al., 1976; Rahe et al., 1978; Chesney et al., in press; Beard et al., in press). A significant positive association was found between CHD incidence and Activity Scale scores in the Minnesota study (Brozek et al., 1966), in which adrenergic response to the cold pressor test was the major predictor of CHD incidence (Keys, Taylor, Blackburn, Brozek, & Anderson, 1971).

Further confirmation was observed in the Framingham study. A cohort of 1822 subjects was administered an extensive questionnaire in 1965-1967 which provided measures of behavior, situational stress, sociocultural mobility and somatic strain

(Haynes et al., 1978). The Framingham Type A Scale (FTAS) is significantly correlated with daily stress, emotional lability, tension, anger symptoms, and ambitiousness. It showed significant correlations with CHD prevalence in both sexes, after controlling for other risk factors. Subjects aged 45–74 and free of CHD ($n = 1674$) were then followed for eight years. There were few associations between psychosocial measures and risk factors such as serum cholesterol or blood pressure. During follow-up Type A men were over twice as likely to develop angina and myocardial infarction than Type Bs, with stronger associations in white than blue collar workers. The respective incidence of angina and infarction was 3.32 and 2.14 times higher in Type A than Type B women. All such associations were significant after controlling for other risk factors (Haynes et al., 1980).

RELATIONSHIP OF CHD TO COMPONENTS
OF TYPE A BEHAVIOR PATTERN

TABP is a syndrome of specific behaviors and reactions that emerge in the interplay of these behavioral attributes and relevant environmental challenges. The S.I. for TABP assessment is designed to assess components of the TABP such as drive and ambition, potential for hostility, competitiveness, speed of activity, and impatience (Rosenman et al., 1964). Analysis of these components showed the CHD incidence in the WCGS to be particularly associated with competitive drive, impatience, and the potential for hostility (Matthews, Glass, Rosenman, & Bortner, 1977). The findings support the hypothesis that is is not just hurried, hard-working, achievement-oriented behavior that is causally related to CHD (Cohen et al., 1975). Indeed it is possible to be hard-working, but not hard-driving and competitive, and the Japanese perhaps exhibit a successful adaptation to the American standard of hard-working success without individual competitiveness or hostility. The findings of a particular relationship between the *competitive-hostility* aspects of TABP and CHD incidence in the WCGS (Matthews et al., 1977) are supported by the association of these attributes in both sexes with the severity of basic coronary atherosclerosis (Williams, Haney, Gentry, & Kong, 1978) and the enhanced adrenergic response to challenge tasks in Type A subjects (Dembroski et al., 1978).

RELATIONSHIP OF TYPE A BEHAVIOR PATTERN
TO PRECIPITATION OF CHD AND
TO CORONARY ATHEROSCLEROSIS

The major clinical manifestations of CHD are myocardial infarction, angina pectoris, and sudden coronary death, the complications of underlying coronary atherosclerosis. One mechanism by which TABP may be causally related to CHD incidence in part because of precipitation of fatal coronary events. The role of psychological stress in precipitating sudden coronary death is well known, the mechanism usually being triggering of ventricular fibrillation by sympathetic nervous system discharge (Lown & Verrier, 1976). Subjects with CHD exhibit increased adrenergic output (Nestel, Verghese, & Lovell, 1967), and exaggerated response to the cold pressor test was a strong predictor of CHD incidence in the Minnesota prospective study (Keys et al., 1971), in which increased CHD incidence was associated with "apparent" TABP, as strongly suggested by the association of CHD risk with high scores on the Activity subscale of the Thurstone Temperament Schedule (Brozek et al., 1966).

TABP is associated with enhanced catecholamine secretion in response to daily work challenges (Friedman, St. George, & Byers, 1960) as well as during specific psychological (Dembroski et al., 1978; Friedman, Byers, Diamant, & Rosenman, 1975) and physical (Haynes, Feinleib, Levine, Scotch, & Kannel, 1978) challenges. In turn, TABP is associated with fatal CHD events (Rosenman et al., 1967) and sudden coronary death from ventricular fibrillation (Friedman, Manwaring, Rosenman, Donlan, Ortega, & Grube, 1973). The potential for enhanced adrenergic output in Type A subjects is shown by their increased physiologic arousal during challenge tests (Glass, 1977; Dembroski et al., 1978; Friedman et al., 1975). As already noted, the anger and hostility facets of TABP, are associated with augmented discharge of norepinephrine, increased prevalance and incidence of CHD, and increased severity of coronary atherosclerosis. Some sequential mechanisms that might relate to triggering of coronary events, including sudden death, are well conceptualized by Nixon (1976).

A second mechanism is by increased risk of coronary thrombosis. The role of psychological stress in precipitating myocardial infarction has been widely noted (Theorell et al., 1971; Kavanagh et al., 1973; Wardwell et al., 1964; Thiel et al., 1973; Nixon, 1976; Engel, 1978) and its association with increased blood clotting and platelet aggregation is well known (Haft & Fani, 1973). TABP is associated with accelerated blood clotting (Friedman, Rosenman, & Carroll, 1958) and with increased platelet aggregation (Jenkins, Thomas, Olewine, Zyzanski, Simpson, & Hames, 1975).

TABP is not only strongly associated with prevalence and incidence of CHD, but also with severity of basic coronary atherosclerosis. Thus it is significantly correlated with the severity of coronary atherosclerosis observed by angiographic study (Zyzanski et al., 1976; Blumenthal et al., 1978; Frank, Meller, Kornfield et al., 1978; Krantz, Sanmarco, Selvester, & Matthews, 1975) as well as to the progression of coronary atherosclerosis over an observed period of 17 months (Krantz et al., 1975), in associations which prevail after multivariate control for the effects of other risk factors. These data confirm our observation of a significantly greater degree of coronary atherosclerosis in Type A men who died during the WCGS follow-up (Friedman, Rosenman, Straus, Wurm, & Kostichek, 1968).

RELATIONSHIP OF TYPE A BEHAVIOR PATTERN TO DEMOGRAPHIC AND SOCIOECONOMIC VARIABLES

There is inadequate knowledge about prevalence of TABP. The WCGS population in 1960 mainly comprised white collar workers in two California urban centers, about half exhibiting TABP (Rosenman et al., 1964), but recent experience in one of the participating companies found higher prevalence (Chesney et al., in press). Most persons can be clarified as exhibiting *mainly* either TABP or the converse Type B pattern, with up to about 20% exhibiting midpoint patterns (Rosenman et al., 1964). TABP appears to be more prevalent in industrialized, densely populated urban areas than in smaller, non-suburban communities, and in an area devoted to relaxation such as Hawaii, the prevalence of TABP is low (Cohen et al., 1975), which may help account for its lower CHD rate compared to Framingham (Gordon et al., 1974).

Little correlation of TABP has been found with *age* (Rosenman et al., 1964; Shekelle et al., 1976), except for lower prevalence at younger ages (Shekelle et al., 1976; Froelichen et al., 1976). TABP shows modest correlations with *social class and level of education* accounting in part for observed small correlations with *occupational status* (Rosenman et al., 1964; Shekelle et al., 1976; Zyzanski et al., submitted for publication; Mettlin, 1976) and *career advancement and achievement* in both sexes (Howard et al., 1977; Glass, 1977; Mettlin, 1976; Waldron et al., 1977). Higher prevalence was observed in *white than in blue collar workers* by us (Rosenman, Bawol, & Oscherwitz, 1977), and in the Chicago (Shekelle et al., 1976) and Framingham (Haynes et al., 1978) study groups.

TABP was less prevalent in black than in white populations studied in Chicago (Shekelle et al., 1976). Cultural differences in TABP are observed between blacks and whites, as previously noted, and in Japanese-American compared to Caucasian men in Hawaii (Cohen et al., 1975).

TABP must be differentiated from psychopathology and is not correlated on psychometric tests with anxiety, somatic complaints, or behavioral correlates of stress (Kavanagh et al., 1973; Caffrey, 1968; Chesney et al., in press; Caplan & Jones, 1975). However, it shows only small correlations with items on standard psychological stress tests (Chesney et al., in press) and none with psychopathology, despite its correlation with stressful life events and current tension (Caplan et al., 1975).

HEREDITARY AND DEVELOPMENTAL ANTECEDENTS OF TYPE A BEHAVIOR PATTERN

Reported family history of CHD is significantly related to CHD incidence at younger ages in the WCGS (Rosenman et al., 1976). Familial similarity of TABP has been found in both sexes (Bortner, Rosenman, & Friedman, 1970). However, there is little evidence of a genetic component for the global TABP (Rosenman et al., 1976; Rahe et al., 1978; Horn, Plomin, & Rosenman, 1976). A modest genetic component is found for certain TABP behavior, including drive, competitiveness, compulsiveness, dominance, sociability, and impulsiveness (Rosenman et al., 1976; Rahe et al., 1978; Horn et al., 1976; Matthews & Krantz, 1976).

It is difficult to separate genetic influences from early learned behavior. Parental attitudes, behaviors, and performance standards influence those of offspring and probably play a role in development of many TABP facets, including competitiveness and achievement-striving (Matthews & Saal, 1978; Matthews, 1977). Since adult modeling and conditioning processes significantly affect competitive and aggressive behavior in offspring, it is not surprising that there is familial similarity of TABP in children (Bortner et al., 1970) or more TABP in children of parents with higher educational levels and occupational status (Bortner et al., 1970; Howard, Cunningham, & Rechnitzer, submitted for publication), in children living in urban than in rural areas (Howard et al., submitted for publication), and in males compared to females (Matthews, 1978). In children, TABP resembles that in adults, with exhibition of enhanced competitiveness, aggressiveness, restlessness, impatience, and achievement-orientation (Howard et al., submitted for publication; Matthews, 1978). There are valid reasons to believe that environment plays a greater role than genetic factors in development of TABP (Rosenman et al., 1976), that TABP often has its origins in childhood (Matthews, 1978), and that cultural factors play an important antecedent role in development of TABP (Cohen et al., 1975).

The antecedents of TABP vary in different individuals, with a different mix of personality attributes, parental-teacher influences, and learned behavior, indicating that the behavioral classification derived from the Structured Interview (Rosenman et al., 1964) or from scores on questionnaire sush as the JAS (Jenkins, Rosenman, & Friedman, 1967; Jenkins, Rosenman, & Zyzanski, 1979) do not represent a linear continuum. TABP is often engendered by socioeconomic factors that do not play a role until occupational careers begin, in keeping with inverse prevalence at younger ages (Shekelle et al., 1976; Mettlin, 1976; Waldron et al., 1977). TABP doubtless is bred by occuptional competitiveness, work loads, conflicting demands, supervisory responsibilities and associated factors (Howard et al., 1977, 1976). The role of such factors is exemplified by its higher prevalence in fully employed females compared to those employed part-time or housewives (Rosenman et al., 1961; Waldron et al., 1977). The relation of TABP to the work setting is recently reviewed (Chesney & Rosenman, 1980).

RELATIONSHIP OF TYPE A BEHAVIOR PATTERN TO OTHER CHD RISK FACTORS AND TO BIOCHEMICAL FINDINGS

The two-fold relative Type A/B risk does not operate through other risk factors, but is a strong, independent factor in the statistical CHD risk (Rosenman et al., 1966, 1970, 1975, 1976; Brand et al., 1976). In the WCGS and other studies, standard risk factors such as smoking (Blumenthal et al., 1978; Howard et al., 1976; Jenkins, Rosenman, & Zyzanski, 1968) show only small correlations with the behavior patterns (Rosenman et al., 1964, 1976). Little correlation is found with resting blood pressure levels (Rosenman et al., 1964; Shekelle et al., 1976; Howard et al., 1976).

We early observed a relationship between certain TABP facets and serum cholesterol, finding significant rise in accountants during occupational deadlines (Friedman et al., 1958). This effect of environmental deadlines has been subsequently confirmed (Rosenman & Friedman, 1974). Such increases are not ascribable to diet (Friedman et al., 1958; Wolf, McCabe, Yamamoto, Adsett, & Schottstaedt, 1961) and occur in association with deadline time urgency, occupational obligations, or annoyance over recent life events (Groen et al., 1962; Friedman et al., 1958; Wolf et al., 1961; Rahe, Rubin, & Arthur, 1974; Clark, Arnold, Foulds, Brown, Eastman, & Parry, 1975). Average serum cholesterols tend to be higher in Type A than Type B subjects in both sexes (Friedman et al., 1959; Rosenman et al., 1961; Rosenman & Friedman, 1963). Type As also exhibit higher fasting and postprandial serum triglyceride levels than their Type B counterparts (Rosenman et al., 1963), accompanied by postprandial sludging of red blood cells in their bulbar conjunctival blood vessels for many hours after ingestion of a meal rich in either saturated or unsaturated triglycerides (Friedman, Rosenman, & Byers, 1964; Friedman, Byers, & Rosenman, 1965). The association of psychological traits with serum lipid-lipoprotein levels has been reviewed elsewhere (Jenkins, Hames, Zyzanski, Rosenman, & Friedman, 1969; Harlan, Oberman, Mitchell, & Graybiel, 1967).

There are no A/B differences in plasma uric acid levels or in glucose metabolism, although Type As may exhibit a hyperinsulinemic response to glucose which does not appear responsible for their higher serum triglyceride levels (Rosenman et al., 1974). Psychological factors are related to the hypothalamic-pituitary-adrenal axis.

Average plasma cortisol and thyroxine levels of Type As and Bs are similar. However, when Type As were challenged with large doses of corticocotropin, most excreted significantly less 17-hydroxycortiocoids than Type Bs, suggesting the possibility that the Type As might be subject to previous, long-standing as well as current excess discharge of ACTH. Indeed, Type As exhibit higher plasma ACTH during waking hours, compared to Type B subjects. Administration of ACTH temporarily abolished the elevation of serum triglycerides in many Type A subjects, but this response was not induced by hydrocortisone administration (Rosenman et al., 1974).

Plasma growth hormone levels were significantly lower in Type A than Type B men and plasma growth hormone response of Type As to infusion of arginine was significantly less than in Type Bs. Growth hormone is necessary for maintenance of plasma cholesterol and administration of growth hormone to Type A men induced a prompt, although temporary, fall of serum cholesterol (Rosenman et al., 1974).

RELATIONSHIP OF TYPE A BEHAVIOR PATTERN TO CATECHOLAMINE METABOLISM

Catecholamines may play an important role in mediating relationships between TABP and both coronary atherosclerosis and CHD incidence. Increased CHD incidence is a 20th-century phenomenon associated with pace of its industrialized societies (Michaels, 1966; White, 1974; Gordon et al., 1974) and acculturation to its accompanied demands (Cohen et al., 1975). Raab early emphasized a role of catecholamines in 20th-century western life (Raab, 1953) and recognized that adrenergic responses were enhanced in individuals with TABP, compared to more relaxed persons (Raab, 1966). Levi pointed out dramatic changes in our environment that are not accompanied by suitable modification of man's genetically determined psychobiological reaction pattern, which has become obsolete, and noted that the stress reactions that promoted survival for Stone Age man when confronting a wolf pack are inappropriate for modern man when confronting a traffic jam or other uniquely new stresses. Levi cogently emphasized that, "in a primitive society, stress reactions prepare the body for violent action, and once this is over, the body returns to normal homeostasis; but modern man's crises do not include escape from a sabre-toothed tiger since his stress is often long-lasting and free-floating and his reaction cannot often be ended by a catharsis of physical exercise, with the result that modern man is constantly poised for fight or flight, but without the civilized possibility of either aggressive fighting or fleeing" (Levi & Anderson, 1975).

It is therefore relevant that subjects with CHD exhibit enhanced catecholamine discharge in response to emotional stress and during physical exertion (Nestel et al., 1967; Raab & Gigee, 1954; Gazes, Richardson, & Woods, 1959). Such enhanced discharge is associated with aggressiveness, competitive drive, anger, and time urgency (Wardwell & Bahnson, 1973; Funkenstein, King, & Drolette, 1957; Elmadjian, Hope, & Lamson, 1958; Von Euler, Gemzell, Levi, & Strom, 1959), which are major TABP facets. TABP is a response style to maintain environment control and leads to chronic performance at maximum capacity, with hyper-reactiveness to actual or perceived threats (Glass, 1977). We and later others have found increased norepinephrine excretion by Type A subjects during working milieus (Friedman et al., 1960) and enhanced secretion during competitive activity (Dembroski et al., 1978; Roskies et al., 1979; Friedman et al., 1975; Simpson et al., 1974). Enhanced norepinephrine discharge is a phasic phenomenon during exposure to the environmental milieu that induces TABP in susceptible individuals who have the desire or need to perform at under maximum capacity to control milieu challenges and threats (Glass, 1977). The Minnesota prospective study supports the importance of catecholamines, finding that the cold pressor test, which reflects adrenergic responsiveness, hence catecholamine secretion, is strongly predictive of CHD incidence (Keys et al., 1971) in a study which also found that the major facets of TABP are similarly associated with CHD incidence (Brozek et al., 1966). Enhanced response to the cold pressor test in Type As (Roskies et al., 1979; DeBacker, Kernitzer, Kiefer, Bogaert, Van Durme, Rustin, Degre, & De Schlaepdriver, 1979) and in patients with atherosclerotic disease is also found by others (Voudoukis, 1971).

RELATIONSHIP OF TYPE A BEHAVIOR PATTERN TO PSYCHOPHYSIOLOGICAL FACTORS

TABP is an interplay between certain behaviors and the environmental milieu, and its overt manifestations represent characterological response of Type As to a milieu perceived as a challenge to their control. Enhanced discharge of norepinephrine occurs when relevant challenge requires rapid and competitive responses by such persons (Friedman et al., 1960, 1975; Obrist, Gaebelein, & Teller et al., 1978; Dembroski & MacDougall, in press). Therefore, autonomic arousal is best studied in dynamic response rather than by static measurements (Obrist et al., 1978). Static measurements have shown no A/B differences in heart rates or blood pressures (Rosenman et al., 1964; Shekelle et al., 1976). However, differences are often observed in exposure to challenge stressors, during which Type As compared to paired Type Bs exhibit significantly greater rise of heart rate, systolic and/or diastolic blood pressure, catecholamine secretion, peripheral vasoconstriction, and ECG changes (Dembroski et al., in press), as during administration of the structured interview, reaction time tasks, cognitive puzzle-solving, exposure to noise and to uncontrollable aversive factors, psychomotor performance tests, and during the cold pressor test. In general, the enhanced response in Type As is greater in males than females (Dembroski et al., in press; Matthews, 1977) and when the challenge is of high rather than low order (Dembroski et al., in press). It is greatest in Type As who exhibit the most competitiveness, impatience, and hostility, the attributes which particularly characterize relationships between TABP and CHD incidence (Haynes et al., 1980; Matthews et al., 1977) and with severity of coronary atherosclerosis (Williams et al., 1978).

At this juncture little is known about relationships between TABP and other physiological factors that might relate to CHD. Type As compared to Type Bs exhibit an enhanced blood clotting time at times of situational stress (Friedman et al., 1958) and enhanced platelet aggregation (Jenkins et al., 1975).

INTERVENTION ON TYPE A BEHAVIOR PATTERN: POSSIBILITIES, METHODS, AND RESULTS

Hesitancy in recognizing the causal role of TABP in CHD and the global definition of the behavior pattern have delayed study of modification of TABP for purposes of prevention. The need appears important since there is little evidence of significant reductions in CHD to date from programs that have altered diet (Mann, 1977; Can I avoid, 1974), habits of physical activity (Werko, 1976), elimination of cigarette smoking (Sparrow et al., 1978; Gordon et al., 1974), or reduction of serum cholesterol or blood pressure (Can I avoid, 1974; Corday et al., 1975; Rosenman et al., 1977; Rosenman, 1979), despite remarkable aura of faith in such measures (Can I avoid, 1974). The importance of these programs cannot be denied, although improved benefits may require their initiation in childhood. However, in adults, significant reduction of CHD incidence may require modification of TABP (Rosenman, 1979, 1978; Rosenman et al., 1978; Rosenman & Friedman, 1977). It should be understood that modification of TABP does not mean an attempt to change a Type A into a Type B, but rather to reduce excessive Type A responses.

The *potential* reduction of CHD that might be afforded by effective modification of TABP has been shown to be statistically significant (Rosenman et al., 1970, 1975). However, effective modification does not loom as simplistic. Many Type A behaviors are considered to be strengths and rewarded as such in the Western world, and TABP is not associated with psychological distress (Chesney et al., 1980). Mettlin emphasized that TABP is considered by many to be an integral factor in the modern occupational career (Mettlin, 1976). Many Type As derive security and pride from their behavior pattern and find it difficult to understand how it may contribute to CHD, particularly in themselves as opposed "to the other fellow." Type A behaviors are often deeply ingrained, sometimes from childhood or by the time vocational careers begin, making it difficult for an impatient Type A to follow a program that cannot be shown to provide definitive proof of possible prophylactic value. Over the past two decades we have found that modification of TABP can be accomplished more readily in post-infarction that in healthy individuals (Rosenman et al., 1977).

There are a number of relevant considerations (Roskies, 1978; Chesney & Rosenman, 1980), first being selection of subjects. Modification of TABP is particularly important for patients with angina pectoris or prior myocardial infarction and for Type A subjects who are at higher risk by reason of subclinical severe coronary atherosclerosis or high levels of other risk factors. A greater selection problem is presented by healthy individuals. Modification of excessive TABP may be appropriate for some Type A individuals with characteristics known to be associated with CHD, including highly competitive subjects who are chronically rushed and hostile in response to environmental stressors. It should be understood that modification does not mean an attempt to change a Type A into a Type B, but only to reduce excessive Type A responses. Indeed, clinical experience has shown that such changes are associated with increased life satisfactions and often with improved productivity (Roskies, Kearney, Spevack, Surkis, Cohen, & Gilman, 1979).

A second consideration concerns which Type A behaviors should be modified since there is a need to select specific targets for intervention. It seems fruitful at this juncture to attempt modification for Type A behaviors that relate particularly to CHD, including excessive competitive drive, habitual severe impatience and time urgency, free-floating hostility, and the hyperresponsiveness of automatic arousal to environmental stressors (Chesney et al., 1980).

A third consideration must be given to methodology. TABP is an interplay of certain behaviors and the environmental milieu. Successful adaptation to Western industrialization was accomplished in Japan without the individual competitiveness that comprises one link between TABP and CHD (Cohen et al., 1975; Matsumoto, 1970). However, in the Western world it is appropriate to advise environmental change only in certain instances. It is possible to alter methods of coping with stress (Lazarus, 1966; Lazarus, Cohen, Folkman, Kanner, & Schaefer, in press; Roskies & Lazarus, 1980) and to reduce autonomic hyperresponsiveness by such methodologies as muscular relaxation, meditation, biofeedback, autogenic training, anxiety management training, stress management training, and instruction in altered perception of stressors (Roskies, 1978; Roskies, Spevack, Surkis, Cohen, & Gilman, 1978; Rahe, Ward, & Hayes, 1979; Lazarus, 1966; Lazarus et al., in press; Roskies et al., 1980; Weiner, 1952; Stoyva & Budzynski, 1974).

One approach to TABP modification teaches coping strategies for stress (Suinn, 1979). Subjects are first relaxed and then trained to visualize an interaction that usually prompts Type A reactions, and then to substitute alternative behaviors less potentially damaging to the cardiovascular system.

Jenni and Wollersheim (1979) found that TABP is more effectively modified by cognitive therapy than by stress-management training. Roskies and associates used two different methods for modification (Roskies, 1978). One is psychoanalytically-oriented and the other is a behaviorally-oriented training program for reduction of anxiety and tension that could be practiced daily at home, finding substantially better results in the behavior therapy group (Roskies et al., 1978). Others have not found that either transcendental meditation or progressive relaxation training are effective in altering TABP (Sime et al., 1978; Thompson, 1976).

Rahe and associates attempted modification by group education and therapy in patients recovering from acute myocardial infarction, with impressive results during four year follow-up. Significantly fewer recurring CHD events and deaths were observed in the cognitive group therapy than in control groups, in this pilot study showing that modification of TABP might be effective for secondary CHD prevention (Rahe et al., 1979).

Our own experience indicates that *enduring* benefit is achieved only if an individual gains adequate insight into the role that TABP plays as a way of life as well as in CHD. The cognitive methods we find most useful are described elsewhere (Rosenman, 1978; Rosenman et al., 1977; Chesney et al., 1980). It seems evident that TABP has a trichotomous origin (Rosenman et al., 1977). The first is concerned with Type A behaviors such as extreme competitive and aggressive drive that often evolves into impatience, hostility, and chronic sense of time urgency. However, TABP emerges only when these traits are "activated." Such activation depends upon the nature of specific environmental stimuli, challenges, demands, and threats to one's control, and particularly upon the individual's perception of the relevance of these challenges. The trichotomous origin thus depends upon behavioral and emotional components, environmental stressors, and the subject's interpretation and responses to them. Successful modification of TABP must consider all three factors and thus probably requires a cognitive methodology in addition to any benefits to be derived from muscular relaxation and techniques for general stress reduction.

The National Heart, Lung, and Blood Institute recently assembled a review panel of more than 50 eminent scientists representing a variety of biomedical and behavioral specialties in order to critically examine the evidence for the association between TABP and CHD. In the opening paragraph of the panel's final report, it was stated that "The Review Panel accepts the available body of scientific evidence as demonstrating that Type A behavior (as defined by the structured interview, JAS, and Framingham scale) is associated with an increased risk of clinically apparent CHD in employed, middle-aged U.S. citizens. This increased risk is over and above that imposed by age, systolic blood pressure, serum, cholesterol, and smoking and appears to be of the same order of magnitude as the relative risk associated with any of these factors" (Cooper, Detre, & Weiss, 1981).

REFERENCES

Abrahams, J. P. & Birren, J. E. Reaction time as a function of age and behavioral predisposition to coronary heart disease. *Journal of Gerontology*, 1973, *28*, 471–478.

Antonovsky, A. Social class and the major cardiovascular diseases. *Journal of Chronic Diseases*, 1968, *21*, 65–106.

Arlow, J. A. Identification of mechanisms in coronary occlusion. *Psychosomatic Medicine*, 1945, *7*, 195–209.

Barry, A. J. Physical activity and psychic stress/strain. *Canadian Medical Association Journal*, 1967, *96*, 848–853.

Blumenthal, J. A., Williams, R., Kong, Y. Schanberg, S. M., & Thompson, L. W. Type A behavior and angiographically documented coronary disease. *Circulation*, 1978, *58*, 634–639.

Bortner, R. W. A short rating scale as a potential measure of Pattern A behavior. *Journal of Chronic Diseases*, 1969, *22*, 87–91.

Bortner, R. W. & Rosenman, R. H. The measurement of Pattern A behavior. *Journal of Chronic Diseases*, 1967, *20*, 525–533.

Bortner, R. W., Rosenman, R. H., & Friedman, M. Familial similarity in Pattern A behavior: Father and sons. *Journal of Chronic Diseases*, 1970, *23*, 39–43.

Brand, R. J. Coronary-prone behavior as an independent risk factor for coronary heart disease. In. T. M. Dembroski, S. M. Weiss, J. L. Shields, S. Haynes, & M. Feinleib (eds.), *Coronary-prone behavior*. New York: Springer-Verlag, 1978.

Brand, R. J., Rosenman, R. H., Jenkins, C. D., Sholtz, R. I., & Zyzanski, S. J. Comparison of coronary heart disease prediction in the Western Collaborative Group Study using the structured interview and the Jenkins Activity Survey assessments of the coronary-prone Type A behavior pattern. *Journal of Chronic Diseases*, in press.

Brand, R. J., Rosenman, R. H., Sholtz, R. I., & Friedman, M. Multivariate prediction of coronary heart disease in the Western Collaborative Group Study compared to the findings of the Framingham Study. *Circulation*, 1976, *53*, 348–355.

Brozek, J., Keys, A., & Blackburn, H. Personality differences between potential coronary and noncoronary subjects. *Annals of the New York Academy of Science*, 1966, *134*, 1057–1064.

Bruhn, J. G. & Wolf, S. Studies reporting "low rates" of ischemic heart disease: A critical review. *American Journal of Public Health*, 1970, *60*, 1477–1495.

Burnam, M. A., Pennebaker, J. W., & Glass, D. C. Time consciousness, achievement striving, and the Type A coronary-prone behavior pattern. *Journal of Abnormal Psychology*, 1975, *84*, 76–79.

Caffrey, B. Behavior patterns and personality characteristics related to prevalence rates of coronary heart disease in American monks. *Journal of Chronic Diseases*, 1969, *22*, 93–103.

Caffrey, B. Factors involving interpersonal and psychological characteristics: A review of empirical findings. *Milbank Memorial Fund Quarterly*, 1967, *45*, 119–139.

Caffrey, B. Reliability and validity of personality and behavioral measures in a study of coronary heart disease. *Journal of Chronic Diseases*, 1968, *21*, 191–204.

Can I avoid a heart attack? Editorial, *Lancet*, 1974, *1*, 605–607.

Caplan, R. D. & Jones, K. W. Effects of work load, role ambiguity, and Type A personality on anxiety, depression, and heart rate. *Journal of Applied Psychology*. 1975, *60*, 713–719.

Carver, C. S. & Glass, D. C. Coronary-prone behavior pattern and interpersonal aggression. *Journal of Personality and Social Psychology*, 1978, *36*, 361–366.

Chesney, M. A., Black, F. W., Chadwick, J. H., & Rosenman, R. H. Psychological correlates of the coronary-prone behavior pattern. *Journal of Behavioral Medicine*, in press.

Chesney, M. A. & Rosenman, R. H. Strategies for modifying Type A behavior. *Consultant*, June 1980, 216–222.

Chesney, M. A. & Rosenman, R. H. Type A behavior in the work setting. In C. Cooper & R. Payne (eds.), *Current issues in occupational stress.* New York: Wiley, 1980.

Clark, D. A., Arnold, E. L., Foulds, E. L., Brown, D. M., Eastmead, D. R., & Parry, E. H. Serum urate and cholesterol levels in Air Force Academy Cadets. *Aviation, Space, and Environmental Medicine*, 1975, *46*, 1044–1075.

Cohen, J. B., Syme, S. L., Jenkins, C. D., Dagan, A., & Zyzanski, S. J. The cultural context of Type A behavior and the risk of CHD. *American Journal of Epidemiology*, 1975, *102*, 434.

Cooper, T., Detre, T., & Weiss, S. J. Coronary-prone behavior and coronary heart disease: A critical review. *Circulation*, 1981, *63*, 1199–1215.

Corday, E. & Corday, S. R. Prevention of heart disease by control of risk factors: The time has come to face the facts. Editorial, *American Journal of Cardiology*, 1975, *35*, 330–333.

DeBacker, G., Kornitzer, M., Kiefer, F., Bogaert, M., Van Durme, J., Ristin, R., Degre, C., & DeSchaepdriver, A. Relation between coronary-prone behavior pattern, excretion of urinary catecholamines, heart rate and rhythm. *Preventive Medicine*, 1979, *8*, 14–22.

Dembroski, T. M. & MacDougall, J. Psychosocial factors and coronary heart disease: A bio-behavioral model. In U. Stockmeier (ed.), *Advances in stress research.* Berlin: Springer-Verlag, in press.

Dembroski, T. M. & MacDougall, J. M. Stress effects on affiliation preferences among subjects possessing the Type A coronary-prone behavior pattern. *Journal of Personality and Social Psychology*, 1978, *36*, 23–33.

Dembroski, T. M., MacDougall, J. M. Shields, J. L., Petitto, J., & Lushene, R. Components of Type A coronary-prone behavior pattern and cardiovascular responses to psychomotor performance challenge. *Journal of Behavioral Medicine*, 1978, *1*, 159–176.

Dembroski, T. M., MacDougall, J. M., & Shields, J. L. Physiologic reactions to social challenge in persons evidencing the Type A coronary-prone behavior pattern. *Journal of Human Stress*, 1977, *3*, 2–9.

Dimsdale, J. E., Hackett, T. P., Hutter, A. M., Jr., Block, P. C., & Catanzo, D. Type A personality and extent of coronary atherosclerosis. *American Journal of Cardiology*, 1978, *42*, 583–586.

Dunbar, H. F. *Psychosomatic diagnosis.* New York: Paul B. Hoeber, 1943.

Elmadjian, F., Hope, J. M., & Lamson, E. T. Excretion of epinephrine and norepinephrine under stress. *Recent Progress in Hormone Research*, 1958, *14*, 513.

Engel, G. L. Psychologic stress, vasodepressor syncope and sudden death. *Annals of Internal Medicine*, 1978, *89*, 403–412.

Enterline, P. E. & Stewart, W. H. Geographic patterns in deaths from coronary disease. *Public Health Reports*, 1959, *71*, 849.

Epstein, F. H. The epidemiology of coronary heart disease: A review. *Journal of Chronic Diseases*, 1965, *18*, 735–774.

Feinleib, M., Brand, R. J., Remington, R., & Zyzanski, S. J. Association of the coronary-prone behavior pattern and coronary heart disease. In T. M. Dembroski, S. M. Weiss, J. L. Shield, S. G. Haynes, & M. Feinleib (eds.), *Coronary-prone behavior.* New York: Springer-Verlag, 1978.

Frank, K. A., Meller, S. S., Kornfield, D. S. et al. Type A behavior and coronary heart disease: Angiographic confirmation. *Journal of the American Medical Association*, 1978, *240*, 761–763.

Friedman, M., Byers, S. O., & Rosenman, R. H. Effect of unsaturated fats upon lipemia and conjunctival circulation. *Journal of the American Medical Association*, 1965, *193*, 882–889.

Friedman, M., Byers, S. O., Diamant, J., & Rosenman, R. H. Plasma catecholamine response of coronary-prone subjects (Type A) to a specific challenge. *Metabolism*, 1975, *4*, 205–210.

Friedman, M., Manwaring, J. H., Rosenman, R. H., Donlon, G., Ortega, P., & Grube, S. M. Instantaneous and sudden death: Clinical and pathological differentiation in coronary artery disease. *Journal of the American Medical Association*, 1973, *225*, 1319–1328.

Friedman, M. & Rosenman, R. H. Association of specific overt behavior pattern with blood and cardiovascular findings. *Journal of the American Medical Association*, 1959, *169*, 1286–1296.

Friedman, M., Rosenman, R. H., & Byers, S. O. Serum lipids and conjunctival circulation after fat ingestion in men exhibiting Type A behavior pattern. *Circulation*, 1964, *29*, 874–886.

Friedman, M., Rosenman, R. H., & Carroll, V. Changes in the serum cholesterol and blood-clotting time in men subjected to cyclic variation of occupational stress. *Circulation*, 1958, *17*, 852–861.

Friedman, M., Rosenman, R. H., Straus, R., Wurm, M., & Kostichek, R. The relationship of behavior pattern A to the state of the coronary vasculature: A study of fifty-one autopsy subjects. *American Journal of Medicine*, 1968, *44*, 525–537.

Friedman, M., St. George, S., & Byers, S. O. Excretion of catecholamines, 17-ketosteroids, 17-hydroxycorticoids, and 5-hydroxyindole in men oexhibiting a particular behavior pattern (A) associated with high incidence of clinical coronary artery disease. *Journal of Clinical Investigation*, 1960, *39*, 758–764.

Froelicher, V. F., Longo, M. R., & McIver, R. G. The effects of chronic exercise on the heart and on coronary atherosclerotic heart disease: A literature survey. USAF School of Aerospace Medicine Report SAM-TR-76-6, Brooks Air Force Base, Texas, 1976.

Funkenstein, D. H., King, S. H., & Drolette, M. E. *Mastery of stress*. Cambridge, Mass.: Harvard University Press, 1957.

Ganeline, I. E. & Kraevskij, J. M. Premorbid personality traits in patients with cardiac ischaemia. *Cardiologia* (Moscow), 1971, *2*, 40–45.

Gazes, P. C., Richardson, J. A., & Woods, E. F. Plasma catecholamine content in myocardial infarction and angina pectoris. *Circulation*, 1959, *19*, 657.

Gildea, E. Special features of personality which are common to certain psychosomatic disorders. *Psychosomatic Medicine*, 1949, *11*, 273–277.

Glass, D. C. *Behavior patterns, stress and coronary disease*. Hillsdale, N.J.: Lawrence Erlbaum, 1977.

Glass, D. C., Snyder, M. L., & Hollis, J. F. Time urgency and the Type A coronary-prone behavior pattern. *Applied Social Psychology*, 1974, *4*, 125–140.

Gordon, T., Garcia-Palmieri, M. R., Kagan, A., Kannel, W. B., & Schiffman, J. Differences in coronary heart disease in Framingham, Honolulu and Puerto Rico. *Journal of Chronic Diseases*, 1974, *27*, 329–337.

Gordon, T., Kannel, W. B., & McGee, D. Death and coronary attacks in men after giving up cigarette smoking—A report from the Framingham Study. *Lancet*, 1974, *2*, 1345–1348.

Gordon, T. & Verter, J. Serum cholesterol, systolic blood pressure and Framingham relative weight as discriminators of cardiovascular disease. The Framingham Study: An epidemiological investigation of cardiovascular disease. Section 23, Washington, D.C.: Government Printing Office, 1969.

Goulet, C., Allard, C., & Poirier, R. Etude epidemiologique d'une population urbine canadienne-Francaise: Factuers Associes au Profile Coronarien. *L'Union Med. du Canada*, 1968, *97*, 1104–1109.

Groen, J. J., Dreyfuss, F., & Guttman, L. Epidemiological, nutritional, and sociological studies of atherosclerotic (coronary) heart disease among different ethnic groups in Israel, progress in biochemical pharmacology. In C. J. Miras, A. N. Howard, & R. Paoletta (eds.), *Recent advances in atherosclllerosis*. Basel: S. Karger AG, 1968.

Groen, J. J., Tjiong, B., Kamminger, C. E., & Willegrands, A. F. The influence of nutrition, individuality and some other factors, including various forms of stress on the serum cholesterol: An experiment of nine months duration in 60 normal human volunteers. *Voeding*, 1962, *13*, 556.

Haft, J. I. & Fani, K. Intravascular platelet aggregation in the heart induced by stress. *Circulation*, 1973, *47*, 353.

Harlan, W. R., Oberman, R. E., Mitchell, R. E., & Graybiel, A. Constitutional and environmental factors related to serum lipid and lipoprotein levels. *Annals of Internal Medicine*, 1967, *66*, 540–551.

Haynes, S. G., Feinleib, M., & Kannel, W. B. The relationship of psychosocial factors to coronary heart disease in the Framingham Study. III. 8 year incidence of CHD. *American Journal of Epidemiology*, 1980, *3*, 37–58.

Haynes, S., Feinleib, M., Levine, S., Scotch, N., & Kannel, W. B. The relationship of psychosocial factors to coronary heart disease in theFramingham Study: Prevalence of coronary heart disease. *American Journal of Epidemiology*, 1978, *107*, 384–402.

Heller, R. F. Type A behavior and coronary heart disease. *British Medical Journal*, 1979, *2*, 368.

Horn, J. M., Plomin, R., & Rosenman, R. Heritability of personality traits in adult male twins. *Behavioral Genetics*, 1976, *6*, 17–30.

Howard, J. H., Cunningham, D. A., & Rechnitzer, P. A. Childhood antecedents of Type A behavior. Submitted for publication.

Raab, W. (ed.). *Prevention of ischemic heart disease.* Springfield, Ill.: Thomas, 1966.

Raab, W. & Gigee, W. Total urinary catechol excretion in cardiovascular and other diseased conditions. *Circulation*, 1954, *9*, 592.

Rahe, R. H., Hervig, L., & Rosenman, R. H. Heritability of Type A behavior. *Psychosomatic Medicine*, 1978, *40*, 478–486.

Rahe, R. H., Rubin, R. T., & Arthur, R. J. The three investigators study serum uric acid, cholesterol and cortisol variability during stress of everyday life. *Psychosomatic Medicine*, 1974, *36*, 258–268.

Rahe, R. H., Ward, H. W., & Hayes, V. Brief group therapy in myocardial infarction rehabilitation: Three to four-year follow up of a controlled trial. *Psychosomatic Medicine*, 1979, *41*, 229–242.

Romo, M. Siltanen, P., Theorell, T., & Rahe, R. H. Work behavior time urgency and life dissatisfactions in subjects with myocardial infarction-A cross-cultural study. *Journal of Psychosomatic Research*, 1974, *18*, 1–6.

Rosenman, R. H. The heart you save may be our own. In J. Chacko (ed.), *Health handbook.* Amsterdam: North-Holland Publishing Co., 1979.

Rosenman, R. H. The interview method of assessment of the coronary-prone behavior pattern. In T. M. Dembroski, S. M. Weiss, J. L. Shields, S. G. Haynes, & M. Feinleib (eds.), *Coronary-prone behavior.* New York: Springer-Verlag, 1978.

Rosenman, R. H. The role of the Type A behavior pattern in ischemic heart disease: Modification of its effects by beta-blocking agents. *British Journal of Clinical Practice*, 1978, *32*, 58–65.

Rosenman, R. H. Role of Type A behavior pattern in the pathogenesis of ischemic heart disease, and modification for prevention. Proceedings of PAAVO NURMI Conference, Helsinki, Finland, September 1977. In *Advances in Cardiology*, 1978, *25*, 1–12.

Rosenman, R. H., Bawol, R. D., & Oscherwitz, M. A 4-year prospective study of the relationship of different habitual vocational physical activity to risk and incidence of ischemic heart disease in volunteer male Federal employees. In P. Milvy (ed.), *The marathon.* New York: Annuals of New York Academy of Sciences, 1977.

Rosenman, R. H., Brand, R. J., Jenkins, C. D., Friedman, M., Straus, R., & Wurm, M. Coronary heart disease in the Western Collaborative Group study: Final follow-up of 8½ years. *Journal of the American Medical Association*, 1975, *233*, 872–877.

Rosenman, R. H., Brand, R. J., Sholtz, R. I., & Friedman, M. Multivariate prediction of coronary heart disease during 8.5 year follow-up in the Western Collaborative Group study. *American Journal of Cardiology*, 1976, *37*, 903–910.

Rosenman, R. H., Brand, R. J., Sholtz, R. I., & Jenkins, C. D. The relationship of corneal arcus to cardiovascular risk factors and the incidence of coronary heart disease. *New England Journal of Medicine*, 1974, *291*, 1322–1323.

Rosenman, R. H. & Friedman, M. Association of specific behavior pattern in women with blood and cardiovascular findings. *Journal of the American Medical Association*, 1961, *24*, 1173–1184.

Rosenman, R. H. & Friedman, M. Behavior patterns, blood lipids, and coronary heart disease. *Journal of the American Medical Association*, 1963, *184*, 934–938.

Rosenman, R. H. & Friedman, M. Modifying Type A behavior pattern. *Journal of Psychosomatic Research*, 1977, *21*, 323–331.

Rosenman, R. H. & Friedman, M. Neurogenic factors in pathogenesis of coronary heart disease. *Medical Clinics of North America*, 1974, *58*, 269–279.

Rosenman, R. H. & Friedman, M. The central nervous system and coronary heart disease. In Braunwald (ed.), *The myocardium: Failure and infarction.* New York: H.P. Publishing Co., Inc., 1974.

Rosenman, R. H. & Friedman, M. The possible role of behavior patterns in proneness and immunity to coronary heart disease. In H. I. Russek & B. L. Zohman (eds.), *Coronary heart disease.* Philadelphia: J.B. Lippincott Co., 1971.

Rosenman, R. H., Friedman, M., Jenkins, C. D., et al. Clinically unrecognized myocardial infarction in the Western Collaborative Group Study. *American Journal of Cardiology*, 1967, *19*, 776–782.

Rosenman, R. H., Friedman, M., Jenkins, C. D., Straus, R., Wurm, M., & Kositcheck, R. The prediction of immunity to coronary heart disease. *Journal of the American Medical Association*, 1966, *198*, 1159–1162.

Rosenman, R. M., Friedman, M., Jenkins, C. D., Straus, R., Wurm, M., & Kositcheck, R. Recurring and fatal myocardial infarction in the Western Collaborative Group Study. *American Journal of Cardiology*, 1967, *19*, 771–775.

Rosenman, R. H., Friedman, M., Straus, R., Jenkins, C. D., Zyzanski, S. J., & Wurm, M. Coronary heart disease in the Western Collaborative Group Study: A follow-up experience of 4½ years. *Journal of Chronic Diseases*, 1970, *23*, 173–190.

Rosenman, R. H., Friedman, M., Straus, R., Wurm, M., Jenkins, C. D., & Messinger, H. E. Coronary heart disease in the Western Collaborative Group Study: A follow-up experience of 2 years. *Journal of the American Medical Association*, 1966, *195*, 86–92.

Rosenman, R. H., Friedman, M., Straus, R., Wurm, M., Kositchek, R., Hahn, W., & Werthessen, N. T. A predictive study of coronary heart disease. The Western Collaborative Group Study. *Journal of the American Medical Association*, 1964, *189*, 15–22.

Rosenman, R. H., Rahe, R. H., Borhani, N. O., & Feinleib, M. Heritability of personality and behavior. Proceedings of the first international congress of twin studies. Rome, Italy, November 1974. *Acta Geneticus Medicus Gemellol*, 1976, *25*, 221–224.

Rosenman, R. H., Sholtz, R. I., & Brand, R. J. A study of comparative blood pressure measures in predicting risk of CHD. *Circulation*, 1976, *54*, 51–58.

Roskies, E. Considerations in developing a treatment program for the coronary-prone (Type A) behavior pattern. In P. Davidson (ed.), *Behavioral medicine: Changing health life styles.* New York: Brunner Mazel, 1978.

Roskies, E., Kearney, H., Spevack, M., Surkis, A., Cohen, C., & Gilman, S. Generalizability and durability of treatment effects in an intervention program for coronary-prone (Type A) managers. *Journal of Behavioral Medicine*, 1979, *2*, 195–207.

Roskies, E. & Lazarus, R. S. Coping theory and the teaching of coping skills. In P. O. Davidson & S. M. Davidson (eds.), *Behavioral medicine: Changing health life styles.* New York: Brunner/Mazel, 1980.

Roskies, E., Spevack, M., Surkis, A., Cohen, C., & Gilman, S. Changing the coronary-prone (Type A) behavior pattern in a non-clinical population. *Journal of Behavioral Medicine*, 1978, *1*, 201–216.

Russek, H. I. Role of emotional stress in the etiology of clinical coronary heart disease. *Diseases of the Chest*, 1967, *52*, 1–9.

Russek, H. I. Stress, tobacco and coronary disease in North American professional groups. *Journal of the American Medical Association*, 1965, *192*, 189–194.

Rustin, R. M., Dramaix, M., Kittle, F., Degre, C., Kornitzer, M., Thilly, C., & de Backer, G. Validation de techniques d'evaluation du profil comportemental "A" utilizees dans de "Projet Belge de Prevention de affections cardiovasculaires," (P.B.S.) *Rev. Evidem. et Saute Publ.*, 1976, *24*, 497–507.

Sales, S. J. & House, J. Job dissatisfaction as a possible risk factor in coronary heart disease. *Journal of Chronic Diseases*, 1971, *23*, 861–873.

Scherwitz, L., Berton, K., & Leventhal, H. Type A assessment and interaction in the behavior pattern interview. *Psychosomatic Medicine*, 1977, *39*, 229–240.

Scherwitz, L., Berton, K., & Leventhal, H. Type A behavior, self-involvement and cardiovascular response. *Psychosomatic Medicine*, 1978, *40*, 593–609.

Schucker, B. & Jacobs, D. R. Assessment of behavioral risks for coronary disease by voice characteristics. *Psychosomatic Medicine*, 1977, *39*, 219–228.

Seltzer, C. Smoking and coronary heart disease. *New England Journal of Medicine*, 1977, *228*, 420–1186.

Shekelle, R. B., Schoenberger, J. A., & Stamler, J. Correlates of the JAS Type A behavior score. *Journal of Chronic Diseases*, 1976, *29*, 381–394.

Sholtz, R. K., Rosenman, R. H., & Brand, R. J. The relationship of reported parental history to the incidence of CHD in the Western Collaborative Group Study. *American Journal of Epidemiology*, 1975, *102*, 350–356.

Sigler, L. H. The mortality from arteriosclerotic and hypertensive heart diseases in the United States. I. Possible relation to the distribution of population and economic status. *American Journal of Cardiology*, 1958, *1*, 176–180.

Sime, W. E. & Parker, C. Physiological arousal in male and female students with either Type A or B behavior patterns. *Medicine and Science in Sports*, 1978, *10*, 51.

Simpson, M. T., Olewine, D. A., Jenkins, C. D., Ramsey, F. H., Zyzanski, S. J., Thomas, G., & James, C. G. Exercise-induced catecholamines and platelet aggregation in the coronary-prone behavior pattern. *Psychosomatic Medicine*, 1974, *36*, 476–487.

Sparrow, D., Dawber, T. R., & Colton, T. The influence of cigarette smoking on prognosis after a first myocardial infarction: A report from the Framingham Study. *Journal of Chronic Disease*, 1978, *31*, 425–433.

Stewart, I. M. G. Coronary disease and modern stress. *Lancet*, 1950, *2*, 867–878.

Stoyva, J. & Budzynski, T. Cultivated low arousal—An anti-stress response. In L. V. DiCara (ed.), *Limbic and autonomic nervous systems research*. New York: Plenum, 1974.

Suinn, R. M. Type A behavior pattern. In R. B. Williams & W. D. Gentry (eds.), *Behavioral approaches to medical treatment*. Cambridge, Mass.: Ballinger, 1979.

Syme, S. I. Psychological factors and coronary heart disease. *International Journal of Psychiatry*, 1968, *5*, 429–433.

Theorell, T., Lind, E., & Floderus, B. The relationship of disturbing life-changes and emotions to the early development of myocardial infarction and other serious illnesses. *International Journal of Epidemiology*, 1975, *4*, 281–293.

Theorell, T. & Rahe, R. H. Psychosocial factors and myocardial infarction. I. An inpatient study in Sweden. *Journal of Psychosomatic Research*, 1971, *15*, 25–31.

Thiel, H. G., Parker, D., & Burce, T. A. Stress factors and the risk of myocardial infarction. *Journal of Psychosomatic Research*, 1973, *17*, 43.

Thompson, P. B. Effectiveness of relaxation techniques in reducing anxiety and stress factors in Type A, post-myocardial infarction patients. Unpublished doctoral dissertation, University of Massachusetts, 1976.

Trulson, F. F. The American diet: Past and present. *American Journal of Clinical Nutrition*, 1959, *7*, 91–97.

Van der Valk, J. M. & Groen, J. J. Personality structure and conflict situations in patients with myocardial infarction. *Journal of Psychosomatic Research*, 1967, *11*, 41–46.

Van Dusch, T. *Lehrbuch der Herzkrankheiten*. Leipzig: Verlag Von Wilhem Engelman, 1868.

Van Egeren, L. F. Social interactions, communications, and the coronary-prone behavior pattern: A psychophysiological study. *Psychosomatic Medicine*, 1979, *41*, 2–19.

Von Euler, V. S., Gemzell, L. A., Levi, L., & Strom, G. Cortical and medullary adrenal activity in emotional stress. *ACTA Endocrinology (Kbh)*, 1959, *30*, 567.

Voudoukis, I. J. Exaggerated cold-pressore response in patients with atherosclerotic vascular disease. *Angiology*, 1971, *22*, 57–62.

Waldron, I., Zyzanski, S., Shekelle, R. B., Jenkins, C. D., & Tennebaum, S. The coronary-prone behavior pattern in employed men and women. *Journal of Human Stress*, 1977, *3*, 2–18.

Wardwell, W. I. & Bahnson, C. B. Behavioral variables and myocardial infarction in the Southeastern Connecticut Heart Study. *Journal of Chronic Diseases*, 1973, *26*, 447–461.

Wardwell, W. I., Hyman, M., & Bahnson, C. B. Socio-environmental antecedents to coronary heart disease in 87 white males. *Social Science Medicine*, 1968, *2*, 165–183.

Wardwell, W. I., Hyman, M., & Bahnson, C. B. Stress and coronary heart disease in three field studies. *Journal of Chronic Diseases*, 1964, *17*, 73–84.

Weidner, G. & Matthews, K. A. Reported physical symptoms elicited by unpredictable events and the Type A coronary-prone behavior pattern. *Journal of Personality and Social Psychology*, 1978, *36*, 1213–1220.

Weiner, H. Some psychological factors related to cardiovascular responses: A logical and empirical analysis. In R. Roessler & W. S. Greenfield (eds.), *Physiological correlates of psychological disorders*. Madison, Wisc.: University of Wisconsin Press, 1952.

Werko, L. Risk factors and coronary heart disease—fact or fancy? *American Heart Journal*, 1976, *91*, 87–98.

White, P. D. The historical background of angina pectoris. *Modern Concepts of Cardiovascular Disease*, 1974, *43*, 109–112.

Williams, R. B., Haney, T., Gentry, W. D., & Kong, Y. Relation between hostility and arteriographically documented coronary atherosclerosis. *Psychosomatic Medicine*, 1978, *40*, 88.

Wolf, S., McCabe, W. R., Yamamoto, J., Adsett, C. A., & Schottstaedt, W. W. Changes in serum lipids in relation to emotional stress during rigid controls of diet and exercise. *Transactions of the American Clinical and Climatological Association*, 1961, *73*, 162–175.

Yudkin, J. Diet and coronary thrombosis, hypothesis and fact. *Lancet*, 1957, *2*, 155–162.

Zyzanski, S. J., Jenkins, C. D., Ryan, T. J., Flessas, A., & Everest, M. Psychological correlates of coronary angiographic findings. *Archives of Internal Medicine*, 1976, *136*, 1234–1237.

Zyzanski, S. J., Wrzesniewski, K., & Jenkins, C. D. Cross-cultural validation of the coronary-prone behavior pattern. Submitted for publication.

17

Biomedical and Psychosocial Predictors of Hypertension in Air Traffic Controllers

C. David Jenkins
University of Texas Medical Branch, Galveston

Michael W. Hurst
Boston University School of Medicine

Robert M. Rose
University of Texas Medical Branch, Galveston

Laurie Anderson and Bernard E. Kreger
Boston University School of Medicine

The Air Traffic Controller Health Change Study, recently conducted at the Boston University School of Medicine, provided an opportunity to study the impact of stress on mental and physical health of about 400 participants with continuing surveillance over a three-year period (Rose, Jenkins, & Hurst, 1978).

The study involved extensive medical, laboratory, psychiatric, psychological, and attitude studies conducted on five occasions, nine months apart at the Boston University Medical Center. It also involved semi-annual blood pressure and hormonal studies of men while they were actually working as air traffic controllers. Finally, each man participated in monthly surveillance for mild and moderate illnesses and injuries. This intensive and comprehensive multidisciplinary study thus provided the opportunity for studying the antecedents of many types of health changes.

The most widespread, serious illness affecting these air traffic controllers was hypertension. Using the Framingham Heart Study criteria for hypertension, 64 percent of our total sample of 416 ATCs were either borderline or definite hypertensives when they entered the study. This was about 50% greater than comparable Framingham prevalence data. Using the same criteria, 64 percent of the intake normotensives became either borderline or definitely hypertensive in the next three years of followup. This new incidence rate was four times that of men the same age in the Framingham Heart Study.

By two other criteria for diagnosis of hypertension, this sample of ATCs had 1.5 to 2.0 times the prevalence rate of hypertension of other large samples of men of similar age (Rose et al., 1978).

This study was supported by a grant from the National Heart, Lung and Blood Institute to the Specialized Center of Research in Hypertension at Boston University School of Medicine (HL 18318-04). Data were derived from the Air Traffic Controller Health Change Study (Contract No. DOT-FA73WA-3211). The contents of this report are the responsibility of the authors and do not necessarily reflect the views of the Department of Transportation, the Federal Aviation Administration or the National Heart, Lung and Blood Institute.

Our reading of the literature has not revealed any other occupational group of similar ages which has hypertension rates higher than those observed here for air traffic controllers.

We were surprised first by the high prevalence and incidence of hypertension in these men, aged 25-39 years, and secondly by the substantial differences in prevalence generated by different diagnostic criteria. For example, the Hanes criterion (DHEW-HRA, 1978) is based on a single blood pressure reading. 140/90 are the cut-off points for borderline hypertension and 160/95 are the cut-off points for definite hypertension. The Framingham Heart Study criterion is based on two blood pressure readings and the rules for diagnosis are somewhat more complex.

For our ATC study we used an additional diagnostic criterion. This involved the two systolic readings being averaged and the two diastolic readings being averaged. Even though the same aboslute thresholds were used for diagnosing borderline and definite hypertension, that is, 140/90 and 160/95, the use of the average rather than the higher of two readings resulted in a lower frequency of men being judged hypertensive, 47 percent in all, as compared to the Framingham or Hanes criteria which found 64 and 55 percent, respectively.

Not only were different frequencies of men judged to be hypertensive by the different diagnostic criteria, but also many men received different diagnoses from the different criteria being applied to the same blood pressure readings. Table 1 shows the percentage of ATCs who received various hypertensive diagnoses at intake using the different criteria.

While 55 percent of men were labeled normotensive by any one or more of the three criteria applied, the three criteria agreed for only about 2/3 of these normotensive men. Similarly, there was about 2/3 agreement for the 30 percent of men who were called definite hypertensives by one or more criteria. The borderline hypertensive diagnosis varied greatly by the different criteria primarily because of the very broad definition of borderline hypertension which the Framingham system uses. The Framingham criterion called many men borderlines who were called normotensives or definites by the two other criteria. In fact, only 36 percent of men called borderline by one or more criteria were so designated uniformly by all three methods.

The reason we emphasize these discrepancies is because they may explain in part why hypertension research has traditionally been so difficult, why so many studies which have identified predictors of hypertension cannot be replicated, and finally, why there is so much controversy about the psychosocial characteristics of hypertensive patients. The confusion in the field may be due to the lack of agree-

Table 1 Agreement among three diagnostic criteria for hypertension: Framingham Heart Study, U.S. Health and Nutrition Examination Survey, and ATC-HCS Research Criterion

Intake diagnosis	Labelled by *any* criterion (%)	Percentage of column 1 agreed upon by *all* 3 criteria (%)
Normotensive	55	66
Borderline	44	36
Definite	30	67

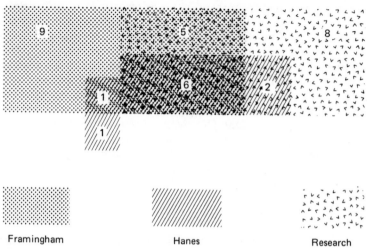

Framingham   Hanes   Research

Figure 1 Psychosocial predictors of hypertension: How they differ by diagnostic criterion.

ment among diagnostic criteria. We are also quite certain that the natural lability of blood pressure—the fact that it changes so rapidly from minute to minute—also makes the use of single, casual resting blood pressure readings a very unstable basis for defining clinical groups.

When faced with this lack of agreement among diagnostic criteria for hypertension, we were perplexed as to which was the "correct" criterion to use. There being no simple answer, we utilized our computer to make a separate search for the predictors of current and future hypertension for each diagnostic criterion. The findings were surprising. In addition to a series of biological variables, we studied the relation of approximately 130 psychological and social variables to the prevalence and incidence of hypertension separately for the three diagnostic criteria. In all, we found 21 psychosocial variables significantly associated with the Framingham criterion, 10 with the Hanes criterion, and 21 with the research criterion. In total, 32 variables were found significant for at least one of the criteria, but only 6 of these 32 were significantly associated with hypertension for all three of the criteria. A graphic display of the overlap and individuality of the predictors for the three criteria is presented in Fig. 1. This finding underscores the importance of diagnostic criteria for hypertension, the noncomparability of these criteria, and the problem of discovering quite different predictors of hypertension depending on which diagnostic scheme is used. This is an issue which needs to be resolved among researchers so that future consistency of research can be achieved.

To simplify discussion for the remainder of this paper, we will focus upon the Framingham diagnostic criterion inasmuch as it is well publicized and widely used. Because of the instability of the diagnosis of borderline hypertension that was observed, the predictive analyses which follow concentrate on definite hypertension. Three groups were defined: (*a*) Men who remained normotensive throughout the study; (*b*) Men who had definite hypertension at intake; and (*c*) Men who were either normotensive or borderline at intake, but who developed definite hypertension before the end of the study. We call these "future cases." From this total number we excluded men who had fewer than 3 of the 5 regular medical examinations plus those who were taking anti-hypertensive drugs which might interfere with their emotional state or their psychological outlook regarding themselves or their work. Despite the high frequency of men with definite hypertension either at the beginning of the study or subsequently, only a very small number were taking anti-hypertensive drugs at any time during these years. This avoidance of drugs was no doubt influenced by the fact that the taking of anti-hypertensive drugs could provide grounds for transfer out of air traffic control work.

This selection of only definite hypertensive cases in the prevalence and incidence categories provides a certainty and stability which increases the likelihood that most of those psychosocial and biological variables found associated with hypertension in the analyses which follow will have a greater chance of being replicated in subsequent studies.

RESULTS

Among the strongest predictors of hypertension were the average and maximum blood pressures recorded by monitoring devices while the men were actually controlling traffic. This data set encompassed about 20,000 blood pressure readings and its final analysis will be the subject of a later paper.

From the variety of physical examination and laboratory test variables collected at baseline, only age, percentage overweight, and pulse rate showed a significant discrimination among normotensives, intake definite hypertensives, and future definite hypertensives using the Framingham diagnostic criterion. As shown in Table 2, the association of age with diagnosis was irregular with intake definites being the oldest, and future cases slightly the youngest. Intake definite (or prevalence) cases were by far the most overweight followed by future cases. Remaining close to ideal weight seems to be most common among men who remained normotensive. Pulse rate at the baseline medical exam was also significantly associated with hypertension, with future cases having an average mid-way between the prevalence cases and the normotensives. The number of significant biological predictors of hypertension was surprisingly small, making it all the more important that we turn to psychosocial variables to increase our understanding of the characteristics of future hypertensives.

We constructed a special questionnaire for this study which dealt specifically with the stresses involved in the daily activities of controlling air traffic. The questionnaire involved many items dealing with attitudes, emotions, and psychophysiologic symptoms which might occur before, during, or after heavy traffic or

Table 2 Predictors of hypertension in the air traffic controller study (Framingham diagnosis)

Biological variables	Averages			F	P
	Normotensive	Intake definite	Future cases		
Sample size	(56)	(54)	(121)		
Age	36.9	38.4	35.5	6.66	0.002
% Overweight	2.7	16.4	9.9	20.04	0.001
Pulse rate (MD exam)	68.6	73.5	70.8	3.30	0.04

Table 3 Predictors of hypertension in the Air Traffic Controller Study (Framingham diagnosis)

Affective states	Averages			F	P
	Normotensive	Intake definite	Future cases		
Sample size	(56)	(54)	(120)		
Anxiety state factor	48.2	46.7	47.7	0.45	0.64
POMS: Tension-anxiety	39.4	40.6	38.1	3.83	0.03
POMS: Depression	40.2	40.1	38.8	4.22	0.02
POMS: Anger	39.3	39.0	38.8	0.26	0.78
Life change stress (PPU)	36.2	23.1	31.2	3.04	0.05
Self-rated L-C distress	321	186	229	3.95	0.02

difficult flight patterns. Many other aspects of ATC work, such as avoiding the feared condition of "burn out," how one discharges tension, the costs and burdens upon one's life as a result of being a controller, commitment to career, and a variety of specific attitudes regarding work, co-workers, management, and one's own styles of coping with stress were asked about. The items and scales thus can be seen to deal with traits, work situations, and the states experienced in common person-situation interactions (Hurst, Jenkins, & Rose, 1978; Rose et al., 1978).

Factor analysis of these scales revealed a general anxiety state factor which was defined by scales reflecting emotional and psychophysiological responses of anxiety state in response to specified circumstances, both during ATC work and off the job. The pattern of correlations of this factor scale with other scales administered suggests that it was in fact a measure of state anxiety on the job for people in this occupation. In addition, we also administered the Profile of Mood States (POMS) and a life change instrument combining the scale of Holmes and Rahe, that of Paykel, Prusoff, and Uhlenhuth, and additional new items. Our life change instrument also provided opportaunity for respondents to rate the amount of the stress they themselves experienced in connection with each life change which had occurred. The relation of these variables to hypertension is shown in Table 3.

This table shows that neither the anxiety state factor nor the POMS anger scale were significantly associated with hypertension despite the theoretical anticipation that they would be. The POMS tension-anxiety scale and depression scale did have significant associations with hypertension, but in a way quite opposite to that which was predicted. Future cases had the lowest average score of all three groups. The findings for the life change distress scales were also contrary to the usual expectation. Persons who remained normotensive reported the greatest amount of life change stress for both ways of scoring these responses. Prevalence cases of hypertension reported the lowest life change distress, and future cases recorded intermediate levels.

While these findings are different from the notion that "stress" directly leads to hypertension, they are consistent with a hypothesis which has gathered considerable support in the last few years, namely, that hypertensives perceive their world in a quite different way from normotensives in that they deny the negatively toned aspect of circumstances around them. This hypothesis is supported by the life change data, which are prospective in nature for future cases and by the POMS tension and anxiety scale. The pattern of scores for the intake definite hypertensives, however, is not fully supportive of this hypothesis inasmuch as they have tension, anxiety, and depression scores quite similar to normotensives. Nevertheless they do see that their life circumstances were particularly free of distress. It may also be that persons who know they are hypertensive avoid life changes.

If emotions and life stress do not provide much help in understanding differences between hypertensives and normotensives, perhaps greater insights can be obtained from considering the ways in which people cope with the problems which confront them. Data for a variety of coping measures are presented in Table 4.

Five significant associations between a larger number of coping scales and hypertension are shown here. "Burn-out" is a condition of feeling that one is losing ability and energy as a function of persisting too long at a difficult career which brings deterioration of one's physical and mental reflexes. Contrary to expectations, normotensives report more burn-out than either prevalence or incidence cases.

Tension discharge rate was designed to be a positive coping mechanism, but the self-report responses to these items imply that current hypertensives discharge tension more quickly and efficiently than do normotensives or future hypertensives. When asked how much of a sacrifice one has to make to continue being an air traffic controller, and how much this career interferes with home life, social life, and achieving other goals and satisfactions, those persons who claimed that being an ATC entailed considerable sacrifice were more heavily concentrated among normotensives. Those who denied their career exacted a cost from them were more likely to be current or future hypertensives.

These findings again are contrary to common expectations. Could it be that this reversal is a function of poor insight or denial on the part of hypertensives? If this be the case, self-report measures would give an untrue picture but the ratings of trained clinicians should yield a different and more accurate set of relationships. The next two variables listed in Table 4 are based on ratings made by qualified psychologists who interviewed the controllers at baseline and rated them on several specific forms of coping, on overall coping skills, and on the general ability of the respondent to handle stress. These ratings were made on a scale of 1 to 5 and hence represent a quite different level of measurement than the self-report scales, all of which were calibrated to have a mean of 50 and a standard deviation of 10.

The interviewer ratings support the self-report data in that future hypertensives are rated as the *best* of all groups in their average overall coping score and rating for handling of stress. Normotensives are intermediate, and current hypertensives do

Table 4 Predictors of hypertension in the Air Traffic Controller Study (Framingham diagnosis)

Coping mechanisms	Averages			F	P
	Normotensive	Intake definite	Future cases		
Sample size	(56)	(54)	(120)		
Avoiding "burn-out"	46.6	49.2	50.7	3.91	0.02
Tension discharge rate	47.9	52.7	48.9	4.07	0.02
Subjective costs of ATC	54.8	47.6	47.5	13.59	0.0001
Rating: Overall coping	3.9	3.5	4.1	3.25	0.04
Rating: Handling stress	3.9	3.3	4.2	13.29	0.004

Table 5 Predictors of hypertension in the Air Traffic Controller Study (Framingham diagnosis)

| Work attitudes | Averages | | | F | P |
	Normotensive	Intake definites	Future cases		
Sample size	(56)	(54)	(121)		
JDI: Work satisfaction	45.0	47.6	49.2	3.56	0.03
JDI: Co-worker satisfaction	49.4	51.5	54.3	4.59	0.01
JAS: Job-involvement	−3.5	−6.5	−3.3	3.67	0.03
Intvw: "Career-investment"	4.4	5.2	5.2	6.11	0.003

clearly the worst of all groups. It is unlikely that interviewers knew anything about the participants' blood pressure. It is possible, however, that many of the intake cases knew of their hypertensive condition for some months or years before entering the ATC study, and this may have influenced the style with which they presented themselves in the interview situation.

Several scales gathered at baseline dealt with the ATCs' work and career attitudes. Four of these scales were significantly associated with hypertensive diagnosis, and these findings, presented in Table 5, are consistent with those previously recorded. On the Job Description Inventory, future hypertensives showed clearly the highest average on satisfaction with work and with co-workers. Normotensives had the lowest averages on both these scales. The JAS job-involvement scale did not differ between normotensives and future cases, but prevalence cases were clearly less job-involved than the other two groups. Interviewer ratings of respondents' career investment showed that psychologists rated both current and future hypertensives as clearly more committed to the ATC career than were those persons who remained normotensive.

A number of other behavioral styles were considered for possible associations with hypertensive diagnosis in Table 6. The JAS Type A and Hard-Driving scales were not significantly associated with hypertension. However, it is interesting to note that the normotensives tended to be closer to the population mid-points whereas both future and current hypertensive cases were somewhat more Type B

Table 6 Predictors of hypertension in the Air Traffic Controller Study (Framingham diagnosis)

| Behavioral styles | Averages | | | F | P |
	Normotensive	Intake definites	Future cases		
Sample size	(56)	(54)	(121)		
JAS: Type A	−2.3	−5.5	−3.7	1.94	0.15
JAS: Hard-driving	1.6	−1.0	−1.1	1.92	0.15
CPI: Achievement by conformity	51.2	48.9	53.2	4.07	0.02
PSS: Impulse control pathology (% positive)	21%	11%	7%	4.31	0.02
"Had fewer friends than most others" when in high school	18%	6%	7%	Chi²	0.03

on these scales. On the CPI scale for achievement by conformity, future cases scored the highest in terms of seeking higher achievement and current cases scored the lowest.

The Psychiatric Status Schedule was included in the psychological interview. The impulse control scale of this standard approach to scoring psychiatric problems involved such questions as whether the subject had had minor violations of the law, gotten into fights, or had become occasionally involved with illegal substances such as marijuana. The most common impulse control problems for our ATCs were minor traffic violations such as speeding. Persons who remained normotensive had the highest frequency of impulse control pathology and future cases of hypertension, the lowest frequency.

The biographical questionnaire administered at the beginning of this study included a question about how many friends the respondent had when in high school. This was intended to be a measure of social relatedness. Current and future hypertensives less frequently reported that they had few friends during their teenage years. This difference was significant by Chi-square.

The question arose as to whether the apparently positive social skills of future hypertensives were a subjective perception or were also supported by the perceptions of colleagues. As part of the ATC study, the controllers in each facility were asked to select three persons whom they judged to be the most competent ATCs, three persons whom they most enjoyed working with and would select as friends for off-the-job activities and also three persons whom they would like to work with on their ideal team. Respondents could select the same or different persons under each of these separate questions. As shown in Table 7, intake definite hypertensives and future cases scored very similarly in frequency of selection by peers. On all three selection tasks, however, normotensives were picked much less often. It appears thus that the self-report is corroborated and that current and future hypertensives do in fact get along better socially than normotensives.

DISCUSSION

As we have discussed these successive series of variables which discriminate among hypertensive categories, we have found that a number of the variables overlap conceptually and seemingly may correlate with one another. Nevertheless, they do present a well-rounded clinical picture. In this sample, future hypertensives were not distinguished by their anxiety states or by their anger. To the degree that their tension and depression differed, it was in the direction of being less tense and discouraged then those who remained normotensive. Both current and future hyper-

Table 7 Predictors of hypertension in the Air Traffic Controller Study (Framingham diagnosis)

| Selections by peers: | Averages | | | | |
	Normotensive	Intake definites	Future cases	F	P
Sample size	(56)	(54)	(121)		
for Competence	1.41	1.93	1.97	3.17	0.04
for Friendliness	1.48	2.09	1.97	3.68	0.03
for Ideal team	1.48	2.09	2.08	4.55	0.01

tensives reported much less life change distress than normotensives. Both by self-report and interviewer ratings, future hypertensives seem to have strong coping mechanisms and to deny that their difficult career was interfering with the rest of their lives. They seemed more satisfied with their work and more invested in their career than normotensives.

Current and future hypertensives were not different from normotensives in the coronary prone behavior pattern. They did, however, seem to strive for achievement by conforming with social norms to a greater degree then did normotensives, and they also were more likely to have good control of their impulses and have more friends then did normotensives. Current and future hypertensives were also more often selected by co-workers for their competence and friendliness.

We have not as yet synthesized from these findings a simple formulation of the psychological or physiological mechanisms which might contribute to the development of hypertension. It may very well be, however, that hypertension resembles other classical psychosomatic diseases, like asthma for example, in which the disease results not directly from exposure to noxious stimuli, nor from the immediate reaction of distressed arousal triggered by such stimuli, but rather emerges more directly from the psychophysiological defenses against noxious stimuli and accompanying pain (Jenkins, 1979). When such defensive styles generalize to inappropriate kinds of situations, increase to hyperactive levels, or persist beyond the time they are really needed, the organisms may finally "pay the price" in the form of a defensive disease such as hypertension.

REFERENCES

DHEW-HRA Publication No. 78-1648. Blood Pressure Levels of Persons Ages 6 Through 74 Years, United States, 1971–1974. (The Health and Nutrition Examination (Survey) Washington, D.C.: U.S. Government Printing Office, 1978.

Framingham Heart Study. Unpublished tabulations of six-year accumulated incidence of hypertension for specific age ranges. Framingham, Massachusetts, U.S.A.

Hurst, M. W., Jenkins, C. D., & Rose, R. M. The assessment of life change stress: A comparative and methodological inquiry. *Psychosomatic Medicine*, 1978, *40*, 126–141.

Jenkins, C. D. Psychosocial modifiers of response to stress. *Journal of Human Stress*, 1979, *5*, 3–15.

Rose, R. M., Jenkins, C. D., & Hurst, M. W. Air Traffic Controller Health Change Study: A Prospective Investigation of Physical, Psychological and Work-Related Changes. A report to the Federal Aviation Administration on research performed under Contract No. DOT-FA73WA-3211. Boston University School of Medicine, 1978. (Available from Department of Psychiatry, University of Texas Medical Branch, Galveston, TX 77550.)

18

Personality Correlates of Elevated Blood Pressure

Anxiety, Unexpressed Anger, and Lack of Assertiveness

Daisy Schalling
Karolinska Institute, and University of Stockholm

Despite extensive research, essential hypertension remains "one of the most complex, puzzling and common diseases known to man" (Weiner, 1979). There is general agreement that psychological factors play a role in the development of hypertension, but much less agreement as to what specific factors are involved and how they work (Weiner, 1979; Henry & Meehan, 1981; Harrell, 1980).

Transient sharp blood pressure increases have been regularly observed in laboratory settings when strong emotions, e.g., anxiety or anger, have been induced by stressful stimuli, but the relevance of such peaks for the pathogenesis of chronic blood pressure elevation is far from clear. Individuals who are prone to strong negative emotions or who live under stressful psychosocial conditions may experience frequent blood pressure rises and undergo changes in their cardiovascular system which eventually lead to essential hypertension. However, the mechanisms that mediate this process are not understood.

In the late thirties, during the first peak of interest in "psychosomatic medicine," psychoanalysts observed that hypertensive patients showed a typical pattern of anxiety and "suppressed rage" (Alexander, 1939; Robbins, 1948; Schwartz, 1940). The joint contributions of anxiety and anger to hypertension were confirmed in the classic study of Wolf and Wolff (1951). In interviews and concomitant physiological recordings in hypertensive patients and controls, dramatic blood pressure increases occurred in subjects (patients and controls) who showed signs of anxiety and also reported being resentful; those who reacted with anxiety and depression showed weaker blood pressure reactions. The early hypothesis that suppressed or unexpressed anger was of special significance has received additional support from experimental studies (e.g., Hokanson & Burgess, 1962) in which lack of opportunity to aggress after laboratory-induced anger retarded subsequent blood pressure drops.

PERSONALITY TRAITS IN HYPERTENSIVE PATIENTS

The studies described above investigated the relation between emotional *states* of anger or anxiety and increases in blood pressure. Other studies have assessed

The research reported was supported by a grant from the Swedish Medical Research Council (4545).

the personality *traits* or habitual behaviors, of hypertensives. Saslow and his collaborators, in a careful and ingenious interview study, found that hypertensive patients were low in assertiveness and high in anxiety (Saslow, Gressel, Shobe, DuBois, & Schroeder, 1950). In another early study, Kalis, Harris, Sokolov, and Carpenter (1957), using the psychodrama technique, found that hypertensive patients behaved in a submissive repetitive way on problems that called for self-assertion.

A follow-up study of 52 patients hospitalized for stroke before the age of 50 is also relevant to this discussion (Espmark, 1973). Thirty-two of these patients reported problems in dealing with aggression earlier in life, e.g., difficulty in showing anger. In cases with severe obesity, Espmark (1979) observed signs of a special personality syndrome ("Eridophobia," Jacobsen, 1965) including hypersensitivity to criticism, difficulties in showing aggressive feelings, and apprehension when confronted with violence in films. This finding is especially noteworthy when the frequent occurrence of obesity in hypertensive groups is taken into account.

The results obtained with self-report personality inventories have generally been consistent with the clinical findings, even though it is difficult to establish correspondence between the clinical observations of suppressed anger or difficulties in expressing anger and the item content or construct validities of the various scales. There is a conceptual problem in distinguishing between reported aggressive acts, hostile attitudes, angry feelings and difficulties in expressing anger, which all presuppose some degree of awareness, and more subtle indicators of (partly unconscious?) "suppressed" anger (Buss, 1961).

Most inventory studies have used scales of aggression and hostility, and there are no scales explicitly aimed at measuring inability to express angry feelings although possibly submissiveness and "assertiveness" scales may be relevant for that purpose. Esler, Julius, Zweifler, Randall, Harburg, Gardiner, and De Quattro (1977) assumed that low scores on a scale of "direct aggressive actions" from the Buss inventory, combined with normal or high scores on "hostile feelings," could be used as an indicator of "suppressed hostility." They found this pattern to characterize patients with mild high renin hypertension, who also had higher scores than controls on the Cattell 16PF scale of submissiveness.

A self-report instrument was recently constructed explicitly for assessing personality traits in hypertensive patients (Baer, Collins, Bourianoff, & Ketchel, 1979). Items relating to anxiety and hostility differentiated between hypertensive and normotensive patients.

WHAT CONCLUSIONS CAN BE DRAWN
FROM PERSONALITY STUDIES
ON HYPERTENSIVE PATIENTS?

Both clinical and psychometric studies suggest links between essential hypertension and high levels or frequent experiences of anxiety and anger. It may be questioned, however, whether results obtained on patients under treatment can be relied upon as evidence of factors related to the *etiology* of essential hypertension because the psychological reactions observed or reported may be consequences rather than causes of the illness. Furthermore, patients who come for treatment for a disease with a paucity of overt symptoms may not be representative of the total population of hypertensive individuals.

The latter possibility was supported by the results of studies by Robinson (1964), showing that hypertensives under medical attention had higher scores on a neuroticism self-report scale than hypertensives selected from the general population, and by Davies (1970), who found that middle-aged hypertensive men whose blood pressure elevation was discovered during a factory screening had *lower* scores on neuroticism than a control group from the same factory. Similarly, Cochrane (1973) found that blood pressure obtained during a health survey procedure was unrelated to emotional instability, as measured by the Eysenck Neuroticism scale, and concluded that the higher neuroticism scores of hypertensive patients may be secondary to the illness, an effect of worrying about having a potentially serious disease.

Another possible explanation of the earlier findings that hypertensive patients have more anxiety and suppressed rage is that the patients available for study are unusually neurotic and hypochondriacal individuals who are more prone to seek medical attention and thus have their hypertension diagnosed. Consequently, when studying the influence of personality factors on the development of hypertension the method of selecting subjects appears to be crucial. Weiner (1979) has suggested that studies are needed on younger individuals in early phases of hypertension, before secondary (mal)adaptive changes have occurred. Hypertension is more common among young people than has been assumed: The prevalence of systolic borderline hypertension across all ages above 20 is 10 percent or more, according to Julius and Schork (1971).

There is a need for personality studies of non-patient, non-self-selected young hypertensive subjects compared to normotensives, which has been a neglected research area (Kaplan, 1978). In an early, well-controlled inventory study of normal subjects, Hamilton (1942) found lower dominance, lower assertiveness and more susceptibility to anger in subjects with elevated blood pressure. The findings were replicated on crossvalidation. In a related interesting and unusual study, Torgersen and Kringlen (1971) found among adult monozygotic twin pairs that higher systolic blood pressure was consistently noted in the twin who, during childhood, had been more submissive.

A PERSONALITY STUDY OF YOUNG MEN
WITH BLOOD PRESSURE ELEVATION

Personality inventories were given to 20 18-year-old "hypertensive" men and a comparison group of 18 normotensive men as part of a large project of research on early stages of hypertension (Schalling and Svensson, 1984). Both groups were selected from a population of military draftees according to strict blood pressure criteria (systolic bp $\geqslant$ 146; diastolic bp $\geqslant$ 90, and systolic bp 124–131, respectively). The general aim of the project was to study group differences in both physiological and psychological dimensions, in conjunction with individualized laboratory stressors. The selection procedures and somatic data have been described in detail by Theorell, Svensson, Löw, and Nerell (1982). The results of an analysis of ballistocardiographic recordings during emotion-provoking interviews were reported by Svensson and Theorell (1982).

Extensive physiological, metabolic, and neuroendocrine studies showed that the hypertensive subjects tended to excrete more adrenaline during a stressful psychological test, but the differences in metabolic and endocrine variables were small. There was no evidence of renal damage in any of the subjects, and only one hypertensive subject was considered in need of treatment, as judged from ECG and chest X-ray (mild left ventricular hypertrophy).

The hypertensive subjects were further subdivided into two subgroups on the basis of plethysmographic digital pulse volume measurements during the interviews. The vasoconstricted (VC) group consisted of subjects who were constantly vaso-constricted during the procedures (pulse volume recording never exceeding 5 mm on the curve); the non-vasoconstricted (NVC) consisted of the remaining subjects who showed variations in pulse volume. There was a trend toward higher aldo-sterone excretion in the NVC group, which could indicate, according to Theorell et al. (1982), that this subgroup might correspond with the "increased blood volume group" in the classification suggested by Weiner (1979); the VC group could correspond with Weiner's "increased peripheral resistance" group. Since Weiner (1979) suggested that physiological heterogeneity among hypertensives might correspond with parallel psychological heterogeneity, personality compari-sons were made between these subgroups.

Personality Measures

The following personality inventory scales were given to the subjects:

1. Four scales from the Eysenck Personality Questionnaire (EPQ) (Eysenck & Eysenck, 1975): Neuroticism (emotionality or overresponsibility associated with autonomic lability), Extraversion (sociability and impulsivity), Psychoticism (de-tachment, hostility, lack of empathy), and Lie (a measure of conventionality or "faking good")

2. The Karolinska Scales of Personality (KSP), which consist of scales con-structed by Schalling and collaborators (Schalling, 1978; Schalling, Cronholm, & Åsberg, 1975; Schalling, Edman, & Åsberg, 1983), and scales with items translated and modified from other published inventories. The scales of main interest in the present context are the three scales of anxiety proneness (items reported in Table 1), for which directed hypotheses are possible: Somatic Anxiety (autonomic dis-turbances, diffuse distress, panic attacks), Muscular Tension (subjective muscular tenseness and aches, difficulty relaxing), and Psychic Activity (cognitive-social anxiety, worrying, slow recovery after stress).

3. A Psychasthenia scale is also included in the KSP. The items in this scale (see Table 1) are similar to those of the Validity scale of the Marke-Nyman Temperament inventory (Coppen, 1966), which is based on the Sjöbring personality model. High scores in Psychasthenia (low in Validity), imply being easily fatigued, sensitive to distraction and time pressure, insecure and submissive (Sjöbring, 1973).

4. Another scale, for which a directed hypothesis is possible with regard to hypertension is Inhibition of Aggression. Items for this scale, which is similar to measures used in assertiveness training programs (e.g., Wolpe & Lazarus, 1966), refer to unexpressed anger and lack of ability to speak up and assert oneself in social situations (see Table 1).

5. Items loading in the two Buss (1961) Aggression and Hostility factors are also included in the KSP. The subscales are for Aggression: Indirect aggression (e.g., slamming doors); Irritability (readiness to explode with negative affect at slight provocation, feelings of irritation); and Verbal aggression (aggression expressed in style and content of speech); and for Hostility: Suspicion (being distrustful, pro-jecting hostility on others); and Guilt (feelings of shame).

The remaining KSP scales are of less interest in the present context except for an Impulsiveness scale.

Table 1 Items in the KSP Anxiety Scales and in the Psychasthenia Scale and the Inhibition of Aggression Scale

---

Somatic Anxiety

My heart sometimes beats hard or irregularly for no real reason.
Sometimes I suddenly start sweating without any particular reason.
Sometimes when upset, I suddenly feel as if my legs were too weak to carry me.
Sometimes my cheeks burn even if it isn't particularly hot.
Quite often, especially when I am tired, I get the feeling that either I or the world around me is changing—a feeling of unreality.
I sometimes have a feeling that I don't get enough air to breathe.
I often feel uncomfortable and ill at ease for no real reason.
I often feel restless, as if I wanted something without knowing what.
I sometimes feel panicky.
I have great difficulty bringing my thoughts together while talking to someone.

Muscular Tension

I often have aches in my shoulders and in the back of my neck.
I often find myself gnashing my jaws together for no real cause.
My body often feels stiff and tense.
My muscles are so tense that I get tired.
Often I find myself holding the newspaper I'm reading too hard.
When trying to fall asleep I often notice that my muscles are really tense.
An unexpected noise makes me jump and startle.
I have difficulty sitting in a relaxed position even in a comfortable chair.
In the late afternoon I often get a headache which feels as if there was an iron band across my forehead.
My hands usually tremble.

Psychic Anxiety (Cognitive-social anxiety)

I often worry about things that other people look upon as trifles.
I worry far in advance when I am going to get started on something.
After buying something I often worry about having made the wrong choice.
It takes me an unusually long time to get over unpleasant events.
I usually don't feel at ease when I meet people I don't know too well.
I don't have much self-confidence.
I am quite self-conscious in most social situations.
I seldom dare to express myself in a discussion because I have the feeling that people think my views are not worth anything.
Even though I know I'm right, I often have great difficulty getting my point across.
I'm the kind of person who is excessively sensitive and easily hurt.

Psychasthenia

I get tired and hurried too easily.
I don't mind being interrupted when I am working with something. (F)
I think I must economize my energy.
In order to get something done I have to spend more energy than most others.
It is easy for me to regain lost sleep. (F)
I can usually concentrate on what I am doing even if the environment is distracting. (F)
I easily feel pressure when I am urged to speed up.
I like to have plenty of time available when I am doing something.
I feel calm and secure even when I am facing new tasks. (F)
I think I get fatigued more easily than most people I know.

Table 1 Items in the KSP Anxiety Scales and in the Psychasthenia Scale and the Inhibition of Aggression Scale (*Continued*)

Inhibition of Aggression

I find it hard to object if I am neglected at a restaurant.
When someone is pushing himself forward in the queue I usually tell him off. (F)
I find it difficult going back to a store to ask if I can exchange an item I have bought.
I think that argument can clear the air sometimes. (F)
I feel embarrassed having to complain when I get too little change back.
When someone is teasing me, I never find a good answer until later.
I have difficulties turning someone down when asked for a favor, even though I don't feel like doing it.
I sometimes wish that I could speak up when I dislike something.
I feel very ill at ease when witnessing a fight in the street.
If someone is scolding me, I become sad rather than angry.

---

6. In view of the great interest in the relation between Type A behavior and cardiovascular illness, two scales were given which have been associated with the Type A as interview measures (Rahe, Hervig, & Rosenman, 1978): The *Gough Adjective Check List* and the *Thurstone Activity Scale.* MacDougall, Dembroski, and Musante (1979) reported that these scales showed higher (although still moderate) correlations with interview-based Type A classification than the more commonly used Jenkins Activity Survey (JAS).

Results

Comparisons of the hypertensive and normotensive subjects by *t*-test yielded significantly higher scores for the hypertensives on all three KSP anxiety scales, the Psychasthenia scale, and the Inhibition of Aggression scale (see Tables 2 and 3). There were no group differences on the Aggression and Hostility scales (sum of subscales), nor on any of the EPQ scales.

The pattern of results in this study was remarkably consistent with earlier findings for both patients and normal subjects. In their self-reports, the young men with blood pressure elevations appeared to be aware of having difficulties in expressing anger and of behaving in a submissive way in everyday life situations. They also seemed aware of a tendency to experience different kinds of anxiety, as described in the items of the anxiety scales (Table 1).

Table 2 Means and standard deviations of three anxiety scales and the Psychasthenia Scale (KSP), from a group of hypertensive young men (HT, $n = 20$), and a comparison group of normotensive men (C_N, $n = 18$)

	HT		C_N		HT-C_N	
	M	SD	M	SD	t	p
Somatic anxiety	19.38	5.33	16.00	3.45	2.15	<0.05
Muscular tension	18.43	5.35	14.50	3.90	2.52	<0.05
Psychic anxiety	21.76	4.61	18.28	3.75	2.52	<0.05
Psychasthenia	24.10	4.78	20.39	2.87	2.78	<0.01

Table 3 Means and standard deviations of modified Buss aggression and hostility factor scales, and the Inhibition of Aggression Scale (KSP) from a group of hypertensive young men (HT, $n = 20$), and a comparison group of normotensive men (C_N, $n = 18$)

	HT		C_N		HT-C_N	
	M	SD	M	SD	t	p
Aggression	36.71	6.00	35.11	4.76	0.70	NS
Hostility	20.81	4.45	19.39	2.52	1.24	NS
Inhibition of aggression	22.95	4.34	19.33	3.12	3.00	<0.01

The anxiety scales used in this study were related to cardiovascular stress reactions in our earlier studies. Patients with high anxiety had more pronounced cardiovascular activation during a stressful interview (Theorell, Schalling, & Åkerstedt, 1977). Further, increases in systolic blood pressure during a stressful interview were positively correlated with scores on Inhibition of Aggression in the less healthy members of twin pairs discordant for coronary heart disease (Theorell, deFaire, Schalling, Adamson, & Askevold, 1979).

The comparison of the VC and NVC subgroups of hypertensives yielded highly interesting results. There were no differences between these groups in the variables that differentiated between the hypertensive and the normotensive subjects, but the NVC group had significantly higher scores on the KSP Impulsiveness scale and marginally higher scores on Aggression (Table 4). The NVC subgroup also had significantly higher scores on one of the two Type A scales (Gough Adjective Check List) and on the EPQ Psychoticism Scale (Table 5). Thus, the personality pattern of the men in the NVC group was similar to that observed in Type A coronary patients.

The psychological differences between the VC and NVC subgroups correspond to one of the physiological differences mentioned above. The NVC subgroup had higher aldosterone excretion which, according to Theorell et al. (1982), may indicate that these men could be identified with Weiner's "increased blood volume" type of essential hypertension. Since the hetereogeneity of the hypertensive population is a major problem for research in this area, it seems important to identify systematic associations between psychological and physiological subgroups.

Summing up, the results of the study suggested that young men with elevated

Table 4 Means and standard deviations of scores in some personality inventory (KSP) scales in two subgroups of hypertensive men, in a group of vasoconstricted men (VC_{HT}, $n = 12$) and a group of non-vasoconstricted men (NVC_{HT}, $n = 7$)

	VC_{HT}		NVC_{HT}			
	M	SD	M	SD	t	p
Impulsiveness	22.67	3.14	26.57	4.35	2.27	<0.05
Aggression	35.83	3.74	40.57	6.80	1.98	<0.10
Hostility	20.67	2.43	21.71	7.23	0.47	NS
Inhibition of aggression	23.00	3.98	22.00	5.42	0.46	NS

Table 5 Means and standard deviations in Type A scales and in the EPQ Psychoticism scale in two subgroups of hypertensive men, a group of vasoconstricted men (VC_{HT}, $n = 12$) and a group of non-vasoconstricted men (NVC_{HT}, $n = 7$)

	VC_{HT}		NVC_{HT}			
	M	SD	M	SD	t	p
Type A scales:						
Gough Adjective Check List	46.83	3.24	50.43	3.82	2.19	<0.05
Thurstone Activity Scale	18.75	5.41	20.43	5.65	0.64	NS
Psychoticism (EPQ)	3.50	2.51	6.29	2.75	2.26	<0.05

blood pressure are, or at least describe or perceive themselves to be, more prone to experience anxiety in the form of autonomic symptoms and muscular tenseness than men with normal blood pressure. They are also more likely to feel more distressed and panicky, as judged from their higher scores on the Somatic Anxiety and Muscular Tension scales, and to be more insecure in interpersonal relations, more anxious and worrying, and less able to relax after stress, as judged from higher scores in Psychic Anxiety. The men with elevated blood pressure also described themselves as easily fatigued and disturbed, and insecure in facing novel tasks and time pressure, as judged from higher Psychasthenia scores. In addition, they find it difficult to assert themselves in social situations, tending to give in and feel embarrassed rather than speaking up, as judged from higher scores in Inhibition of Aggression.

The findings of the present study are also very much in line with the behavior observed by Harburg and his collaborators (1964) in an ingenious study of "experimental yielding" in college males with elevated blood pressure. The subjects first rated their attitudes on selected topics, e.g., juvenile delinquency. Then, students with high and low blood pressure, matched in pairs with maximal disagreement in attitude, were called back to discuss and try to reach a compromise on the selected topic. After the discussion, they made new ratings both overtly in the presence of the companion, and privately after the session. Yielding was higher in the hypertensive students; 76 percent were above the median in private yielding, as compared to 29 percent of the students with low blood pressure, a highly significant difference. The high blood pressure students also had significantly higher scores on the Cattell submissiveness scale.

Individuals with elevated blood pressure appear to be submissive and unassertive, unable to express anger, anxious and insecure in social relations, and unwilling to enter into competition. While the pathogenic mechanisms are not known, submissive and withdrawal responses in psychosocial interactions have been associated with activation of the pituitary-adrenal cortical system in animal research with monkeys and rats in natural conditions (Henry & Stephens, 1977, p. 119). It has been suggested that a similar mechanism may operate in the early pathophysiology of essential hypertension in man (Henry, 1976). Adrenocorticotropic responses are assumed to develop in individuals who perceive themselves as not coping effectively and who fail to attain their expectations; there is evidence of a preponderance of pituitary-adrenocortical response over the sympathetic adrenal-medullary response in low-renin hypertension (Henry, 1976).

HYPERTENSIVE AND CORONARY–PRONE
PERSONALITY PATTERN–SAME OR DIFFERENT?

Since the Type A personality was found in patients with coronary disease by Rosenman, Friedman, and their collaborators, it has been at least implicitly assumed in many papers that Type A was also associated with hypertension. Rosenman, Friedman, Strauss, Wurm, Jenkins, and Messinger (1966) reported higher blood pressure for Type A individuals (although not for a group older than 50) and there are other reports of high blood pressure in groups classified as Type A by interview. However, Shekelle, Schoenberger, and Stamler (1976) used the Jenkins JAS self-report scale to measure Type A and found no relation between personality type and blood pressure for men or women. Jenkins (1980) also found no relation between Type A scale measures and hypertension in male air traffic controllers, and Waldron (1978) reported a negative correlation between JAS Type A and diastolic blood pressure in a group of women.

Persons with Type A personality are described as highly competitive and hard-driving, with overtly expressed irritability and impatience. In view of the literature on hypertensive personality patterns reviewed above, the hypertensive in many ways seems to be the opposite of the "coronary prone" Type A; he is rather submissive than competitive, he does not show his anger, and is not good at asserting himself. Thus, in the present perspective, there seems to be no solid basis for assuming a single personality pattern that would constitute a vulnerability for cardiovascular disease in general. In an excellent discussion on these problems, Henry and Meehan (1981) give some clues to the differences between "coronary" and "hypertensive" personality. They assume that the potential coronary disease victim has signs of "suppressed depression," whereas, the subject prone to essential hypertension or with mild hypertension rather seems to suppress anger and hostility. They discuss at length the possible underlying neuroendocrine differences associated with differential activation of the pituitary adrenal-cortical system and the adrenal-medullary system. It would certainly lead too far in the present context to try to elucidate the implication of this model. Continued research with combined psychological and physiological approaches on young individuals at risk for different types of cardiovascular disease, including long term follow-up, is needed to increase our understanding of this complicated issue.

REFERENCES

Alexander, F. Emotional factors in essential hypertension. Presentation of a tentative hypothesis. *Psychosomatic Medicine*, 1939, *1*, 173–179.

Baer, P. E., Collins, F. H., Bourianoff, G. G., & Ketchel, M. F. Assessing personality factors in essential hypertension with a brief self-report instrument. *Psychosomatic Medicine*, 1979, *41*, 321–330.

Buss, A. H. *The Psychology of Aggression.* New York: Wiley, 1961.

Cochrane, R. Hostility and neuroticism among unselected essential hypertensives. *Journal of Psychosomatic Research*, 1973, *17*, 215–218.

Coppen, A. The Marke-Nyman temperament scale, an English translation. *British Journal of Medical Psychology*, 1966, *39*, 55–59.

Davies, M. Blood pressure and personality. *Journal of Psychosomatic Research*, 1970, *14*, 89–104.

Esler, M., Julius, S., Zweifler, A., Randall, O., Harburg, E., Gardiner, H., & DeQuattro, V. Mild high-renin essential hypertension. Neurogenic human hypertension? *New England Journal of Medicine*, 1977, *296*, 405–411.

Espmark, S. Stroke before 50. A follow-up study of vocational and psychological adjustment. *Scandinavian Journal of Rehabilitation Medicine*, Suppl. 2, 1973.

Espmark, S. Psychosocial disturbances in obesity. In M. Mancini, B. Lewis, & F. Contaldo (eds.), *Medical Complications of Obesity*. London: Academic Press, 1979.

Eysenck, H. J. & Eysenck, S. B. G. *Manual of the Eysenck Personality Questionnaire*. London: Hodder and Stoughton, 1975.

Hamilton, J. A. Psychophysiology of blood pressure. I. Personality and behavior ratings. *Psychosomatic Medicine*, 1942, *4*, 125–133.

Harburg, E., Julius, S., McGinn, N. F., McLeod, J., & Hoobler, S. W. Personality traits and behavioral patterns associated with systolic blood pressure levels in college males. *Journal of Chronic Diseases*, 1964, *17*, 405–414.

Harrell, J. P. Psychological factors and hypertension. A status report. *Psychological Bulletin*, 1980, *87*, 482–501.

Henry, J. P. Understanding the early psychophysiology of essential hypertension. *Geriatrics*, 1976, *30*, 59–72.

Henry, J. P. & Meehan, J. P. Psychosocial stimuli, physiological specificity and cardiovascular disease. In H. Weiner, M. A. Hofer, & A. J. Stunkard (eds.), *Brain, Behavior and Bodily Disease*. New York: Raven Press, 1981.

Henry, J. P. & Stephens, P. M. *Stress, Health and the Social Environment. A Sociobiological Approach to Medicine*. New York: Springer, 1977.

Hokanson, J. E. & Burgess, M. The effects of three types of aggression on vascular processes. *Journal of Abnormal and Social Psychology*, 1962, *64*, 446–449.

Jacobsen, E. *Psykoneuroser* (Psychoneuroses). Copenhagen: Munksgaard, 1965.

Jenkins, C. D. Hypertension in air traffic controllers. Paper given in NIAS International Conference on Stress and Anxiety, 1980.

Julius, S. & Schork, M. A. Borderline hypertension—A critical review. *Journal of Chronic Diseases*, 1971, *23*, 723–754.

Kalis, B. L., Harris, R. E., Sokolov, M., & Carpenter, L. G. Response to psychological stress in patients with essential hypertension. *American Heart Journal*, 1957, *53*, 572–578.

Kaplan, N. M. *Clinical Hypertension*, pp. 366–384. Baltimore: Williams & Wilkins, 1978.

MacDougall, J. M., Dembroski, T. M., & Musante, L. The structured interview and questionnaire methods of assessing coronary-prone behavior in male and female college students. *Journal of Behavioral Medicine*, 1979, *2*, 71–83.

Rahe, K., Hervig, L., & Rosenman, R. H. Heritability of Type A behavior. *Psychosomatic Medicine*, 1978, *40*, 478–486.

Robbins, L. L. Psychological factors in essential hypertension. *Bulletin of the Menninger Clinic*, 1948, *12*, 195–202.

Robinson, J. O. A possible effect of selection on the test scores of a group of hypertensives. *Journal of Psychosomatic Research*, 1964, *8*, 239–243.

Rosenman, R. H., Friedman, M., Strauss, R., Wurm, M., Jenkins, D., & Messinger, H. Coronary heart disease in the Western Collaborative Group Study. *Journal of the American Medical Association*, 1966, *195*, 86–95.

Saslow, G., Gressel, G. C., Shobe, F. O., DuBois, P. H., & Schroeder, H. A. The possible etiological relevance of personality factors in arterial hypertension. *Proceedings of the Association for Research in Nervous and Mental Disease*, 1950, *29*, 881–889.

Schalling, D. Psychopathy-related personality variables and the psychophysiology of socialization. In R. D. Hare & D. Schalling (eds.), *Psychopathic Behaviour. Approaches to Research*. Chichester: Wiley, 1978.

Schalling, D., Cronholm, B., & Åsberg, M. Components of state and trait anxiety as related to personality and arousal. In L. Levi (ed.), *Emotions, their Parameters and Measurement*, pp. 603–617. New York: Raven Press, 1975.

Schalling, D., Edman, G., & Åsberg, M. Impulsive cognitive style and inability to tolerate boredom. In M. Zuckerman (ed.), *Biological Bases of Sensation Seeking, Impulsivity and Anxiety*, pp. 123–145. Hillsdale, N.J.: Erlbaum, 1983.

Schalling, D. & Svensson, J. Blood pressure and personality. *Personality and Individual Differences*, 1984, *5*, 41–51.

Schwartz, L. A. An analyzed case of essential hypertension. *Psychosomatic Medicine*, 1940, *2*, 468–486.

Shekelle, R. B., Schoenberger, J. A., & Stamler, J. Correlates of the JAS Type A behavior pattern score. *Journal of Chronic Diseases*, 1976, *29*, 381–394.

Sjöbring, H. Personality structure and development. A model and its application. *Acta Psychia-trica Scandinavica*, Suppl. 244, 1973.

Svensson, J. C. & Theorell, T. Cardiovascular effects of anxiety induced by interviewing young hypertensive male subjects. *Journal of Psychosomatic Research*, 1982, *26*, 359–370.

Theorell, T., de Faire, U., Schalling, D., Adamson, U., & Askevold, F. Personality traits and psychophysiological reactions to a stressful interview in twins with varying degrees of coronary heart disease. *Journal of Psychosomatic Research*, 1979, *23*, 89–99.

Theorell, T., Schalling, D., & Åkerstedt, T. Circulatory reaction in coronary patients during interview–A noninvasive study. *Biological Psychology*, 1977, *5*, 233–243.

Theorell, T., Svensson, J., Löw, H., & Nerell, G. Clinical characteristics of 18-year-old men with elevated blood pressure. *Acta Medica Scandinavica*, 1982, *211*, 87–93.

Torgersen, S. & Kringlen, E. Blood pressure and personality. A study of the relationship be-tween intrapair differences in systolic blood pressure and personality in monozygotic twins. *Journal of Psychosomatic Research*, 1971, *15*, 183–191.

Waldron, J. The coronary-prone behavior pattern, blood pressure, employment and socio-economic status in women. *Journal of Psychosomatic Research*, 1978, *22*, 79–87.

Weiner, H. *Psychobiology of Essential Hypertension*. New York: Elsevier, 1979.

Wolf, S. & Wolff, H. G. A summary of experimental evidence relating life stress to the patho-genesis of hypertension in man. In E. T. Bell (ed.), *Hypertension: A Symposium*. Minneapo-lis: University of Minnesota Press, 1951.

Wolpe, J. & Lazarus, A. A. *Behavior Therapy Techniques*. Oxford: Pergamon Press, 1966.

19

Validation in Lithuania of the Type A Coronary-prone Behavior Pattern as Measured by the JAS

A. Appels
Rijksuniversiteit Limburg, Maastricht, Holland

C. D. Jenkins
University of Texas Medical Branch, Galveston

A. Gostautas
Kaunas Medical Institute, Kaunas, Lithuania SSR

F. Nijhuis
Rijksuniversiteit Limburg, Maastricht, Holland

The coronary-prone or Type A behavior pattern refers to a hard-driving, aggressive, competitive, rushed, job-devoted way of living, which is associated with a significantly increased risk of coronary heart disease in American populations (Friedman & Rosenman, 1959; Dembroski, 1978). The presence or absence of this behavior is evaluated by a structured interview (Rosenman, 1978). Because the administration and assessment of the interview is time-consuming and requires special training, several psychologists have tried to design a questionnaire to measure the behavior pattern.

The Jenkins Activity Survey (JAS) is the best available questionnaire for assessing the Type A behavior pattern (Jenkins, Zyzanski, & Rosenman, 1979). The structured interview procedure was used as the criterion for the construction of the JAS and this test has been shown to have concurrent and predictive validity.

The American way of living seems so much connected with this behavior pattern that one may wonder whether it is a risk factor for coronary heart disease (CHD) in other cultures as well. The findings of a Belgian study have revealed that the JAS, when properly translated and scored, shows a strong correspondence with the structured interview. This indicates that both methods are sufficiently robust to retain their properties when translated, but does not establish their validity for predicting CHD (Kittel, Kornitzer, Zyzanski, Jenkins, Rustin, & Degré, 1978).

The first evidence that the JAS is linked to CHD in a European country is provided by a study in which patients from the Center of Cardiological Rehabilitation at Inowroclaw (Poland) were compared to patients who were treated for rheumatic diseases and to healthy controls. It was found that coronary patients scored significantly more in the Type A direction than men who were free of CHD (Zyzanski, Wrzesniewski, & Jenkins, 1979).

While the Belgian and the Polish findings indicate that the coronary prone behavior pattern may have some validity outside the U.S., evidence that the behavior pattern has the same cardiovascular meaning as in the U.S. must come from prospective studies. Such studies are currently being conducted, but it will take a few years before the results are available. The preparatory work, however, already provides some indication so as to warrant the inclusion of the JAS in these studies.

METHOD

In 1972 a feasibility study about operational and behavioral components of health intervention programs started simultaneously in Kaunas, Lithuania SSR, and Rotterdam, Holland. The main goal of this project, which was inaugurated by the World Health Organization, was to study the relations between operational procedures employed in a screening program, demographic and psychosocial characteristics of potential participants, and participation and adherence to the intervention program (Burema, Sturmans, & Valkenburg, 1974). The JAS was used in this study to determine whether the coronary prone behavior pattern was related to participation and adherence in a health intervention program. If Type As, because of their constant feeling of living under the pressure of time, participated to a lesser degree than Type Bs, a screening program for cardiovascular risk factors would miss a significant group.

This chapter is limited to the Lithuanian part of the study; the Dutch part has been published elsewhere (Appels, Haes, & Schuurman, 1977).

The 1969 Form A of the JAS was translated into Lithuanian by Dr. Gostautas and back-translated into English by an independent translator. Rewordings for a small number of items were necessary in order to find Lithuanian terms that were more comparable to the intent of the original wording. Each reformulation was discussed with Jenkins.

The JAS provides an overall measure of the Type A coronary-prone behavior pattern, as well as scores on three component dimensions that were derived by a factor analysis of the JAS items. The data available at the time the Lithuanian translation was made indicated that the overall measure had the highest validity and that the validity of the subscales still had to be further established. Therefore, it was decided to derive an overall Type A score, using a maximum likelihood method (LOGOG) designed by Bock and Kolakowski (Bock, 1972; Kolakowski & Bock, 1973).

The JAS items were analyzed by the LOGOG method, which extracts more information from the answers given to multiple-choice questions than using a simpler pass-fail model. The starting point for the LOGOG method is the assumption that the responses of subjects who do not give the correct answer to a multiple-choice question are not uniformly distributed among the wrong (less representative) response alternatives. Suppose, for example, that one wishes to measure knowledge of geography and asks whether Rome, Naples, or Vienna is the capital of Italy. The answer, Vienna, indicates less knowledge than the answer, Naples. Thus, "wrong" answers can be used to make inferences about latent traits such as geographical knowledge or Type A behavior pattern by taking into account the degree to which each response alternative is chosen as a function of the trait that one wishes to measure.

In using the LOGOG model, it was assumed that the coronary-prone behavior pattern is a continuous, normally distributed variable, which underlies the correlation of test items with symptoms of cardiovascular disease. For each item a traceline is postulated at the boundary between any two response alternatives. Together they form an ogive which expresses the cumulative probability of a subject responding to the categories below the boundary as a function of the latent trait.

In essence, the LOGOG model uses a multivariate logistic function with two parameters to express the probability of occurrence of each response alternative for each item. One of these parameters characterizes the response alternatives and the second trait-parameter characterizes the respondent. The following steps are required in the computation of these parameters:

1. The subjects are divided into five fractiles that correspond to the categories employed in assessment by the interview method: Type A-1 (strong Type A), A-2 (Type A), A/B (intermediate), B-3 (weak B), B-4 (strong B). For each fractile the class intervals and the median values of the latent trait were calculated.

2. The parameters are obtained by solving the maximum likelihood equations using the Newton-Raphson technique.

3. Using these estimated parameters, new provisional values of the latent trait are then obtained from step 1 by solving the maximum likelihood equations.

4. Steps 1, 2, and 3 are repeated until the estimations of the parameters in successive cycles agree at a predetermined level of accuracy. The parameters are assumed to have reasonable accuracy when the slope divided by its standard error is equal to or larger than 2.00. In this case, the probability that the slope differs significantly from zero is 98 percent.

In constructing the Dutch adaptation of the JAS, the parameters for 36 items met these requirements; the same parameters were used to compute LOGOG Type A scores in Kaunas. In addition, scores for each individual were computed for the JAS Type A scale and the three JAS subscales: "Hard-driving" (H); "Job Involvement" (J); and "Speed and Impatience" (S). These scores were based on item parameters derived by Jenkins from the Western Collaborative Group Study (Jenkins, Rosenman, & Friedman, 1967). The following three criteria were available to study the concurrent validity of the JAS: (a) currently being treated for one or more cardiovascular risk factors; (b) presence or absence of angina pectoris, as measured by the Rose Questionnaire (Rose & Blackburn, 1969); and (c) previous myocardial infarction (as shown on the ECG).

RESULTS AND DISCUSSION

The hypotheses to be tested were that persons: (a) who were being treated for one or more cardiovascular risk factors, or (b) who suffered from angina pectoris, or (c) who had had a myocardial infarction in the past, would have higher mean scores on the JAS scales than healthy persons, i.e., persons who were free of cardiovascular risk factors and who had no previous history of cardiovascular disease. Univariate F tests were used to test these hypotheses.

Using criteria (a) or (c), no differences were found for any of the JAS scales. For criterion (b), the single most important available criterion measure, the mean scores for persons suffering from angina pectoris were significantly higher on the Type A scale as computed by the LOGOG method, and on JAS Factor H (Hard-driving). The mean JAS scores for men who did or did not suffer from angina pectoris at screening are reported in Table 1.

Table 1 Mean JAS scores for men who did or did not suffer from angina pectoris at screening

JAS Scale	No angina		Angina		
	N^a	Mean	N^a	Mean	*F*-ratio
Type A LOGOG	1432	0.02	149	0.28	8.88[b]
Type A	1668	1.1	167	1.5	0.61
Factor H	1670	8.1	165	9.4	4.30[c]
Factor J	1663	−12.4	165	−12.2	0.18
Factor S	1674	−1.8	167	−0.8	2.42

[a]The number of subjects for each mean differed because subjects with missing data on those JAS items that contributed to the computations of a particular scale score were eliminated.
[b]$p < 0.01$.
[c]$p < 0.05$.

The results provide evidence that the JAS measures psychological factors that are relevant for cardiovascular disease. Given the major differences between Lithuanian and American socio-cultural conditions, these findings are especially interesting. It should be noted that a positive association was also found between JAS scores and level of occupation and education for Lithuanian subjects in the present study.

In addition to the validation study of the JAS scales, the discriminating power of each JAS item was determined by comparing the distributions of responses of men with and without angina pectoris. A total of 15 items significantly discriminated between the two groups. These items provide a representative description of Lithuanian men with cardiovascular disease which confirms the construct validity of the Type A coronary-prone personality pattern.

The men who suffered from angina pectoris tended to describe themselves as persons who: often experienced annoyance at work; lost their appetite under pressure; were inclined to solve problems immediately; did not like to listen to long stories; often hurried even if there was enough time; walked while waiting for someone who was late; and who wanted to be the first in everything they did. They also reported that they were rated by their wives as too active; were, according to other people, easily irritated; liked competition in the job; were hot tempered; felt displeased when interrupted during work; often made lists of things to be done; had the feeling that they approached life more seriously than others do; and had given up hobbies because of lack of time.

Since the LOGOG Type A scores in the present study were based on item parameters established in a Dutch validation study, some of the items which significantly discriminated between men with and without angina pectoris were not included in the LOGOG equation. Conversely, some items that were included in both the LOGOG equation and the JAS scale scores did not discriminate. Therefore, the scale scores as computed in this study may underestimate the concurrent validity of the Lithuanian adaptation of the JAS. Further adaptation and refinement of the JAS will be necessary to improve the Lithuanian Form of the questionnaire, and additional studies will be needed to determine which items correlate with other forms of CHD.

The correspondence between the Lithuanian data presented in this study and the results of investigations in the United States and other countries support the generalizability of the Type A behavior pattern and the JAS. Until more data are available on the predictive power of the component scales of the JAS, important questions about the cross-cultural validity of the JAS subscales cannot be answered.

REFERENCES

Appels, A., Haes, W. de, & Schuurman, J. Een test ter meting van het "coronary prone behavior pattern" Type A. *Nederlands Tijdschrift Psychologie*, 1977, *34*, 181–188.

Bock, R. D. Estimating item parameters and latent ability when responses are scored in two or more nominal categories. *Psychometrika*, 1972, *37*, 29–51.

Burema, L., Sturmans, R., & Valkenburg, H. A. De Kaunas-Rotterdam Intervention Study (KRIS I: doelstellingen. *Tijdschrift Sociale Geneeskunde*, 1974, *52*, 790–796.

Dembroski, Th. (ed.). *Coronary Prone Behavior*. New York: Springer, 1978.

Friedman, M. & Rosenman, R. H. Association of specific overt behavior pattern with blood and cardiovascular findings. *Journal of the American Medical Association*, 1959, *169*, 1286–1296.

Jenkins, C. D., Rosenman, R. H., & Friedman, M. Development of an objective psychological test for the determination of the coronary-prone behavior pattern in employed men. *Journal of Chronic Disease*, 1967, *20*, 371–379.

Jenkins, C. D., Zyzanski, S., & Rosenman, R. H. *Jenkins Activity Survey Manual*. New York: The Psychological Corporation, 1979.

Kittel, F., Kornitzer, M., Zyzanski, S., Jenkins, C. D., Rustin, C. D., & Degré, C. Two methods of assessing the Type A coronary prone behavior pattern in Belgium. *Journal of Chronic Disease*, 1978, *31*, 147–155.

Kolakowski, D. & Bock, R. D. *Maximum Likehoood Item Analysis and Test Scoring: Logistic Model for Multiple Item Responses*. Chicago: National Educational Resources Inc., 1973.

Rose, G. A. & Blackburn, H. *Mèthodes d'Enquete sur les maladies cardiovasculaires*. Genève: Organisation Mondiale de la Santé, 1969.

Rosenman, R. H. The interview method of assessment of the coronary prone behavior pattern. In T. M. Dembroski, S. M. Wiess, J. L. Shields, S. G. Haynes, & M. Feinlieb (eds.), *Coronary-Prone Behavior*. New York: Springer-Verlag, 1978.

Zyzanski, S., Wrzesniewski, K., & Jenkins, C. D. Cross-cultural validation of the coronary prone behavior pattern. *Social Science and Medicine*, 1979, *13*, 405–412.

Appendix

PARTICIPANTS, NIAS FIRST INTERNATIONAL CONFERENCE ON STRESS AND ANXIETY FEBRUARY 7–9, 1980

P. Allen, Department of Psychology, University of Wisconsin

V. L. Allen, Department of Psychology, University of Wisconsin (NIAS Fellow, 1980)

A. Appels, Faculty of Medicine, University of Limburg

J. W. Atkinson, Department of Psychology, University of Michigan, Ann Arbor; Visiting Professor, University of Leiden

C.-J. N. Bailey, Department of Linguistics, Technical University of Berlin (NIAS Fellow, 1980)

F. C. Bakker, Department of Psychology and Physical Education, Free University of Amsterdam

J. Bastiaans, Faculty of Medicine, Department of Psychiatry, University of Leiden

D. Bauman, Institute for Perception (TNO), Soesterberg

B. Bonke, Faculty of Medicine, Department of Medical Psychology, Erasmus University, Rotterdam

W. R. Bowerman, Research Associate, Bureau of Child Research, University of Kansas (NIAS Visitor, 1980)

I. Bressers, Department of Psychology, University of Limburg

M. Cernea, The World Bank, Washington, D.C. (NIAS Fellow, 1980)

F. Cohen, Curator, Museum Boerhaave, Leiden (NIAS Fellow, 1980)

P. B. Defares, Department of Psychology, University of Wageningen (NIAS Fellow, 1980)

E. Dekker, Director, Netherlands Heart Foundation, The Hague

Y. Dekking, Department of Psychology, University of Utrecht

N. van Dijkhuizen, Bureau of Organizational Psychology, The Royal Dutch Navy, The Hague

C. L. Ekkers, Netherlands Institute for Preventive Health Care (TNO), Leiden

P. R. J. Falger, Department of Medical Psychology, University of Limburg

M. F. Fresco, Department of Philosophy, Leiden University (NIAS Fellow, 1980)

N. H. Frijda, Psychological Laboratory, University of Amsterdam

N. H. Frijling, Department of Psychology, Leiden University

A. W. K. Gaillard, Institute for Perception (TNO), Soesterberg

B. de Gelder, Department of Psychology, University of Tilburg (NIAS Fellow, 1980)

E. Goudsmit, Department of Psychology, University of Amsterdam

W. J. A. van den Heuvel, Stichting Koningin Wilhelmina Fonds, Rotterdam

C. H. L. Janssen, Department of Clinical Psychology and Psychotherapy, University of Tilburg

R. D. de Jong, Department of Clinical Psychology, Psychotherapy, and Preventive Medicine, University of Utrecht

A. A. Jorna, Institute for Perception (TNO), Soesterberg
A. A. Kaptein, Institute of Social Medicine, Leiden University
P. Cohen-Kettenis, Department of Clinical Psychology, University of Utrecht
H. W. Krohne, Sozialwissenschaften, University of Osnabruck, FRG
L. Laux, Psychology Institute, Johannes Gutenberg University, Mainz, FRG
A. C. Linssen, Psychology Laboratory, University of Amsterdam
J. L. M. Nass, Department of Psychology, Leiden University
J. F. Orlebeke, Department of Experimental Psychology, Free University, Amsterdam
M. van Overloop, Royal Dutch Navy, The Hague
G. Pask, Department of Cybernetics, Brunel University (NIAS Fellow, 1980)
L. Pinxten, Department of Psychology, University of Limburg
H. M. van der Ploeg, Department of Psychiatry, University of Leiden
K. Polenske, Department of Urban Studies and Planning, MIT (NIAS Fellow, 1980)
J. Pruyn, Department of Social Psychology, Erasmus University, Rotterdam
R. W. Ramsay, Psychology Laboratory, University of Amsterdam (NIAS Fellow, 1980)
W. D. Reitsma, Institute of Perception (TNO), Soesterberg
K. Cogan-Rittenberg, Bonn, FRG
R. Rombouts, Max-Planck Institute for Psychiatry, Munich, FRG
C. Roy, University of St. Andrews, Scotland
A. F. Sanders, Department of Psychology, University of Tilburg
P. Schreuers, Institute for Clinical Psychology, University of Utrecht
R. Schwarzer, Pedagogische Hochschule Rheinland, Aachen, FRG
J. Snel, Department of Psychology, University of Amsterdam
P. Sonderegger, Max-Planck Institute for Psychiatry, Munich, FRG
C. D. Spielberger, Department of Psychology, University of South Florida, Tampa (NIAS Fellow, 1980)
W. Stevens, Director, Medical Biological Laboratory, Rÿswÿk
W. Stiggelbout, Netherlands Heart Foundation
C. Thorne, University of Sussex, UK (NIAS Fellow, 1980)
F. Verhage, Department of Medical Psychology, Erasmus University, Rotterdam
A. J. J. M. Vingerhoets, Department of Psychology, University of Tilburg
A. Visser, Department of Social Psychology, Free University, Amsterdam
P. Visser, Department of Psychology, University of Amsterdam
R. van der Vlist, Department of Psychology, University of Leiden (NIAS Fellow, 1980)
J. Baroness van Dedem-Wevschede, Jeigersma Clinic, University of Leiden
P. Werre, Psychiatric Center Rosenburg, The Hague
P. Westerhof, Department of Psychology, University of Wageningen
J. A. M. Winnubst, Psychology Laboratory, University of Nijmegen
C. de Wolff, Department of Psychology, University of Nijmegen
J. Whyte, Department of Psychology, Queen's University of Belfast (NIAS Visitor, 1980)

PARTICIPANTS, NIAS SECOND INTERNATIONAL CONFERENCE ON STRESS AND ANXIETY JUNE 19–21, 1980

P. Allen, Department of Psychology, University of Wisconsin
V. L. Allen, Department of Psychology, University of Wisconsin (NIAS Fellow, 1980)

A. Appels, Faculty of Medicine, University of Limburg

J. W. Atkinson, Department of Psychology, University of Michigan, Ann Arbor; Visiting Professor, University of Leiden

C.-J. N. Bailey, Department of Linguistics, Technical University of Berlin (NIAS Fellow, 1980)

F. C. Bakker, Department of Psychology and Physical Education, Free University of Amsterdam

K. W. Bash, Psychiatric Clinic, University of Bern, Switzerland

J. Bastiaans, Faculty of Medicine, Department of Psychiatry, University of Leiden

B. Bonke, Faculty of Medicine, Department of Medical Psychology, Erasmus University, Rotterdam

A. G. Bouwman, Institute for Perception (TNO), Soesterberg

W. R. Bowerman, Research Associate, Bureau of Child Research, University of Kansas (NIAS Visitor, 1980)

M. Brandjes, Department of Psychology, SOPS, University of Wageningen

J. J. C. B. Bremer, Department of Psychology, University of Limburg

M. Bremer-Schulte, Department of Psychology, University of Limburg

G. Bresa, Institute of Psychiatry, University of Rome

I. Bressers, Department of Psychology, University of Limburg

S. Breznitz, Department of Psychology, University of Haifa

D. Brom, Department of Psychology, SOPS, University of Wageningen

M. Cernea, The World Bank, Washington, D.C. (NIAS Fellow, 1980)

T. Cox, Department of Psychology, University of Nottingham

F. S. A. M. van Dam, Department of Psychology, University of Amsterdam

P. B. Defares, Department of Psychology, University of Wageningen (NIAS Fellow, 1980)

Y. Dekking, Department of Psychology, University of Utrecht

T. Dembroski, Department of Psychology, Eckerd College, St. Petersburg, Florida

N. van Dijkhuizen, Bureau of Organizational Psychology, The Royal Dutch Navy, The Hague

P. M. W. Dijkstra, Medical Faculty of Maastricht, Department of Psychology, University of Limburg

C. L. Ekkers, Netherlands Institute for Preventive Health Care (TNO), Leiden

R. Erdman, Department of Clinical Psychology, Erasmus University, Rotterdam

H. J. Eysenck, Institute of Psychiatry, University of London

P. R. J. Falger, Department of Medical Psychology, University of Limburg

C. Faucheux, Department of Psychology, University of Paris

N. H. Frijda, Psychological Laboratory, University of Amsterdam

A. W. K. Gaillard, Institute for Perception (TNO), Soesterberg

A. Garssan, Psychiatric Clinic, Research Department, University of Utrecht

B. de Gelder, Department of Psychology, University of Tilburg (NIAS Fellow, 1980)

E. Goudsmit, Department of Psychology, University of Amsterdam

J. A. Gray, Department of Psychology, University of Oxford

P. Grossman, Department of Psychology, SOPS, University of Wageningen

V. L. Hamilton, Department of Psychology, Reading University

V. Hodapp, Psychology Institute, Johannes Gutenberg University

I. Janis, Department of Psychology, Yale University

C. D. Jenkins, School of Medicine, Program on Behavioral Epidemiology, Boston University

R. D. de Jong, Department of Clinical Psychology, Psychotherapy, and Preventive Medicine, University of Utrecht

Author Index

Anatomy and Physiology of Speech

McGraw-Hill Series in Speech

Glen E. Mills, *Consulting Editor in General Speech*

John J. O'Neill, *Consulting Editor in Speech Pathology*

Armstrong and Brandes: THE ORAL INTERPRETATION OF LITERATURE

Baird: AMERICAN PUBLIC ADDRESSES

Baird: ARGUMENTATION, DISCUSSION, AND DEBATE

Baird and Knower: ESSENTIALS OF GENERAL SPEECH

Baird, Becker, and Knower: GENERAL SPEECH COMMUNICATION

Black and Moore: SPEECH: CODE, MEANING, AND COMMUNICATION

Carrell and Tiffany: PHONETICS

Gibson: A READER IN SPEECH COMMUNICATIONS

Hahn, Lomas, Hargis, and Vandraegen: BASIC VOICE TRAINING FOR SPEECH

Hasling: THE MESSAGE, THE SPEAKER, THE AUDIENCE

Kaplan: ANATOMY AND PHYSIOLOGY OF SPEECH

Kruger: MODERN DEBATE

Ogilvie: SPEECH IN THE ELEMENTARY SCHOOL

Ogilvie and Rees: COMMUNICATION SKILLS: VOICE AND PRONUNCIATION

Powers: FUNDAMENTALS OF SPEECH

Reid: TEACHING SPEECH

Robinson and Becker: EFFECTIVE SPEECH FOR THE TEACHER

Wells: CLEFT PALATE AND ITS ASSOCIATED SPEECH DISORDERS